HEALTH CARE BOOK OF LISTS

RICHARD K. THOMAS, PH.D.
LOUIS G. POL, PH.D.
WILLIAM F. SEHNERT, JR., M.B.A.

GR PRESS, INC.

950417

ISBN: 1-878205-25-0
Library of Congress Card Catalog Number: 93-085846

Printed in the United States of America

TABLE OF CONTENTS

INTRODUCTION

The 1980s witnessed an explosion in the demand for statistics on health and health care. Although health care had been the fastest growing industry in the economy since World War II, its ability to generate data–particularly accessible, usable data–had not kept pace. Certain characteristics of health care–its fragmentation, its discontinuities and the proprietary status of many health care organizations, among other factors–had prevented the development of the strong data component in health care that was so well-developed in other industries.

HEALTH CARE: A CHANGING INDUSTRY

Despite decades of steady growth, it was not until the 1980s that the health care industry began to change in terms of its basic orientation and organization. During that decade the industry underwent a radical transformation. Concern over the rising cost of health care resulted in the implementation of a variety of cost containment measures. Significant shifts in power occurred as hospitals, physicians, various levels of government, and insurers jockeyed for position.

One of the most important developments during the 1980s was the realization that health care was, in fact, a business, not a charity or community service. This realization was prompted in part by the introduction of unprecedented competition into the industry. Hospitals, faced with overcapacity, decreasing utilization and declining compensation for their services, were forced to begin seriously competing in order to maintain their respective shares of the market. Changes were occurring in consumer preferences and provider practice patterns that channeled customers away from the traditional sources of care, particularly hospitals. These developments meant that the "hip pocket" management approach that had characterized health care was forced to give way to analytical decision-making.

Paralleling these changes in the delivery system was a paradigmatic shift away from a "medical care" framework toward a "health care" framework. *Medical care* is narrowly defined and refers primarily to those functions of the health care system that are under the influence of medical doctors. This concept encompasses the "clinical" or treatment aspects of care, rather than the nonmedical aspects of health care. *Health care* refers to any function that might be directly or indirectly related to preserving, maintaining or enhancing health status. Not only does this concept include formal health-preserving activities (e.g., visiting a health professional), but also such informal activities as preventive care, exercise, proper diet, and so forth. This shift in orientation resulted in a broadening of what was considered important in terms of health data.

Along with these trends, the industry developed an unprecedented interest in accountability. Despite the high ethical standards of the industry, operational accountability had not been a prominent characteristic of health care. In fact, cost accounting procedures were virtually unknown and, when data were available, the information often remained proprietary and, thus, not available to the public. During the 1980s the number of entities demanding accountability increased dramatically. Health care providers found themselves assailed on all sides by regulators, consumer groups, government financing agencies, policy setters and others, all demanding data that were not readily available. Health care providers themselves, especially hospitals, realized that they did not have the data they needed for their own internal purposes.

THE MUSHROOMING DEMAND FOR HEALTH DATA

These developments of the 1980s resulted in an increased demand for health-related data. Although the health industry generates massive amounts of data, the information available has tended to be highly decentralized. As the providers of health services came to face the demands long addressed by other industries, the lack of appropriate data became increasingly obvious. Like other industries, health care was having to deal with a more demanding consumer, increasing market differentiation, unprecedented product development decisions, and complex distribution choices–all without the requisite market data. Health care organizations that in the past had had little interest or need for market data now realized that data gathering and analysis was a necessary part of their operations.

The growth in the demand for health-related data has not been limited to the providers of health care. Decisions relating to the provision and financing of care, as well as to medical education and research, are more and more being made by individuals and organizations *outside* of health care. At the national and state levels, these include politicians, agencies financing health care, and policy-setters; at the institutional level (e.g., hospitals, physician groups), these parties include government financing agencies, insurers, and employers. This shift in decision-making has resulted in a changed emphasis with regard to data demands. The emphasis for clinicians has historically been on epidemiologically-oriented data; for non-clinicians the emphasis is on market-oriented data. To a great extent, the interest has shifted from internal data (e.g., patient characteristics) to external data (e.g., utilization projections).

Outside of health care, journalists, writers and other commentators require increasing amounts of health data and they need it at ever-increasing levels of sophistication. Others demanding additional data include policy analysts, government decision-makers, and business coalitions.

The health care industry has always presented something of a paradox when it comes to data. Despite the fact that an incredible amount of data on health and health care is generated, these data are often unpublicized, inaccessible and/or difficult to interpret. The data historically generated suffered from a lack of any standard reporting format, thus limiting the comparability of much of the data. Much important information is buried in government reports and/or in obscure journals that the casual researcher would not be aware of or in proprietary research that is inaccessible to the general public. Even published statistics are often of such detail and/or complexity that the typical reader cannot easily locate the specific statistic sought. Too often, the important information is buried under the minutia provided in such reports.

The problems related to health data, along with the mushrooming demand, have led to the development of a strong health data industry. Several commercial data vendors have added health data to their inventories and a few health-specific data vendors have emerged. These vendors have not only repackaged existing data into a more palatable form, but also now develop their own databases. Health consumer data became available for the first time and by the late 1980s at least three major nationwide surveys were being conducted by private health data vendors.

ORGANIZATION OF THE BOOK

The book is divided into eleven separate sections related to different aspects of health care, followed by one section of demographic data. There are obviously different ways in which this material could be grouped and, in this case, there was a tendency to group material from the perspective of someone within health care who uses the data for applied research. Most entries, in fact, could be placed in more than one section. Each section is preceded by an introduction to the material being presented. The introduction provides information on the state of the data for that particular topic, discusses any unique characteristics or problems, reviews major sources of those data, and otherwise lays the groundwork for the tables that follow.

The book includes exactly 338 tables, with the data presented in a simplified format for ease of use. In addition to the data itself, each table includes other information that in some cases may prove more valuable than the data. Information is provided for each table that indicates the source of the data and the references or organizations to access if additional information is required. In addition, definitions are provided if the meaning of a term is not clear or if it is a term that is unique to health care. For each table, caveats or qualifications are provided when they have a bearing on the quality and/or meaning of the figures. One final feature is an interpretation of the data presented. This is not necessary in every case, but is beneficial in instances where a casual review of the data may be misleading.

The currency of the data was an important consideration in compiling these tables. Every attempt has been made to provide the most current data available. In some cases, tables were omitted because it was felt that providing dated information related to a rapidly changing environment would do more harm than good. When "older" data are provided, it is with the understanding that they are the latest figures available *and* there has not been significant change in conditions since the data were issued.

The data sources discussed are limited to those that provide data for the United States, although an occasional table may include data for international comparisons.

Section I

DATA ON HEALTH STATUS

The basic data required for any analysis of health services or any health planning activity are those related to the health status of the population. *Health status* refers to the level of morbidity, disability and mortality characterizing a particular population. Despite the importance of health status, there is no widely accepted measure of the health status of individuals or populations available. As a result, a variety of different measures are utilized. Ultimately, the variables that are examined in determining health status depend on the objectives of the analysis being undertaken.

The most common measures of health status are those referred to as "outcome" measures. These include mortality rates and either prevalence or incidence figures for morbidity and disability within the population. They are referred to as outcome measures because they presumably reflect the end result of the operation of the health care system. Most of the tables in this section present data of this type. Analysts sometimes use "process" measures as indicators of health status–i.e., the extent to which members of the population avail themselves in the existing health services. Process measures are based on the assumption that the use of health services correlates positively with health status. These indicators are discussed in the section on health care utilization.

Health status data are collected in a variety of ways and are available from a variety of sources. Some of these data are compiled through registries or other sources of official figures. Death registries, based on death certificate files, would be an example, as would statistics maintained by the Centers for Disease Control and Prevention (CDCP) on the incidence of "reportable" diseases. Although mortality statistics are virtually complete, the data on morbidity and disability from these sources is spotty. In fact, there is no official registry for most health conditions and, at this point in 1992, AIDS is not even classified as a "reportable" condition–i.e., one that must be reported by law. The major sources of registry-based health status data are the National Center for Health Statistics (NCHS) and the CDCP. Both of these are

Federal agencies with responsibility for compiling and disseminating data for the nation.

The other source of health status data is surveys of various types. The most common source of such data is community sample surveys in which data are obtained directly from members of the population with regard to their health status. This approach is particularly useful for collecting information on morbidity and disability, conditions for which there are few official sources of data. Much of what we know about the prevalence of various health problems within the population comes from this source. NCHS is probably the leading collector of this type of data, although some private organizations have started collecting and disseminating health status data based on sample surveys they have conducted. Regardless of the source, sample surveys have inherent drawbacks. A variety of sampling and nonsampling errors can effect the quality of the data and statistics from such surveys should be interpreted cautiously.

Another source of health status data is the surveys conducted on health facilities. For example, patient records can be sampled for the nation's hospitals or physician practices. These data indicate the types of conditions for which patients are being treated and/or hospitalized and, thus, provide an indicator of the population's health status. NCHS is also a leading source of this type of data. Other categories of these data are, in fact, based not on a sample but on the entire population. For example, the Health Care Financing Administration (HCFA), the federal agency that administers the Medicare program, makes data available on the entire treated Medicare population. Additional information on the utilization of hospitals and physicians is included in the section on health services utilization.

Statistics on deaths are reported in a separate section on mortality. Although health status data are collected for both physical and mental health conditions, statistics on mental health status are presented in the separate section on mental health. Behavioral patterns that affect health status (e.g., alcohol consumption) are presented in this section.

I-1. GLOBAL ASSESSMENTS
SELF-ASSESSMENT OF HEALTH BY SELECTED CHARACTERISTICS
1990

Characteristic	Percent Reporting Their Health As:			
	Excellent	Very good	Good	Fair/Poor
Total	40.5%	28.5%	22.0%	8.9%
Age				
Under 15 years	52.8	28.1	16.6	2.4
Under 5 years	53.2	28.1	15.8	2.9
5-14 years	52.6	28.1	17.1	2.2
15-44 years	43.1	30.9	20.6	5.4
45-64 years	29.2	27.1	27.7	16.0
65 years and over	17.1	22.9	32.3	27.7
65-74 years	18.9	23.5	32.6	25.1
75 years and over	14.5	21.9	31.9	31.7
Sex:				
Male	42.5	28.3	20.8	8.4
Female	38.7	28.8	23.2	9.3
Race:				
White	42.1	29.0	20.8	8.1
Black	31.1	25.3	28.5	15.1
Family income:				
Less than $14,000	28.1	24.3	28.9	18.6
$14,000-$24,999	34.6	29.6	25.0	10.8
$25,000-$34,999	40.6	30.2	21.7	7.5
$35,000-$49,999	45.9	29.7	19.1	5.3
$50,000 or more	52.1	28.0	16.0	4.0
Geographic region:				
Northeast	43.1	28.1	21.6	7.2
Midwest	41.7	29.3	21.1	7.9
South	37.3	27.8	23.8	11.2
West	42.2	29.1	20.6	8.1
Location of residence:				
Within MSA	41.6	28.5	21.5	8.5
Outside MSA	36.7	28.7	24.1	10.4

Source: Based on data collected by the National Center for Health Statistics and published in **Health, United States, 1991**. National Center for Health Statistics (NCHS) conducts a variety of surveys from which health-related data are drawn. Additional data, including some unpublished data, on this topic are available from NCHS (Hyattsville, MD).

Methodology: These data were collected by the NCHS by means of the 1990 National Health Interview Survey. In 1990, over 40,000 households were interviewed, representing over 100,000 persons.

Qualifications: The National Health Interview Survey is faced with the same drawbacks that characterize all sample surveys. The size and representativeness of the sample, questionnaire design, interviewer skills, and a variety of other factors may affect the quality of the data. The NCHS is the major health data collection agency in the United States and has a reputation for rigorous research methodology. Since respondents were asked to report the existence of hypertension, some misreporting is possible.

Interpretation: There are substantial differences in the reporting of self-assessed health status for all of the characteristics examined except for region of the country. The differences are the greatest for race, income, and age. Note that there may be interaction among the variables that may exacerbate some of the differences.

I-2. RISK FACTORS
RANKINGS ON HEALTH STATUS OVERALL AND FOR SPECIFIC FACTORS
1990

Rank	State	Rank by Health Status Factor				
		Lifestyle	Access	Disability	Disease	Mortality
1	Utah	1	20	6	6	5
1	Minnesota	6	6	28	3	3
3	New Hampshire	6	2	28	12	8
4	Hawaii	5	5	1	19	2
5	Nebraska	4	14	41	5	9
5	Connecticut	16	1	21	25	9
7	Massachusetts	17	3	28	30	6
7	Wisconsin	9	16	28	11	6
7	Iowa	12	16	45	10	3
10	Kansas	17	7	28	9	9
10	Colorado	12	22	6	4	13
12	Vermont	12	14	28	16	14
12	North Dakota	2	44	28	2	1
15	Virginia	20	9	12	16	21
16	New Jersey	19	4	21	41	19
17	Rhode Island	23	10	41	37	9
18	Montana	3	41	12	7	16
19	Ohio	26	20	28	16	20
20	Pennsylvania	22	11	45	40	21
20	Indiana	29	23	28	14	29
22	California	31	12	4	39	21
23	Michigan	38	24	21	14	34
24	South Dakota	9	43	28	7	18
24	Maryland	34	7	12	43	30
26	Oklahoma	23	25	21	28	37
26	Wyoming	20	42	9	1	30
26	Delaware	29	16	21	42	4
26	Missouri	26	28	45	37	27
30	Washington	12	25	11	49	16
30	Texas	31	34	5	24	21
32	North Carolina	38	25	21	30	37
33	Idaho	8	46	12	13	34
34	Georgia	38	29	12	30	48
34	Tennessee	45	31	28	30	37
34	New York	48	12	12	45	40
34	Illinois	41	36	12	26	30
38	Kentucky	43	38	28	28	40
39	Alabama	43	39	41	19	45
39	Arkansas	41	40	45	30	34
39	Arizona	34	32	6	47	21
39	South Carolina	45	33	12	36	50
43	Oregon	26	36	21	50	21

(Continued on next page)

I-2. RISK FACTORS
RANKINGS ON HEALTH STATUS OVERALL AND
FOR SPECIFIC FACTORS
1990 *(Continued from previous page)*

Rank	State	Rank by Health Status Factor				
		Lifestyle	Access	Disability	Disease	Mortality
44	Florida	50	29	45	45	27
45	New Mexico	31	50	2	19	30
45	Louisiana	47	45	12	27	44
47	Nevada	49	34	9	48	40
47	Mississippi	34	47	28	19	49
49	West Virginia	34	49	45	30	45
50	Alaska	23	48	2	44	45

Source: Based on data collected by Northwestern National Life Insurance Company and published in **Medical Benefits**, September 15, 1990. Northwestern National Life Insurance Company (NWNL) is a national health insurance company. **Medical Benefits** is a semi-monthly publication devoted to health care costs. For additional information on state health status or a copy of the report, contact NWNL (Minneapolis).

Methodology: Rankings were developed by NWNL on 17 components of health status for each state. These 17 components were grouped into five major categories and these categories were weighted and combined to produce an overall health status rating.

Qualifications: Any rating scale has inherent problems and should be utilized with caution. The weightings applied to the various measures examined could influence the final score for overall health status. (In fact, a change in the weighting system utilized resulted in a significant change in rankings between 1989 and 1990.) The choice of the components to be utilized in itself represents something of a value judgment. Since the overall score is a composite of the weighted components, states with similar scores may actually be quite different in terms of their health status characteristics.

Definitions: "Lifestyle" refers to a measurement of behaviors and their consequences that impact health, including smoking, motor vehicle deaths, violent crime, obesity, hypertension, lack of exercise and education. "Access" refers to a measurement of the availability of health care (as a result of insurance), the availability of medical care providers, use of prenatal care, and state and local expenditures on health care for low income persons. "Disability" refers to a measurement of the limitations of daily activity on a state's population due to chronic and acute ill health. "Disease" refers to a measurement of the prevalence of heart disease, cancer, AIDS, tuberculosis, and hepatitis among the state's population. "Mortality" refers to a measurement of age- and race-adjusted death rates, race-adjusted infant mortality rates, and years of life lost due to death before age 65.

Interpretation: There appears to be a great deal of diversity among states in terms of health status and within the individual states among the separate indicators. Some states, however, are consistently low on the indicators. Utah is consistently ranked highest because of the influence of its Mormon population. Southern states and rural states are generally ranked lower on such measures, but there are some exceptions.

I-3. RISK FACTORS
SELECTED RISK FACTORS FOR SELECTED STATES
1988

State	Being overweight	Sedentary lifestyle	Current smokers	Binge drinking	Drinking and driving	Seat belt non-use
Alabama	22.5%	57.8%	26.2%	10.7%	1.6%	47.8%
Arizona	20.0	53.0	23.8	16.6	2.9	35.8
California	20.9	48.8	22.4	15.8	3.9	18.4
Connecticut	19.7	57.6	26.8	17.3	3.8	25.2
D.C.	23.0	66.7	20.2	7.1	2.2	20.9
Florida	22.3	52.6	24.2	13.6	2.5	21.5
Georgia	18.8	61.7	25.3	16.5	3.1	33.9
Hawaii	16.4	53.3	23.8	19.6	3.6	6.5
Idaho	17.9	51.0	20.3	14.0	3.2	37.5
Illinois	22.7	57.8	27.0	18.0	2.9	32.5
Indiana	24.1	60.2	27.5	15.3	3.5	30.1
Iowa	20.1	58.3	22.4	15.3	3.2	23.7
Kentucky	23.0	67.1	34.4	8.3	1.4	52.5
Maine	21.5	58.6	26.6	14.7	2.9	49.2
Maryland	18.8	64.4	25.3	8.9	1.5	18.9
Massachusetts	21.4	52.9	26.6	18.4	4.6	49.6
Michigan	25.0	NA	26.4	23.3	4.9	22.4
Minnesota	10.9	53.5	22.5	22.6	5.9	26.7
Missouri	23.0	59.0	26.0	15.3	2.7	24.9
Montana	15.6	46.4	19.9	21.0	6.0	28.8
Nebraska	22.5	60.5	21.0	17.0	4.3	51.3
New Hampshire	19.5	55.4	18.1	17.5	3.5	52.4
New Mexico	14.7	51.8	24.5	13.4	3.0	20.2
New York	20.8	73.6	24.1	13.6	1.8	24.1
North Carolina	20.6	63.7	26.3	11.9	3.1	13.1
North Dakota	23.3	57.5	22.3	21.7	5.9	60.5
Ohio	21.9	63.1	26.3	17.0	3.6	27.8
Oklahoma	18.0	59.7	24.6	10.4	3.4	33.6
Rhode Island	18.2	64.8	24.7	8.2	2.6	47.0
South Carolina	21.5	65.4	26.0	9.8	1.4	48.7
South Dakota	22.9	56.8	21.3	19.3	6.0	67.4
Tennessee	20.1	67.3	30.0	9.0	2.2	32.5
Texas	18.6	59.7	23.9	16.9	3.9	15.4
Utah	18.2	50.3	14.7	7.3	1.5	33.3
Washington	20.4	45.3	24.8	18.3	4.0	16.0
West Virginia	24.4	66.0	26.8	9.1	1.4	56.1
Wisconsin	28.0	55.4	23.2	25.3	6.2	23.4
Median Prevalence	20.9	58.0	25.7	15.3	3.2	30.1

Source: Based on data collected by the Centers for Disease Control and Prevention (CDCP) within the U.S. Public Health Service and published in Morbidity and Mortality Weekly Report, Vol. 39, No. SS-2. The Centers for Disease Control and Prevention are charged with tracking the spread of communicable diseases. For additional information on risk factors contact the CDCP (Atlanta).

Methodology: Based on data collected by means of the Behavioral Risk Factor Surveillance System (BRFSS) coordinated by the Centers for Disease Control and Prevention. Thirty-six states and the District of Columbia participate in this data collection effort.

Qualifications: The figures used in the table are based on self-reports by respondents and are characterized by the shortcomings associated with this type of information. The wording of such questions is always problematic as are the premises underlying some of the questions. Since not all states participate it is not possible to develop national statistics.

Definitions: "Being overweight" refers to a body mass index of 27.8 or more for males and 27.3 or more for females. "Sedentary lifestyle" refers to less than three 20-minute sessions of leisure-time activity per week. "Current smokers" refers to those currently smoking cigarettes regularly. "Binge drinking" refers to having five or more drinks on one occasion at least once in the last month. "Seat belt non-use" refers to those indicating sometimes, seldom or never using seat belts.

Interpretation: There appears to be no consistent patterns for the states with regard to these risk factors. States tend to vary from factor to factor in terms of their ranking (i.e., the typical state is higher than average on some factors and lower than average on others).

I-4. CANCER PREVALENCE
CANCER PREVALENCE RATES FOR SELECTED
CANCER SITES BY RACE AND SEX*
1988

	White Male	White Female	Black Male	Black Female
All sites	436.1	341.7	512.5	327.0
Colon	40.6	28.9	41.5	35.7
Rectum	18.2	10.7	15.0	9.1
Pancreas	10.4	7.4	15.9	13.5
Lung and bronchus	80.6	41.0	119.4	41.3
Prostate gland	101.9	NA	136.0	NA
Non-Hodgkin's lymphoma	17.4	11.6	11.8	7.2
Breast	NA	112.9	NA	96.5
Uterus	NA	29.0	NA	28.5
Ovary	NA	15.4	NA	10.3

*Rates are age-adjusted and based on cases per 100,000 population.

Source: Based on data collected by the National Cancer Institute and published in **Health, United States, 1990.** The National Cancer Institute (NCI) is the major federal source of statistics on cancer. For additional information contact NCI (Washington).

Methodology: Based on data collected from surveillance programs in selected cities and states. These figures are generalized to the total population.

Qualifications: These figures reflect the known cases of cancer only. They do not include individuals with undiagnosed cancer.

Interpretation: There is considerable variation in the type (i.e., site affected) of cancer characterizing different age/sex groupings within the population. Some forms of cancer are more prevalent among one of the sexes (even excluding sites unique to either sex) and some are more prevalent among either whites or blacks.

I-5. CANCER INCIDENCE
ESTIMATED NEW CANCER CASES BY SEX AND SPECIFIC SITE
1990

| Site | Distribution by Site | |
	Males	Females
Skin	3%	3%
Oral	4	2
Lung	20	11
Pancreas	3	3
Stomach	3	< 2
Colon and rectum	15	15
Prostate	20	0
Urinary	10	4
Leukemia/Lymphomas	7	6
Breast	< 1	29
Ovary	0	4
Uterus	0	9
All other	15	14

Source: Based on data compiled by the American Cancer Society and published in **Medical Benefits** (March 15, 1990). The American Cancer Society (Atlanta) is the major private source of cancer statistics.

Methodology: These American Cancer Society figures are derived from estimates of newly diagnosed cancer cases made using data from the National Cancer Institute (Surveillance, Epidemiology, and End Results Program). Rates based on 1984-86 studies have been applied to the 1990 U.S. population.

Definitions: "All other" includes reported cancer cases for which no site was specified. "Breast" cancer refers to invasive cancer only. "Skin" cancer refers to melanoma only.

Qualifications: These are estimates using known rates that are several years old. The estimates are only accurate to the extent that incidence rates have not changed since 1986. Figures for non-melanoma skin cancer and carcinoma were not provided.

Interpretation: The major differences in cancer incidence by sex reflect anatomical differences (i.e., breast, uterine, and prostate cancer). Some other differences among the sexes reflect lifestyle differences (e.g., lung and oral cancer).

I-6. CANCER INCIDENCE
ESTIMATED NEW CANCER CASES BY SEX BY SITE
1990

| Site | Estimated New Cases (in 1,000s) | | |
	Male	Female	Total
All sites	520.0	520.0	1,040.0
Digestive organs	121.3	115.5	236.8
Genital organs	113.1	71.9	185.0
Respiratory system	115.0	58.7	173.7
Breast	0.9	150.0	150.9
Urinary organs	51.0	22.0	73.0
Blood and lymph tissues	28.9	25.9	54.8
Oral	20.4	10.1	30.5
Leukemias	15.7	12.1	27.8
Skin	14.8	12.8	27.6
Brain/central nervous system	8.5	7.1	15.6
Endocrine glands	4.0	9.6	13.6
Connective tissue	3.0	2.7	5.7
Bone	1.2	0.9	2.1
Eye	0.9	0.8	1.7
All other	21.3	19.9	41.2

Source: Based on data compiled by the American Cancer Society and published in **Medical Benefits** (March 15, 1990). The American Cancer Society (Atlanta) is the major private source of cancer statistics.

Methodology: These American Cancer Society figures are derived from estimates made using data form the National Cancer Institute (Surveillance, Epidemiology, and End Results Program). Rates based on 1984-86 studies have been applied to the 1990 U.S. population.

Definitions: "All other" includes reported cancer cases for which no site was specified. "Breast" cancer refers to invasive cancer only. "Skin" cancer refers to melanoma only.

Qualifications: These are estimates using known rates that are several years old. The estimates are only accurate to the extent that incidence rates have not changed since 1986. Figures for non-melanoma skin cancer and carcinoma were not provided.

Interpretation: Four sites (digestive system, genital organs, respiratory system, and the breast) accounted for over 75% of the new cancer cases in 1990. Considerable variation exists in the incidence of cancer at the various sites between males and females.

I-7. ACUTE CONDITIONS
SELECTED ACUTE CONDITIONS BY AGE
1989

Condition	All Ages	Incidence Rate*					
		Under 5 Years	5 to 17 Years	18 to 24 Years	25 to 44 Years	45 to 64 Years	65 Years and over
All Acute Conditions	181.3	369.5	252.2	180.8	165.4	113.6	100.2
Infective and Parasitic Diseases	20.1	53.2	41.3	15.4	13.5	8.6	5.9
Respiratory Conditions	95.2	175.8	138.7	100.0	89.7	60.1	42.0
Common Cold	29.1	73.1	34.4	34.2	26.2	17.4	14.4
Influenza	50.4	61.8	81.2	48.3	51.1	34.7	19.9
Acute Bronchitis	3.6	9.8	4.8	3.2	3.1	1.7	2.5[a]
Digestive System Conditions	5.9	11.0	6.3	6.5	4.5	4.1	7.6
Acute Ear Infections	8.7	62.1	11.9	3.6	2.9	1.8	0.5[a]

*Rates are reported as cases per 100 population.
Figures with the superscript[a] do not meet an acceptable level of statistical reliability.

Source: Based on data collected by the National Center for Health Statistics and published in "Current Estimates from the National Health Interview Survey" in **Vital Health Statistics**, Series 10, No. 176, 1990. The National Center for Health Statistics (NCHS) conducts a variety of surveys from which health-related data are drawn. Additional data, including some unpublished data, on this topic are available from NCHS (Hyattsville, MD).

Methodology: These data were collected by means of the 1989 National Health Interview Survey. In 1989, 45,711 households were interviewed representing 116,929 persons. Respondents indicated whether they or any family members have had the condition in the last three months. The condition must have been associated with at least one doctor visit or at least one day of restricted activity. The data reflect responses for the civilian noninstitutionalized population.

Definitions: An "acute condition" is one that caused certain types of impacts associated with health, such as a visit to the doctor or a day spent in bed. In general, acute conditions have rapid asset, last a relatively short period of time, and typically have no lasting impact on a person's health.

Qualifications: The National Health Interview Survey is faced with the same drawbacks that characterize all sample surveys. The size and representativeness of the sample, questionnaire design, interviewer skills, and a variety of other factors may affect the quality of the data. The NCHS is the major health data collection agency in the United States and has a reputation for rigorous research methodology. Since respondents were asked to report the existence of hypertension, some misreporting is possible.

Interpretation: Respiratory conditions account for approximately half of the identified acute conditions. The incidence of acute conditions decreases steadily as age increases.

I-8. CHRONIC CONDITIONS
SELECTED REPORTED CHRONIC CONDITIONS BY AGE
1990

Condition	All Ages	Under 18 Years	18 to 44 Years	45 to 64 Years	65 to 74 Years	75 Years and over
		Prevalence Rate*				
Arthritis	125.3	3.0	47.9	249.1	428.1	535.2
Orthopedic Impairment	111.7	28.8	136.3	161.5	168.2	183.9
Dermatitis	35.3	31.0	37.7	37.0	33.2	33.1
Diabetes	25.3	0.6[a]	10.1	50.4	102.2	79.7
Cataracts	24.1	0.9[a]	2.5	22.1	112.2	218.4
Heart Disease	78.5	18.9	38.1	118.7	257.1	333.9
Hypertension	110.2	1.8[a]	55.7	218.3	354.1	392.0
Hearing Impairment	94.7	21.0	57.1	150.0	264.1	411.0
Ulcer	18.1	1.6[a]	19.5	28.6	33.3	32.9
Frequent Indigestion	23.4	1.7[a]	27.6	32.7	44.6	36.5
Frequent Constipation	16.2	6.7	12.4	14.3	33.9	83.5
Chronic Sinusitis	131.3	56.7	149.0	181.9	154.1	148.1

*Rates are reported as existing cases per 1,000 population.

Figures with the superscript[a] do not meet acceptable levels of statistical reliability.

Source: Based on data collected by the National Center for Health Statistics and published in "Current Estimates from the National Health Interview Survey" in **Vital Health Statistics**, Series 10, No. 181, 1991. The National Center for Health Statistics (NCHS) conducts a variety of surveys from which health-related data are drawn. Additional data, including some unpublished data, on this topic are available from NCHS (Hyattsville, MD).

Methodology: These data were collected by means of the 1990 National Health Interview Survey. In 1989, over 40,000 households were interviewed, representing over 100,000 persons. Respondents indicated whether they or any family members have had the condition that was first noticed more than three months before the reference date of the interview or is a condition that ordinarily has a duration of more than three months. These data reflect responses from civilian noninstitutionalized population.

Definition: "Chronic condition" refers to a health condition that has a slow onset, lasts a prolonged period of time, and has some type of lasting impact on the individual's health status.

Qualifications: The National Health Interview Survey is faced with the same drawbacks that characterize all sample surveys. The size and representativeness of the sample, questionnaire design, interviewer skills, and a variety of other factors may affect the quality of the data. The NCHS is the major health data collection agency in the United States and has a reputation for rigorous research methodology. Since respondents were asked to report the existence of hypertension, some misreporting is possible.

Interpretation: Arthritis and related conditions represent the largest category of chronic conditions, followed by hearing and visual impairments. The prevalence of acute conditions increases steadily as age increases.

I-9. NOTIFIABLE DISEASES
SELECTED NOTIFIABLE DISEASE RATES
1989

Disease	Cases	Incidence Rate*
Diphtheria	3	<1
Hepatitis A	35,821	14
Hepatitis B	23,419	9
Mumps	5,712	2
Pertussis (whooping cough)	4,157	2
Poliomyelitis, total	5	<1
Paralytic	5	<1
Rubella (German measles)	396	<1
Rubeola (measles)	18,193	7
Salmonellosis, excluding typhoid fever	47,812	19
Shigellosis	25,010	10
Tuberculosis	23,495	9
Varicella (chicken pox)	185,441	12
Sexually transmitted diseases		
Syphilis	110,797	45
Primary and secondary	44,540	18
Early latent	43,898	18
Late and late latent	21,418	9
Congenital	941	<1
Gonorrhea	733,151	297
Chancroid	4,692	2
Granuloma inguinale	7	<1
Lymphogranuloma venereum	189	<1

*Rates are reported cases per 100,000 population.

Source: Based on data collected by the Centers for Disease Control and Prevention (CDCP) and published in **Health, United States, 1990.** The Centers for Disease Control and Prevention (Atlanta) are charged with tracking the spread of communicable diseases. The best source of CDCP data is its publication **Mortality and Morbidity Weekly Review.**

Methodology: Health care providers and officials are required by law to report certain diseases to disease control authorities. These data are usually reported at the county level to the local health department. These data are compiled at the national level by the CDCP.

Qualifications: The extent to which reportable diseases are actually reported varies from disease to disease. There is certainly some underreporting for each of these diseases. These diseases that are considered reportable reflect historical disease patterns and more "contemporary" conditions (e.g., AIDS) may not be included.

Interpretation: The diseases for which reporting are required are those that are communicable and not necessarily those that pose the greatest threat to the population's health.

I-10. HYPERTENSION
HYPERTENSION RATES BY AGE AND SELECTED CHARACTERISTICS
1987

Characteristic	Prevalence Rate*			
	Under 45	46-64	64-74	75+
Sex:				
Male	41.8	244.3	348.9	247.9
Female	37.0	259.1	426.9	388.8
Race:				
White	35.7	237.6	376.1	337.5
Black	64.3	374.3	495.0	326.0
Family income:				
Less than $10,000	46.3	333.0	412.3	336.9
$10,000-$19,999	47.9	277.5	373.7	396.6
$20,000-$34,999	35.4	261.7	413.5	350.0
$35,000 or more	37.3	210.3	368.2	251.6

*Rates are reported cases per 1,000 population.

Source: Based on data collected through the National Health Interview Survey conducted by the National Center for Health Statistics. Reprinted in the Metropolitan Life **Statistical Bulletin**, April-June, 1989. The **Statistical Bulletin** published by Metropolitan Life Insurance Company reprints data from a variety of sources, including statistics on the experiences of the large Metropolitan Life insured population, data not available elsewhere.

Methodology: These data were collected by the NCHS by means of the 1987 National Health Interview Survey. These figures are based on data collected by means of personal interviews conducted annually from a national sample of between 36,000 and 46,000 households. Respondents were asked if they ever had hypertension.

Qualifications: The National Health Interview Survey is faced with the same drawbacks that characterize all sample surveys. The size and representativeness of the sample, questionnaire design, interviewer skills, and a variety of other factors may affect the quality of the data. The NCHS is the major health data collection agency in the United States and has a reputation for rigorous research methodology. Since respondents were asked to report the existence of hypertension, some misreporting is possible.

Interpretation: There are differences in the prevalence of hypertension based on age, sex, race and income. Age affects differences found between the other demographic characteristics. While the prevalence of hypertension generally increases with age, there is a substantial increase in its prevalence after age 45. Ironically, the hypertension rate for those 75 and over is lower than that of the 65-74 cohort, presumably reflecting the higher mortality rate of hypertensives.

I-11. DISABILITY
LIMITATION OF ACTIVITY DUE TO CHRONIC CONDITIONS
BY SELECTED CHARACTERISTICS
1990

| Characteristic | Percent Reporting | |
	Limitation in Activity	Inability to Perform Major Activity
Total	12.9%	3.9%
Sex:		
Male	12.9	4.4
Female	13.0	3.4
Race:		
White	12.8	3.6
Black	15.5	6.5
Age:		
Under 15	4.7	0.4
15-44	8.5	2.4
45-64	21.8	8.6
65 and over	37.5	10.2
Family Income:		
Less than $14,000	22.9	9.6
$14,000-$24,999	14.8	4.8
$25,000-$34,999	11.6	3.0
$35,000-$49,999	10.4	2.3
$50,000 or more	8.4	1.7

Source: Based on data collected by the National Center for Health Statistics and published in **Health, United States, 1991.** National Center for Health Statistics (NCHS) conducts a variety of surveys from which health-related data are drawn. Additional data, including some unpublished data, on this topic are available from NCHS (Hyattsville, MD).

Methodology: These data were collected by the NCHS by means of the 1990 National Health Interview Survey. In 1990, over 40,000 households were interviewed, representing over 100,000 persons.

Definition: "Chronic condition" refers to a health condition that has a slow onset, lasts a prolonged period of time, and has some type of lasting impact on the individual's health status.

Qualifications: The National Health Interview Survey is faced with the same drawbacks that characterize all sample surveys. The size and representativeness of the sample, questionnaire design, interviewer skills, and a variety of other factors may affect the quality of the data. The NCHS is the major health data collection agency in the United States and has a reputation for rigorous research methodology. Since respondents were asked to report the existence of hypertension, some misreporting is possible.

Interpretation: The level of limitation in activity from chronic conditions varies based on a variety of characteristics. The degree of limitation increases with age and decreases with income. Blacks tend to have higher levels of limitations than do whites.

I-12. DISABILITY
PERSONS IN NURSING HOMES REQUIRING ASSISTANCE BY AGE
1985

Activity Requiring Assistance	Persons Requiring Assistance			
	< 65	65-74	75-84	> 84
Total	173,100	212,100	509,000	597,300
Bathing	65.6%	76.9%	88.5%	91.9%
Dressing	54.0	64.2	71.0	77.3
Using Toilet Room	37.7	49.3	55.1	62.2
Transferring	37.0	46.3	54.1	62.8
Eating	29.0	32.9	32.3	39.1

Source: Based on data collected by the National Center for Health Statistics and published in "Nursing Home Utilization by Current Residents" in **Vital and Health Statistics**, Series 13, No. 102, 1989. The National Center for Health Statistics (NCHS) conducts a variety of surveys from which health-related data are drawn. Additional data, including some unpublished data, on this topic are available from NCHS (Hyattsville, MD).

Methodology: These data were collected by means of the National Nursing Home Survey, which is a sample survey of nursing homes, their residents, discharges, and the staff in the coterminous U.S. Nurses at each institution referred to medical records in order to provide the information needed.

Definitions: "Nursing homes" include all types of nursing and related care homes with three or more beds set up and staffed for use by residents and routinely providing nursing and personal care services. Residential care facilities are excluded. These include community care facilities in California, adult congregate living facilities in Florida, family care homes in Kentucky, and adult foster care homes in Michigan.

Qualifications: Therefore, the data are subject to sampling and nonsampling error. The sample frame consisted of 20,479 nursing and related care facilities of which 1,079 were included in the survey. The response rate was 93 percent. Percentages may not total 100 because of rounding.

Interpretation: After age 65 the number (and proportion) in the nursing home population requiring assistance in daily activities increases steadily.

I-13. DISABILITY
BED DAYS ASSOCIATED WITH ACUTE CONDITIONS
1989

Condition	All Ages	Bed Disability Rate*					
		Under 5 Years	5 to 17 Years	18 to 24 Years	25 to 44 Years	45 to 64 Years	65 Years and over
All Acute Conditions	344.4	447.7	409.7	321.7	300.3	279.2	415.7
Infectious and Parasitic Diseases	35.3	77.3	78.9	31.2	21.1	13.3	17.1[a]
Respiratory Conditions	172.3	252.0	251.5	159.2	148.8	132.1	137.1
Common Cold	29.5	68.1	34.5	36.4	26.7	20.7	12.7[a]
Influenza	107.9	137.5	176.6	91.0	92.7	87.4	70.9
Acute Bronchitis	8.0	12.6[a]	8.8[a]	12.8[a]	7.5	5.9[a]	3.8[a]
Digestive System Conditions	13.0	3.5[a]	10.9[a]	6.1[a]	9.1	18.2	30.6
Acute Ear Infections	9.2	57.7	15.3	1.7[a]	2.0[a]	3.7[a]	3.2[a]

*Rates are based on bed days per 100 persons.
Figures with the superscript[a] do not meet acceptable standards of statistical reliability.

Source: Based on data collected by the National Center for Health Statistics and published in "Current Estimates from the National Health Interview Survey" in **Vital Health Statistics**, Series 10, No. 176. The National Center for Health Statistics (NCHS) conducts a variety of surveys from which health-related data are drawn. Additional data, including some unpublished data, on this topic are available from NCHS (Hyattsville, MD).

Methodology: These data were collected by means of the 1989 National Health Interview Survey. In 1989, 45,711 households were interviewed, representing 116,929 persons. Respondents indicated whether they or any family members have had the condition in the last three months. Any acute condition not associated with at least one doctor visit or at least one day of restricted activity was excluded. The data represent the civilian noninstitutionalized population.

Definitions: An "acute condition" is one that caused certain types of impacts associated with health, such as a visit to the doctor or a day spent in bed. In general, acute conditions have rapid asset, last a relatively short period of time, and have no lasting impact on a person's health. A "bed day" is one during which a person stayed in bed more than half a day because of illness or injury.

Qualifications: The National Health Interview Survey is faced with the same drawbacks that characterize all sample surveys. The size and representativeness of the sample, questionnaire design, interviewer skills, and a variety of other factors may affect the quality of the data. The NCHS is the major health data collection agency in the United States and has a reputation for rigorous research methodology. Since respondents were asked to report the existence of hypertension, some misreporting is possible.

Interpretation: The number of bed days associated with acute conditions generally decreases as age increases, up until age 65. While the incidence of most acute conditions decreases with age, digestive system problems among those 65 and over account for the upturn in bed days among this age group.

I-14. MEASLE CASES
LEADING COUNTIES FOR REPORTED CASES OF MEASLES
AMONG PRESCHOOL-AGED CHILDREN
1989

County	Number of Measles Cases Reported
Cook County, Illinois	1,758
Los Angeles County, California	756
Harris County, Texas	729
Milwaukee County, Wisconsin	341
San Bernadino County, California	291
Orange County, California	228
Fresno County, California	155
Dallas County, Texas	126
Hudson County, New Jersey	100
San Diego County, California	83
Riverside County, California	66
Hillsborough County, Florida	61
Hartford County, Connecticut	42
Cuyahoga County, Ohio	36
Queens County, New York	35
Washington, D.C.	26
Duvall County, Florida	26
Total for all urban counties	5,047

Source: Based on data compiled by the Centers for Disease Control and Prevention (CDCP) of the U.S. Public Health Department. The Centers for Disease Control and Prevention are charged with tracking the spread of communicable diseases. The best source of CDCP data is its publication **Mortality and Morbidity Weekly Review.**

Methodology: Health care providers and officials are required by law to report certain diseases to disease control authorities. These data are usually reported at the county level to the local health department. These data are compiled at the national-level by the CDCP.

Qualifications: Statistics on communicable diseases are compiled from reports made to local health departments and, occasionally, from data obtained in community surveys. Although the reporting of specified communicable diseases by health professionals is required by law, reporting has been found to be less than complete.

Interpretation: The reported number of measles cases in 1989 constitutes some thing of an epidemic. The Chicago area accounts for a disproportionate share of the nation's measles cases.

I-15. MORBIDITY RATES
REPORTED CASES OF MEASLES BY AGE
1989

Age Cohort	Cases	Rate*
0-4	6,035	32.4
5-9	1,491	8.2
10-14	1,969	11.7
15-19	3,889	21.3
20-24	1,337	6.8
25 and over	1,387	0.9
Total	16,108	6.5

*Rates are reported as cases per 100,000 population.

Source: Based on data complied by the Centers for Disease Control and Prevention (CDCP) of the U.S. Public Health Department and reprinted in the Metropolitan Life **Statistical Bulletin**, January-March, 1990. The **Statistical Bulletin** published by Metropolitan Life Insurance Company reprints data from a variety of sources including the experiences of the large Metropolitan Life insured population, data not available elsewhere. The Centers for Disease Control and Prevention are charged with tracking the spread of communicable diseases. The best source of CDCP data is its publication **Mortality and Morbidity Weekly Review.**

Methodology: Based on data reported to the Centers for Disease Control and Prevention by state and territorial health departments during 1989. Health care providers and officials are required by law to report certain diseases to disease control authorities. These data are usually reported at the county level to the local health department. These data are compiled at the national level by the CDCP.

Qualifications: Statistics on communicable diseases are compiled from reports made to local health departments and, occasionally, from data obtained in community surveys. Although the reporting of specified communicable diseases by health professionals is required by law, reporting has been found to be less than complete.

Interpretation: While the highest incidence of measles is found among very young children, the number of cases among older children and even adults is not insubstantial. The rates for 1989 are several times higher in every age category than they were in 1988, indicating the existence of something of an epidemic of measles.

I-16. AIDS CASES
REPORTED CASES OF AIDS BY EXPOSURE GROUP
1989

HIV exposure group	Number	Percent
Homosexual/bisexual men	19,652	55.8%
Intravenous-drug users		
Women and heterosexual men	7,970	22.6
Homosexual/bisexual men	2,138	6.1
Persons with hemophilia		
Adult/adolescent	296	0.8
Child	26	<0.1
Transfusion recipients		
Adult/adolescent	768	2.2
Child	40	0.1
Heterosexual contacts	1,562	4.4
Persons born in countries where		
heterosexual transmission predominates	392	1.1
Perinatal	547	1.6
No identified risk	1,848	5.2
Total	36,238	100.0

Source: Based on data collected by the Centers for Disease Control and Prevention (CDCP) within the U.S. Public Health Service and published in **Morbidity and Mortality Weekly Report**, February 5, 1990. The Centers for Disease Control and Prevention (Atlanta) are charged with tracking the spread of communicable diseases.

Methodology: Based on data reported to the Centers for Disease Control and Prevention by state and territorial health departments during 1989. Health care providers and officials are required by law to report certain diseases to disease control authorities. These data are usually reported at the county level to the local health department. These data are compiled at the national level by the CDCP.

Definitions: "Reported cases of AIDS" refers to those individuals who have been identified as infected on the basis of AIDS tests and who have been subsequently reported to public health authorities.

Qualifications: Since the reporting of AIDS cases is not required by law, the figures compiled can be assumed to be some fraction of the total number of AIDS cases within the population.

Interpretation: AIDS continues to be concentrated among homosexual males and intravenous-drug users of both sexes. However, the proportion represented by heterosexuals and non-drug users has increased in recent years.

I-17. AIDS CASES
REPORTED AIDS CASES BY SELECTED
DEMOGRAPHIC CHARACTERISTICS
1990*

Characteristic	Number of Cases	Percent Distribution by Characteristic
Total	33,215	100.0%
Sex:		
Male	29,050	89.0
Female	3,599	11.0
Race/Ethnicity:		
White	17,834	54.6
Black	10,198	31.2
Hispanic	4,256	13.0
Other	361	1.1
Age:		
Under 13	566	1.7
13-19	120	0.4
20-29	6,352	19.1
30-39	15,166	45.7
40-49	7,653	23.0
50-59	2,377	7.2
60 and over	981	3.0

*Figures through September 30, 1990, only.

Source: Based on data collected by the Centers for Disease Control and Prevention (CDCP) within the U.S. Public Health Service and published in **Morbidity and Mortality Weekly Report,** February 5, 1990. The Centers for Disease Control and Prevention (Atlanta) are charged with tracking the spread of communicable diseases.

Methodology: Based on data reported to the Centers for Disease Control and Prevention by state and territorial health departments during 1990. Health care providers and officials are required by law to report certain diseases to disease control authorities. These data are usually reported at the county level to the local health department. These data are compiled at the national level by the CDCP.

Definitions: "Reported cases of AIDS" refers to those individuals who have been identified as infected on the basis of AIDS tests and who have been subsequently reported to public health authorities. Figures for sex, race, and age refer to individuals 13 or older only. Figures for whites and blacks exclude Hispanics.

Qualifications: Since the reporting of AIDS cases is not required by law, the figures compiled can be assumed to be some fraction of the total number of AIDS cases within the population.

Interpretation: There are significant differences in the prevalence of AIDS for various sex, race and age groups. AIDS patients are disproportionately male, black and Hispanic, and aged 20 to 49.

I-18. AIDS CASES
ACQUIRED IMMUNODEFICIENCY SYNDROME (AIDS)
RATE BY STATE
1989

State	Incidence Rate of Reported AIDS Cases*
Total	13.4
Alabama	5.4
Alaska	2.6
Arizona	7.6
Arkansas	3.0
California	22.2
Colorado	11.5
Connecticut	13.6
Delaware	11.5
District of Columbia	84.1
Florida	27.5
Georgia	18.0
Hawaii	14.2
Idaho	2.1
Illinois	9.7
Indiana	4.9
Iowa	2.0
Kansas	4.0
Kentucky	2.9
Louisiana	10.4
Maine	4.0
Maryland	13.5
Massachusetts	13.0
Michigan	5.3
Minnesota	4.4
Mississippi	5.7
Missouri	8.5
Montana	1.5
Nebraska	2.7
Nevada	17.1
New Hampshire	4.1
New Jersey	28.9
New Mexico	6.3
New York	35.8
North Carolina	5.7
North Dakota	0.9
Ohio	4.5
Oklahoma	4.5
Oregon	8.0
Pennsylvania	9.3

(Continued on next page)

I-18. AIDS CASES
ACQUIRED IMMUNODEFICIENCY SYNDROME (AIDS)
RATE BY STATE
1989 *(Continued from previous page)*

State	Incidence Rate of Reported AIDS Cases*
Rhode Island	8.4
South Carolina	8.0
South Dakota	0.8
Tennessee	5.2
Texas	12.5
Utah	4.9
Vermont	2.2
Virginia	7.1
Washington	10.4
West Virginia	2.0
Wisconsin	2.8
Wyoming	2.7

* Rates are based on reported cases per 100,000 population.

Source: Based on data collected by the Centers for Disease Control and Prevention (CDCP) within the U.S. Public Health Service and published in **Morbidity and Mortality Weekly Report**, February 5, 1990. The Centers for Disease Control and Prevention (Atlanta) are charged with tracking the spread of communicable diseases.

Methodology: Based on data reported to the Centers for Disease Control and Prevention by state and territorial health departments during 1989. Health care providers and officials are required by law to report certain diseases to disease control authorities. These data are usually reported at the county level to the local health department. These data are compiled at the national level by the CDCP.

Definitions: "Reported cases of AIDS" refers to those individuals who have been identified as infected on the basis of AIDS tests and who have been subsequently reported to public health authorities.

Qualifications: Since the reporting of AIDS cases is not required by law, the figures compiled can be assumed to be some fraction of the total number of AIDS cases within the population. The time period used refers to the twelve months ending September 30, 1989.

I-19. AIDS CASES
20 WORST LARGE CITIES FOR AIDS
1981-1990

City	Number of AIDS Cases Reported
New York, New York	28,595
Los Angeles, California	10,194
San Francisco, California	8,933
Houston, Texas	4,481
Newark, New Jersey	4,136
Chicago, Illinois	3,722
Philadelphia, Pennsylvania	3,156
Atlanta, Georgia	3,075
Dallas, Texas	2,643
Boston, Massachusetts	2,471
Ft. Lauderdale, Florida	2,402
San Diego, California	2,237
Oakland, California	1,950
Baltimore, Maryland	1,792
Jersey City, New Jersey	1,656
Nassau-Suffolk, New York	1,574
Seattle, Washington	1,541
Tampa, Florida	1,481
New Orleans, Louisiana	1,380
West Palm Beach, Florida	1,358
Total for Large Cities	130,161

Source: Based on data compiled by the Centers for Disease Control and Prevention (CDCP) of the U.S. Public Health Department and reprinted by the Children's Defense Fund in **Maternal and Child Health in America's Cities** (Special Report Three), January, 1991. The Children's Defense Fund (Washington) is a private organization established as a voice for the children of the United States. The Centers for Disease Control and Prevention are charged with tracking the spread of communicable diseases. The best source of CDCP data is its publication **Mortality and Morbidity Weekly Review**.

Methodology: Based on data reported to the Centers for Disease Control and Prevention by state and territorial health departments during 1989. Health care providers and officials are required by law to report certain diseases to disease control authorities. These data are usually reported at the county level to the local health department. These data are compiled at the national level by the CDCP.

Definitions: "Large cities" for these computations are those with populations of 500,000 or more. The term "city" generally refers to the population within the actual corporate boundaries of the city and may not include adjacent suburbs and urbanized areas. "AIDS" is the acronym for acquired immune deficiency syndrome.

Qualifications: Since the reporting of AIDS cases is not required by law, the figures compiled can be assumed to be some fraction of the total number of AIDS cases within the population. The time period used refers to the twelve months ending September 30, 1989. The reporting period for these data ends with September, 1990.

Interpretation: AIDS cases are concentrated within the nation's urban areas. Among American cities, three urban areas (New York, Los Angeles, and San Francisco) account for over one-third of the cases.

I-20. AIDS CASES
TEN WORST LARGE CITIES FOR AIDS AMONG CHILDREN
1981-1990

City	Number of Pediatric AIDS Cases Reported
New York, New York	693
Miami, Florida	156
Newark, New Jersey	123
Los Angeles, California	88
Washington, D.C.	62
West Palm Beach, Florida	54
Philadelphia, Pennsylvania	52
Boston, Massachusetts	51
Chicago, Illinois	48
Ft. Lauderdale, Florida	46
Total for Large Cities	2,205

Source: Based on data compiled by the Centers for Disease Control and Prevention (CDCP) of the U.S. Public Health Department and reprinted by the Children's Defense Fund in **Maternal and Child Health in America's Cities** (Special Report Three), January, 1991. The Children's Defense Fund (Washington) is a private organization established as a voice for the children of the United States. The Centers for Disease Control and Prevention are charged with tracking the spread of communicable diseases. The best source of CDCP data is its publication **Mortality and Morbidity Weekly Review.**

Methodology: Based on data reported to the Centers for Disease Control and Prevention by state and territorial health departments during 1989. Health care providers and officials are required by law to report certain diseases to disease control authorities. These data are usually reported at the county level to the local health department. These data are compiled at the national level by the CDCP.

Definitions: "Large cities" for these computations are those with populations of 500,000 or more. The term "city" generally refers to the population within the actual corporate boundaries of the city and may not include adjacent suburbs and urbanized areas. "AIDS" is the acronym for acquired immune deficiency syndrome. "Pediatric" here refers to children under 13 years of age.

Qualifications: Since the reporting of AIDS cases is not required by law, the figures compiled can be assumed to be some fraction of the total number of AIDS cases within the population. The time period used refers to the twelve months ending September 30, 1989. The reporting period for these data ends with September, 1990.

Interpretation: Pediatric AIDS was not initially identified as a problem but has now become a major concern. Nearly half of the pediatric AIDS cases are concentrated in three urban areas (New York, Miami, and Newark).

I-21. DEVELOPMENTAL PROBLEMS
CHILDREN WITH DELAY IN GROWTH OR DEVELOPMENT BY DEMOGRAPHIC AND SOCIAL CHARACTERISTICS
1988

Characteristic	Percent of Children
All children 17 years and under	4.0%
Race/Ethnicity:	
White	4.4
Black	2.1
Hispanic	3.4
Family Income:	
Less than $10,000	5.4
$10,000-$24,999	4.0
$25,000-$39,999	4.0
$40,000 or more	3.9
Place of Residence:	
Metropolitan area	3.8
Non-metropolitan area	4.7
Overall Health Status:	
Excellent, very good or good	3.7
Fair or poor	15.2
Family structure:	
Biological mother and father	3.6
Biological mother and stepfather	3.7
Biological mother only	4.5
All other arrangements	4.8

Source: Based on data collected by the National Center for Health Statistics and published in **Advance Data**, Number 190, November 16, 1990. The National Center for Health Statistics (NCHS) conducts a variety of surveys from which health-related data are drawn. Additional data, including some unpublished data, on this topic is available from NCHS (Hyattsville, MD).

Methodology: These data were collected by NCHS by means of the 1988 National Health Interview Survey of Child Health. These figures are based on data collected by means of personal interviews from a national sample of 17,110 children under the age of 18. The parents of the children were asked a series of questions concerning the child's historical developmental delays, learning disabilities and emotional or behavioral problems.

Definitions: The "Hispanic" category can include both black and white respondents. "Family income" refers to the combined income for members living together in that family as a household unit. A "Metropolitan Area" is an urban area designated by the Census Bureau as a Metropolitan Statistical Area (MSA).

Qualifications: The National Health Interview Survey of Child Health is faced with the same drawbacks that characterize all sample surveys. The size and representativeness of the sample, questionnaire design, interviewer skills and a variety of other factors may affect the quality of the data. Since respondents were asked to report the incidence of this condition, some misreporting is possible due to the fact that a condition of the child may have gone undetected or unrecognized by the parent.

Interpretation: Differences in the distribution of child development problems appear to be influenced by income, family structure, health status, and urban or rural residence. Race and ethnicity appear to be less important than these other factors.

I-22. LEARNING DISABILITIES
CHILDREN EVER HAVING A LEARNING DISABILITY BY DEMOGRAPHIC AND SOCIAL CHARACTERISTICS
1988

Characteristic	Percent of Children
All children 13-17 years	**6.5%**
Race/Ethnicity:	
White	6.7
Black	6.2
Hispanic	5.8
Family Income:	
Less than $10,000	8.4
$10,000-$24,999	7.2
$25,000-$39,999	6.2
$40,000 or more	5.8
Place of Residence:	
Metropolitan area	6.5
Non-metropolitan area	6.5
Overall Health Status:	
Excellent, very good or good	6.3
Fair or poor	15.1
Family structure:	
Biological mother and father	5.5
Biological mother and stepfather	9.1
Biological mother only	7.5
All other arrangements	8.3

Source: Based on data collected by the National Center for Health Statistics and published in **Advance Data,** Number 190, November 16, 1990. The National Center for Health Statistics (NCHS) conducts a variety of surveys from which health-related data are drawn. Additional data, including some unpublished data, on this topic is available from NCHS (Hyattsville, MD).

Methodology: These data were collected by NCHS by means of the 1988 National Health Interview Survey of Child Health. These figures are based on data collected by means of personal interviews from a national sample of 17,110 children under the age of 18. The parents of the children were asked a series of questions concerning the child's historical developmental delays, learning disabilities and emotional or behavioral problems.

Definitions: Respondents were included who had ever had a learning disability, not just those reporting a learning disability at the time of the survey. The "Hispanic" category can include both black and white respondents. "Family income" refers to the combined income for members living together in that family as a household unit. A "Metropolitan Area" is an urban area designated by the Census Bureau as a Metropolitan Statistical Area (MSA).

Qualifications: The National Health Interview Survey of Child Health is faced with the same drawbacks that characterize all sample surveys. The size and representativeness of the sample, questionnaire design, interviewer skills and a variety of other factors may affect the quality of the data. Since respondents were asked to report the incidence of this condition, some misreporting is possible due to the fact that a condition of the child may have gone undetected or unrecognized by the parent.

Interpretation: The distribution of learning disability problems within the population appears to be influenced by income, family structure, and health status.

I-23. EMOTIONAL/BEHAVIORAL PROBLEMS
CHILDREN EVER HAVING AN EMOTIONAL OR BEHAVIORAL PROBLEM BY DEMOGRAPHIC AND SOCIAL CHARACTERISTICS
1988

Characteristic	Percent of Children
All children 13-17 years	13.4%
Race/Ethnicity:	
White	14.2
Black	10.3
Hispanic	12.0
Family Income:	
Less than $10,000	15.8
$10,000-$24,999	14.5
$25,000-$39,999	13.4
$40,000 or more	12.8
Place of Residence:	
Metropolitan area	13.7
Non-metropolitan area	12.4
Overall Health Status:	
Excellent, very good or good	13.1
Fair or poor	23.3
Family structure:	
Biological mother and father	8.3
Biological mother and stepfather	23.6
Biological mother only	19.1
All other arrangements	22.2

Source: Based on data collected by the National Center for Health Statistics and published in **Advance Data,** Number 190, November 16, 1990. The National Center for Health Statistics (NCHS) conducts a variety of surveys from which health-related data are drawn. Additional data, including some unpublished data, on this topic is available from NCHS (Hyattsville, MD).

Methodology: These data were collected by NCHS by means of the 1988 National Health Interview Survey of Child Health. These figures are based on data collected by means of personal interviews from a national sample of 17,110 children under the age of 18. The parents of the children were asked a series of questions concerning the child's historical developmental delays, learning disabilities and emotional or behavioral problems.

Definitions: Respondents were included who had ever had an emotional or behavioral problem that lasted three months or more. The "Hispanic" category can include both black and white respondents. "Family income" refers to the combined income for members living together in that family as a household unit. A "Metropolitan Area" is an urban area designated by the Census Bureau as a Metropolitan Statistical Area (MSA).

Qualifications: The National Health Interview Survey of Child Health is faced with the same drawbacks that characterize all sample surveys. The size and representativeness of the sample, questionnaire design, interviewer skills and a variety of other factors may affect the quality of the data. Since respondents were asked to report the incidence of this condition, some misreporting is possible due to the fact that a condition of the child may have gone undetected or unrecognized by the parent.

Interpretation: The distribution of childhood emotional or behavioral problems within the population appears to be influenced by family structure, health status and (to a lesser extent) income.

I-24. HEALTH BEHAVIOR
HEALTH-PROMOTING PRACTICES BY U.S. ADULTS
1990

Health-Promoting Behavior	Proportion of U.S. Adults
Do not smoke	74%
Avoid smoking in bed	91
Wear seat belt	65
Avoid driving after drinking	81
Smoke detector in home	86
Socialize regularly	84
Frequent strenuous exercise	34
Drink alcohol moderately	91
Avoid home accidents	78
Limit fat in diet	56
Maintain proper weight	22
Obey speed limit	53
Annual blood pressure test	85
Control stress	71
Consume fiber	59
Limit cholesterol in diet	49
Adequate vitamins and minerals	59
Annual dental examination	75
Limit sodium in diet	51
Limit sugar in diet	46
7-8 hours sleep per night	61

Source: Based on data collected for **Prevention Magazine** and published as "The Prevention Index" (1990).

Methodology: Telephone interviews were conducted nationwide by Louis Harris and Associates with around 1,300 randomly-selected adults.

Qualifications: All sample surveys are characterized by inherent drawbacks. The size and representativeness of the sample questionnaire design, interviewer skills, and other factors may affect the quality of the data. The Louis Harris polling organization, however, has a long history of quality survey research.

Interpretation: U.S. adults have become increasingly health conscious and have improved their participation in health-related behaviors. Nevertheless, large segments of the population (representing tens of millions of people) still do not subscribe to healthy behavior.

I-25. SMOKING HABITS
CIGARETTE SMOKING STATUS BY AGE
1987

Age	Never Smoked	Former Smoker	Current Smoker
All Ages	48.4%	22.8%	28.8%
18 to 24 years	64.9	8.0	27.1
25 to 44 years	47.2	19.6	33.2
45 to 64 years	39.3	29.8	30.9
65 to 74 years	44.2	36.8	19.0
75 years and over	61.5	29.6	8.9

Source: Based on data collected by the National Center for Health Statistics and published in "Smoking and Other Tobacco Use: United States, 1987 in **Vital and Health Statistics**, Series 10, No. 169. The National Center for Health Statistics (NCHS) conducts a variety of surveys from which health-related data are drawn. Additional data, including some unpublished data, on this topic are available from NCHS (Hyattsville, MD).

Methodology: These data were collected by the NCHS by means of the 1987 National Health Interview Survey. These figures are based on data collected annually from a nationwide sample of between 36,000 and 46,000 households.

Definitions: "Never smoked" refers to a person who has never smoked or has smoked less than 100 cigarettes in their lifetime. A "former smoker" is a person who has smoked 100 or more cigarettes in their lifetime, but does not currently smoke. A "current smoker" has smoked 100 or more cigarettes in their lifetime and is still smoking. Data are for the population age 18 and over.

Qualifications: The National Health Interview Survey is faced with the same drawbacks that characterize all sample surveys. The size and representativeness of the sample, questionnaire design, interviewer skills, and a variety of other factors may affect the quality of the data. The NCHS is the major health data collection agency in the United States and has a reputation for rigorous research methodology. Since respondents were asked to report the existence of hypertension, some misreporting is possible.

I-26. SMOKING HABITS
CIGARETTES SMOKING STATUS BY SEX AND RACE
1990

Sex/Race Group	Current Smokers
All sexes/races	25.4%
All males:	28.0
White males	27.6
Black males	32.2
All females:	23.1
White females	23.9
Black females	20.4

Source: Based on data collected by the National Health Interview Survey conducted by the National Center for Health Statistics (NCHS) within the Department of Health and Human Services. Published in **Advance Data**, No. 204, July 1, 1991. NCHS is the principal federal agency for the compilation and dissemination of health-related data. Additional data, including some unpublished data, on this topic is available from NCHS (Hyattsville, MD).

Methodology: These data were collected by the NCHS by means of the 1990 National Health Interview Survey. These figures are based on data collected by means of personal interviews conducted annually of a national sample of between 36,000 and 46,000 households. This question was asked only of those 18 and over.

Definitions: "Current smokers" includes those 18 and over who have smoked at least 100 cigarettes and who now smoke.

Qualifications: The National Health Interview Survey is faced with the same drawbacks that characterize all sample surveys. The size and representativeness of the sample, questionnaire design, interviewer skills, and a variety of other factors may affect the quality of the data. The NCHS is the major health data collection agency in the United States, however, and has a reputation for rigorous research methodology.

I-27. DRUG ABUSE
COCAINE ADDICTION ESTIMATES BY STATE
1988

State	Total Addicts	Addiction Rate*	U.S. Rank By Rate
Alabama	22,000	5.5	27
Alaska	3,700	7.1	19
Arizona	43,000	12.7	4
Arkansas	8,400	3.5	39
California	325,000	11.8	6
Colorado	34,000	10.4	7
Connecticut	24,000	7.5	18
Delaware	2,700	4.2	33
District of Columbia	20,000	32.9	1
Florida	93,000	7.7	17
Georgia	48,000	7.7	16
Hawaii	9,400	8.7	12
Idaho	3,100	3.1	41
Illinois	142,000	12.2	5
Indiana	14,000	2.5	44
Iowa	7,800	2.8	42
Kansas	13,000	5.4	28
Kentucky	13,500	3.6	38
Louisiana	29,000	76.5	23
Maine	2,900	2.5	45
Maryland	47,000	10.3	8
Massachusetts	30,000	5.2	30
Michigan	61,000	6.6	22
Minnesota	26,000	6.1	26
Mississippi	6,200	2.4	46
Missouri	46,000	9.0	10
Montana	1,700	2.1	48
Nebraska	7,900	4.9	31
Nevada	23,000	22.4	3
New Hampshire	3,500	3.3	40
New Jersey	66,000	8.6	13
New Mexico	12,800	8.5	15
New York	434,000	24.4	2
North Carolina	40,000	6.3	25
North Dakota	1,400	2.1	49
Ohio	57,000	5.3	29
Oklahoma	22,500	16.9	20
Oregon	17,000	6.4	24
Pennsylvania	81,000	6.8	21
Rhode Island	3,900	3.9	35
South Carolina	12,600	3.7	37
South Dakota	800	1.1	51

(Continued on next page)

I-27. DRUG ABUSE
COCAINE ADDICTION ESTIMATES BY STATE

1988 *(Continued from previous page)*

State	Total Addicts	Addiction Rate*	U.S. Rank By Rate
Tennessee	23,000	4.7	32
Texas	144,000	8.6	14
Utah	6,500	3.9	36
Vermont	1,200	2.2	47
Virginia	53,000	9.0	11
Washington	18,000	4.0	34
West Virginia	3,800	2.0	50
Wisconsin	47,000	9.9	9
Wyoming	1,300	2.7	53

*Rate is based on number of addicts per 1,000 population.

Source: Based on data collected by the National Institute on Drug Abuse. The National Institute on Drug Abuse is the major federal source of substance abuse data.

Methodology: The National Institute on Drug Abuse periodically conducts a National Household Survey on Drug Abuse on a sample of the U.S. population 12 years and older.

Definitions: "Addiction" is defined in terms of standards developed by the National Institute on Drug Abuse.

Qualifications: The National Household Survey on Drug Abuse is faced with the same drawbacks that characterize all sample surveys. The size and representativeness of the sample, questionnaire design, interviewer skills and a variety of other factors may affect the quality of the data. It is particularly difficult to elicit accurate responses on issues as sensitive as substance use.

Interpretation: The rate of cocaine addiction varies widely by state. The rates range from a high of 32.9 cocaine addicts per 1,000 population in the District of Columbia to a low of 1.1 per 1,000 in South Dakota.

I-28. SUBSTANCE ABUSE
USE OF SELECTED SUBSTANCES
BY YOUTHS AND YOUNG ADULTS
1990

| | Percent Using | | |
	Cigarettes	Alcohol	Marijuana
Total 12-17 years	12%	25%	5%
Males 12-17	12	25	6
Females 12-17	11	24	4
Total 18-25 years	32	63	13
Males 18-25	36	74	17
Females 18-25	27	53	9

Source: Based on data collected by the National Institute on Drug Abuse and published in **Health, United States, 1991.** The National Institute on Drug Abuse is the major federal source of substance abuse data.

Methodology: The National Institute on Drug Abuse periodically conducts a National Household Survey on Drug Abuse on a sample of the U.S. population 12 years and older.

Definitions: "Use" refers to use of the substance at least once during the month prior to the interview.

Qualifications: The National Household Survey on Drug Abuse is faced with the same drawbacks that characterize all sample surveys. The size and representativeness of the sample, questionnaire design, interviewer skills and a variety of other factors may affect the quality of the data. It is particularly difficult to elicit accurate responses on issues as sensitive as substance use.

I-29. SUBSTANCE USE

TRENDS IN USE OF SELECTED SUBSTANCES
BY YOUTHS AND YOUNG ADULTS
1974-1990

	Percent Using:					
	Cigarettes		Alcohol		Marijuana	
	Age: 12-17	18-25	12-17	18-25	12-17	18-25
1990	12%	32%	25%	63%	5%	13%
1988	12	35	25	65	6	15
1985	15	37	31	71	12	22
1982	15	40	27	68	12	27
1979	*	*	37	76	17	35
1977	22	47	31	70	17	27
1976	23	49	32	69	12	25
1974	25	49	34	69	12	25

*Data not comparable due to changed definitions.

Source: Based on data collected by the National Institute on Drug Abuse and published in Health, **United States, 1991**. The National Institute on Drug Abuse is the major federal source of substance abuse data.

Methodology: The National Institute on Drug Abuse periodically conducts a National Household Survey on Drug Abuse on a sample of the U.S. population 12 years and older.

Definitions: "Use" refers to use of the substance at least once during the month prior to the interview.

Qualifications: The National Household Survey on Drug Abuse is faced with the same drawbacks that characterize all sample surveys. The size and representativeness of the sample, questionnaire design, interviewer skills and a variety of other factors may affect the quality of the data. It is particularly difficult to elicit accurate responses on issues as sensitive as substance use.

Interpretation: The use of cigarettes, alcohol, and marijuana by youths and young adults generally decreased between 1974 and 1990. However, this survey question does not address the heaviness of use among admitted users and thus limited conclusions can be drawn concerning the extent of substance abuse among youths and young adults.

I-30. OCCUPATIONAL INJURY/ILLNESS
TRENDS IN OCCUPATIONAL INJURY AND ILLNESS
1980-1989

Year	Total Incidence Rate*	Incidence Rate Involving Lost Workdays*	Lost Workdays Rate*
1989	8.6	4.0	78.7
1988	8.6	4.0	76.1
1987	8.3	3.8	69.9
1986	7.9	3.6	65.8
1985	7.9	3.6	64.9
1984	4.0	3.7	63.4
1983	7.6	3.4	58.5
1982	7.7	3.5	58.7
1981	8.3	3.8	61.7
1980	8.7	4.0	65.2

* Rates are based on incidents per 100 full-time employees.

Source: Based on data compiled by the Bureau of Labor Statistics in the U.S. Department of Labor and published in **Source Book of Health Insurance Data** by the Health Insurance Association of America. The Bureau of Labor Statistics (BLS) is the major federal source of work-related data.

Methodology: Data were compiled by the U.S. Department of Labor from the various industries.

Qualifications: What constitutes an industrial injury or illness is a matter of definition. Not all injuries and illnesses are reported to the Department of Labor.

Interpretation: The incidence of occupational injury and illness declined during the mid-1980s but went back up toward the end of the decade. The number of workdays lost increased steadily during the mid- to late-1980s.

I-31. OCCUPATIONAL INJURIES/ILLNESSES
OCCUPATIONAL INJURIES/ILLNESSES AND LOST WORKDAYS
BY INDUSTRY
1988

	Incidence Rate*		Lost Workdays Rate*	
	Injuries	Illnesses	Injuries	Illnesses
Agriculture, forestry & fishing	101.9	4.6	952.1	18.9
Mining	64.4	1.9	1,113.2	12.9
Construction	656.5	6.9	6,396.8	43.0
Manufacturing	2,464.8	176.7	20,254.7	2,071.2
Transportation and public utilities	464.8	9.0	6,165.6	67.7
Wholesale and retail trade	1,534.8	15.3	11,933.5	225.2
Finance, insurance and real estate	119.4	3.1	1,022.6	54.3
Services	1,031.9	23.3	9,104.6	162.8

*Rates are based on incidence per 1,000 employees.

Source: Based on data compiled by the Bureau of Labor Statistics in the U.S. Department of Labor and published in **Source Book of Health Insurance Data** by the Health Insurance Association of America. The Bureau of Labor Statistics (BLS) is the major federal source of work-related data.

Methodology: Data were compiled by the U.S. Department of Labor from the various industries.

Definitions: "Total cases" include fatalities. The "agriculture, forestry, and fishing" category excludes farms with fewer than 11 employees.

Qualifications: What constitutes an industrial injury or illness is a matter of definition. Not all injuries and illnesses are reported to the Department of Labor.

Interpretation: The rates of occupational injury and illness varies substantially from industry to industry. Manufacturing accounts by far for the highest rate of both injuries and illnesses.

I-32. DISABILITY
AVERAGE LENGTH OF DISABILITY AND PERCENT OF LOSS OF TIME CLAIMS BY TYPE OF CONDITION
1990-1991

Type of Condition	Average Length of Disability (in weeks)	Percent of All Loss of Time Claim Dollars
Eye, ear, nose and throat	4.3	2.9%
Respiratory system	3.8	2.0
Heart disease	10.0	6.2
Other circulatory disorders	6.8	2.6
Digestive system	5.8	6.0
Maternity	9.1	21.8
Genitourinary	5.6	5.2
Alcohol and drug abuse	4.2	1.9
Mental and behavioral	6.6	2.2
Musculoskeletal	8.3	15.5
Cancer	12.9	4.8
Accidents	6.6	18.6
Miscellaneous diagnoses	6.2	10.3
All Diagnoses	7.1	100.0

Source: Based on data collected by the Mutual of Omaha Companies and published in their report, **Current Trends in Health Care Costs and Utilization** (1991 edition). Mutual of Omaha (Omaha) is a leading health insurer and, as such, generates a large amount of data on the health care of its employees.

Methodology: Utilizing a sample of records from enrollees in Mutual of Omaha group health plans, the company develops statistics related to the cost and utilization of health care for this population. Statistical tests are utilized to assure the validity of the data.

Definitions: "Disability" refers to claims in which insurance plan enrollees claimed payment of loss of work time.

Qualifications: Since these data are based on a sample of records they are subject to sampling error. The accuracy of the data is also a function of the accuracy of the codes applied to the records. These statistics refer only to Mutual of Omaha enrollees in group health plans and may not be entirely representative of the total U.S. population.

Interpretation: Cancer and heart problems account for the greatest amount of disability among Mutual of Omaha enrollees. Maternity cases account for the largest share of loss-of-time claims, followed by accidents and musculo-skeletal problems.

DATA ON FERTILITY

Fertility data have a longer history than most other health-related information in the United States because there has been a good-quality birth registration system in place for six decades. Fertility data are obtained primarily from vital event (birth) registries, censuses and surveys. Registry data are maintained primarily by the National Center for Health Statistics (NCHS) which is also responsible for most of the surveys that collect fertility data. In addition, hospitals and other health organizations that provide obstetrical services have their own internal databases which include a great deal of detailed information about the mothers and children who have been patients at these facilities. As the inherent connection between health care and characteristics of children born (e.g., the birth weight of a newborn) has become more obvious, increased emphasis has been placed on fertility data.

The basic source of birth data is the information compiled for birth registration. These registries include some data on the health and demographic characteristics of the child and mother along with limited data on the father. These data are initially collected for individual births and first aggregated at the county level, though data for smaller units of geography are available. When combined with age-specific population and size data, birth rates can be calculated. By combining birth rates with population projections, along with assumptions about birth rate changes, a birth forecast for a specific area becomes possible. Further analysis using characteristics of mothers and babies facilitates the forecasting of needs for services specific to mothers and children.

On the decennial census items related to fertility have been limited historically to the issue of the number of children ever born. This information becomes useful when cross-tabulated by factors known or thought to be related to differences in births, such as age, marital status, and employment status. Birth projections for a market area can be fine-tuned by accounting for the way a population's birth expectancy is shaped by its demographic composition. Because census data are available for very small units of geography, these rates can be calculated for virtually any type of market or service area.

The National Family Growth Survey (NFGS) conducted by NCHS provides data at the national level for fertility and fertility-related activity and behavior such as type of contraceptive used. The NFGS is the latest in a long line of national level fertility studies that date back to the 1950s. These surveys have allowed demographers and others to: 1) chart the narrowing of fertility differentials across religious groups, 2) observe historical shifts in preference for type of contraceptives; and 3) provide insight into the reduction of black-white fertility differences. Other NCHS surveys include items on fertility-related behavior. Several surveys conducted by private vendors also address such behavior.

Birth registration is an ongoing phenomenon, making methods of measuring change necessary. Combining registry data with internal records (e.g. hospital or clinic) improves the value of the data immensely and broadens their application. National survey data present an opportunity to compare local area trends with national ones. In additional, these national data provide insights into phenomena that are not being measured or seen at the local level.

Fertility data are available at the national level through **Vital and Health Statistics** reports produced by the National Center for Health Statistics, surveys conducted by NCHS, and as a part of the Census Bureau's Current Population Survey (CPS). At the state and local level, birth data are available from agencies and planning boards, with original birth certificates being filed with the local health department which is often a good source of such data.

While most aggregated fertility data are available in published form, micro-data (individual birth records with identifying personal information removed) can be obtained from national and state sources on computer tape. In the near future, these data will be placed on CD-ROM. Survey data are available on both computer tape and on CD-ROM.

II-1. BIRTHS
ANNUAL BIRTHS TO U.S. WOMEN
1945-1991

Year	Births (in millions)	Year	Births (in millions)
1991	4.1	1967	3.5
1990	4.2	1966	3.6
1989	4.0	1965	3.8
1988	3.9	1964	4.0
1987	3.8	1963	4.1
1986	3.8	1962	4.2
1985	3.7	1961	4.3
1984	3.7	1960	4.3
1983	3.6	1959	4.2
1982	3.7	1958	4.3
1981	3.6	1957	4.3
1980	3.6	1956	4.2
1979	3.5	1955	4.1
1978	3.3	1954	4.1
1977	3.3	1953	4.0
1976	3.2	1952	3.9
1975	3.1	1951	3.8
1974	3.2	1950	3.6
1973	3.1	1949	3.6
1972	3.3	1948	3.6
1971	3.6	1947	3.8
1970	3.7	1946	3.4
1969	3.6	1945	2.9
1968	3.5		

Sources: Data published in **U.S. Bureau of the Census** in Historical Statistics of the U.S. Colonial Times to 1970, Part 1, Series B1-4 and Statistical Abstract of the United States 1990. Core source data came from the annual reports, **Vital Statistics of the United States**, published by the National Center for Health Statistics. "Annual Summary of Births, Marriages, Divorces, and Deaths: United States, 1991." **Monthly Vital Statistics Report**, Vol. 40, No. 13, 1992.

Methodology: These data are based on information coded by the National Center for Health Statistics (NCHS) from copies of original birth certificates received from state registration offices. The data are provided to NCHS through the Vital Statistics Cooperative Program (VSCP).

Interpretation: The total number of annual births increased steadily after World War II until 1957, remained high until the mid-1960s, and fell through the late 1970s. Births increased again during the 1980s and once again are at or near levels seen during the baby boom.

II-2. BIRTHS
ANNUAL BIRTHS BY RACE
1960-1989

	Total	White	Births By Race (in 1,000s) Percent	Black	Percent	Other	Percent
1989	4,041	3,132	77.5%	709	17.5%	200	5.0%
1985	3,761	2,991	79.5	608	16.2	161	4.3
1980	3,612	2,899	80.3	589	16.3	124	3.4
1975	3,144	2,552	81.2	511	16.3	81	2.5
1970	3,731	3,091	82.8	572	15.3	68	1.9
1965	3,760	3,124	83.0	581	15.4	55	1.6
1960	4,258	3,601	84.6	602	14.1	55	1.3

Source: Based on data collected by the National Center for Health Statistics and published in "Advance Report of Final Natality Statistics, 1989." **Monthly Vital Statistics Report**, Vol. 40, No. 8, 1992.

Methodology: These data are based on information coded by the National Center for Health Statistics (NCHS) from copies of original birth certificates received from state registration offices. The data are provided to NCHS through the Vital Statistics Cooperative Program (VSCP).

Qualifications: Race designation in 1989 was based on race of mother. Prior to 1989 designation was based on race of child as it appeared on the birth certificate.

Interpretation: The proportion of all births that are black or other races has increased steadily since 1960.

II-3. BIRTHS
BIRTHS AND BIRTH RATES BY AGE OF MOTHER
1989

Age Group	Number of Births	Birth Rate*
Under 15 years	11,486	1.4
15-19 years	506,503	58.1
20-24 years	1,077,598	115.4
25-29 years	1,263,098	116.6
30-34 years	842,395	76.2
35-39 years	293,878	29.7
40-44 years	44,401	5.2
45-49 years	1,599	0.2
Total	4,040,958	69.2

*Rates are expressed as births per 1,000 women in the age range specified

Source: Based on data collected by the National Center for Health Statistics and published in **Monthly Vital Statistics Report,** Vol. 40, No. 8, 1991.

Methodology: These data are based on information coded by the National Center for Health Statistics (NCHS) from copies of original birth certificates received from state registration offices. The data are provided to NCHS through the Vital Statistics Cooperative Program (VSCP).

Qualifications: Fertility statistics are usually based on data compiled from birth certificates. The quality of data entered on birth certificates may vary from locality to locality. Since the NCHS must compile fertility data for the entire United States there is a considerable time lag before this information can be made available.

Interpretation: Births and birth rates peak at ages 20 to 29. However, in 1989 over 800,000 births occurred to mothers who were in their early 30s and over 300,000 to women 35 and older.

II-4. BIRTHS
TEN STATES WITH THE LARGEST NUMBER OF BIRTHS
1990

State	Number
California	617,704
Texas	329,976
New York	302,084
Florida	199,481
Illinois	192,545
Pennsylvania	172,145
Ohio	165,546
Michigan	157,674
New Jersey	120,654
Georgia	114,818
United States Total	4,179,000

Source: Based on data collected by the National Center for Health Statistics and published in "Annual Summary of Births, Marriages, Divorces, and Deaths: United States, 1990" in **Monthly Vital Statistics Report**, Vol. 40, No. 8, 1991.

Methodology: These data are based on information coded by the National Center for Health Statistics (NCHS) from copies of original birth certificates received from state registration offices. The data are provided to NCHS through the Vital Statistics Cooperative Program (VSCP).

Interpretation: The top ten states accounted for about 57 percent of all births in the U.S. in 1990.

II-5. BIRTHS
PERCENT OF CHILDREN BORN TO UNMARRIED
WOMEN BY RACE OF CHILD
1970-1989

		Race of Child		
Year	White	Black	Native American	Chinese
1989	19.2	65.7	52.7	4.2
1985	14.5	60.1	40.7	3.7
1980	11.0	55.2	33.5	3.3
1975	7.0	49.0	27.9	3.3
1970	5.5	37.4	19.8	3.0

Source: Based on data compiled by the National Center for Health Statistics and published in **Health, United States, 1991.**

Methodology: These data are based on information coded by the National Center for Health Statistics (NCHS) from copies of original birth certificates received from state registration offices. The data are provided to NCHS through the Vital Statistics Cooperative Program (VSCP).

Qualifications: Fertility statistics are usually based on data compiled from birth certificates. The quality of data entered on birth certificates may vary from locality to locality. Since the NCHS must compile fertility data for the entire United States there is a considerable time lag before this information can be made available.

Interpretation: The percentage of births born to unmarried mothers has increased markedly since 1970. Blacks and Native Americans report much higher rates of illegitimacy than do whites and Chinese.

II-6. FERTILITY RATES
TOTAL FERTILITY RATE BY RACE
1970-1989

	All Races	White	Black
1989	2,014.0	1,885.0	2,554.5
1985	1,842.5	1,754.0	2,196.0
1980	1,839.5	1,748.5	2,266.0
1975	1,774.0	1,686.0	2,243.0
1970	2,480.0	2,385.0	3,098.7

Source: Based on data collected by the National Center for Health Statistics and published in "Advance Report of Final Natality Statistics, 1988" in **Monthly Vital Statistics Report,** Vol. 40, No. 8, 1991.

Methodology: These data are based on information coded by the National Center for Health Statistics (NCHS) from copies of original birth certificates received from state registration offices. The data are provided to NCHS through the Vital Statistics Cooperative Program (VSCP).

Definitions: The "total fertility rate" (TFR) is the hypothetical number of children a group of 1,000 15-year-old females would have throughout their childbearing years assuming no change in age-specific birth rates. While age-specific fertility rates may change over the childbearing interval, the TFR is a good measure for ascertaining relative differences and changes in fertility rates over time.

Interpretation: Total fertility rates have declined since 1970, though recently a slight upturn has been seen. Black-white rate differences in the total fertility rate narrowed during this time period.

II-7. FERTILITY RATES
AGE-SPECIFIC AND TOTAL FERTILITY RATES BY RACE AND ETHNICITY
1989

	Fertility Rates*			
Age Group	All Races	White	Black	Hispanic
Under 15	1.4	0.7	5.0	2.3
15-19 years	58.1	48.5	110.4	100.8
20-24 years	115.4	108.0	157.1	184.4
25-29 years	116.6	116.1	112.6	146.6
30-34 years	76.2	76.6	65.1	92.1
35-39 years	29.7	29.3	26.8	43.5
40-44 years	5.2	4.9	5.5	10.4
45-49 years	0.2	0.2	0.3	0.6
Total Fertility Rate	2,014.0	1,885.0	2,554.5	2,902.0

*Rates are expressed as births per 1,000 women in the age and race/ethnicity category specified

Source: Based on data collected by the National Center for Health Statistics and published in "Advance Report of Final Natality Statistics, 1989." **Monthly Vital Statistics Report,** Vol. 40, No. 8, 1991.

Methodology: These data are based on information coded by the National Center for Health Statistics (NCHS) from copies of original birth certificates received from state registration offices. The data are provided to NCHS through the Vital Statistics Cooperative Program (VSCP). Data for Hispanics are for the 47 states reporting births by Hispanic origin.

Definitions: The total fertility rate (TFR) is a hypothetical number of children a group of 1,000 15-year-old females would have throughout their childbearing years assuming no change in age-specific birth rates. While age-specific fertility rates may change over the childbearing interval, the TFR is a good measure for ascertaining relative differences and changes in fertility rates over time.

Interpretation: Black birth rates overall are higher than those of whites and Hispanic rates exceed those of blacks. Significant differences exist among the racial groups in terms of age-specific fertility rates.

II-8. TEENAGE BIRTHS
TOP LARGE CITIES FOR TEENAGE BIRTHS
1987

City	Percent of Births to Teenagers
Baltimore, Maryland	22.9
Detroit, Michigan	21.8
Cleveland, Ohio	20.8
Memphis, Tennessee	19.6
Milwaukee, Wisconsin	19.3
New Orleans, Louisiana	18.7
Dallas, Texas	18.6
Chicago, Illinois	18.5
San Antonio, Texas	18.5
Philadelphia, Pennsylvania	17.1
Washington, D.C.	16.3
Indianapolis, Indiana	16.2
Average for all large cities	15.9
United States average	12.4

Source: Based on data compiled by the National Center for Health Statistics. Reprinted by the Children's Defense Fund in **Maternal and Child Health in America's Cities** (Special Report Three), January, 1991. The Children's Defense Fund (Washington) is a private organization established as a voice for the children of the United States. For more information, refer to the detailed statistics published by the NCHS in **Vital Statistics for the United States**. Additional data, including some unpublished data, on this topic, is available from NCHS (Hyattsville, MD).

Methodology: The National Center for Health Statistics (NCHS) compiles fertility data from death registration information collected at the local level.

Definitions: "Large cities" for these computations are those with populations of 500,000 or more. The term "city" generally refers to the population within the actual corporate boundaries of the city and may not include adjacent suburbs and urbanized areas.

Qualifications: Fertility statistics are usually based on data compiled from birth certificates. The quality of data entered on birth certificates may vary from locality to locality. Since the NCHS must compile fertility data for the entire United States there is a considerable time lag before this information can be made available. It is possible that the teenage fertility rates have changed since 1987.

II-9. BIRTH WEIGHT
PERCENT LOW BIRTH WEIGHT BABIES BY AGE AND RACE OF MOTHER
1989

Age Group	All Races	White	Black
All Ages	7.0	5.7	13.2
Under 15	13.4	10.2	15.8
15-19	9.3	7.5	13.2
15	11.3	8.6	14.4
16	10.6	8.6	13.7
17	9.6	7.9	13.2
18	9.1	7.5	12.8
19	8.5	6.9	12.9
20-24	7.2	5.8	12.6
25-29	6.2	5.1	13.2
30-34	6.5	5.4	14.1
35-39	7.2	6.1	14.3
40-44	8.4	7.4	14.3
45-49	10.5	10.6	15.9

Source: Based on data collected by the National Center for Health Statistics and published in "Advance Report of Final Natality Statistics, 1989" in **Monthly Vital Statistics Report**, Vol. 40, No. 8, 1992.

Methodology: These data are based on information coded by the National Center for Health Statistics (NCHS) from copies of original birth certificates received from state registration offices. The certificates contain data on race and birth weight of live births along with other information. The data are provided to NCHS through the Vital Statistics Cooperative Program (VSCP).

Definitions: "Low birth weight" is defined as a live birth of less than 2,500 grams (5 pounds, 9 ounces).

Qualifications: Fertility statistics are usually based on data compiled from birth certificates. The quality of data entered on birth certificates may vary from locality to locality. Since the NCHS must compile fertility data for the entire United States there is a considerable time lag before this information can be made available.

Interpretation: The likelihood of low birth weight decreases as the mother's age increases until the 35-39 cohort. The likelihood increases for older cohorts. Black babies are more likely to be born at low birth weight.

II-10. BIRTH WEIGHT
WORST LARGE CITIES FOR "LOW" BIRTH WEIGHT BIRTHS
1987

City	Percent of Births With Low Birthweights
Detroit, Michigan	13.6%
Washington, D.C.	13.5
Baltimore, Maryland	12.2
New Orleans, Louisiana	11.4
Memphis, Tennessee	11.3
Philadelphia, Pennsylvania	10.9
Chicago, Illinois	10.5
Cleveland, Ohio	9.9
New York, New York	9.4
Boston, Massachusetts	9.3
Average for all large cities	9.2
United States average	6.9

Source: Based on data compiled by the National Center for Health Statistics. Reprinted by the Children's Defense Fund in **Maternal and Child Health in America's Cities** (Special Report Three), January, 1991. The Children's Defense Fund (Washington) is a private organization established as a voice for the children of the United States. For more information, refer to the detailed statistics published by the NCHS in **Vital Statistics for the United States.** Additional data, including some unpublished data, on this topic, is available from NCHS (Hyattsville, MD).

Methodology: The National Center for Health Statistics (NCHS) compiles fertility data from birth registration information collected at the local level.

Definitions: "Large cities" for these computations are those with populations of 500,000 or more. The term "city" generally refers to the population within the actual corporate boundaries of the city and may not include adjacent suburbs and urbanized areas. "Low birthweight" refers to babies weighing less than 2,500 grams (5.5 pounds) at birth.

Qualifications: Birthweight statistics are usually based on data compiled from birth certificates. The quality of data entered on birth certificates may vary from locality to locality. Since the NCHS must compile fertility data for the entire United States there is a considerable time lag before this information can be made available. It is possible that the incidence of low birthweight births has changed since 1987.

II-11. BIRTH WEIGHT
TRENDS IN "LOW" BIRTH WEIGHT BIRTHS BY RACE
1950-1989

	Percent of Births With Low Birthweights		
Year	Total	White	Nonwhite
1989	7.0%	5.7%	11.6%
1988	6.9	5.6	11.5
1987	6.9	5.7	11.3
1986	6.8	5.6	11.2
1985	6.8	5.6	11.2
1984	6.7	5.6	11.1
1983	6.8	5.6	11.2
1982	6.8	5.6	11.2
1981	6.8	5.7	11.4
1980	6.8	5.7	11.5
1975	7.4	6.3	12.4
1970	7.9	6.8	13.3
1965	8.3	7.2	13.8
1960	7.7	6.9	13.0
1955	7.6	6.8	11.7
1950	7.5	7.1	10.2

Source: Based on data compiled by the National Center for Health Statistics. Reprinted by the Children's Disease Fund in **Maternal and Child Health: Special Interim Report on Prenatal Care, Low-Birthweight Births, and Public Health Service Year 2000 Objectives**, September, 1990. The Children's Defense Fund (Washington) is a private organization established as a voice for the children of the United States.

Methodology: The National Center for Health Statistics (NCHS) compiles fertility data from birth registration information collected at the local level.

Definitions: "Low birthweight" refers to babies weighing less than 2,500 grams (5.5 pounds) at birth. "Nonwhite" includes blacks and all other races.

Qualifications: Birthweight statistics are usually based on data compiled from birth certificates. The quality of data entered on birth certificates may vary from locality to locality. Since the NCHS must compile fertility data for the entire United States there is a considerable time lag before this information can be made available. It is possible that the incidence of low birthweight births has changed since 1988.

Interpretation: Low birthweight is a major cause of mortality and disability among infants. These figures indicate that virtually no progress was made in reducing the percentage of low birthweight babies during the 1980s after a decade of steady improvement. Rates for nonwhites historically have been higher than those for whites. Blacks tend to have the highest rate (13.5% in 1989) among the racial groups included in the nonwhite category.

II-12. BIRTH WEIGHT
TRENDS IN "VERY LOW" BIRTHWEIGHT BIRTHS BY RACE
1979-1989

| Year | Percent of Births With Very Low Birthweights | | |
	Total	White	Nonwhite
1989	1.28%	0.95%	2.84%
1988	1.24	0.92	2.78
1987	1.24	0.94	2.73
1986	1.21	0.93	2.66
1985	1.21	0.94	2.65
1984	1.19	0.92	2.56
1983	1.19	0.93	2.55
1982	1.18	0.92	2.51
1981	1.16	0.90	2.47
1980	1.15	0.90	2.44
1979	1.15	0.90	2.37

Source: Based on data compiled by the National Center for Health Statistics. Reprinted by the Children's Disease Fund in **Maternal and Child Health: Special Interim Report on Prenatal Care, Low-Birthweight Births, and Public Health Service Year 2000 Objectives,** September, 1990. The Children's Defense Fund (Washington) is a private organization established as a voice for the children of the United States. For more information, refer to the detailed statistics published by the NCHS in Vital Statistics for the United States. Additional data, including some unpublished data, on this topic, is available from NCHS (Hyattsville, MD).

Methodology: The National Center for Health Statistics (NCHS) compiles fertility data from birth registration information collected at the local level.

Definitions: "Low birthweight" refers to babies weighing less than 2,500 grams (5.5 pounds) at birth. "Nonwhite" includes blacks and all other races.

Qualifications: Birthweight statistics are usually based on data compiled from birth certificates. The quality of data entered on birth certificates may vary from locality to locality. Since the NCHS must compile fertility data for the entire United States there is a considerable time lag before this information can be made available. It is possible that the incidence of low birthweight births has changed since 1988.

Interpretation: Very low birthweight is a major cause of mortality and disability among infants. These figures indicate that virtually no progress was made in reducing the percentage of low birthweight babies during the 1980s after a decade of steady improvement. Rates for nonwhites historically have been higher than those for whites. Blacks tend to have the highest rate (3.5% in 1989) among the racial groups included in the nonwhite category.

II-13. WANTEDNESS OF CHILDREN
WOMEN WITH WANTED AND UNWANTED CHILDREN BY AGE
1982 AND 1988

| | Percent of Wanted Conceptions | | | | Percent Unwanted Conceptions* | |
| | Total | | Mistimed | | Total | |
Age Group	1988	1982	1988	1982	1988	1982
15-24	91.1%	94.3%	42.6%	43.8%	8.6%	5.7%[a]
25-34	90.8	93.1	23.3	18.5	9.0	6.7
35-44	82.2	82.7	12.2	11.3[a]	17.6	17.1

*The percentages refer to the proportion of all births in the last five years to sample women that were either wanted or unwanted. Figures including a superscript[a] do not meet acceptable standards of reliability or precision.

Source: Based on data collected by the National Center for Health Statistics and published in "Wanted and Unwanted Childbearing in the United States: 1973-88" in **Advance Data**, No. 189, 1990. The National Center for Health Statistics (NCHS) conducts a variety of surveys from which health-related data are drawn. Additional data, including some unpublished data, on this topic are available from NCHS (Hyattsville, MD).

Methodology: These data come from cycle III (1982) and cycle IV (1988) of the National Family Growth Survey (NSFG), which in 1988 contained 8,450 women age 18 to 44 in the civilian noninstitutionalized population. The NSFG interview includes information on a number of topics related to childbearing, family planning, and maternal and infant health.

Definitions: Pregnancies that ended in a live birth within five years of the survey data have been classified as "wanted" or "unwanted" in this table. A wanted birth is one where the women had stopped, or not used, a contraceptive because she wanted a pregnancy, or became pregnant while using a contraceptive, but had wanted, or probably wanted, another baby at some time. Births that were wanted, but occurred sooner than desired, have been subclassified mistimed. Births not meeting the wanted criteria were classified unwanted.

Qualifications: Because the data come from a sample survey, they are subject to both sampling and nonsampling error.

Interpretation: While the vast majority of births are wanted on conception, a large proportion are mistimed. The proportion of births that are unwanted at birth rose between acceptable 1982 and 1988.

II-14. FECUNDITY STATUS
FECUNDITY STATUS BY PARITY AND AGE FOR WOMEN 15-44
1982 AND 1988

	Surgically Sterile Contraceptive		Surgically Sterile Noncontraceptive		Impaired Fecundity		Fecund	
	1988	1982	1988	1982	1988	1982	1988	1982
Parity 0								
15-24 years	0.2[a]	0.1[a]	0.0	0.0	4.1	4.1	95.7	95.8
25-34 years	3.1[a]	3.3[a]	1.6[a]	1.8[a]	13.4	14.7	82.0	80.2
35-44 years	15.8	10.3[a]	9.2	12.7	21.4	25.7	53.6	51.3
Parity 1 or More								
15-24 years	9.8	9.0	0.7[a]	0.6[a]	7.7	5.2	81.8	85.2
25-34 years	32.8	28.1	3.3	6.1	7.8	8.1	56.1	57.8
35-44 years	52.3	42.7	12.5	19.0	8.5	10.1	26.7	28.1

Figures including a superscript[a] do not meet standards of reliability or precision.

Source: Based on data compiled by the National Center for Health Statistics and published in "Fecundity and Infertility in the United States, 1965-1988" in **Advance Data**, No. 192, 1990. The National Center for Health Statistics (NCHS) conducts a variety of surveys from which health-related data are drawn. Additional data, including some unpublished data, on this topic are available from NCHS (Hyattsville, MD).

Methodology: These data come from cycle III (1982) and cycle IV (1988) of the National Family Growth Survey (NSFG), which in 1988 contained 8,450 women age 18 to 44 in the civilian noninstitutionalized population. The NSFG interview includes information on a number of topics related to childbearing, family planning, and maternal and infant health.

Definitions: "Fecundity" is the physical ability of a woman or couple to presently have children. In the 1982 and 1988 National Family Growth Surveys, the source of data for the table above, women were classified surgically sterile if they or their husband or partner had had a sterilizing operation. "Impaired fecundity" refers to difficulties experienced in conceiving. "Fecund" is a residual category and refers to women who are not surgically sterile or fecundity impaired. "Parity 0" means that the women have not had a live birth. "Parity 1" or more means that they have had 1 or more births.

Qualifications: Because the data come from a sample survey, they are subject to both sampling and nonsampling error.

Interpretation: Rates of contraceptive and noncontraceptive sterility and of impaired fecundity increase as women age. The rate of contraceptive sterility rose between 1982 and 1988.

II-15. FAMILY PLANNING
PERCENT OF WOMEN WHO HAD ONE OR MORE FAMILY PLANNING VISITS BY AGE AND RACE
1982 AND 1988

Age	Whites		Blacks	
	1982	1988	1982	1988
15-19	28.6%	29.2%	43.4%	40.9%
20-24	59.9	59.8	65.1	65.5
25-29	55.9	54.5	56.7	52.1
30-34	33.4	34.8	38.3	38.0
35-39	19.4	17.0	20.0	15.6
40-44	7.0	5.7	7.9	8.0

Source: Based on data collected by the National Center for Health Statistics and published in "Use of Family Services in the United States: 1982 and 1988" in **Advance Data**, No. 184, 1990. National Center for Health Statistics (NCHS) conducts a variety of surveys from which health-related data are drawn. Additional data, including some unpublished data, on this topic are available from NCHS (Hyattsville, MD).

Definitions: In the 1982 and 1988 National Family Growth Surveys, women were asked a series of questions regarding the use of medical services. If they responded yes to one or more of these services, they were classified as having used family planning services. The services include: to get a new method of birth control, renew a prescription or get supplies for a method already being used, and to get counseling about birth control, among others.

Methodology: These data were collected by means of the 1982 and 1988 National Family Growth Surveys (NFGS), which in 1988 contained 8,450 women age 18 to 44 in the civilian noninstitutionalized population. The NFGS interview includes information on a number of topics related to childbearing, family planning, and maternal and infant health.

Qualifications: Because the data come from a sample survey, they are subject to both sampling and nonsampling error. The standard errors for the 1988 figures appearing in this table are five percent or less.

Interpretation: A higher proportion of blacks report family planning visits than whites at all ages. The age group for which the highest proportion reports family planning visits were those 20 to 29 years of age.

II-16. CONTRACEPTIVE USE
CONTRACEPTIVE USE FOR WOMEN BY STATUS AND RACE
1982 AND 1988

| | Percent Reporting Use | | | |
| | Whites | | Blacks | |
Contraceptive Status	1988	1982	1988	1982
Number of Women (in 1,000s)	47,077	45,367	7,679	6,985
Sterile	30.5%	27.7%	29.6%	23.7%
Pregnant or Post Partum	4.8	4.8	5.0	5.6
Seeking Pregnancy	3.7	4.0	3.9	5.0
Other Nonuser	23.8	26.2	26.9	29.6
Nonsurgical Contraceptors	37.2	37.2	34.6	35.7
Pill	18.4	15.1	21.6	19.8
IUD	1.1	3.9	1.7	4.7
Diaphragm	3.8	5.0	1.1	1.8
Condom	9.2	7.2	5.8	3.2

Source: Based on data collected by the National Center for Health Statistics and published in "Contraceptive Use in the United States," 1973-88" in **Advance Data**, No. 182, 1990. The National Center for Health Statistics (NCHS) conducts a variety of surveys from which health-related data are drawn. Additional data, including some unpublished data, on this topic are available from NCHS (Hyattsville, MD).

Methodology: These data were collected by means of the 1982 and 1988 National Family Growth Surveys (NSFG), which in 1988 contained 8,450 women age 18 to 44 in the civilian noninstitutionalized population. The NSFG interview includes information on a number of topics related to childbearing, family planning, and maternal and infant health.

Definitions: A woman was classified as "sterile" if she reported that it was impossible for her to have a baby for any reason. "Other nonusers" include women who have never had intercourse and those not having intercourse in the last three months. The "nonsurgical contraceptor" subcategory percentages do not sum to the total of the category due to omitted categories. These categories include foam, douche, periodic abstinence and withdrawal.

Qualifications: Because the data come from a sample survey, they are subject to both sampling and nonsampling error. The standard errors for the 1988 figures appearing in this table are five percent or less.

Interpretation: About 30 percent of all women in their childbearing years are surgically sterile. Among the nonsurgical contraceptors, pills are the most widely used form of contraceptive.

II-17. CONTRACEPTIVE USE
CONTRACEPTIVE USE FOR WOMEN 15-44 BY MARITAL STATUS
1988

| Method | All Statuses | Percent by Marital Status | | |
		Currently Married	Widowed, Separated or Divorced	Never Married
Female Sterilization	28.5%	31.4%	50.7%	6.4%
Male Sterilization	11.7	17.3	3.6	1.8
Pill	30.7	20.4	25.3	59.0
IUD	2.0	2.0	3.6	1.3
Diaphram	5.7	6.2	5.3	4.9
Condom	14.6	14.3	5.9	19.6

Source: Based on data collected by the National Center for Health Statistics and published in "Contraceptive Use in the United States," 1973-88" in **Advance Data**, No. 182, 1990. The National Center for Health Statistics (NCHS) conducts a variety of surveys from which health-related data are drawn. Additional data, including some unpublished data, on this topic are available from NCHS (Hyattsville, MD).

Methodology: These data were collected by means of the 1982 and 1988 National Family Growth Surveys (NSFG), which in 1988 contained 8,450 women age 18 to 44 in the civilian noninstitutionalized population. The NSFG interview includes information on a number of topics related to childbearing, family planning, and maternal and infant health.

Qualifications: Because the data come from a sample survey, they are subject to both sampling and nonsampling error. The standard errors for the 1988 figures appearing in this table are five percent or less.

Interpretation: While currently married women are dependent upon four major sources of contraception, widowed, separated, divorced, and never married women rely most heavily on only two sources.

II-18. STERILIZATION
POSTPARTUM STERILIZATION RATES BY AGE, RACE AND MARITAL STATUS
1987

Characteristic	Percent Sterilized After Delivery
Age:	
Under 20 years	0.6%
20-24 years	7.2
25-29 years	9.7
30-34 years	12.9
35 years and over	18.5
Race:	
White	8.9
Nonwhite	10.4
Race not reported	8.4
Marital Status:	
Married	9.7
Unmarried	8.2
Marital status not reported	8.5
Total	9.2

Source: Based on data from the National Hospital Discharge Survey conducted by the National Center for Health Statistics. Additional data, including some unpublished data, on this topic are available from NCHS (Hyattsville, MD). Reprinted in the Metropolitan Life **Statistical Bulletin**, April-June, 1990. The **Statistical Bulletin** published by Metropolitan Life Insurance Company reprints data from a variety of sources.

Methodology: The National Hospital Discharge Survey is used by NCHS to collect data annually on the characteristics of patients hospitalized in "short-stay" hospitals. Data collection is based on a sample of approximately 200,000 medical records each year. Information is collected on patient demographics, circumstances of the hospitalization, diagnosis and treatment and characteristics of the facility. Data from the sample are weighted up to produce national estimates.

Definitions: "Postpartum sterilization" refers to sterilization procedures performed at the time of childbirth.

Qualifications: Since the survey is based on a sample of administrative records, all of the drawbacks related to sample surveys apply. In addition, the quality of the data also depend heavily on the completeness and accuracy of the medical records examined. The figures are based on less than 10,000 sterilization cases thereby limiting the statistical validity and precision.

Interpretation: The rate of postpartum sterilization procedures performed varies with age, race and marital status. The strongest association appears to be age. The frequency of the performance of this procedure has been demonstrated to be as much a function of practice patterns as it is of medical necessity.

II-19. STERILIZATION
POSTPARTUM STERILIZATION RATES FOR ALL DELIVERIES
AND INITIAL CESAREAN DELIVERIES
1970-1987

| Year | Percent Sterilized At Time of Delivery | |
	Total Deliveries	Initial Cesarean
1987	24.4%	17.4%
1986	24.1	17.4
1985	22.7	16.3
1984	21.1	15.0
1983	20.3	14.3
1982	21.1	15.0
1981	17.9	12.5
1980	16.5	12.1
1975	10.4	7.8
1970	5.5	4.2

Source: Based on data from the National Hospital Discharge Survey conducted by the National Center for Health Statistics. Additional data, including some unpublished data, on this topic are available from NCHS (Hyattsville, MD). Reprinted in the Metropolitan Life **Statistical Bulletin**, April-June, 1990. The **Statistical Bulletin** published by Metropolitan Life Insurance Company reprints data from a variety of sources.

Methodology: The National Hospital Discharge Survey is used by NCHS to collect data annually on the characteristics of patients hospitalized in "short-stay" hospitals. Data collection is based on a sample of approximately 200,000 medical records each year. Information is collected on patient demographics, circumstances of the hospitalization, diagnosis and treatment and characteristics of the facility. Data from the sample are weighted up to produce national estimates.

Definitions: "Cesarean" refers to surgical removal of the baby through the abdomen rather than through natural vaginal delivery. "Initial cesareans" are those performed on females with no previous cesareans.

Qualifications: Since the survey is based on a sample of administrative records, all of the drawbacks related to sample surveys apply. In addition, the quality of the data also depend heavily on the completeness and accuracy of the medical records examined. The figures are based on less than 10,000 deliveries thereby limiting the statistical validity and precision.

Interpretation: The rate of cesarean procedures performed increased dramatically between 1970 and 1987. The greatest growth in the use of this procedure was during the 1970s, with some leveling off noted by the late 1980s. The frequency of the performance of this procedure has been demonstrated to be as much a function of practice patterns as it is of medical necessity. The decline in the growth rate during the mid-1980s can probably be attributed to evidence as to the lack of necessity for it in many cases and to the adverse publicity surrounding alleged excessive unnecessary procedures. Nevertheless, the cesarian rate in the U.S. remains high by most standards.

II-20. PRENATAL CARE
INFANTS BORN TO WOMEN RECEIVING LATE OR NO
PRENATAL CARE BY RACE
1969-1989

	Percent of Infants Born To Women with No or Late Prenatal Care		
Year	Total	White	Black
1989	6.4%	5.2%	11.9%
1988	6.1	5.0	10.9
1987	6.1	5.0	11.1
1986	6.0	5.0	10.6
1985	5.7	4.7	10.0
1984	5.6	4.7	9.6
1983	5.6	4.7	9.7
1982	5.5	4.5	9.6
1981	5.2	4.3	9.1
1980	5.1	4.3	8.8
1975	6.0	5.0	10.5
1970	7.9	6.2	16.6

Source: Based on data compiled by the National Center for Health Statistics and reprinted by the Children's Disease Fund in **Maternal and Child Health: Special Interim Report on Prenatal Care, Low-Birthweight Births, and Public Health Service Year 2000 Objectives**, September, 1990. The Children's Defense Fund (Washington) is a private organization established as a voice for the children of the United States. For more information, refer to the detailed statistics published by the NCHS in Vital Statistics for the United States. Additional data, including some unpublished data on this topic, are available from NCHS (Hyattsville, MD).

Methodology: The National Center for Health Statistics (NCHS) compiles fertility data from birth registration information collected at the local level.

Definitions: "Late prenatal care" refers to care initiated after the sixth month of pregnancy.

Qualifications: Prenatal care statistics are usually based on data compiled from birth statistics. The quality of data entered on birth certificates may vary from locality to locality. Since the NCHS must compile fertility data for the entire United States there is a considerable time lag before this information can be made available. It is possible that the amount of prenatal care has changed since 1988.

Interpretation: Access to and the timeliness of prenatal care are important factors in the prevention of premature births. Prematurity typically results in low birthweight and low birthweight is a major cause of mortality and disability among infants. These figures indicate that virtually no progress was made in improving participation in prenatal care during the 1980s after a decade of steady improvement. Blacks have historically received less prenatal care than have whites.

II-21. LEGAL ABORTIONS
LEGAL ABORTIONS
1973-1989

Year	Number of Abortions (in 1,000s)	Abortions Per 100 Live Births
1989	1,397	34.6
1985	1,329	35.4
1980	1,298	35.9
1975	855	27.2
1973	616	19.6

Source: Based on data collected by the National Center for Health Statistics and published in **Health, United States, 1991,** tables 12 and 13. The National Center for Health Statistics (NCHS) conducts a variety of surveys from which health-related data are drawn. Additional data, including some unpublished data, on this topic are available from NCHS (Hyattsville, MD).

Methodology: The National Center for Health Statistics (NCHS) compiles data from the 13 states who participate in the federal abortion reporting program.

Qualifications: These figures are estimates extrapolated from data for the 13 participating states and not actual data. Abortions are often underreported so these figures should be interpreted with caution.

Interpretation: The total number of legal abortions has been stable at about 1.3 million a year since 1980.

Section III

DATA ON MORTALITY

The major source of data on mortality in the U.S. is the national registration system coordinated by the National Center for Health Statistics (NCHS). By law, death certificates must be completed and processed for each person who dies. To be included in the death registry, a state must agree to include a standard set of inquiries on the certificate and demonstrate a high rate of coverage; that is, at least 90 percent of all deaths must be registered. Deaths are reported at the county level and the aggregated to the state and national levels. Today, more than 99 percent of all deaths in the U.S. are registered. Given this level of coverage, mortality data for even very small units of geography are highly accurate.

The standard death certificate includes a basic set of demographic items (e.g., age, sex, and race) along with information on the immediate and underlying causes of death. Data are available for a variety of levels of geography. The geographic specificity of the data, when combined with demographic and cause of death information, generates useful information for studying a variety of phenomena. For example, the comparison of cause-specific mortality rates by age can provide valuable insight into the impact of inadequate health care and environmental hazards on the overall quality of life.

The study of infant mortality is a special case where mortality data can provide insight into the effect of environmental, social, and health services factors on health status. The infant mortality rate is often regarded as a surrogate measure for the quality of life in a given area. Specifically, high rates of infant mortality have been linked to environmental hazards and the lack of proper prenatal and postnatal care. Infant mortality rates may be seen as both an indication of the quality of health care in existence in a particular area and as a measure of the degree to which health care standards must be improved in order to meet some specified target.

Hospitals and other health organizations constitute another source of data on the mortality experiences of their patients. Health care providers often maintain internal databases on mortality. These data bases serve some useful purposes, such as determining death rates by type of procedure. Some of these institutional data are compiled by the Health Care Financing Administration (for Medicare patients) and by NCHS. Some hospitals and physicians have achieved unwanted notoriety because they have "unexpectedly" high mortality rates. However, often these data are used without a clear understanding of the conditions and socioeconomic status characterizing the patients treated. That is, higher death rates should be expected for physicians and hospitals that treat and admit sicker, less advantaged patients. Without "fair" comparisons, the wrong conclusions are likely to be drawn.

Mortality data are available at the national level through **Vital and Health Statistics** reports produced by the National Center for Health Statistics. Information for specific causes of death such as accidents, AIDs and cancer are available from other public and private agencies (e.g., AIDs mortality data from the Centers for Disease Control and Prevention). At the state and local level, state, regional, and local health planning boards and health departments are sources of mortality data.

While most aggregated mortality data are available in published form, microdata (individual death records with identifying personal information removed) can be obtained from national and state sources on computer tape. In the near future, these data will also be available on CD-ROM.

III-1. DEATHS
NUMBER OF ANNUAL DEATHS
1935-1991

Year	Deaths in (1,000s)
1991	2,165
1990	2,162
1985	2,084
1980	1,990
1975	1,893
1970	1,921
1965	1,828
1960	1,712
1955	1,529
1950	1,452
1945	1,402
1940	1,417
1935	1,393

Sources: Data published in **U.S. Bureau of the Census.** Historical Statistics of the United States, Colonial Times to 1970. Bicentennial Edition, Part I, 1975; U.S. Bureau of the Census. Statistical Abstract of the United States, 1990, table 107, 1990; U.S. Department of Health and Human Services, National Center for Health Statistics, Advance Report of Final Mortality Statistics, 1984. Monthly Vital Statistics Report, Vol. 35, No. 6, 1986; U.S. Department of Health and Human Services, National Center for Health Statistics. "Births, Marriages, Divorces and Deaths for 1991" in Monthly Vital Statistics Report, Vol. 40, No. 12, 1992.

Methodology: These data are based on information coded by the National Center for Health Statistics (NCHS) from copies of original death certificates received from state registration offices.

Qualifications: Mortality statistics are usually based on data compiled from death certificates. Research has indicated that the quality of death registration data is less than optimal. Variations in definitions and the existence of multiple causes of death limit the precision of mortality statistics.

Interpretation: The number of deaths have increased each year since 1935 due to an increase in population size and the aging of the population.

III-2. CAUSE OF DEATH
DEATH RATES FOR THE 15 LEADING CAUSES
1991

Rank	Cause of Death	Death Rates*	% of Total Deaths
	All Causes	854.0	100.0%
1	Diseases of the Heart	283.3	33.2
2	Malignant Neoplasms, Including Neoplasms of Lymphatic and Hematopoietic Tissues	202.9	23.8
3	Cerebrovascular Diseases	56.8	6.7
4	Accidents and Adverse Effects	36.2	4.2
5	Chronic Obstructive Pulmonary Diseases and Related	35.2	4.1
6	Pneumonia and Influenza	29.6	3.5
7	Diabetes Mellitus	19.7	2.3
8	Suicide	11.9	1.4
9	Human Immunodeficiency Virus Infection	11.8	1.4
10	Homicide and Legal Intervention	10.8	1.3
11	Chronic Liver Disease and Cirrhosis	9.8	1.1
12	Nephritis, Nephrotic Syndrome and Nephrosis	8.7	1.0
13	Septicemia	7.7	0.9
14	Atherosclerosis	6.7	0.8
15	Certain Conditions Originating in the Perinatal Period	6.6	0.8
	All Other Causes	116.3	13.5

*Rates are based on the number of cause-specific deaths per 100,000 population.

Source: Based on data compiled by the National Center for Health Statistics and published in "Annual Summary of Births, Marriages, Divorces and Deaths: United States, 1991," **Monthly Vital Statistics Report**, Vol. 40, No. 13, 1992.

Methodology: These data are based on information coded by the National Center for Health Statistics (NCHS) from copies of original death certificates received from state registration offices. The ranking is based on total deaths attributable to that cause.

Qualifications: Mortality statistics are usually based on data compiled from death certificates. Research has indicated that the quality of death registration data is less than optimal. Variations in definitions and the existence of multiple causes of death limit the precision of mortality statistics.

Interpretation: Diseases of the heart and cancer account for 57 percent of all deaths. In 1989 most of the leading causes of death were related to lifestyle or environmental factors.

III-3. CAUSE OF DEATH
DEATH RATES FOR THE FOUR LEADING CAUSES BY STATE
1988

| State | Death Rates by Cause* | | | |
	Heart Disease	Cancer	Stroke	Accidents
United States	311	197	61	40
Alabama	324	206	71	54
Alaska	89	86	16	74
Arizona	252	180	44	49
Arkansas	359	226	89	52
California	250	168	56	37
Colorado	196	135	40	34
Connecticut	319	212	54	31
Delaware	356	218	45	44
District of Columbia	356	264	64	39
Florida	384	253	72	44
Georgia	267	171	64	50
Hawaii	167	39	39	29
Idaho	237	159	60	55
Illinois	341	202	60	38
Indiana	318	204	70	39
Iowa	359	218	78	41
Kansas	323	200	71	40
Kentucky	338	215	69	46
Louisiana	303	191	58	44
Maine	330	227	64	40
Maryland	276	201	51	33
Massachusetts	344	223	64	30
Michigan	327	194	57	35
Minnesota	276	188	70	35
Mississippi	353	201	76	55
Missouri	359	213	71	44
Montana	257	192	57	47
Nebraska	321	198	72	38
Nevada	258	193	40	43
New Hampshire	278	195	56	28
New Jersey	356	224	55	32
New Mexico	190	145	42	57
New York	376	216	54	32
North Carolina	299	196	74	50
North Dakota	308	193	65	36
Ohio	345	212	62	35
Oklahoma	340	197	71	44
Oregon	281	211	72	45
Pennsylvania	401	237	67	38
Rhode Island	354	242	64	30

(Continued on next page)

III-3. CAUSE OF DEATH
DEATH RATES FOR THE FOUR LEADING CAUSES BY STATE
1988 *(Continued from previous page)*

State	Heart Disease	Death Rates by Cause*		
		Cancer	Stroke	Accidents
South Carolina	294	177	75	56
South Dakota	364	190	73	40
Tennessee	328	201	76	49
Texas	242	154	48	39
Utah	175	101	41	35
Vermont	289	183	57	42
Virginia	269	184	58	37
Washington	253	179	60	38
West Virginia	397	232	70	48
Wisconsin	321	202	70	35
Wyoming	192	146	49	53

*Rates are reported as deaths per 1,000 population.

Source: Based on data compiled by the National Center for Health Statistics (NCHS) and published in the **NCHS Monthly Vital Statistics Report.** Additional data, including some unpublished data, on this topic are available from NCHS (Hyattsville, MD).

Methodology: The National Center for Health Statistics compiles mortality data from death registration information collected at the local level.

Definitions: "Heart disease" refers to the various forms of heart or cardiovascular disease. "Cancer" is officially recorded as malignant neoplasms. "Stroke" is officially recorded as cerebrovascular diseases.

Qualifications: Mortality statistics are usually based on data compiled from death certificates. Research has indicated that the quality of death registration data is less than optimal. Variations in definitions and the existence of multiple causes of death limit the precision of mortality statistics.

Interpretation: There are clear differences in the rates of mortality for the leading causes by state, reflecting differences in demographic makeup and lifestyles.

III-4. CAUSE OF DEATH
DEATH RATES FOR THE LEADING CAUSES
1920-1990

	Death Rate*				
Cause of Death	**1920**	**1940**	**1960**	**1980**	**1990**
All causes	1,298.9	1,076.4	954.7	874.1	861.9
Heart Disease	159.6	292.5	369.0	335.9	289.0
Cancer	83.4	120.3	149.2	182.4	201.7
Stroke	93.0	90.9	108.0	75.0	57.9
Accidents	71.0	73.6	52.3	46.9	37.3
Pneumonia and influenza	207.3	70.3	37.3	23.2	31.3
Tuberculosis	113.1	45.9	6.1	0.1	0.7
Infant mortality (all causes)	85.8	47.0	26.0	12.5	9.4
Maternal mortality (all causes)	799.0	376.0	37.1	9.0	8.2

*Rates are reported as deaths per 100,000 population.

Source: Based on data compiled by the National Center for Health Statistics (NCHS) and published in the **NCHS Monthly Vital Statistics Report.** Additional data, including some unpublished data, on this topic are available from NCHS (Hyattsville, MD).

Methodology: The National Center for Health Statistics compiles mortality data from death registration information collected at the local level.

Definitions: "Cancer" is officially recorded as malignant neoplasms. "Stroke" is officially recorded as cerebrovascular diseases. "Infant mortality" refers to deaths to infants under one year per 1,000 live births. "Maternal mortality" refers to maternal deaths per 100,000 live births.

Qualifications: Mortality statistics are usually based on data compiled from death certificates. Research has indicated that the quality of death registration data is less than optimal. Variations in definitions and the existence of multiple causes of death limit the precision of mortality statistics. These shortcomings are particularly significant for the elderly who may be characterized by multiple health problems at the time of death. A variety of diseases may be grouped under any major category.

Interpretation: There have been significant shifts in the leading causes of death since early in this century. The leading cause of death in 1920, pneumonia and influenza, has dropped far down the list. Another leading cause, tuberculosis, is no longer even mentioned as a significant cause of death. Cancer accounted for less than 7% of the deaths in 1920 but for over 22% by the late 1980s.

III-5. DEATH RATES
DEATH RATES BY AGE
1991

Age	Death Rate*
Under 1 year	901.8
1-4 years	46.7
5-14 years	24.0
15-24 years	107.1
25-34 years	137.4
35-44 years	222.7
45-54 years	458.2
55-64 years	1,162.4
65-74 years	2,568.7
75-84 years	5,932.3
85 years and over	14,784.4
All Ages	854.0

*Death rates are expressed per 100,000 persons in the age range specified.

Source: Based on data compiled by the National Center for Health Statistics and published in "Annual Summary of Births, Marriages, Divorces, and Deaths: United States, 1990" in **Monthly Vital Statistics Report**, Vol. 40, No. 13, 1992.

Methodology: These data are based on information coded by the National Center for Health Statistics (NCHS) from copies of original death certificates received from state registration offices. The denominators used in calculating the raters are population estimates produced by the U.S. Bureau of the Census.

Qualifications: Mortality statistics are usually based on data compiled from death certificates. Research has indicated that the quality of death registration data is less than optimal. Variations in definitions and the existence of multiple causes of death limit the precision of mortality statistics.

Interpretation: These age-specific death rates illustrate the classic J curve of mortality. The rate is high for those under 1 year of age, falls sharply during the adolescent and young adult years, and then rises steadily, especially beyond age 60.

III-6. DEATH RATES
TEN LEADING CAUSES OF DEATH FOR THE ELDERLY
1987

Cause of Death	Total	Death Rate*	
		Males	Females
Heart Disease	2,075	2,356	1,883
Cancer	1,060	1,397	829
Stroke	435	399	460
COPD and related	216	322	143
Pneumonia and influenza	203	232	183
Diabetes mellitus	95	90	99
Accidents	87	109	71
Atherosclerosis	72	64	77
Kidney disease/failure	61	72	54
Septicemia	53	55	52

*Rates are reported as deaths per 100,000 population for persons age 65 and over.

Source: Based on data collected by the National Center for Health Statistics and reprinted in the Metropolitan Life **Statistical Bulletin,** April-June, 1990. The **Statistical Bulletin** published by Metropolitan Life Insurance Company reprints data from a variety of sources including statistics on the experiences of the large Metropolitan Life insured population, data not available elsewhere. Additional data, including some unpublished data, on this topic is available from NCHS (Hyattsville, MD).

Methodology: The National Center for Health Statistics compiles mortality data from death registration information collected at the local level.

Definitions: "Cancer" is officially recorded as malignant neoplasms. "Stroke" is officially recorded as cerebrovascular diseases. "COPD" is the abbreviation for chronic obstructive pulmonary disease. "Kidney disease/failure" is officially recorded as nephritis, nephrotic syndrome and nephrosis.

Qualifications: Mortality statistics are usually based on data compiled from death certificates. Research has indicated that the quality of death registration data is less than optimal. Variations in definitions and the existence of multiple causes of death limit the precision of mortality statistics. These shortcomings are particularly significant for the elderly who may be characterized by multiple health problems at the time of death. A variety of diseases may be grouped under any major category; in order to determine exactly which diseases are included under a heading, refer to the detailed statistics published by the NCHS in Vital Statistics for the United States.

Interpretation: Of the ten leading causes of death among the elderly, the top three causes account for the vast majority of the deaths. There are clear differences in the rates of accidental death based on sex. Males experience higher rates of death for all but three causes.

III-7. CANCER DEATHS
ESTIMATED CANCER DEATHS BY SEX AND SITE
1990

Site	Estimated Deaths (in 1,000s)		
	Male	Female	Total
All sites	270.0	240.0	510.0
Digestive organs	64.6	58.3	122.9
Genital organs	54.1	30.6	84.7
Respiratory system	95.9	51.2	147.1
Breast	0.3	44.0	44.3
Urinary organs	12.6	7.4	20.0
Blood and lymph tissues	14.9	13.8	28.7
Oral	5.6	2.8	8.4
Leukemias	9.8	8.3	18.1
Skin	5.7	3.1	8.8
Brain/central nervous system	6.0	5.1	11.1
Endocrine glands	0.8	1.0	1.8
Connective tissue	1.5	1.6	3.1
Bone	0.6	0.5	1.1
Eye	0.1	0.1	0.2
All other	21.0	19.3	40.3

Source: Based on data compiled by the American Cancer Society and published in **Medical Benefits** (March 15, 1990). The American Cancer Society (Atlanta) is the major private source of cancer statistics. Medical Benefits is a semi-monthly publication devoted to health care costs.

Methodology: These American Cancer Society figures are derived from estimates made using data from the National Cancer Institute (Surveillance, Epidemiology, and End Results Program). Rates based on 1984-86 studies have been applied to the 1990 U.S. population.

Definitions: "All other" includes reported cancer cases for which no site was specified. "Breast" cancer refers to invasive cancer only. "Skin" cancer refers to melanoma only.

Qualifications: These are estimates using known rates that are several years old. The estimates are only accurate to the extent that incidence rates have not changed since 1986. Figures for non-melanoma skin cancer and carcinoma were not provided.

Interpretation: Two cancer sites (digestive organs and the respiratory system) accounted for over half the estimated cancer deaths in 1990. Considerable variation exists in the incidence of cancer at the various sites between males and females.

III-8. CANCER DEATHS
ESTIMATED CANCER DEATHS BY SEX AND SPECIFIC SITE
1990

Site	Distribution by Site	
	Males	Females
Skin	2%	1%
Oral	2	1
Lung	34	21
Pancreas	5	5
Stomach	3	< 1
Colon and rectum	11	13
Prostate	11	0
Urinary	5	3
Leukemia/Lymphomas	8	7
Breast	< 1	18
Ovary	0	5
Uterus	0	4
All other	19	21

Source: Based on data compiled by the American Cancer Society and published in **Medical Benefits** (March 15, 1990). The American Cancer Society (Atlanta) is the major private source of cancer statistics. Medical Benefits is a semi-monthly publication devoted to health care costs.

Methodology: These American Cancer Society figures are derived from estimates made using data from the National Cancer Institute (Surveillance, Epidemiology, and End Results Program). Rates based on 1984-86 studies have been applied to the 1990 U.S. population.

Definitions: "All other" includes reported cancer cases for which no site was specified. "Breast" cancer refers to invasive cancer only. "Skin" cancer refers to melanoma only.

Qualifications: These are estimates using known rates that are several years old. The estimates are only accurate to the extent that incidence rates have not changed since 1986. Figures for non-melanoma skin cancer and carcinoma were not provided.

III-9. INFANT MORTALITY
TRENDS IN INFANT MORTALITY BY RACE
1940-1991

	Infant Mortality Rate*		
Year	Total	White	Black
1991	9.0	7.4	17.3
1988	10.1	8.6	17.9
1986	10.4	8.9	18.0
1985	10.6	9.3	18.2
1984	10.8	9.4	18.4
1983	11.2	9.7	19.2
1982	11.5	10.1	19.6
1981	11.9	10.5	20.0
1980	12.6	11.0	21.4
1975	16.1	14.2	26.2
1970	10.0	17.8	32.6
1965	24.7	21.5	41.7
1960	26.0	22.9	44.3
1955	26.4	23.6	43.1
1950	29.2	26.8	43.9
1945	38.3	35.6	56.2
1940	47.0	43.2	72.9

*Rates are reported as deaths within the first year of life per 1,000 live births.

Source: Based on data compiled by the National Center for Health Statistics and reprinted by the Children's Defense Fund in **Maternal and Child Health in America's Cities** (Special Report Three), January, 1991. The Children's Defense Fund (Washington) is a private organization established as a voice for the children of the United States. For more information, refer to the detailed statistics published by the NCHS in **Vital Statistics for the United States.** Additional data, including some unpublished data, on this topic, are available from NCHS (Hyattsville, MD).

Methodology: The National Center for Health Statistics (NCHS) compiles mortality data from death registration information collected at the local level.

Definitions: "Infant mortality" refers to deaths within the first year of life.

Qualifications: Mortality statistics are usually based on data compiled from death certificates. Research has indicated that the quality of death registration data is less than optimal. Variations in definitions and the existence of multiple causes of death limit the precision of mortality statistics. These shortcomings are not as serious in calculating infant mortality rates as they are for other calculations.

Interpretation: Although the infant mortality rate has declined steadily since 1940 (and actually since 1900), significant disparities remain between blacks and whites.

III-10. INFANT MORTALITY
INFANT MORTALITY RATES BY RACE AND SEX
1940-1991

| | Infant Mortality Rates* | | | | | |
| | All Races | | White | | Black | |
	Male	Female	Male	Female	Male	Female
1991	10.0	7.8	8.4	6.4	19.4	15.1
1988	11.0	8.9	9.5	7.4	19.0	16.1
1980	13.9	11.2	12.3	9.6	23.3	19.4
1970	22.4	17.5	20.0	15.4	36.2	29.0
1960	29.3	22.6	26.0	19.6	49.1	39.4
1950	32.8	25.5	30.2	23.1	48.3	39.4
1940	52.5	41.3	48.3	37.8	81.1	64.6

*Rates are expressed as deaths per 1,000 live births.

Source: Based on data compiled by the National Center for Health Statistics and published in "Advance Report of Final Mortality Statistics, 1988" in **Monthly Vital Statistics Report,** Vol. 39, No. 7 (Supplement), table 13, 1990 and **Monthly Vital Statistics Report,** Vol. 40, No. 12, 1992. Additional data including some unpublished data, on this topic may be available from NCHS (Hyattsville, MD).

Methodology: These data are based on information coded by the National Center for Health Statistics (NCHS) from copies of original death certificates received from state registration offices. The certificates contain the needed data: age, sex and race of decedent along with other information.

Definitions: "Infant deaths" are deaths that occur from birth through the first year of life. Infant mortality rates are calculated by dividing the number of infant deaths (classified by race and sex for this table) by the total number of live births (again, classified by race and sex for this table).

Qualifications: Mortality statistics are usually based on data compiled from death certificates. Research has indicated that the quality of death registration data is less than optimal. Variations in definitions and the existence of multiple causes of death limit the precision of mortality statistics. These shortcomings are not as serious in calculating infant mortality rates as they are for other calculations.

Interpretation: Infant mortality rates have dropped precipitously since 1940 for all age/sex combinations. Infant mortality rates for blacks and males remain higher than those for whites and females.

III-11. INFANT MORTALITY
RANKINGS ON INFANT MORTALITY BY STATE
1991

State	Infant Mortality Rate*
District of Columbia	20.0
Delaware	12.7
Georgia	12.4
Mississippi	11.3
Alabama	11.2
North Carolina	11.0
South Carolina	10.7
Arkansas	10.4
Illinois	10.3
Missouri	10.2
Michigan	9.9
Oklahoma	9.9
Tennessee	9.7
Virginia	9.7
Louisiana	9.6
Ohio	9.5
New York	9.4
Pennsylvania	9.4
Indiana	9.4
Kansas	9.4
Alaska	9.0
South Dakota	9.0
West Virginia	9.0
North Dakota	9.0
Florida	8.9
Idaho	8.7
Arizona	8.7
New Jersey	8.6
New Mexico	8.5
Colorado	8.3
Kentucky	8.2
Maryland	8.1
Wisconsin	8.1
Oregon	7.6
Montana	7.6
California	7.8
Rhode Island	7.8
Texas	7.7
Iowa	7.7
Washington	7.4
Connecticut	7.4
Nebraska	7.4
Minnesota	7.3
Wyoming	7

(Continued on next page)

III-11. INFANT MORTALITY
RANKINGS ON INFANT MORTALITY BY STATE
1991 *(Continued from previous page)*

State	Infant Mortality Rate*
Nevada	7.1
Massachusetts	6.8
Hawaii	6.5
New Hampshire	6.5
Maine	6.3
Vermont	6.1
Utah	6.0

*Rates are reported as deaths within the first year of life per 1,000 live births.

Source: Based on data compiled by the National Center for Health Statistics and published in "Annual Summary of Births, Marriages, Divorces and Deaths: United States, 1991," **Monthly Vital Statistics Report,** Vol. 40, No. 13, 1992.

Methodology: The National Center for Health Statistics compiles mortality data from death registration information collected at the local level.

Definitions: "Infant mortality" refers to deaths within the first year of life.

Qualifications: Mortality statistics are usually based on data compiled from death certificates. Research has indicated that the quality of death registration data is less than optimal. Variations in definitions and the existence of multiple causes of death limit the precision of mortality statistics. These shortcomings are not as serious in calculating infant mortality rates as they are for other calculations.

Interpretation: Although the infant mortality rate has declined steadily since 1940 (and actually since 1900), significant disparities remain among the states. The states with the highest infant mortality rates are primarily rural Southern states, although the District of Columbia and Delaware are exceptions.

III-12. INFANT MORTALITY RATES
TEN WORST LARGE CITIES FOR INFANT MORTALITY
1987

City	Infant Mortality Rate*
Detroit, Michigan	19.7
Washington, D.C.	19.3
Baltimore, Maryland	19.2
Memphis, Tennessee	17.7
Philadelphia, Pennsylvania	17.3
Chicago, Illinois	16.6
New Orleans, Louisiana	15.8
Cleveland, Ohio	15.5
Indianapolis, Indiana	13.3
New York, New York	12.7
Total United States	10.1

*Rates are reported as deaths within the first year of life per 1,000 live births.

Source: Based on data compiled by the National Center for Health Statistics and reprinted by the Children's Defense Fund in **Maternal and Child Health in America's Cities (Special Report Three)**, January, 1991. The Children's Defense Fund (Washington) is a private organization established as a voice for the children of the United States. For more information, refer to the detailed statistics published by the NCHS in Vital Statistics for the United States. Additional data, including some unpublished data, on this topic is available from NCHS (Hyattsville, MD).

Methodology: The National Center for Health Statistics compiles mortality data from death registration information collected at the local level.

Definitions: "Large cities" for these computations are those with populations of 500,000 or more. The term "city" generally refers to the population within the actual corporate boundaries of the city and may not include adjacent suburbs and urbanized areas.

Qualifications: Mortality statistics are usually based on data compiled from death certificates. Research has indicated that the quality of death registration data is less than optimal. Variations in definitions and the existence of multiple causes of death limit the precision of mortality statistics. These shortcomings are not as serious in calculating infant mortality rates as they are for other calculations.

III-13. NEONATAL MORTALITY
WORST LARGE CITIES FOR NEONATAL MORTALITY
1987

City	Neonatal Mortality Rate*
Washington, D.C.	14.4
Detroit, Michigan	13.9
Baltimore, Maryland	12.5
Memphis, Tennessee	11.6
Philadelphia, Pennsylvania	11.6
Chicago, Illinois	10.3
New Orleans, Louisiana	10.4
Cleveland, Ohio	9.3
Indianapolis, Indiana	9.2
New York, New York	8.6
Boston, Massachusetts	8.4
Milwaukee, Wisconsin	7.6
Jacksonville, Florida	7.5
Houston, Texas	7.4
Phoenix, Arizona	6.9
Dallas, Texas	6.6
San Diego, California	6.6
Average for all large cities	8.6
United States average	6.5

*Rates are reported as deaths within the first 28 days of life per 1,000 live births.

Source: Based on data compiled by the National Center for Health Statistics and reprinted by the Children's Defense Fund in **Maternal and Child Health in America's Cities** (Special Report Three), January, 1991. The Children's Defense Fund (Washington) is a private organization established as a voice for the children of the United States. For more information, refer to the detailed statistics published by the NCHS in **Vital Statistics for the United States**. Additional data, including some unpublished data, on this topic, is available from NCHS (Hyattsville, MD).

Methodology: The National Center for Health Statistics compiles mortality data from death registration information collected at the local level.

Definitions: "Large cities" for these computations are those with populations of 500,000 or more. The term "city" generally refers to the population within the actual corporate boundaries of the city and may not include adjacent suburbs and urbanized areas. "Neonatal" refers to the first 28 days of life.

Qualifications: Mortality statistics are usually based on data compiled from death certificates. Research has indicated that the quality of death registration data is less than optimal. Variations in definitions and the existence of multiple causes of death limit the precision of mortality statistics. These shortcomings are not as serious in calculating infant mortality rates as they are for other calculations.

Interpretation: The neonatal mortality component of infant mortality reflects somewhat different causative factors than does postneonatal mortality. Neonatal mortality is more likely to reflect the presence of birth defects or complications related to childbirth. Postneonatal mortality is more a function of factors associated with the infant's environment during the first year of life.

III-14. POSTNEONATAL MORTALITY
WORST LARGE CITIES FOR POSTNEONATAL MORTALITY
1987

City	Postneonatal Mortality Rate*
Baltimore, Maryland	6.6
Cleveland, Ohio	6.2
Memphis, Tennessee	6.0
Detroit, Michigan	5.8
Chicago, Illinois	5.8
Philadelphia, Pennsylvania	5.7
New Orleans, Louisiana	5.4
Jacksonville, Florida	5.2
Washington, D.C.	4.9
Milwaukee, Wisconsin	4.6
Columbus, Ohio	3.6
Indianapolis, Indiana	4.1
New York, New York	4.1
Los Angeles, California	4.0
San Francisco, California	4.0
Houston, Texas	4.0
San Jose, California	3.9
Dallas, Texas	3.7
Average for all large cities	4.7
United States average	3.6

*Rates are reported as deaths between the first 28 days of life and one year per 1,000 live births.

Source: Based on data compiled by the National Center for Health Statistics and reprinted by the Children's Defense Fund in **Maternal and Child Health in America's Cities** (Special Report Three), January, 1991. The Children's Defense Fund (Washington) is a private organization established as a voice for the children of the United States. For more information, refer to the detailed statistics published by the NCHS in **Vital Statistics for the United States**. Additional data, including some unpublished data, on this topic, is available from NCHS (Hyattsville, MD).

Methodology: The National Center for Health Statistics compiles mortality data from death registration information collected at the local level.

Definitions: "Large cities" for these computations are those with populations of 500,000 or more. The term "city" generally refers to the population within the actual corporate boundaries of the city and may not include adjacent suburbs and urbanized areas. "Postneonatal" refers to the period between the first 28 days of life and one year.

Qualifications: Mortality statistics are usually based on data compiled from death certificates. Research has indicated that the quality of death registration data is less than optimal. Variations in definitions and the existence of multiple causes of death limit the precision of mortality statistics. These shortcomings are not as serious in calculating infant mortality rates as they are for other calculations.

Interpretation: The neonatal mortality component of infant mortality reflects somewhat different causative factors than does postneonatal mortality. Neonatal mortality is more likely to reflect the presence of birth defects or complications related to childbirth. Postneonatal mortality is more a function of factors associated with the infant's environment during the first year of life.

III-15. MATERNAL MORTALITY
MATERNAL MORTALITY RATES BY AGE AND RACE
1989

Maternal	
All races	**Mortality Rate***
All ages	7.9
Under 20 years	5.8
20-24 years	6.4
25-29 years	6.7
30-34 years	10.0
35 years and over	15.3
White:	
All ages	5.6
Under 20 years	5.2
20-24 years	4.9
25-29 years	4.8
30-34 years	6.4
35 years and over	9.7
Black:	
All ages	18.4
Under 20 years	7.0
20-24 years	13.5
25-29 years	17.9
30-34 years	33.8
35 years and over	57.5

*Deaths per 100,000 live births

Source: Data collected by the National Center for Health Statistics and published in Health, **United States, 1991**, table 38. Additional data including some unpublished data, on this topic may be available from NCHS (Hyattsville, MD).

Methodology: These data are based on information coded by the National Center for Health Statistics (NCHS) from copies of original death certificates received from state registration offices.

Qualifications: Mortality statistics are usually based on data compiled from death certificates. Research has indicated that the quality of death registration data is less than optimal. Variations in definitions and the existence of multiple causes of death limit the precision of mortality statistics.

Interpretation: Maternal mortality rates generally increase with the age of the mother. Black maternal mortality rates are more than three times higher than those for whites.

III-16. OCCUPATIONAL DISEASE
DEATHS FOR SELECTED OCCUPATIONAL DISEASES FOR MALES 25 AND OVER
1970-1989

Cause of Death	Number of Deaths				
	1970	1975	1980	1985	1989
Malignant neoplasm of peritoneum and pluera mesothelioma	602	591	552	571	565
Coalminers pneumoconiosis	1155	973	977	947	725
Asbestosis	25	43	96	130	261
Silicosis	351	243	202	138	130

Source: Based on data computed by the National Institute for Occupational Safety and Health and compiled by the Division of Vital Statistics of the National Center for Health Statistics (NCHS). For more information refer to the detailed statistics published by the NCHS. Additional data, including some unpublished data, may be available from NCHS (Hyattsville, MD).

Methodology: The National Center for Health Statistics compiles mortality data from death registration information collected at the local level.

Definitions: "Occupational disease" refers to a health condition contracted during the course of employment in a specific industry. This table classifies deaths according to underlying cause.

Qualifications: Mortality statistics are usually based on data compiled from death certificates. Research has indicated that the quality of death registration data is less than optimal. Thus, mortality statistics should be interpreted with caution.

III-17. ACCIDENTAL DEATHS
TYPES OF ACCIDENTAL DEATHS
1988

Cause of Death	Number	Death Rate*
Motor vehicle accidents	49,000	19.9
Falls	12,000	4.9
Poisonings by solids and liquids	5,300	2.2
Drownings	5,000	2.0
Fire and associated deaths	5,000	2.0
Suffocations (Ingested objects)	3,600	1.5
Firearms	1,400	0.6
Poisonings by gases and vapors	1,000	0.4
All other types	13,700	5.6
Total	96,000	39.1

*Rates are reported as deaths per 100,000 population.

Source: Data collected by the National Center for Health Statistics (NCHS) and published in **Accident Facts**, 1989 edition. The National Safety Council is an independent non-profit education and service organization.

Methodology: The National Center for Health Statistics compiles mortality data from death registration information collected at the local level.

Qualifications: Mortality statistics are usually based on data compiled from death certificates. Research has indicated that the quality of death registration data is less than optimal. Thus, mortality statistics should be interpreted with caution. Figures are rounded to nearest 1,000.

Interpretation: Motor vehicle accidents account for one-half of the nation's accidental deaths.

III-18. ACCIDENTAL DEATHS
ACCIDENTAL DEATH RATES BY SEX AND AGE
1986-87

	Death Rate*	
Age Group	Males	Females
1-4	24.0	16.4
5-14	16.7	7.8
15-19	68.5	25.2
20-24	83.6	21.5
25-29	66.4	17.2
30-34	56.9	14.9
35-44	49.0	14.3
45-54	46.2	15.4
55-64	51.6	20.5
65+	108.6	71.2
Total	55.3	24.1

*Rates are reported as deaths per 100,000 population.

Source: Based on data collected by the National Center for Health Statistics and reprinted in the Metropolitan Life **Statistical Bulletin**, January-March 1990. The **Statistical Bulletin** published by Metropolitan Life Insurance Company reprints data from a variety of sources, including statistics on the experiences of the large Metropolitan Life insured population, data not available elsewhere. Additional data, including some unpublished data, on this topic is available from NCHS (Hyattsville, MD).

Methodology: The National Center for Health Statistics (NCHS) compiles mortality data from death registration in information collected at the local level.

Qualifications: Mortality statistics are usually based on data compiled from death certificates. Research has indicated that the quality of death registration data is less than optimal. Variations in definitions and the existence of multiple causes of death limit the precision of mortality statistics.

Interpretation: There are clear differences in the rates of accidental death based on age and sex. Males experience higher rates of accidental death at all ages (and for all causes) than do females. The chances of accidental death remain relatively constant throughout the adult years for both males and females. However, there is a dramatic increase in the accidental death rate for those 65 and over of both sexes.

III-19. ACCIDENTAL DEATHS
MOTOR VEHICLE DEATH RATES FOR TEN LARGEST METROPOLITAN AREAS
1987

Metropolitan Area	Rank	Deaths Number	Rate*
United States Total		48,289	19.8
Dallas-Fort Worth, Tx	1	691	18.2
Los Angeles-Long Beach, CA	2	1,530	18.0
Houston, TX	3	533	15.6
Detroit, MI	4	634	15.0
Philadelphia,PA-NJ	5	691	14.2
Washington, DC-MD-VA	6	457	13.5
Chicago, IL	7	982	13.4
San Francisco-Oakland, CA	8	424	11.9
Boston-Lowell-Brockton-Lawrence-Haverhill, MA	9	434	11.6
New York, NY-NJ	10	986	10.5

*Rates are based on deaths per 100,000 population.

Source: Based on data collected by the National Center for Health Statistics (NCHS) and published in the Metropolitan Life **Statistical Bulletin**, January-March, 1991. The **Statistical Bulletin** published by Metropolitan Life Insurance Company reprints data from a variety of sources including statistics on the experiences of the large Metropolitan Life insured population, data not available elsewhere. Additional data, including some unpublished data, on this topic is available from NCHS (Hyattsville, MD).

Methodology: The National Center for Health Statistics compiles mortality data from death registration information collected at the local level.

Definitions: "Metropolitan areas" refers to metropolitan statistical areas (MSAs) as established by the U.S. Office of Management and Budget from 1980 Census boundaries are used as denominator to be consistent with deaths for MSAs published by the National Center for Health Statistics (NCHS).

Qualifications: Mortality statistics are usually based on data compiled from death certificates. Research has indicated that the quality of death registration data is less than optimal. Variations in definitions and the existence of multiple causes of death limit the precision of mortality statistics.

III-20. AIDS DEATHS
DEATHS AND DEATH RATES FOR HUMAN IMMUNODEFICIENCY VIRUS INFECTION (AIDS)
1991

	AIDS	
	Number	Death Rate*
All Ages	29,850	11.8
Under 15 years	370	0.7
15-24 years	650	1.8
25-34 years	9,590	22.1
35-44 years	12,450	31.6
45-54 years	4,700	18.0
55 years and over	2,060	3.9
Age Not Stated	20	–

*Rates are expressed per 100,000 persons in the age range specified.

Source: Based on data collected by the National Center for Health Statistics (NCHS) and published in "Annual Summary of Births, Marriages, Divorces, and Deaths: United States, 1991" in **Monthly Vital Statistics Report,** Vol. 40, No. 13, 1992. Additional data on this topic may be available from the NCHS (Hyattsville, MD).

Methodology: These data are based on information coded by the National Center for Health Statistics (NCHS) from copies of original death certificates received from state registration offices. The data for the rate denominators are population estimates produced by the U.S. Bureau of the Census. The data are provisional and based upon a 10 percent sample of deaths.

Qualifications: Mortality statistics are usually based on data compiled from death certificates. Research has indicated that the quality of death registration data is less than optimal. Thus, mortality statistics should be interpreted with caution.

Interpretation: The highest concentration (75%) of AIDS deaths are in the age range 25 to 44.

III-21. AIDS DEATHS
DISTRIBUTION OF AIDS DEATHS BY SELECTED DEMOGRAPHIC CHARACTERISTICS
1991

Characteristic	Percent Distribution by Characteristic
Total	100%
Sex:	
Male	87.5%
Female	12.5
Race/Ethnicity:	
White	66.8%
Black	33.2
Age:	
Under 15	1.2%
15-24	2.2
24-34	32.1
35-44	41.7
45-54	15.7
55 and over	6.9

Source: Based on data collected by the Centers for Disease Control and Prevention (CDCP) within the U.S. Public Health Service and published in **Monthly Vital Statistics Report**, Vol. 40, No. 13, 1992. The Centers for Disease Control and Prevention are charged with tracking the spread of communicable diseases. For additional statistics on AIDS contact the CDCP (Atlanta).

Methodology: Based on data reported to the Centers for Disease Control and Prevention by state and territorial health departments during 1989.

Definitions: "Reported cases of AIDS" refers to those who have been identified as infected on the Basis of AIDS tests and who have been subsequently reported to public health authorities. Figures for sex, race, and age refer to individuals 13 or older only. Figures for whites and blacks exclude Hispanics.

Qualifications: Since the reporting of AIDS cases is not required by law, the figures compiled can be assumed to be some fraction of the total number of AIDS cases within the population.

III-22. SURGICAL MORTALITY
MORTALITY RATES FOR THE 25 TOP PROCEDURES
1990

Surgical Procedure	Mortality Rate*
Low cervical cesarean section	< 0.1
Total cholecystectomy (gall bladder removal)	0.8
Total abdominal hysterectomy	0.1
Left heart cardiac catheterization	0.6
Repair of obstetric laceration	< 0.1
Transurethral prostatectomy	0.5
Intervertebral disc excision	0.1
Appendectomy	0.2
Low forceps delivery with episiotomy	< 0.1
Balloon angioplasty	1.1
Biopsy of esophagus, stomach and/or duodenum	3.1
Open reduction of fracture with internal fixation femur	4.0
Combined right/left heart cardiac catheterization	1.7
Cystoscopy (examination of bladder with cystoscope)	1.6
Vacuum extraction delivery with episiotomy	< 0.1
Debridement wound (removal of foreign material)	5.3
Vaginal hysterectomy	< 0.1
Open reduction of fracture with internal fixation tibia/fibula	0.2
Venous catheterization	20.3
Total knee replacement	.5
Unilateral simply mastectomy	0.2
Contrast myelogram	0.7
Dilation and curettage post delivery	< 0.1
Fetal monitoring intrauterine	0.1
Closed biopsy of large bowel	2.3

*Rates reported as deaths per 100 cases.

Source: Based on data collected by the National Center for Health Services Research and published in **HealthWeek** (February 25, 1991). Additional data, including some unpublished data, on this topic are available from NCHS (Hyattsville, MD). (**HealthWeek** ceased publication at the end of 1991.)

Methodology: The National Center for Health Statistics (NCHS) conducts a variety of surveys from which health-related data are drawn.

Definitions: "Procedure" refers to the principal procedure in cases where more than one procedure is involved. These procedures are calculated from non-federal, short-stay general hospitals only.

Qualifications: Mortality may not be directly related to the surgical procedure but to another procedure or to some other condition related to the admission.

Interpretation: The overall mortality rate for hospital patients is quite low. The mortality rate associated with most of the frequent procedures is even lower than the average. In fact, only two procedures (venous catheritization and biopsy of large bowel) carry mortality rates significantly higher than the average. These, however, are diagnostic procedures and are thus not likely to have contributed directly to the patient's expiration.

III-23. YEARS LOST

YEARS OF POTENTIAL LIFE LOST FOR SELECTED CAUSES OF DEATH
1988

Cause of Death	Years Lost*	Years lost per 100,000 Population under 65
All Causes	12,276,000	5,698
Heart disease	1,485,000	689
Cerebrovascular disease	249,000	116
Malignant neoplasms	1,826,000	847
Chronic obstructive pulmonary disease	133,000	62
Pneumonia and influenza	182,000	84
Chronic liver disease and cirrhosis	237,000	110
Diabetes mellitus	134,000	62
Accidents and adverse effects	1,405,000	1,556
Suicide	476,000	527
Homicide and legal intervention	241,000	267
Human immunodeficiency infection virus	272,000	301

*Rounded to the nearest thousand

Source: Based on data compiled by the National Center for Health Statistics (NCHS) and published in **Health, United States, 1990.** Additional data including some unpublished data on this topic may be available from NCHS (Hyattsville, MD).

Methodology: Mortality statistics are compiled by the NCHS from copies of original death certificates received from state registration offices. Lost years of life are calculated using life tables.

Definitions: "Cerebrovascular disease" is commonly referred to as "stroke." "Malignant neoplasms" are generally referred to as "cancer."

Qualifications: Mortality statistics are usually based on data compiled from death certificates. Research has indicated that the quality of death registration data is less than optimal. Thus, mortality statistics should be interpreted with caution.

Interpretation: Although the major killers (heart disease, cancer, and stroke) account for a large portion of the lost years of potential life, other causes of death account for a rate of lost years out of proportion to their death rate. Accidents, homicide, suicide, and AIDS account for a disproportionate amount of the lost life because of the young average age of the victims of these causes of death.

III-24. YEARS LOST
YEARS OF POTENTIAL LIFE LOST BY RACE AND SEX
1988

		Years Lost Per 100,000
Race/Sex Category	Years Lost*	Population Under 65
All races and sexes	12,276,000	5,698
White males	5,972,000	5,972
White females	3,096,000	3,448
Black males	1,844,000	13,845
Black females	1,057,000	7,352

*Rounded to nearest thousand

Source: Based on data compiled by the National Center for Health Statistics (NCHS) and published in **Health, United States, 1990.** Additional data including some unpublished data on this topic may be available from NCHS (Hyattsville, MD).

Methodology: Mortality statistics are compiled by the NCHS from copies of original death certificates received from state registration offices. Lost years of life are calculated using life tables.

Qualifications: Mortality statistics are usually based on data compiled from death certificates. Research has indicated that the quality of death registration data is less than optimal. Thus, mortality statistics should be interpreted with caution.

Interpretation: The number of lost years due to death is proportionately higher for males than for females and for blacks than for whites. Males and blacks have higher overall death rates than females and whites. In addition, males, and particularly black males, are more likely to suffer from causes of death that occur at a relatively young age.

III-25. LIFE EXPECTANCY
LIFE EXPECTANCY IN YEARS AT BIRTH BY RACE AND SEX
1940-1991

	All Races		White		Black	
	Male	Female	Male	Female	Male	Female
1991	72.2	79.1	73.0	79.7	65.6	74.3
1980	70.0	77.4	70.7	78.1	65.3	73.6
1970	67.1	74.7	68.0	75.6	61.3	69.4
1960	66.6	73.1	67.4	74.1	61.1	66.3
1950	65.6	71.1	66.5	72.2	59.1	62.9
1940	60.8	65.2	62.1	66.6	51.5	54.9

Source: Based on data compiled by the National Center for Health Statistics and published in "Annual Summary of Births, Marriages, Divorces and Deaths: United States, 1991," **Monthly Vital Statistics Report,** Vol. 40, No. 13, 1992.

Methodology: These data are based on information coded by the National Center for Health Statistics (NCHS) from copies of original death certificates received from state registration offices. The certificates contain the needed data: age, sex and race of decedent along with other information.

Definitions: Life expectancy at birth is the average number of years from birth a hypothetical cohort of 100,000 persons could expect to live given that current age-specific mortality rates remain constant over their life course. These age-specific mortality rates can be refined to include sex and race. The rate denominator data (population figures) come from decennial census data for years ending in zero and population estimates data for intercensal years.

Qualifications: While the figures seen here are lower than the average number of years that will actually be lived by these groups (mortality rates are decreasing, therefore life expectancy is increasing) they are good indicators for assessing differences across groups as well as relative change over time.

Interpretation: Whites have markedly higher life expectancies than do blacks. Females outlive males by nearly seven years on the average.

III-26. LIFE EXPECTANCY
EXPECTED YEARS OF LIFE AT SELECTED AGES BY SEX AND RACE
1988

Selected Ages	Whites		Blacks		All Other Races	
	Males	Females	Males	Females	Males	Females
0	72.1	78.9	65.1	73.8	67.4	75.5
25	48.9	55.0	42.9	50.8	45.0	52.4
45	30.6	35.8	26.7	32.6	28.2	33.0
65	14.9	18.7	13.6	17.1	14.5	18.0
85	5.0	6.3	5.6	6.8	5.8	7.1

Source: Based on calculations by the National Center for Health Statistics and reprinted in the Metropolitan Life **Statistical Bulletin,** April-June 1990. The **Statistical Bulletin** published by Metropolitan Life Insurance Company reprints data from a variety of sources including statistics on the experiences of the large Metropolitan Life insured population, data not available elsewhere. Additional data, including some unpublished data, on this topic are available from NCHS (Hyattsville, MD).

Methodology: Life expectancy is calculated based on the statistical averages of the experiences of individuals residing within the population.

Interpretation: Life expectancy is greater for females than males at every age. However, among the oldest cohorts the gap in additional expected years of life tends to narrow, suggesting that the less hardy among the males have expired.

III-27. LIFE EXPECTANCY
EXPECTED YEARS OF LIFE AT SELECTED AGES
1979-81 AND 1988

	Years of Expected Life	
Selected Ages	1979-81 Average	1988
0	73.9	74.9
15	60.2	61.0
25	50.8	51.6
35	41.4	42.2
45	32.3	33.0
55	23.9	24.4
65	16.5	16.9
75	10.5	10.6
85	6.0	6.0

Source: Based on calculations by the National Center for Health Statistics and reprinted in the Metropolitan Life **Statistical Bulletin**, April-June 1990. The **Statistical Bulletin** published by Metropolitan Life Insurance Company reprints data from a variety of sources including statistics on the experiences of the large Metropolitan Life insured population, data not available elsewhere. Additional data, including some unpublished data, on this topic are available from NCHS (Hyattsville, MD).

Methodology: Life expectancy is calculated based on the statistical averages of the experiences of individuals residing within the population.

Qualifications: 1988 figures are provisional (i.e., not finalized by the NCHS).

Interpretation: Although life expectancy in the United States has continued to increase, the year to year improvements during the 1980s were small relative to the gains in life expectancy made in previous decades.

DATA ON HEALTH FACILITIES AND ORGANIZATIONS

The U.S. has a long history of data collection related to health facilities. Because of the active role played by government at the federal, state and local levels in the development of health care facilities, a great deal of information has been collected. Just as important has been the role of government in the licensing and accreditation of health care facilities. These accreditation activities generally occur at the state level and result in the compilation of a great deal of data on hospitals and other facilities.

In recent years, the process has become somewhat more complicated due to the proliferation of the types of organizations that are providing health services. The facilities that historically served as settings for the provision of most care were the physician's office, the hospital and the nursing home. The 1970s and 1980s witnessed the emergence of minor emergency centers, freestanding surgery centers, and a variety of other settings for care. This development complicated the collection of data on health care facilities and ultimately opened the door for the development of new sources of such data.

The data collected on health care facilities may cover a wide variety of topics. Data elements include characteristics of the facility (e.g., number of beds, number of employees) and services provided (e.g., types of diagnostic tests). These are fairly straightforward since there are industry standards and accreditation requirements that have served to standardized reporting of such data. Facility databases are also likely to include financial data and this is somewhat more problematic due to the variations in financial record keeping and reporting from facility to facility. Some facility databases may also include patient data; although such information has been rare in the past, it is becoming increasingly important.

There are three major sources of facility data: state accrediting and licensing agencies, associations of facilities, and commercial data vendors. In addition, the Federal government, because of its role in the funding of facility construction in the past and its current role as financing entity for such programs as Medicare and Medicaid, maintains significant amounts of data on health facilities. State agencies typically have responsibility for maintaining standards and controlling licensure. As such they serve as useful sources of data, although the quality and nature of the data are likely to vary from state to state. Data from government sources are typically available in printed form and less frequently as computerized databases.

The best-known of the associations collecting facility data is the American Hospital Association (AHA). For much of this century the AHA has been essentially the last word on hospitals in the U.S. Its annual survey of hospitals (and some other facilities as well) has made it the leading on-going source of such data. The AHA is joined by associations of other types of facilities which also collect data on their member organizations. The American Health Care Association maintains data on over 10,000 nursing homes and long-term care facilities, while other associations maintain data on minor emergency centers, health maintenance organizations or hospital transplant facilities. Information on physician groups is difficult to come by but the Medical Group Management Association maintains information available nowhere else (at least for participating groups). The data collected by associations are maintained in a variety of forms and with varying degrees of accessibility. Established databases like that of the AHA may be available in both printed and computerized formats. Less well-established databases may take a variety of forms and have various levels of accessibility for the public.

Because of the increasing demand for facilities data and the proliferation of organizations that provide health services, a number of commercial data vendors have begun to collect data and create databases for selected types of facilities. This has been particularly the case for such innovative services as freestanding emergency centers, surgicenters, and diagnostic centers that do not have accrediting agencies and may not have developed national associations. These private sources often maintain computerized databases which are made available to the public in a variety of forms. In some cases the data are relatively inexpensive, while in others the costs are quite high.

One other source of facility data is the general interest health care publications and the publications of the respective associations. The journals of associations of facilities frequently print tables or listings of the relevant facilities. General interest publications like Modern Health Care magazine sometimes conduct annual surveys of hospitals or other facilities.

IV-1. Community Health
STATE RANKINGS FOR SELECTED COMMUNITY HEALTH SERVICES
1990

State	Score
Vermont	17
New Hampshire	16
Rhode Island	16
Connecticut	15
Ohio	15
Colorado	14
New York	12
North Carolina	12
Wisconsin	12
Utah	11
Delaware	10
Maine	10
Oregon	10
Pennsylvania	10
Virginia	10
Alabama	9
Alaska	9
Kentucky	9
Maryland	9
Massachusetts	9
Minnesota	9
Missouri	9
Nebraska	9
New Jersey	9
Washington	9
Arkansas	8
Georgia	8
Michigan	8
North Dakota	8
South Carolina	8
California	7
District of Columbia	7
Illinois	7
Indiana	7
Kansas	7
Oklahoma	7
Tennessee	7
Arizona	6
Florida	6
Iowa	6
Louisiana	6
New Mexico	6
South Dakota	6

(Continued on next page)

IV-1. COMMUNITY HEALTH
STATE RANKINGS FOR SELECTED COMMUNITY HEALTH SERVICES
1990 *(Continued from previous page)*

State	Score
West Virginia	6
Nevada	5
Texas	5
Mississippi	4
Montana	4
Idaho	3
Wyoming	3
Hawaii	2

Source: Published in the **Orlando Sentinel** (9/12/90) based on Associated Press sources.

Methodology: Rankings were developed based on a score calculated for each state. States were evaluated in terms of their hospital services, outpatient and community support services, vocational rehabilitation services and housing and services for seriously emotionally disturbed children. A score between 0 and 5 was given to each state for each of these five categories. The total of the five scores determined each state's rank.

Qualifications: Assessments such as this often rely heavily on subjective evaluations of the services being rated. They also vary depending on who is doing the rating and what criteria are being utilized. The choice of services to be evaluated is also a consideration. This rating scale assumes that each of the five categories of services are equal in importance, although this is unlikely to be the case.

Interpretation: Interpretation of these rankings is difficult if they are meant to indicate relative standing in terms of overall health services. It is conceivable that the top ranking state received three excellent ratings and two poor ratings, but that can not be determined from the data provided. It is clear from the scores of the lowest ranking states that they received very low evaluations on all or most of the services.

IV-2. HOSPITALS
SUMMARY STATISTICS COMMUNITY HOSPITALS
1990

Characteristic	Number
Facilities:	
Community hospitals	5,384
Hospital beds	927,000
Utilization:	
Admissions	31,181,000
Inpatient days	225,972,000
Average stay in days (adults)	7.2
Surgical operations	21,915,000
Outpatient visits	301,329,000
Occupancy rate	66.8
Personnel (Full-time equivalents):	
Total personnel employed	3,370,705
Employees per bed	3.4

Source: Data collected by the American Hospital Association (AHA) and published in **Hospital Statistics**. The AHA is the national association of hospitals and, based on data collected from the nation's hospitals, annually publishes **Hospital Statistics** and the **AHA Guide to Health Care Facilities**. The AHA maintains the nation's most extensive data base on hospitals and maintains information beyond that published in its annual guides. Additional, and sometimes unpublished, data can be obtained from the AHA's data office (Chicago).

Methodology: Data in AHA publications are collected through annual surveys of AHA member hospitals.

Definitions: "Community hospitals" include all hospitals (other than state and federal facilities) that provide general care rather than specialty care.

Qualifications: Although most hospitals are members of the AHA, some are not and are not, therefore, likely to participate in the survey. Some members fail to participate (and are listed as nonresponding). The AHA may obtain some of the missing data from other sources, but this does mean there may be some slippage in the data quality. In addition, the AHA must rely on self-reports from the hospitals and this raising the question of the completeness and the accuracy of the data. There is also the problem of timeliness of the data. The magnitude of the data collection, processing and publishing effort means there is a certain time lag between the data can be disseminated (e.g., the 1990 guide contains data for the 1989 fiscal year).

IV-3. HOSPITAL REVENUES
HOSPITAL REVENUES BY TYPE OF HOSPITAL
(in millions of dollars)
1980-1989

Type of Hospital	Amount of Revenue		
	1980	1985	1989
Total	$102,399	$167,938	$232,752
Non-Federal	93,707	154,956	216,830
Community	85,601	143,311	200,927
Inpatient	74,404	119,119	156,468
Outpatient	11,197	24,192	44,459
Noncommunity	8,106	11,645	15,903
Federal	8,692	12,982	15,923

Type of Hospital	Percent Distribution		
	1980	1985	1989
Total	100%	100%	100%
Non-Federal	92	92	93
Community	84	85	86
Inpatient	73	71	67
Outpatient	11	14	19
Noncommunity	8	7	7
Federal	8	8	7

Type of Hospital	Annual Percent Growth		
	1980	1985	1985
Total	-	6.8%	10.0%
Non-Federal	-	6.7	10.1
Community	-	6.7	10.2
Inpatient	-	4.4	8.6
Outpatient	-	19.3	16.2
Noncommunity	-	7.3	9.5
Federal	-	8.2	7.4

Source: Based on data collected by Health Care Financing Administration (HCFA) within the U.S. Department of Health and Human Services. HCFA, as the organization responsible for the administration of the Medicare program, is the primary source of Medicare statistics. Additional data are available directly from HCFA (Washington, D.C.) or through its publications such as **Health Care Financing Review**.

Methodology: The data are drawn from the universe of hospitals participating in the Medicare program, representing 99% of all short-term non-federal hospitals.

Definitions: "Community hospitals" include all hospitals (other than State and Federal facilities) that provide general care rather than specialty care. "Noncommunity hospitals" include non-federal long-term care hospitals, psychiatric hospitals, alcoholism and chemical dependency hospitals, units of institutions such as prison hospitals and college infirmaries, chronic disease hospitals, and some institutions for the mentally retarded.

IV-4. HOSPITALS
HOSPITAL BEDS AND OCCUPANCY RATES
1980-90

Year	Number of Beds	Percent Change	Occupancy Rates	Percent Change
1990*	922,022	-0.9%	64.8	-0.5%
1989	930,994	-1.3	65.2	0.6
1988	942,306	-1.3	64.5	0.6
1987	954,458	-0.9	64.1	1.1
1986	963,133	-1.2	63.4	-0.3
1985	974,559	-1.8	63.6	-4.5
1984	992,616	-1.1	66.6	-7.8
1983	1,003,658	0.6	72.2	-3.2
1982	997,720	1.1	74.6	-1.6
1981	986,917	1.7	75.8	-0.1
1980	970,456	1.2	75.9	1.9

*Estimate based on January through November 1990 data.

Source: Data collected by the American Hospital Association (AHA) and published in **Hospital Statistics**. The AHA is the national association of hospitals and, based on data collected from the nation's hospitals, annually publishes **Hospital Statistics** and the **AHA Guide to Health Care Facilities**. Although hospital-oriented, these publications contain some information on other facilities. The AHA maintains the nation's most extensive data base on hospitals and maintains information beyond that published in its annual guides. Additional, and sometimes unpublished, data can be obtained from the AHA's data office (Chicago).

Methodology: The National Hospital Panel Survey is a monthly survey of a randomly selected sample of 1800 community hospitals. There are approximately 5,800 community hospitals in the U.S.

Definitions: Hospital "occupancy rate" is determined by the number of occupied beds divided by the number of operating beds.

Interpretation: The average occupancy declined with the decline in admission and length of stay recorded during the 1980s. This decline is a direct result of implementation of Medicare's prospective payment system (PPS), the program by which Medicare pays a hospital a predetermined amount depending on the admitting diagnosis. This program encourages hospitals to limit admissions and work toward early discharge.

IV-5. HOSPITALS
COMMUNITY HOSPITAL OPENINGS AND CLOSINGS
1980-1988

Year	Hospital Openings	Hospital Closings
1988	10	83
1987	27	79
1986	23	72
1985	29	49
1984	26	45
1983	18	25
1982	34	23
1981	20	27
1980	10	45

Source: Data collected by the American Hospital Association (AHA) and published in **Hospital Statistics**. The AHA is the national association of hospitals and, based on data collected from the nation's hospitals, annually publishes **Hospital Statistics** and the **AHA Guide to the Health Care Field**. Although hospital-oriented, these publications contain some information on other facilities. The AHA maintains the nation's most extensive data base on hospitals and maintains information beyond that published in its annual guides. Additional, and sometimes unpublished, data can be obtained from the AHA's data office (Chicago).

Methodology: Based on data maintained by the American Hospital Association.

Interpretation: Few hospitals are opening annually, while the number of closures is at historical highs. Half of the hospital closings occur in rural America and contain fewer than 100 beds.

IV-6. HOSPITALS
COMMUNITY HOSPITAL EXPENSES
1965-1990

Year	Total Expenses ($ in billions)	Adjusted Expense Per Admission
1990	$217,113	$5,021
1989	195,377	4,586
1988	177,770	4,194
1987	161,322	3,860
1986	146,032	3,527
1985	134,043	3,226
1980	79,340	1,836
1975	38,492	1,017
1970	20,261	608
1965	9,220	315

Source: Data collected by the American Hospital Association (AHA) and published in **Hospital Statistics**. The AHA is the national association of hospitals and, based on data collected from the nation's hospitals, annually publishes **Hospital Statistics** and the **AHA Guide to the Health Care Field**. Although hospital-oriented, these publications contain some information on other facilities. The AHA maintains the nation's most extensive data base on hospitals and maintains information beyond that published in its annual guides. Additional, and sometimes unpublished, data can be obtained from the AHA's data office (Chicago).

Methodology: The National Hospital Panel Survey is a monthly survey of a randomly selected sample of 1,800 community hospitals. There are approximately 5,800 community hospitals in the United States.

Interpretation: Hospital expenses have increased annually since records have been kept, with the increases accelerating in recent years. The growth rate exceeds the rate of inflation.

IV-7. HOSPITAL SERVICES
DISTRIBUTION OF SELECTED SERVICES AMONG COMMUNITY HOSPITALS
1990

Service	Percent of Hospitals Providing
Ambulatory surgery	94.7%
Birthing rooms	65.1
Blood bank	69.1
Emergency department	93.5
Outpatient alcoholism/chemical dependency	20.5
Physical therapy	84.5
Trauma care	12.9
Volunteer services	67.8
Outpatient rehabilitation	51.5
Outpatient department	85.2
Home health care	35.6
Hospice program	16.2

Source: Data collected by the American Hospital Association (AHA) and published in **Hospital Statistics**. The AHA is the National Association of Hospitals and, based on data collected from the nation's hospitals, annually publishes **Hospital Statistics** and the **AHA Guide to the Health Care Field**. The AHA maintains the nation's most extensive data base on hospitals and maintains information beyond that published in its annual guides. Additional, and sometimes unpublished, data can be obtained from the AHA's data office (Chicago).

Methodology: Data in AHA publications are collected through annual surveys of AHA member hospitals.

Definitions: "Community hospitals" include all hospitals (other than state and federal facilities) that provide general care rather than specialty care.

Qualifications: Although most hospitals are members of the AHA, some are not and are not, therefore, likely to participate in the survey. Some members fail to participate (and are listed as nonresponding). The AHA may obtain some of the missing data from other sources, but this does means there is some slippage in the data quality. In addition, the AHA must rely on self-reports from the hospitals and this raising the question of the completeness and the accuracy of the data. There is also the problem of timeliness of the data. The magnitude of the data collection, processing, and publishing effort means there is a certain time lag between the data can be disseminated (e.g., the 1990 guide contains data for the 1989 fiscal year). Most, but not all, reporting hospitals provided information. To the extent that the reporting hospitals were representative, these figures are accurate.

IV-8. HOSPITALS
DISTRIBUTION OF COMMUNITY HOSPITALS BY SIZE CATEGORY
AND COMMUNITY TYPE
1990

Type	Number
Total community hospitals	5,384
Urban community hospitals	2,924
6-24 beds	34
25-49	174
50-99	439
100-199	785
200-299	619
300-399	375
400-499	218
500 or more	280
Rural community hospitals	2,460
6-24 Beds	192
25-49	761
50-99	824
100-199	521
200-299	120
300-399	33
400-499	4
500 or more	5

Source: Data collected by the American Hospital Association (AHA) and published in **Hospital Statistics.** The AHA is the national association of hospitals and, based on data collected from the nation's hospitals, annually publishes **Hospital Statistics** and the **AHA Guide to the Health Care Field.** The AHA maintains the nation's most extensive data base on hospitals and maintains information beyond that published in its annual guides. Additional, and sometimes unpublished, data can be obtained from the AHA's data office (Chicago).

Methodology: Data in AHA publications are collected through annual surveys of AHA member hospitals.

Definitions: "Community hospitals" include all hospitals (other than state and federal facilities) that provide general care rather than specialty care.

Qualifications: Although most hospitals are members of the AHA, some are not and are not, therefore, likely to participate in the survey. Some members fail to participate (and are listed as nonresponding). The AHA may obtain some of the missing data from other sources, but this does means there is some slippage in the data quality. In addition, the AHA must rely on self-reports from the hospitals and this raising the question of the completeness and the accuracy of the data. There is also the problem of timeliness of the data. The magnitude of the data collection, processing, and publishing effort means there is a certain time lag between the data can be disseminated (e.g., the 1990 guide contains data for the 1989 fiscal year).

Interpretation: The trend over the past two decades has been toward larger hospitals and has involved the closing or consolidation of many small (fewer than 100 beds) facilities. However, the 50-90 bed hospital is still the most common size facility in rural areas.

IV-9. HOSPITALS
CHARACTERISTICS OF GENERAL HOSPITALS BY OWNERSHIP TYPE
1990

Type of Hospital	Number	Beds	Admissions
Nongovernment not-for-profit	3,085	645,658	22,578,707
Investor-owned (for-profit)	693	96,764	2,978,930
Local government	1,358	143,557	4,395,916
State government	94	24,225	816,499
Federal government	305	76,856	1,630,541

Source: Data collected by the American Hospital Association (AHA) and published in **Hospital Statistics**. The AHA is the national association of hospitals and, based on data collected from the nation's hospitals, annually publishes **Hospital Statistics** and the **AHA Guide to the Health Care Field**. The AHA maintains the nation's most extensive data base on hospitals and maintains information beyond that published in its annual guides. Additional, and sometimes unpublished, data can be obtained from the AHA's data office (Chicago).

Methodology: Data in AHA publications are collected through annual surveys of AHA member hospitals.

Definitions: "Nongovernment not-for-profit" hospitals are usually religious-affiliated institutions.

Qualifications: Although most hospitals are members of the AHA, some are not and are not, therefore, likely to participate in the survey. Some members fail to participate (and are listed as nonresponding). The AHA may obtain some of the missing data from other sources, but this does mean there is some slippage in the data quality. In addition, the AHA must rely on self-reports from the hospitals and this raising the question of the completeness and the accuracy of the data. There is also the problem of timeliness of the data. The magnitude of the data collection, processing and publishing effort means there is a certain time lag between the data can be disseminated (e.g., the 1990 guide contains data for the 1989 fiscal year).

IV-10. HOSPITAL BEDS
DISTRIBUTION OF HOSPITAL BEDS BY HOSPITAL SIZE
1990

Bed-size category	Beds	
	Number	Percent
6-24	4,427	0.5%
25-49	35,420	3.8
50-99	90,394	9.7
100-199	183,867	19.8
200-299	179,670	19.4
300-399	138,938	15.0
400-499	99,833	10.7
500+	195,811	21.1

Source: Data collected by the American Hospital Association (AHA) and published in **Hospital Statistics**. The AHA is the national association of hospitals and, based on data collected from the nation's hospitals, annually publishes **Hospital Statistics** and the **AHA Guide to the Health Care Field.** The AHA maintains the nation's most extensive data base on hospitals and maintains information beyond that published in its annual guides. Additional, and sometimes unpublished, data can be obtained from the AHA's data office (Chicago).

Methodology: Data in AHA publications are collected through annual surveys of AHA member hospitals.

Definitions: "Community hospitals" include all hospitals (other than state and federal facilities) that provide general care rather than specialty care.

Qualifications: Although most hospitals are members of the AHA, some are not and are not, therefore, likely to participate in the survey. Some members fail to participate (and are listed as nonresponding). The AHA may obtain some of the missing data from other sources, but this does means there is some slippage in the data quality. In addition, the AHA must rely on self-reports from the hospitals and this raising the question of the completeness and the accuracy of the data. There is also the problem of timeliness of the data. The magnitude of the data collection, processing, and publishing effort means there is a certain time lag between the data can be disseminated (e.g., the 1990 guide contains data for the 1989 fiscal year).

Interpretation: Although very large hospitals are uncommon, because of the size of those that do exist, they account for a disproportionate share of the nation's hospital beds. Note the relative small portion of beds accounted for by hospitals in the 400-499 size category.

IV-11. HEALTH-RELATED CORPORATIONS
HEALTH-RELATED CORPORATIONS AMONG THE
100 FASTEST GROWING COMPANIES
1990

Company (Headquarters)	Product(s)	Rank Within Top 100
Diagnostak (Albuquerque, NM)	Mail order prescription drugs, imaging centers	5
Coventry (Nashville, TN)	Health maintenance organizations, insurance	9
Columbia Hospital (Fort Worth, TX)	Hospitals, surgery centers	12
T2 Medical (Alpharetta, GA)	Home health, cancer therapy	13
Qual-Med (Monte Vista, CA)	Health maintenance organizations	15
Medical Imaging Centers (San Diego, CA)	Diagnostic equipment	16
IVAX	Pharmaceutical R&D, diagnostics	17
Integrated Health Services (Hunt Valley, MD)	Geriatric care	38
Vencor (Louisville, KY)	Long-term care	41
Scimed Life Systems (Maple Grove, MN)	Surgical equipment	42
Lifetime (Boston, MA)	Home health, hospital staffing	45
Amgen (Thousand Oaks, CA)	Blood products	46
Ransay HMO (Coral Gables, FL)	Health maintenance organization	49
Healthsouth Rehabilitation (Birmingham, AL)	Rehabilitation Services	50
MDT (Torrance, CA)	Sterilization equipment	63
Chiron (Emeryville, CA)	Vaccine	67
Novacare (Valley Forge, PA)	Therapist recruitment & training	69
Foundation Health (Rancho Cordova, CA)	Military health care	81
Medco Containment Services (Montvale, NJ)	Mail order pharmaceuticals	85
Carenetwork (Milwaukee, WI)	Health maintenance organizations	86
Surgical Care Affiliates (Nashville, TN)	Surgery centers	95
Century Medicorp (Los Angeles, CA)	Health maintenance organizations, hospitals	99
Tokos Medical (Santa Ana, CA)	Pregnancy care	100

Source: Based on figures provided by corporations. Compiled by William O'Neil and Co. (Los Angeles) and published by **Fortune** (October 7, 1991).

Methodology: O'Neil and Company accessed its database of publicly-traded companies with at least three years of operating results. After companies with one or more quarters of losses were excluded, the remainder were ranked on sales growth. Banking, finance and insurance companies were excluded from the analysis.

Qualifications: Some corporations that were tangentially involved in health care were excluded from this list. Some companies that may have been eligible for the list may have failed to submit information.

Interpretation: Twenty-three of the top 100 fastest-growing companies in 1990 were in the health care field. Most were built on innovative delivery of goods or services or on technology breakthroughs. Only computer production and sales could count more corporations within the top 100.

IV-12. HOSPITALS
25 LARGEST HOSPITALS BASED ON ADMISSIONS
1989

Name	Admissions	Average Daily Census	Percent Occupancy
LAC-University of Southern California Medical Center (Los Angeles, CA)	76,261	1,234	89.6%
James M. Jackson Memorial Hospital (Miami, FL)	54,729	1,176	82.6
Health One Corp. (Minneapolis, MN)	53,308	987	66.8
Baptist Memorial Hospital (Memphis, TN)	45,361	1,122	76.6
St. Luke's-Roosevelt Hospital Center (New York, NY)	43,743	NA	88.0
The Presbyterian Hospital in the City of New York (New York, NY)	41,549	1,095	89.0
Catholic Medical Center of Brooklyn & Queens Inc. (Jamaica, NY)	40,682	1,137	94.2
Dallas County Hospital District-Parkland Memorial Hospital (Dallas, TX)	40,585	696	81.1
Harris County Hospital District (Houston, TX)	40,572	769	82.6
Grady Memorial Hospital (Atlanta, GA)	40,336	732	78.6
Society of the New York Hospital (New York, NY)	39,988	1,182	83.6
Montefiore Medical Center (Bronx, NY)	39,579	975	80.6
Medical Center of Delaware (Wilmington, NC)	39,409	750	80.0
Baylor University Medical Center (Dallas, TX)	39,065	726	69.1
Florida Hospital (Orlando, FL)	38,557	742	73.2
Riverside Methodist Hospital (Columbus, OH)	38,279	722	82.8
Fairfax Hospital (Falls Church, VA)	37,751	570	86.9
William Beaumont Hospital (Royal Oak, MI)	37,627	716	77.1
Methodist Hospital of Indiana (Indianapolis, IN)	37,607	743	77.4
Johns Hopkins Hospital (Baltimore, MD)	36,361	810	85.1
The Methodist Hospital (Houston, TX)	35,322	812	67.3
Barnes Hospital (St. Louis, MO)	35,174	758	74.8
Brigham and Women's Hospital (Boston, MA)	35,105	621	86.3
Beth Israel Medical Center (New York, NY)	34,413	NA	92.5

Source: Based on data collected by the American Hospital Association and published in **HealthWeek** (July 29, 1991). The AHA is the national association of hospitals and, based on data collected from the nation's hospitals, annually publishes **Hospital Statistics** and the **AHA Guide to the Health Care Field**. The AHA maintains the nation's most extensive data base on hospitals and maintains information beyond that published in its annual guides. (HealthWeek ceased publication at the end of 1991.)

Methodology: Data in AHA publications are collected through annual surveys of AHA member hospitals.

Qualifications: Hospitals use a variety of methods for calculating admissions and determining which facilities are counted in their admission totals. Also, reporting procedures may vary from state to state. These factors should be investigated further prior to use of these statistics.

IV-13. HOSPITAL ALLIANCES
TOTAL BEDS AND TOTAL FACILITIES FOR THE TOP 10 HOSPITAL ALLIANCES
1990

Company	Total Beds	Total Number of Facilities
Voluntary Hospitals of America, Inc. (Irving, TX)	221,975	853
American Healthcare Systems (San Diego, CA)	144,937	1,090
The SunHealth Network (Charlotte, NC)	63,000	230
Consolidated Catholic Health Care (Oakbrook, IL)	32,500	150
Premier Hospitals Alliance, Inc. (Westchester, IL)	31,658	76
University Hospital Consortium, Inc. (Oakbrook, IL)	27,550	52
HFN Inc. (Oak Brook, IL)	20,185	68
InterHealth (St. Paul, MN)	13,851	216
Pacific Health Alliance (San Mateo, CA)	10,114	53
Catholic Health Alliance for Metro Chicago (Chicago, IL)	6,500	22

Source: Based on data collected by the American Hospital Association and through a telephone survey by **HealthWeek**. Published in **HealthWeek** (March 25, 1991). The AHA is the national association of hospitals and, based on data collected from the nation's hospitals annually publishes **Hospital Statistics** and the **AHA Guide to the Health Care Field**. The AHA maintains the nation's most extensive data base on hospitals and maintains information beyond that published in its annual guides. Additional, and sometimes unpublished, data can be obtained from the AHA's data office (Chicago). (**HealthWeek** ceased publication at the end of 1991.)

Methodology: Data in AHA publications are collected through annual surveys of AHA member hospitals.

Definitions: "Hospital alliances" are organizations comprised of individual hospitals and hospital systems for purposes of improving efficiency, sharing information and a variety of other purposes.

Qualifications: Although most hospitals are members of the AHA, some are not and are not, therefore, likely to participate in the survey. Some members fail to participate (and are listed as nonresponding). The AHA may obtain some of the missing data from other sources, but this does means there is some slippage in the data quality. In addition, the AHA must rely on self-reports from the hospitals and this raising the question of the completeness and the accuracy of the data. There is also the problem of timeliness of the data. The magnitude of the data collection, processing, and publishing effort means there is a certain time lag between the data can be disseminated (e.g., the 1990 guide contains data for the 1989 fiscal year).

Interpretation: There are only a few major hospital alliances. However, some of them are quite large (with hundreds of institutional members). The 18 largest alliances, based on number of beds, include approximately one-third of the nation's hospitals among their members.

IV-14. MANAGEMENT COMPANIES
LARGEST INVESTOR-OWNED HOSPITAL MANAGEMENT COMPANIES
1991

Hospitals Company	Beds Owned/ Owned/Managed	Hospitals Managed
Quorum Health Group	179	20,821
Hospital Corporation of America	131	24,667
Charter Medical Corporation	108	10,375
HealthTrust	88	11,833
Humana	85	17,846
Psychiatric Institute of America (NME)	75	6,121
Hospital Management Professionals	61	7,737
Paracelsus Healthcare Corporation	58	6,901
American Medical Holdings	57	11,642
Community Psychiatric Centers	50	4,883
Brim & Associates	45	2,881
National Medical Enterprises	41	7,934
Epic Healthcare Group	37	4,399
Universal Health Services	35	3,961
Rehab Hospital Services Corporation	27	2,436
American Healthcare Management	17	2,203
Republic Health Corporation	16	3,790

Source: Based on data from the Federation of American Health Systems, supplemented by data compiled by HealthWeek Publications (Manhasset, NY). Published in **HealthWeek** (June 3, 1991). The Federation of American Health Systems is an association of multi-unit health care organizations. (**HealthWeek** ceased publication at the end of 1991.)

Methodology: Based on data published in the directory of the Federation of American Health Systems, 1991 edition.

Definitions: "Investor-owned hospital management companies" include those who own, manage or both own and manage hospitals. This list includes systems that include 2,000 beds or more under ownership or management.

Qualifications: The hospital management industry continues to experience reorganization with mergers and divestitures common. Specific figures should be verified prior to their use by the reader.

IV-15. HOSPITAL RATINGS
HIGHEST-RATED HOSPITALS FOR CANCER TREATMENT
1990

Hospital (Location)	Percent of Physicians Choosing
Memorial Sloan-Kettering Institute (New York, NY)	71%
M.D. Anderson Cancer Center (Houston, TX)	62
Johns Hopkins Hospital (Baltimore, MD)	62
Dana-Farber Cancer Institute (Boston, MA)	42
Stanford University Hospital (Stanford, CA)	42
UCLA Medical Center (Los Angeles, CA)	38
Duke University Hospital (Durham, NC)	36
University of Pennsylvania Medical Center (Philadelphia, PA)	33
The Mayo Clinic (Rochester, MN)	33
Massachusetts General Hospital (Boston, MA)	29
University of California at San Francisco Medical Center (San Francisco, CA)	27
University of Chicago Hospitals (Chicago, IL)	27
University of Washington Medical Center (Seattle, WA)	24
Barnes Hospital (St. Louis, MO)	20
National Institute of Health Clinical Center (Bethesda, MD)	20
University Medical Center (Tucson, AZ)	20

Source: Based on a survey of physicians conducted by and published in **U.S. News & World Report** (April 30, 1990). Copyright, April 30, 1990, by **U.S. News & World Report**.

Methodology: Based on a survey of 400 physicians representing twelve specialties. Each physician was asked to identify the top 10 hospitals in his or her specialty. Although ratings by "experts" can provide a reasonable rating system, these ratings are subjective. If a more objective criterion were used, the ratings might be different.

Qualifications: Like all "opinion" surveys, this one may reflect biases on the part of the respondents.

IV-16. HOSPITAL RATINGS
HIGHEST-RATED PEDIATRICS HOSPITALS
1990

Hospital (Location)	Percent of Physicians Choosing
Children's Hospital (Boston, MA)	74%
Children's Hospital and Medical Center (Seattle, WA)	23
Children's Hospital of Philadelphia (Philadelphia, PA)	49
Johns Hopkins Hospital (Baltimore, MD)	40
Children's Hospital Los Angeles (Los Angeles, CA)	40
St. Louis Children's Hospital (St. Louis, MO)	34
Texas Children's Hospital (Houston, TX)	32
Children's Hospital Medical Center (Cincinnati, OH)	30
Children's Memorial Medical Center (Chicago, IL)	28
Children's Hospital of Pittsburgh (Pittsburgh, PA)	26
Duke University Hospital (Durham, NC)	26
Children's Hospital National Medical Center (Washington, DC)	23
Stanford University Hospital (Stanford, CA)	20

Source: Based on a survey of physicians conducted by and published in **U.S. News & World Report** (April 30, 1990). Copyright, April 30, 1990, by **U.S. News & World Report**.

Methodology: Based on a survey of 400 physicians representing twelve specialties. Each physician was asked to identify the top 10 hospitals in his or her specialty. Although ratings by "experts" can provide a reasonable rating system, these ratings are subjective. If a more objective criterion were used, the ratings might be different.

Qualifications: Like all "opinion" surveys, this one may reflect biases on the part of the respondents.

IV-17. HOSPITAL RATINGS
HIGHEST-RATED HOSPITALS FOR HEART CARE
1990

Hospital (Location)	Percent of Physicians Choosing
Massachusetts General Hospital (Boston, MA)	71%
The Mayo Clinic (Rochester, MN)	71
The Cleveland Clinic (Cleveland, OH)	51
Duke University Hospital (Durham, NC)	49
Brigham and Women's Hospital (Boston, MA)	46
Emory University Hospital (Atlanta, GA)	37
Johns Hopkins Hospital (Baltimore, MD)	37
Stanford University Hospital (Stanford, CA)	37
University of Alabama at Birmingham Hospital (Birmingham, AL)	31
Columbia-Presbyterian Medical Center (New York, NY)	26
University of Pennsylvania Medical Center (Philadelphia, PA)	23
Methodist Hospital (Houston, TX)	20

Source: Based on a survey of physicians conducted by and published in **U.S. News & World Report** (April 30, 1990). Copyright, April 30, 1990, by **U.S. News & World Report.**

Methodology: Based on a survey of 400 physicians representing twelve specialties. Each physician was asked to identify the top 10 hospitals in his or her specialty. Although ratings by "experts" can provide a reasonable rating system, these ratings are subjective. If a more objective criterion were used, the ratings might be different.

Qualifications: Like all "opinion" surveys, this one may reflect biases on the part of the respondents.

IV-18. HOSPITAL SYSTEMS
TEN LARGEST HOSPITAL SYSTEMS RANKED BY REVENUE
1990

System (Headquarters)	Revenue ($ Millions)
Kaiser Foundation Hospitals (Oakland, CA)	$8,443.0
Humana (Louisville, KY)	4,852.0
National Medical Enterprises (Santa Monica, CA)	3,742.1
Daughters of Charity National Health System (St. Louis, MO)	3,195.6
UniHealth America (Burbank, CA)	2,600.0
New York City Health and Hospitals Corp. (New York, NY)	2,550.9
American Medical International (Dallas, TX)	2,546.1
HealthTrust - The Hospital Co. (Nashville, TN)	1,856.9
Mercy Health Services (Farmington Hills, MI)	1,398.0
Sisters of Charity Health Care Systems (Cincinnati, OH)	1,125.0

Source: Based on the Annual Survey of Hospitals conducted by and published in **Modern Healthcare** (May 20, 1991).

Methodology: Data are collected annually by means of a survey of multi-hospital systems. These data are based on response from 171 multi-hospital systems.

Definitions: "Gross revenues" includes bad debts but excludes discounts taken by Medicare, Medicaid, and other third-party payors. "Hospitals" refers to general acute care facilities, although some other types of hospitals may be owned by the systems.

Qualifications: Since these data are based on voluntary responses, there have been occasions when some systems may not have been represented. Also, the information is based on self-reports by organizations that may use different accounting methods or definitions. Revenues for some of the systems include income from health insurance plans, psychiatric hospitals, or rehabilitation hospitals.

IV-19. HOSPITAL SYSTEMS
TEN LARGEST HOSPITAL SYSTEMS RANKED BY TOTAL FACILITIES
1990

System (Headquarters)	Number of Facilities
Quorum Health Group (Nashville, TN)	174
National Medical Enterprises (Santa Monica, CA)	150
Hospital Corp. of America (Nashville, TN)	139
Charter Medical Corp. (Macon, GA)	104
HealthTrust - The Hospital Co. (Nashville, TN)	86
Humana (Louisville, KY)	81
Brim (Portland, OR)	69
Hospital Management Professionals (Brentwood, TN)	65
Paracelsus Healthcare Corp. (Pasadena, CA)	60
Daughters of Charity National Health System (St. Louis, MO)	50
Mercy Health Services (Farmington Hills, MI)	50

Source: Based on the Annual Survey of Hospitals conducted by and published in **Modern Healthcare** (May 20, 1991).

Methodology: Data are collected annually by means of a survey of multi-hospital systems. These data are based on response from 171 multi-hospital systems.

Definitions: "Facilities" refers to general acute care hospitals, although some of the systems ranked include psychiatric, rehabilitation and/or substance abuse hospitals. This figure includes facilities worldwide.

Qualifications: Since these data are based on voluntary responses, there have been occasions when some systems may not have been represented. Also, the information is based on self-reports by organizations that may use different accounting methods or definitions.

IV-20. HOSPITAL SYSTEMS
TEN LARGEST CATHOLIC HOSPITAL SYSTEMS
1990

System (Headquarters)	Beds	Facilities
Daughters of Charity National Health System (St. Louis, MO)	13,766	44
Mercy Health Services (Farmington, MI)	7,942	41
Catholic Health Corp. (Omaha, NE)	4,903	41
Sisters of Charity Health Care Systems (Cincinnati, OH)	4,903	22
SCH Health Care System (Houston, TX)	4,533	11
Mercy Health System (Cincinnati, OH)	4,445	19
Eastern Mercy Health System (Radnor, PA)	4,378	13
Sisters of Mercy Health System-St. Louis (St. Louis, MO)	3,951	14
Hospital Sisters Health System (Springfield, IL)	3,821	14
Health Care Corp. of Sisters of St. Joseph (St. Louis, MO)	3,765	15
Sisters of Providence (Seattle, WA)	3,712	15

Source: Based on the Annual Survey of Hospitals conducted by and published in **Modern Healthcare** (May 20, 1991).

Methodology: Data are collected annually by means of a survey of multi-hospital systems. These data are based on response from 171 multi-hospital systems.

Definitions: "Facilities" refers to general acute care hospitals, although some of the systems ranked include psychiatric, rehabilitation and/or substance abuse hospitals. This figure includes facilities worldwide.

Qualifications: Since these data are based on voluntary responses, there have been occasions when some systems may not have been represented. Also, the information is based on self-reports by organizations that may use different accounting methods or definitions.

IV-21. HOSPITAL SYSTEMS
TOP 10 NON-CATHOLIC CHURCH-AFFILIATED HOSPITAL SYSTEMS
RANKED BY TOTAL BEDS
1990

Name (Location)	Beds	Facilities
Baptist Memorial Healthcare System (Memphis, TN)	4,157	19
Adventist Health System/Sunbelt (Orlando, FL)	3,075	18
Adventist Health System/West (Roseville, CA)	2,860	17
U.S. Health Corp. (Columbus, OH)	2,717	6
Methodist Health Systems (Memphis, TN)	2,627	13
Fairview Hospitals & Health Care Services (Minneapolis, MN)	2,292	6
Evangelical Health Systems (Oak Brook, IL)	1,952	5
Methodist Hospital System (Houston, TX)	1,859	2
Baylor Health Care System (Dallas, TX)	1,784	5
Baptist Medical Centers (Birmingham, AL)	1,668	6

Source: Based on the Annual Survey of Hospitals conducted by and published in **Modern Healthcare** (May 20, 1991).

Methodology: Data are collected annually by means of a survey of multi-hospital systems. These data are based on response from 171 multi-hospital systems.

Definitions: "Facilities" refers to acute care hospitals and includes operations worldwide.

Qualifications: Since these data are based on voluntary responses, there have been occasions when some systems may not have been represented. Also, the information is based on self-reports by organizations that may use different accounting methods or definitions.

IV-22. HOSPITAL SYSTEMS
TEN LARGEST PUBLIC HOSPITAL SYSTEMS RANKED BY TOTAL BEDS
1990

Name (Location)	Beds	Facilities
New York City Health and Hospitals Corp. (New York, NY)	10,061	13
County of Los Angeles-Dept. of Health (Los Angeles, CA)	4,363	6
State of Hawaii-Dept. of Health (Honolulu, HI)	1,181	11
Charlotte-Mecklenburg Hospital Authority (Charlotte, NC)	973	2
Metrohealth System (Cleveland, OH)	748	2
Kennestone Regional Health Care Systems (Marietta, GA)	738	3
DCH Healthcare Authority (Tuscaloosa, AL)	734	3
Boston City Hospital (Boston, MA)	713	3
Wake Medical Center (Raleigh, NC)	656	5
Spartanburg Hospital System (Spartanburg, SC)	631	2

Source: Based on Annual Survey of Hospitals conducted by and published in **Modern Healthcare** (May 20, 1991).

Methodology: Data are collected annually by means of a survey of multi-hospital systems. These data are based on response from 171 multi-hospital systems.

Definitions: "Facilities" refers to acute care hospitals and includes operations worldwide.

Qualifications: Since these data are based on voluntary responses, there have been occasions when some systems may not have been represented. Also, the information is based on self-reports by organizations that may use different accounting methods or definitions.

IV-23. HOSPITAL SYSTEMS
TEN LARGEST INVESTOR-OWNED HOSPITAL SYSTEMS
RANKED BY TOTAL BEDS
1990

System (Location)	Beds	Facilities
Quorum Health Group (Nashville, TN)	19,498	174
Hospital Corp. of America (Nashville, TN)	18,799	85
Humana (Louisville, KY)	17,252	81
HealthTrust-The Hospital Co. (Nashville, TN)	11,621	85
American Medical International (Dallas, TX)	10,337	44
Hospital Management Professionals (Brentwood, TN)	8,574	64
National Medical Enterprises (Santa Monica, CA)	7,414	38
Paracelsus Healthcare Corp. (Pasadena, CA)	6,904	57
Brim (Portland, OR)	5,370	69
Epic Healthcare Group (Dallas, TX)	4,303	39

Source: Based on Annual Survey of Hospitals conducted by and published in **Modern Healthcare** (May 20, 1991).

Methodology: Data are collected annually by means of a survey of multi-hospital systems. These data are based on response from 171 multi-hospital systems.

Definitions: "Facilities" refers to acute care hospitals and includes operations worldwide.

Qualifications: Since these data are based on voluntary responses, there have been occasions when some systems may not have been represented. Also, the information is based on self-reports by organizations that may use different accounting methods or definitions.

IV-24. HOSPITAL SYSTEMS
THE 10 HOSPITAL SYSTEMS WITH LARGEST FOREIGN HOLDINGS
RANKED BY BEDS OWNED
1990

System (Headquarters)	Total Beds	Facilities	No. of countries
Paracelsus Healthcare Corp. (Pasadena, CA)	5,305	38	5
Hospital Corp. of America (Nashville, TN)	1,087	10	2
National Medical Enterprises (Santa Monica, CA)	864	3	2
Medlantic Healthcare Group (Washington, DC)	570	1	1
Healthcare Management Group (Macon, GA)	502	1	1
Humana (Louisville, KY)	483	3	2
Mercy Health Services (Farmington Hills, MI)	215	2	2
Universal Health Services (Philadelphia, PA)	190	3	1
Sisters of Sorrowful Mother Ministry Corp. (Milwaukee, WI)	107	1	1
Shriners Hospitals for Crippled Children (Tampa, FL)	100	2	2

Source: Based on the Annual Survey of Hospitals conducted by and published in **Modern Healthcare** (May 20, 1991).

Methodology: Data are collected annually by means of a survey of multi-hospital systems. These data are based on response from 171 multi-hospital systems.

Definitions: "Facilities" refers to acute care hospitals owned or managed outside the U.S.

Qualifications: Since these data are based on voluntary responses, there have been occasions when some systems may not have been represented. Also, the information is based on self-reports by organizations that may use different accounting methods or definitions.

IV-25. REHABILITATION HOSPITALS
LEADING OPERATORS OF REHABILITATION HOSPITALS
RANKED BY TOTAL OWNED/MANAGED BEDS
1990

Name (Headquarters)	Beds	Facilities	No. States
National Medical Enterprises (Santa Monica, CA)	2,436	27	10
Continental Medical Systems (Mechanicsburg, PA)	1,089 *	16	9
HealthSouth Rehabilitation Corp. (Birmingham, AL)	942	9	6
Advantage Health Corp. (Woburn, MA)	438 *	4	2
Rehab Systems Co. (Camp Hill, MA)	406 *	7	4
Healthcare International (Austin, TX)	319	3	NA
Mediplex Group (Wellesley, MA)	306	3	3
Daughters of Charity National Health System (St. Louis, MO)	254	1	1
ReLife (Birmingham, AL)	200 *	3	3
Allied Services (Scranton, PA)	192	2	2
Detroit Medical Center (Detroit, MI)	175	1	1
Baylor Health Care System (Dallas, TX)	172	2	1
Baptist Medical System (Little Rock, AR)	168	1	1
Renaissance America (Atlanta, GA)	160	2	2
Medlantic Healthcare Group (Washington, DC)	160	1	1

NA = not available
* Includes some managed beds

Source: Based on the Annual Survey of Hospitals conducted by and published in **Modern Healthcare** (May 20, 1991).

Methodology: Data are collected annually by means of a survey of health-related facilities.

Definitions: "Facilities" refers to rehabilitation hospitals only.

Qualifications: Since these data are based on voluntary responses, there have been occasions when some systems may not have been represented. Also, the information is based on self-reports by organizations that may use different accounting methods or definitions.

IV-26. NURSING HOMES
NURSING HOME CHAINS (RANKED BY NUMBER OF BEDS)
1990

Chains (Headquarters)	Total Beds	Total Facilities
Beverly Enterprises (Fort Smith, AR)	93,917	867
The Hillhaven Corp. (Tacoma, WA)	42,467	363
ARA Living Centers (Houston, TX)	24,592	230
Manor Care (Silver Springs, MD)	22,100	164
Good Samaritan Society (Sioux Falls, SD)	20,040	205
Life Care Centers of America (Cleveland, TN)	17,545	128
HCR Corp (Toledo, OH)	17,529	136
Unicare Health Facilities (Milwaukee, WI)	15,917	144
Texas Health Enterprises, Inc. (Denton, TX)	14,608	125
National Heritage, Inc. (Dallas, TX)	9,872	89
National Health Corp. (Murfreesboro, TN)	8,887	74
Diversified Health Services (Plymouth Meeting, PA)	7,616	32
Care Enterprises (Tustin, CA)	6,514	65
Meritcare (Pittsburgh, PA)	6,170	59
Meridian Healthcare (Towson, MD)	5,500	36
Integrated Health Services, Inc. (Hunt Valley, MD)	5,487	41
Britthaven, Inc. (Hookerton, NC)	5,486	53
Brian Center Management Corp. (Hickory, NC)	4,800	39
Horizon Healthcare Corp. (Albuquerque, NM)	4,800	46
Geriatric & Medical Center, Inc. (Philadelphia, PA)	4,660	24
Genesis Health Ventures (Milwaukee, WI)	4,444	31
American Medical Services, Inc. (Milwaukee, WI)	4,406	29
HCM, Inc. (Jackson, MS)	4,005	44
Meadowbrook Health Care Services, Inc. (Orange City, FL)	3,804	29
Medical Facilities of America (Roanoake, VA)	3,621	27

Source: Based on data from the American Health Care Association (Washington, D.C.) and published in **HealthWeek** (January 28, 1991). (**HealthWeek** ceased publication at the end of 1991.)

Qualifications: Some facilities counted in the totals for the nursing home chains may not be nursing homes in the traditional sense, but "life care centers" or some other type of residential arrangement.

Interpretation: During the 1980s the nursing home industry under went considerable consolidation. A number of large chains emerged to account for an increasing portion of nursing homes and nursing home beds.

IV-27. NURSING HOMES
NURSING HOMES AND NURSING HOME BY STATE
1991

State	Number of Nursing Homes	Number Nursing Beds
Alabama	219	22,289
Alaska	15	875
Arizona	132	15,595
Arkansas	248	26,338
California	1,290	132,032
Colorado	204	19,854
Connecticut	240	28,669
Delaware	41	4,471
District of Columbia	16	3,138
Florida	554	65,837
Georgia	364	38,528
Hawaii	43	3,505
Idaho	70	5,659
Illinois	792	100,587
Indiana	590	64,263
Iowa	463	44,950
Kansas	415	29,767
Kentucky	282	24,211
Louisiana	327	36,681
Maine	146	10,080
Maryland	217	27,665
Massachusetts	540	51,594
Michigan	439	49,927
Minnesota	472	48,403
Mississippi	162	14,691
Missouri	469	47,446
Montana	99	7,056
Nebraska	237	18,464
Nevada	36	3,497
New Hampshire	76	7,321
New Jersey	306	44,317
New Mexico	71	6,558
New York	619	103,516
North Carolina	320	29,658
North Dakota	83	7,123
Ohio	988	92,518
Oklahoma	409	33,758
Oregon	176	15,165
Pennsylvania	690	610
Rhode Island	100	9,808
South Carolina	147	14,099
South Dakota	118	8,530

(Continued on next page)

IV-27. NURSING HOMES
NURSING HOMES AND NURSING HOME BY STATE
1991 *(Continued from previous page)*

State	Number of Nursing Homes	Number Nursing Beds
Tennessee	300	35,551
Texas	1,127	115,148
Utah	90	6,913
Vermont	48	3,585
Virginia	258	30,989
Washington	287	28,256
West Virginia	122	10,849
Wisconsin	418	49,297
Wyoming	38	2,859
Total	15,913	1,690,481

Source: Based on data collected by the Health Care Financing Administration (HCFA) within the U.S. Department of Health and Human Services. HCFA, as the organization responsible for the administration of the Medicare program is a primary source of nursing home statistics. Additional data are available directly from HCFA (Washington, D.C.) or through its publications such as **Health Care Financing Review.**

Methodology: HCFA maintains a registry of all health care facilities that provide services to Medicare and Medicaid enrollees.

Definitions: "Nursing homes" includes only those beds that are certified to care for Medicare and/or Medicaid patients. Over three-months of nursing facilities are certified by HCFA.

Qualifications: This list excludes over 4,000 facilities that are not certified by HCFA.

IV-28. CONTINUING CARE CENTERS
LARGEST OPERATORS OF CONTINUING CARE RETIREMENT COMMUNITIES
RANKED BY NUMBER OF APARTMENTS OWNED OR LEASED
1990

Corporation (Headquarters)	Facilities	Apartments	Nursing Home Beds Attached
Covenant Benevolent Institutions (Chicago, IL)	12	2,494	803
Catholic Health Corp. (Omaha, NE)	11	1,259	-
Sisters of Charity Health Care Systems (Cincinnati, OH)	5	1,039	210
Franciscan Sisters of the Poor Health System (Brooklyn Heights, NY)	5	847	719
Lutheran General Health Care System (Park Ridge, IL)	4	846	245
Franciscan Sisters of Allegany Health (St. Petersburg, FL)	4	821	129
Catholic Healthcare West (San Francisco, CA)	4	674	59
Brim (Portland, OR)	5	659	-
Alexian Brothers Health Systems (Elk Grove Village, IL)	2	563	185
Baptist Health Care (Pensacola, FL)	2	481	90
Manor HealthCare Corp. (Silver Springs, MD)	3	450	545
HRHS (Huntington Valley, PA)	2	449	150
Holy Cross Health System Corp. (South Bend, IN)	3	446	171
School Sisters of St. Francis (Milwaukee, WI)	16	350	837
CSJ Health System of Wichita (Wichita, KS)	4	342	213

Source: Based on the Annual Survey of Hospitals conducted by and published in **Modern Healthcare** (May 20, 1991).

Methodology: Data are collected annually by means of a survey of health-related facilities.

Definitions: "Facilities" refers to continuing care retirement communities only.

Qualifications: Since these data are based on voluntary responses, there have been occasions when some systems may not have been represented. Also, the information is based on self-reports by organizations that may use different accounting methods or definitions.

IV-29. FREESTANDING FACILITIES
HOSPITAL-OPERATED FREESTANDING FACILITIES BY TYPE OF FACILITY
1990

Type of Facility	Number
Surgery center	94
Urgent care	721
Diagnostic imaging	282
Birthing center	9
Industrial medicine	243
Psychiatric care	113
Health club	53
Sports medicine	116
Rehabilitation center	151
Chemical-dependency treatment center	101
Pain clinic	30
Cancer center	60
Other services	251

Source: Based on the Annual Survey of Hospitals conducted by and published in **Modern Healthcare** (May 20, 1991).

Methodology: Data are collected annually by means of a survey of multi-hospital systems. These data are based on response from 171 multi-hospital systems.

Definitions: "Freestanding facilities" refers to health care facilities physically separated from the operating hospital.

Qualifications: Since these data are based on voluntary responses, there have been occasions when some systems may not have been represented. Also, the information is based on self-reports by organizations that may use different accounting methods or definitions.

Interpretation: The number of free-standing facilities operated by hospitals has increased in recent years. Urgent care facilities have been by far the most popular facilities developed by hospitals.

IV-30. PSYCHIATRIC HOSPITALS
LEADING OPERATORS OF PSYCHIATRIC HOSPITALS RANKED BY BEDS
OWNED/MANAGED
1990

Name (Headquarters)	Beds	Facilities	No. States
Charter Medical Corp. (Macon, GA)	7,696	87	27
Hospital Corp. of America (Nashville, TN)	6,224 *	54	18
National Medical Enterprises (Santa Monica, CA)	6,156 **	72	26
Healthcare International (Austin, TX)	1,540	18	4
Universal Health Services (Philadelphia, PA)	854	11	7
Comprehensive Care Corp. (Chesterfield, MO)	519 ***	10	1
Nu-Med (Encino, CA)	461	6	6
SCN Health Corp. (Louisville, KY)	416	1	1
Daughters of Charity National Health System (St. Louis, MO)	346	5	5
Samaritan Foundation (Phoenix, AZ)	335	4	1
Mercy Health Services (Farmington Hills, MI)	255	3	1
Incarnate World Health Services (San Antonio, TX)	254	1	1
County of Los Angeles-Dept. of Health (Los Angeles, CA)	242	2	1
Hospital Management Associates (Naples, FL)	226	3	9
UniHealth America (Burbank, CA)	200	4	1
Paracelsus Healthcare Corp. (Pasadena, CA)	198	3	1
Catholic Health Corp. (Omaha, NE)	181	1	2
Nebraska Methodist Health System (Omaha, NE)	181	1	1
Intermountain Health Care (Salt Lake City, UT)	152	2	1
Albert Einstein Healthcare Foundation (Philadelphia, PA)	147	1	1

* Includes 540 managed beds
** Includes 51 managed beds
*** Includes 134 managed beds

Source: Based on the Annual Survey of Hospitals conducted by and published in **Modern Healthcare** (May 20, 1991).

Methodology: Data are collected annually by means of a survey of multi-hospital systems. These data are based on response from 171 multi-hospital systems.

Definitions: "Facilities" refers to acute care hospitals owned or managed outside the U.S.

Qualifications: Since these data are based on voluntary responses, there have been occasions when some systems may not have been represented. Also, the information is based on self-reports by organizations that may use different accounting methods or definitions.

IV-31. HEALTH MAINTENANCE ORGANIZATIONS
HEALTH MAINTENANCE ORGANIZATIONS
1976-1990

Year	Number of Plans	Enrollment**
1990	572	33,028
1989	604	31,883
1987	647	29,232
1986	623	25,725
1985*	478	21,005
1984	304	15,101
1982	264	10,807
1980	235	9,078
1978	202	7,450
1976	174	5,987

*Reporting procedures changed in 1985
**In 1,000s

Source: Data collected by the Office of Health Maintenance Organizations and Interstudy and published in **Health, United States, 1991.** The Office of Health Maintenance Organizations is the agency within the U.S. Public Health Service with responsibility for statistics on HMOs. Interstudy (Excelsior, MN) is an organization established to monitor the activities of health maintenance organizations.

Methodology: The Office of Health Maintenance Organizations (HMOs) periodically conducts a census of the nation's HMOs. Interstudy publishes an annual report on HMOs based on records the organization maintains and data it collects from HMOs.

Qualifications: The definition of "health maintenance organization" has been undergoing change. The characteristics of HMOs have also changed since the concept was introduced in the 1970s. A realistic comparison of these figures over time must consider these changes.

Interpretation: The number of health maintenance organizations nationwide grew steadily through 1987 after which consolidation and shakeouts among HMOs reduced the number. Despite the downturn in number, enrollment continues to climb, more than tripling during the decade of the 80s.

IV-32. HEALTH MAINTENANCE ORGANIZATIONS
ENROLLMENT RATE IN HEALTH MAINTENANCE ORGANIZATIONS
BY GEOGRAPHIC REGION
1980-1990

	Enrollment Rate*		
Region	1980	1985**	1990
Northeast	31.4	79.4	145.6
Midwest	28.1	96.8	126.2
South	8.3	37.5	70.5
West	121.8	172.5	232.1

*Rate is based on enrollees per 1,000 population.
**Reporting procedures changed in 1985.

Source: Data collected by the Office of Health Maintenance Organizations and Interstudy and published in **Health, United States, 1991.** The Office of Health Maintenance Organizations is the agency within the U.S. Public Health Service with responsibility for statistics on HMOs. Interstudy (Excelsior, MN) is an organization established to monitor the activities of health maintenance organizations.

Methodology: The Office of Health Maintenance Organizations (HMOs) periodically conducts a census of the nation's HMOs. Interstudy publishes an annual report on HMOs based on records the organization maintains and data it collects from HMOs.

Definitions: A health maintenance organization (HMO) is an alternative form of health care financing that features a prepayment arrangement. A monthly premium is paid and, theoretically, this covers any health care cost incurred. HMOs generally place restrictions on the hospitals and physicians that can be utilized by their enrollees.

Qualifications: The definition of "health maintenance organization" has been undergoing change. The characteristics of HMOs have also changed since the concept was introduced in the 1970s. A realistic comparison of these figures over time must consider these changes.

Interpretation: The west coast was the site of early successful health maintenance organizations. The Northeast and the Midwest have witnessed major penetration of HMOs while the South, with more traditional medical practice patterns, lags behind the rest of the nation.

IV-33. HEALTH MAINTENANCE ORGANIZATIONS
TEN HIGHEST RATED HMOs
1990

HMO	Service area	Model type	Type
Kaiser Foundation Health Plan	San Francisco	Group	National chain
HMO Pennsylvania (U.S. Healthcare)	Philadelphia	IPA	Regional chain
Group Health Cooperative	Seattle	Network	Local independent
Group Health, Inc.	Minneapolis	Staff	Local independent
Kaiser Foundation Health Plan	Los Angeles	Group	National chain
M.D. Individual Practice Association	Washington	IPA	Local independent
Share Health Plan of Minn.	Minneapolis	Network	National chain
HealthAmerica Corp. of PA	Pittsburgh	Network	Regional chain
Harvard Community Health Plan	Boston	Group	Local independent
Kaiser Foundation Health Plan	Portland	Group	National chain

Source: Based on evaluations by Health Plan Management Services (HPMS) and published in **The HMO Buyers Guide.** The book and more information on HPMS is available from Health Plan Management Services (Atlanta, GA).

Methodology: Based on evaluations made of the nation's health maintenance organizations by HPMS. Each HMO was rated in terms of financial stability, cost control potential and the comprehensiveness of its provider network. Each HMO is rated in absolute terms and then compared to other HMOs within its service area.

Definitions: "HMOs" are health maintenance organizations which involve a prepayment financing mechanism rather than the "indemnity" approach utilized by commercial insurance and Blue Cross plans. "Model type" refers to the organizational relationship between the HMO and various providers (e.g., hospitals and physicians).

Qualifications: Any rating scale has inherent problems and should be utilized with caution. The weightings applied to the various measures examined could influence the final score for the HMOs examined. These ratings may be influenced by the relative importance of an HMO within its local service area.

IV-34. HEALTH MAINTENANCE ORGANIZATIONS
HEALTH MAINTENANCE ORGANIZATION ENROLLMENT
BY STATE
1989

State	Number of HMOs	Enrollment	Percent of population in HMOs
Total	590	32,492,784	13.2%
Alabama	8	180,624	4.4
Alaska	0	0	0.0
Arizona	16	597,896	17.1
Arkansas	5	55,739	2.3
California	51	8,439,810	29.8
Colorado	17	657,637	19.9
Connecticut	13	621,260	17.9
Delaware	6	118,247	17.9
District of Columbia	4	449,534	72.9
Florida	35	1,300,862	10.6
Georgia	8	285,616	4.5
Guam	3	58,337	44.7
Hawaii	6	240,816	21.9
Idaho	2	19,878	2.0
Illinois	28	1,513,833	13.0
Indiana	12	399,916	7.2
Iowa	8	222,270	7.8
Kansas	11	208,153	8.3
Kentucky	7	205,688	5.5
Louisiana	9	237,110	5.4
Maine	3	24,903	2.1
Maryland	12	684,656	14.8
Massachusetts	19	1,455,308	24.7
Michigan	17	1,408,058	15.3
Minnesota	10	767,041	17.8
Mississippi	0	0	0.0
Missouri	17	526,802	10.2
Montana	1	2,858	0.4
Nebraska	5	61,798	5.1
Nevada	2	93,157	8.8
New Hampshire	3	113,058	10.4
New Jersey	16	879,465	11.4
New Mexico	5	190,507	12.6
New York	37	2,567,431	14.3
North Carolina	12	326,679	5.0
North Dakota	2	20,047	3.0
Ohio	34	1,294,173	11.9
Oklahoma	6	169,032	5.2

(Continued on next page)

IV-34. HEALTH MAINTENANCE ORGANIZATIONS
HEALTH MAINTENANCE ORGANIZATION ENROLLMENT
BY STATE

1989 *(Continued from previous page)*

State	Number of HMOs	Enrollment	Percent of population in HMOs
Oregon	10	652,044	23.6
Pennsylvania	20	1,257,801	10.5
Rhode Island	4	212,612	21.4
South Carolina	6	74,665	2.2
South Dakota	1	28,540	4.0
Tennessee	8	231,096	4.7
Texas	29	1,197,199	7.1
Utah	6	226,178	13.4
Vermont	1	26,571	4.8
Virginia	14	386,318	6.4
Washington	10	655,428	14.1
West Virginia	1	66,482	3.5
Wisconsin	30	1,057,078	21.8
Wyoming	1	2,594	0.5

Source: Published by InterStudy, **The InterStudy Edge**, 1989, Volume 4. These figures are based on reports provided to InterStudy by the nation's health maintenance organizations (HMOs). InterStudy is an organization established to monitor the activities of health maintenance organizations.

Definitions: A health maintenance organization (HMO) is an alternative form of health care financing that features a prepayment arrangement. A monthly premium is paid and, theoretically, this covers any health care cost incurred. HMOs generally place restrictions on the hospitals and physicians that can be utilized by their enrollees.

Interpretation: HMO penetration varies widely from state to state and is a function of the nature of the industry, the progressiveness of the population, and the influence of organized medicine and traditional insurers.

IV-35. HEALTH MAINTENANCE ORGANIZATIONS
HEALTH MAINTENANCE ORGANIZATION ENROLLMENT BY STATE
JANUARY 1, 1990

State	Pure HMOs No. of Plans	Enrollment	Percent of Population Enrolled	Open Ended HMOs No. of Plans	Enrollment
All plans	575	33,092,954	13.3%	84	857,995
Alabama	8	212,207	5.2	0	0
Alaska	0	0	0	0	0
Arizona	14	548,162	15.4	3	5,284
Arkansas	4	50,495	2.1	1	900
California	47	8,693,538	29.9	7	22,834
Colorado	18	661,039	19.9	4	13,264
Connecticut	13	634,856	19.6	1	11,862
Delaware	6	111,605	14.8	2	2,504
D.C.	4	468,843	77.6	0	0
Florida	31	1,319,655	10.4	5	29,090
Georgia	8	297,603	4.6	2	16,724
Guam	3	65,008	49.6	0	0
Hawaii	6	243,671	22.0	0	0
Idaho	2	23,820	2.3	0	0
Illinois	28	1,501,523	12.9	1	2,521
Indiana	13	372,088	6.7	0	0
Iowa	7	300,398	10.6	0	0
Kansas	11	217,609	8.7	1	2,112
Kentucky	7	217,848	5.8	1	84,889
Louisiana	9	235,751	5.4	3	3,359
Maine	3	30,295	2.5	0	0
Maryland	12	747,136	15.9	4	44,142
Massachusetts	19	1,482,798	25.1	2	2,238
Michigan	17	1,421,657	15.3	3	30,607
Minnesota	11	713,604	16.4	8	355,489
Mississippi	0	0	0	0	0
Missouri	17	529,747	10.3	4	17,178
Montana	1	3,410	0.4	0	0
Nebraska	5	85,314	5.3	1	2,700
Nevada	3	91,709	8.3	1	7,200
New Hampshire	2	111,308	10.0	1	357
New Jersey	15	901,375	11.7	3	8,399
New Mexico	5	193,800	12.7	1	310
New York	37	2,646,416	14.7	4	44,396
North Carolina	12	309,073	4.7	1	4,994
North Dakota	2	10,900	1.7	0	0
Ohio	35	1,353,359	12.4	2	3,740
Oklahoma	6	162,748	5.0	0	0
Oregon	9	657,016	23.3	2	3,926

(Continued on next page)

IV-35. HEALTH MAINTENANCE ORGANIZATIONS
HEALTH MAINTENANCE ORGANIZATION ENROLLMENT BY STATE
JANUARY 1, 1990 *(Continued from previous page)*

State	No. of Plans	Pure HMOs Enrollment	Percent of Population Enrolled	Open Ended HMOs No. of Plans	Enrollment
Pennsylvania	21	1,329,450	11.0	1	3,925
Rhode Island	4	220,856	22.1	2	4,099
South Carolina	4	70,240	2.0	0	0
South Dakota	1	26,522	3.7	0	0
Tennessee	8	197,189	4.0	1	4,827
Texas	27	1,190,812	7.0	4	96,479
Utah	6	224,653	13.2	3	17,730
Vermont	1	33,128	5.8	0	0
Virginia	13	364,584	6.0	1	143
Washington	10	678,883	14.3	1	528
West Virginia	1	70,766	3.8	0	0
Wisconsin	29	1,058,487	21.7	3	9,245
Wyoming	0	0	0	0	0

Source: Data collected by InterStudy and published in **The InterStudy Edge**, 1990, Volume 2. InterStudy (Excelsior, MN) is a research institute that specializes in the study of health maintenance organizations and other alternative mechanisms for financing health care. InterStudy is the nation's leading source of information on HMOs and related organizations.

Methodology: These figures are based on reports provided to InterStudy by the nation's health maintenance organizations (HMOs).

Definitions: A health maintenance organization (HMO) is an alternative form of health care financing that features a prepayment arrangement. A monthly premium is paid and, theoretically, this covers any health care cost incurred. "Pure HMOs" require enrollees to utilize only selected providers. "Open-ended HMOs" allow use of non-HMO providers at the point of service but require a higher consumer contribution.

Interpretation: HMO penetration varies widely from state to state and is a function of the nature of the industry, the progressiveness of the population, and the influence of organized medicine and traditional insurers.

IV-36. HEALTH MAINTENANCE ORGANIZATIONS
25 FASTEST GROWING HMOs (RANKED BY ENROLLMENT INCREASE)
JAN. 1-JULY 1, 1990

Health Maintenance Organization	Enrollment	Enrollees Added
Kaiser Foundation (Southern California)	2,236,511	70,069
Humana Medical Plan	373,899	69,299
PacifiCare of California	474,472	67,243
Kaiser Foundation (Northern California)	2,402,539	44,343
Keystone Health Plan East	105,141	36,593
Western Ohio Health Care Plan	141,419	33,854
Bay State Health Care	315,730	30,807
FHP (California Region)	301,649	29,867
PruCare of New Jersey	72,169	25,794
HMO of New Jersey	378,000	25,000
U.S. HealthCare	120,000	24,000
Health Net	762,000	21,508
Health Power	30,500	19,104
M.D. IPA Health Plan	164,000	18,000
Lincoln National Health Plan	94,791	17,150
CareAmerica Health Plans	117,745	16,705
Intergroup Prepaid Health Services of Arizona	197,500	16,349
Family Health Net of Ohio	29,000	19,543
Kaiser Foundation Health Plan of Georgia	136,070	15,758
Physicians Health Plan of Ohio	154,099	15,726
Capitol Health Care	60,005	15,164
Harvard Community Health Plan	415,336	14,644
TakeCare Corp.	229,000	14,000
FHP (Arizona Region)	72,968	13,989
Pilgrim Health Care	149,905	13,813

Source: Data collected by InterStudy and published in **HealthWeek** (July 1, 1991). InterStudy (Excelsior, MN) is a research institute that specializes in the study of health maintenance organizations and other alternative mechanisms for financing health care. InterStudy is the nation's leading source of information on HMOs and related organizations. (**HealthWeek** ceased publication at the end of 1991.)

Methodology: Based on data compiled by the staff of InterStudy.

Definitions: A health maintenance organization (HMO) is an alternative form of health care financing that features a prepayment arrangement. A monthly premium is paid and, theoretically, this covers any health care cost incurred. HMOs generally place restrictions on the hospitals and physicians that can be utilized by their enrollees.

IV-37. MANAGED CARE
TOP 25 NATIONAL MANAGED CARE FIRMS RANKED BY
ENROLLMENT IN LICENSED HMOs
JANUARY 1990

Company	HMO Enrollment	Total Number of Plans
Kaiser Permanente Medical Care Program	6,245,385	12
Blue Cross & Blue Shield Plan HMO-USA	4,439,133	85
Cigna Healthplan, Inc. (Equicore Healthplan Inc.)	1,443,554	49
Aetna Health Plan (Partners National Health Plan)	1,138,985	27
Health Insurance Plan of Greater New York	1,051,097	3
U.S. Healthcare, Inc.	1,005,000	6
United Health Care Corp.	723,536	18
Prudential Health Care System	677,077	43
PacifiCare Health Systems, Inc.	568,041	6
Humana, Inc.	514,540	18
FHP, Inc.	509,713	5
Sanus Corp. Health Systems, Inc.	468,439	5
Group Health Cooperative of Puget Sound	443,041	1
Lincoln National Corp.	431,047	1
MetLife HealthCare Management Corp.	352,486	29
Maxicare Health Plans, Inc.	316,000	7
Independent Health Association, Inc.	247,774	3
Community Health Plan	178,379	5
Heritage National Healthplan Services	173,000	4
HMO America, Inc.	170,342	1
Health Care Corporation of America	146,956	3
Qual-Med, Inc.	138,388	6
Physicians Health Services, Inc.	132,729	4
Mercy Alternative	107,381	2
Travelers Health Network, Inc.	101,027	10

Source: Published in **HealthWeek**, April 5, 1991. (**HealthWeek** ceased publication at the end of 1991.)

Methodology: Based on data collected through a survey of health maintenance organizations.

Definitions: A health maintenance organization (HMO) is an alternative form of health care financing that features a prepayment arrangement. A monthly premium is paid and, theoretically, this covers any health care cost incurred. HMOs generally place restrictions on the hospitals and physicians that can be utilized by their enrollees.

IV-38. INSURANCE CARRIERS
25 LARGEST COMMERCIAL HEALTH AND ACCIDENT INSURANCE
COMPANIES BASED ON PREMIUMS
1989

Insurer (Headquarters)	Total Premiums*
Prudential Insurance Co. of America (Newark)	$5,638,000,000
Metropolitan Life Insurance Co. (New York)	2,328,000,000
Aetna Life Insurance Co. (Hartford)	2,078,000,000
Principal Mutual Life Insurance Co. (Des Moines)	1,978,000,000
American Family Life Assurance Co. of Columbus (Columbus)	1,958,000,000
Travelers Insurance Co. (Hartford)	1,868,000,000
Connecticut General Life Insurance Co. (Hartford)	1,528,000,000
Mutual of Omaha Insurance Co. (Omaha)	1,528,000,000
Continental Assurance Co. (Chicago)	1,508,000,000
Guardian Life Insurance Co. of America (New York)	1,478,000,000
Provident Life & Accident Insurance Co. (Chattanooga)	985,450,000
Lincoln National Life Insurance Co. (Fort Wayne)	823,740,000
Employers Health Insurance Co. (Green Bay)	821,770,000
First Equicor Life Insurance Co. (Hartford)	820,930,000
State Farm Mutual Automobile Insurance Co. (Bloomington)	810,330,000
New York Life Insurance Co. (New York)	804,860,000
Bankers Life & Casualty Co. (Chicago)	759,840,000
Unum Life Insurance Co. of America (Portland)	731,640,000
Massachusetts Mutual Life Insurance Co. (Springfield)	697,670,000
Hartford Life & Accident Insurance Co. (Hartford)	661,410,000
Combined Insurance Co. of America (Chicago)	660,380,000
Life Insurance Co. of North America (Philadelphia)	658,710,000
Time Insurance Co. (Milwaukee)	654,790,000
John Hancock Mutual Life Insurance Co. (Boston)	594,180,000
Mutual Benefit Life Insurance Co. (Newark)	562,800,000

*Rounded to nearest $1,000.

Source: Published in **HealthWeek** (February 11, 1991). (**HealthWeek** ceased publication at the end of 1991.)

Methodology: Based on a survey of the nation's insurors.

Definitions: "Commercial" insurers excludes insurance organizations established on a not-for-profit basis (e.g., Blue Cross Association). "Total premiums" are all premiums minus dividends paid.

IV-39. MALPRACTICE INSURERS
TOP 20 MEDICAL MALPRACTICE INSURANCE WRITERS RANKED
BY TOTAL VALUE OF PREMIUMS WRITTEN
1989

Company	Direct Premiums Written ($1,000)	Market Share
The St. Paul Companies Inc.	$638,041	12.4%
Medical Liability Mutual Insurance Co.	304,244	5.9
CNA Insurance Co.	287,397	5.6
Medical Protective Co.	203,300	4.0
Farmers Insurance Group	194,319	3.8
American International Group	180,078	3.5
Illinois State Medical Inter-Insurance Exchange	172,052	3.3
Medical Malpractice Insurance Association	165,665	3.2
Southern California Physicians Ins. Exchange	150,150	2.9
Health Care Ins. Exchange/Princeton Ins. Co.	146,828	2.9
PIE Mutual Insurance Co.	145,825	2.8
The Doctor's Company Insurance Group	145,485	2.8
Phico Insurance Co.	129,104	2.5
Medical Inter-Insurance Exchange of New Jersey	102,357	2.0
Physicians Reciprocal Insurers	101,106	2.0
Norcal Mutual Insurance Co.	86,406	1.7
MAG Mutual Insurance Co.	71,893	1.4
Mutual Insurance Company of America	68,608	1.3
Health Care Indemnity, Inc.	64,785	1.3
Medical Mutual Liability Ins. Society of Maryland	63,609	1.2

Source: Published in **HealthWeek**, August 12, 1991. (**HealthWeek** ceased publication at the end of 1991.)

Methodology: Based on a survey of the nation's malpractice insurors.

IV-40. PHYSICIAN GROUPS
25 LARGEST GROUP PRACTICES
1988

Group (Location)	Total FTE Physicians	Annual Outpatient Visits	Annual Inpatient Admits	Number of Employees
The Permanente Medical Group (Oakland, CA)	2,628	9,635,622	176,728	25,000
Southern California Permanente Medical Group (Pasadena, CA)	2,500	6,594,264	142,605	26,000
Mayo Clinic (Rochester, MN)	1,500	319,699	63,046	16,499
Henry Ford Health Care Corp. (Detroit, MI)	725	1,847,866	34,052	8,579
Group Health Cooperative of Puget Sound (Seattle, WA)	547	1,564,537	32,038	7,417
Cleveland Clinic Foundation (Cleveland, OH)	454	756,691	31,377	9,093
Northwest Permanente P.C Physicians and Surgeons (Portland, OR)	403	1,602,243	NA	5,113
Geisinger Foundation (Danville, PA)	374	1,010,556	37,934	1,227
Scott & White Clinic (Temple, TX)	323	798,587	17,035	1,965
Ochsner Clinic (New Orleans, LA)	300	680,000	18,200	1,550
Scripps Clinic & Research Foundation (La Jolla, CA)	271	687,343	7,297	3,225
Park Nicollet Medical Center (Minneapolis, MN)	270	1,500,000	-	1,500
Marshfield Clinic (Marshfield, WI)	262	611,612	17,738	1,650
Virginia Mason Medical Center (Seattle, WA)	250	481,000	12,866	2,750
Fargo Clinic Ltd. (Fargo, ND)	245	1,071,691	-	1,476
Gunderson Clinic Ltd. (Lacrosse, WI)	241	627,100	-	1,050
Group Health Inc. (Minneapolis, MN)	240	1,753,923	NA	2,600
Carle Clinic Association (Urbana, IL)	218	850,000	13,000	1,520
Guthrie Clinic Ltd. (Sayre, PA)	204	700,000	-	700
Dean Medical Center (Madison, WI)	200	496,323	-	1,000
LCF Foundation Inc. (Burlington, MA)	200	NA	NA	NA
Dakota Clinic Ltd. (Fargo, ND)	190	NA	NA	NA
Lovelace Medical Center (Albuquerque, NM)	189	670,272	9,735	1,911
Kelsey-Seybold Clinic (Houston, TX)	175	NA	NA	NA
Physicians Plus Medical Group (Madison, WI)	165	500,000	-	750

Source: Data compiled by the Medical Group Management Association (MGMA) and published in **HealthWeek** (May 30, 1989). MGMA is a major association for the nation's physician group practices. (**HealthWeek** ceased publication in 1991.)

Methodology: Based on data compiled by MGMA from member groups and other sources. Some data were collected by **HealthWeek** staff.

Definitions: FTE means full-time-equivalent. "Group practices" does not include groups that are affiliated with colleges and universities. "Employees" excludes physicians.

DATA ON HEALTH SERVICES UTILIZATION

The demand for data on the utilization of health services has grown probably faster than that for any other type of health-related information. Historically, there has been an interest in "who uses health care" but over the past decade this mostly academic interest in health services utilization has become almost an obsession. There has been an increase in the appreciation of the fact that the demand for health care is highly elastic. Utilization (in terms of both type and volume of services) tends to rise or fall depending on a variety of factors, the least of which is probably the level of actual illness within the population. Utilization patterns are, of course, of interest to any organization that wants to predict or influence the demand for a particular service.

During the 1990s the most urgent demand developed on the part of those who were paying for health care. As health care costs have escalated, the pattern of utilization has become the focal point for intensive research, since it is this behavior that explains health care expenditures. Today, both providers of health service and insurers have an urgent need for this information. Agencies like the Federal Health Care Financing Administration (which administers Medicare) require detailed utilization data in order to evaluate the appropriateness of services being provided Medicare enrollees. Business coalitions increasingly need such information to evaluate the quality of services their enrollees are receiving.

As researchers have learned more about the processes through which individuals come to use (or not use) a particular health service, an appreciation of the complexity of this process has grown. Health care consumers differ from the consumers of other types of goods and services. A variety of motives may be involved and the nature of health problems may serve to influence the decisions that are made. These decisions may also be influenced by demographic characteristics, socioeconomic characteristics, psychographic factors, social group influences, cultural preferences and any number of other factors. Not only do the characteristics of the patients themselves impact on utilization, but variations in the practice patterns of providers (especially physicians) also influence utilization.

Today, health services utilization is heavily influenced by nonmedical factors, with decisions concerning treatment increasingly being made by individuals and organizations that are not involved in the clinical management of the patient. For example, to a certain extent the best predictor of an individual's health behavior is the type of insurance program in which he or she is involved.

Until the 1980s limited data on the use of health services were available. However, since then the amount, quality and accessibility of such data have increased markedly. The main source of these data has always been the federal government and this remains so today. The government's role as the national data collector has placed it in the forefront of the compilation of data related to health services utilization. Since the introduction of the Medicare and Medicaid programs, however, the federal government has demonstrated a much more urgent need for utilization data. The spiraling cost of government-subsidized health care has required the federal government to become as knowledgeable about the use of health services as possible.

There are certain government agencies that provide the majority of the data on the use health services. These include the National Center for Health Statistics (NCHS), the Centers for Disease Control and Prevention (CDCP), and the Heath Care Financing Administration (HCFA). The NCHS is considered the "census bureau" of health, since it is charged with compiling and disseminating health-related data obtained from a variety of sources. Along with the CDCP, the NCHS collects data through registration programs, monitoring activities and surveys. In fact, it is the surveys of the NCHS (e.g., the National Health Interview Survey, the National Ambulatory Medical Care Survey and the Hospital Discharge Survey) that provide the basis for much of what is known about the use of health services. HCFA is the agency that administers the Medicare program and, as such, is the major compiler of data related to the financing of health care. This, of necessity, involves the Administration in the collection of data on utilization. There are other government agencies (such as the National Institutes of Health) that collect utilization data incidental to other research activities. Over the past decade, the various federal agencies have increased their efforts not only in data collection but in making the information easily and inexpensively available to the public in accessible form.

The other major source of utilization data is private organizations. Commercial data vendors have become increasingly active in the collection and dissemination of utilization data. As the health care industry has become more competitive, these vendors have attempted to meet the demand for timely, comprehensive and accessible data. One method of collecting such data is through the establishment of databases on institutions (e.g., hospitals, minor emergency clinics, health maintenance organizations) and the subsequent extraction of information from these institutions with regard to their utilization. A second approach is taken by other vendors and research organizations who query members of the general public with regard to the health products and services they utilize. There are at least three major (50,000 or more households) nationwide surveys currently being conducted by vendors annually. These directly elicit information from members of the public with regard to their health care consumption patterns.

Much of the data collected by commercial vendors is proprietary and may only be released to clients who participate in certain of the vendor programs. Some of the information is available for purchase by the public. There are few research organizations (e.g., those funded by foundations or university research programs) that collect such data on an episodic basis and this information is generally available to the public.

V-1. HOSPITALS
HOSPITAL DISCHARGES AND DISCHARGE RATES BY AGE AND SEX
1989

Age Category	Total		Males		Females	
	Discharges	Rate*	Discharges	Rate*	Discharges	Rate*
Under 15 years	2,597,000	48.2	1,521,000	55.1	1,077,000	40.9
15-44 years	11,848,000	102.8	3,405,000	59.8	8,443,000	144.9
45-64 years	6,271,000	135.0	3,179,000	142.8	3,092,000	127.9
65 years and over	10,230,000	330.2	4,478,000	354.4	5,752,000	313.5

*The rate is stated in terms of the number of dischargers per 1,000 population.

Source: Based on data collected through the National Hospital Discharge Survey conducted by the National Center for Health Statistics. The National Center for Health Statistics (NCHS) conducts a variety of surveys from which health-related data are drawn. Additional data, including some unpublished data, on this topic are available from NCHS (Hyattsville, MD).

Methodology: The National Hospital Discharge Survey is used by NCHS to collect data annually on the characteristics of patients hospitalized in "short-stay" hospitals. Data collection is based on a sample of approximately 200,000 medical records each year. Information is collected on patient demographics, circumstances of the hospitalization, diagnosis and treatment and characteristics of the facility. Data from the sample are weighted up to produce national estimates.

Definitions: Includes all patients discharged (whether dead or alive) from all non-Federal hospitals except for newborn babies. Figures were rounded to nearest thousand.

Qualifications: Since the survey is based on a sample of administrative records, all of the drawbacks related to sample surveys apply. In addition, the quality of the data also depend heavily on the completeness and accuracy of the medical records examined. The age breakdown shown is commonly utilized for comparing utilization rates. It should be noted, however, that major variations exist within each age cohort.

Interpretation: The rate of hospitalization varies by age and, less dramatically, by sex.

V-2. HOSPITALS
HOSPITAL DISCHARGES BY AGE
1965-1989

| | **Discharge Rate*** | | | | |
	1965	1970	1975	1980	1989
All Ages	150.0	144.3	159.2	167.7	143.1
Under 15 Years	72.2	66.8	70.4	71.6	48.2
15 to 44 Years	175.1	154.6	152.4	150.2	102.8
45 to 64 Years	172.9	154.6	191.8	194.8	135.0
65 to 74 Years	213.9	253.2	291.6	315.9	330.2**
75 Years and Over	313.8	359.1	409.7	489.1	NA

*The discharge rate is reported as the number of discharges per 1,000 population.
**Rate for age 65 and over.

Source: Based on data collected by the National Center for Health Statistics and published in "Trends in Hospital Utilization: United States, 1965-86." **Vital and Health Statistics**, Series 13, No. 101, 1989 and "1989 Summary: National Hospital Discharge Survey." **Advance Data**, No. 199, 1991. The National Center for Health Statistics (NCHS) conducts a variety of surveys from which health-related data are drawn. Additional data, including some unpublished data, on this topic are available from NCHS (Hyattsville, MD).

Methodology: The National Hospital Discharge Survey is used by NCHS to collect data annually on the characteristics of patients hospitalized in "short-stay" hospitals. Data collection is based on a sample of approximately 200,000 medical records each year. Information is collected on patient demographics, circumstances of the hospitalization, diagnosis and treatment and characteristics of the facility. Data from the sample are weighted up to produce national estimates.

Definitions: "Hospitals" refer to non-federal hospitals with six beds or more for patient use and those in which the average length of stay for all patients is less than 30 days (short-stay hospital). Rate per 1,000 population is calculated by dividing the number of age-specific discharges by the age-specific population and multiplying that quotient by 1,000. "Discharge" refers to the formal release of a patient by a hospital. Newborn infants are excluded.

Qualification: The data come from the National Hospital Discharge Survey and are subject to sampling and nonsampling error. The survey's methodology has changed little over the 22-year period covered in this table, though the sample size of hospitals has increased significantly since 1965. The base population data for the rates come from the U.S. Census Bureau's population estimates.

V-3. HOSPITALS
HOSPITAL UTILIZATION RATES SELECTED INDICATORS
1970-1989

	1970	1980	1985	1989
Patients Discharged (In 1,000s)	39,127	37,832	35,056	30,947
Discharges per 1,000 Population	144	168	148	126
Days of Care per 1,000 Persons	1,122	1,217	954	815
Average Stay in Days	8.0	7.3	6.5	6.5
Beds Used per Day (per 100,000 civilian population)	321	337	261	223

Source: Based on data collected by the National Center for Health Statistics in the National Hospital Discharge Survey and published in **Statistical Abstract of the United States**, 1992 table 173.

Methodology: The National Hospital Discharge Survey is used by NCHS to collect data annually on the characteristics of patients hospitalized in "short-stay" hospitals. Data collection is based on a sample of approximately 200,000 medical records each year. Information is collected on patient demographics, circumstances of the hospitalization, diagnosis and treatment and characteristics of the facility. Data from the sample are weighted up to produce national estimates.

Qualifications: Since the survey is based on a sample of administrative records, all of the drawbacks related to sample surveys apply. In addition, the quality of the data also depends heavily on the completeness and accuracy of the medical records examined.

Interpretation: The reduction in all of these measures reflects the trend toward greater reliance on outpatient services.

V-4. HOSPITALS
AVERAGE LENGTH OF STAY FOR HOSPITAL PATIENTS
BY AGE
1965-1990

	Average Number of Days per Stay				
	1965	1970	1975	1980	1990
All Ages	7.8	7.8	7.7	7.3	6.7
Under 15 Years	4.9	4.7	4.6	4.4	5.8
15 to 44 Years	5.9	5.7	5.7	5.2	5.4
45 to 64 Years	9.8	9.3	9.0	8.2	6.7
65 to 74 Years	12.2	12.0	11.1	10.0	8.0
75 Years and Over	14.0	13.3	12.2	11.4	8.9

Source: Based on data collected by the National Center for Health Statistics and published in "Trends in Hospital Utilization: United States, 1965-86." **Vital and Health Statistics,** Series 13, No. 101. Hyattsville, Maryland: Public Health Service, 1989 and **Health, United States, 1991**, table 81. The National Center for Health Statistics (NCHS) conducts a variety of surveys from which health-related data are drawn. Additional data, including some unpublished data, on this topic are available from NCHS (Hyattsville, MD).

Methodology: The National Hospital Discharge Survey is used by NCHS to collect data annually on the characteristics of patients hospitalized in "short-stay" hospitals. Data collection is based on a sample of approximately 200,000 medical records each year. Information is collected on patient demographics, circumstances of the hospitalization, diagnosis and treatment and characteristics of the facility. Data from the sample are weighted up to produce national estimates.

Definitions: "Hospitals" refer to hospitals with six beds or more for patient use and those in which the average length of stay for all patients is less than 30 days (short-stay hospital) are included as the base for the data. "Average length of stay" is the total number of patient days accumulated at the time of discharge. A stay of less than one day (admission and discharge is counted as one day, and for multiple-day stays the day of admission but not the day of discharge is counted toward the total). Newborn infants are excluded.

Qualification: The data come from the National Hospital Discharge Survey and are subject to sampling and nonsampling error. The survey's methodology has changed little over the 22-year period covered in this table, though the sample size of hospitals has increased significantly since 1965.

V-5. HOSPITALS
TRENDS IN HOSPITAL DISCHARGES BY SEX
1980-1989

| Year | Discharge Rate* | |
	Male	Female
1989	103.9	127.4
1988	105.8	130.2
1987	115.0	141.2
1986	119.8	146.2
1985	123.5	152.7
1984	131.8	164.7
1983	139.9	174.4
1982	140.5	176.5
1981	141.0	179.5
1980	140.0	178.1

*Discharge rate is reported as discharged patients per 1,000 population.

Source: Based on data from the National Hospital Discharge Survey conducted by the National Center for Health Statistics (NCHS) and published in **Health, United States**, 1990. Additional data, including some unpublished data, are available from NCHS (Rockville, MD).

Methodology: The National Hospital Discharge Survey is used by NCHS to collect data annually on the characteristics of patients hospitalized in "short-stay" hospitals. Data collection is based on a sample of approximately 200,000 medical records each year. Information is collected on patient demographics, circumstances of the hospitalization, diagnosis and treatment and characteristics of the facility. Data from the sample are weighted up to produce national estimates.

Definitions: "Hospitals" refers to non-federal short-stay hospitals. Rates are age adjusted.

Qualifications: Since the survey is based on a sample of administrative records, all of the drawbacks related to sample surveys apply. In addition, the quality of the data also depend heavily on the completeness and accuracy of the medical records examined.

Interpretation: Hospital discharge rates for both males and females declined steadily through the 1980s, with a substantial drop occurring mid-decade after the introduction of the Medicare prospective payment system.

V-6. HOSPITALS
HOSPITAL LENGTH OF STAY (LOS):
FOR ALL ADULTS AND ADULTS AGE 65 AND OVER,
1980-1990

Year	All Adults Length of Stay	Percent Change	Age 65 and Over Length of Stay	Percent Change
1990*	6.6	0.0%	8.7	-1.1%
1989	6.6	0.0%	8.8	0.0%
1988	6.6	0.0%	8.8	-0.7%
1987	6.6	0.8%	8.9	1.0%
1986	6.6	0.6%	8.8	0.4%
1985	6.6	-1.7%	8.8	-2.1%
1984	6.7	-5.1%	9.0	-7.5%
1983	7.0	-2.0%	9.7	-4.4%
1982	7.2	-0.7%	10.1	-4.4%
1981	7.2	0.4%	10.4	-0.1%
1980	7.2	-	10.4	-

*Estimate based on January through November 1990 data.

Source: Based on data collected by the American Hospital Association through its annual panel survey of community hospitals. The AHA maintains the nation's most extensive data base on hospitals and maintains information beyond that published in its annual guides. Additional, and sometimes unpublished, data can be obtained from the AHA's data office (Chicago).

Methodology: The National Hospital Panel Survey is a monthly survey of a randomly selected sample of 1,800 community hospitals. There are approximately 5,800 community hospitals in the U.S.

Qualifications: Since this survey involves a sample of all hospitals, the data are subject to sampling error.

Interpretation: The average length of stay was generally stable in the early 1980s before the implementation of Medicare's prospective payment system (PPS). The introduction of PPS in 1983 had a demonstrable effect on length of stay resulting in significant declines for both elderly and non-elderly patients.

V-7. HOSPITALS
SELECTED INDICATORS OF HOSPITAL UTILIZATION
1970-1990

	1970	1980	1985	1990
Patients Discharged (In 1,000s)	29,127	37,832	35,056	30,788
Discharges per 1,000 Population	144	168	148	123
Days of Care per 1,000 Persons	1,122	1,217	954	792
Average Stay in Days	8.0	7.3	6.5	6.4

Source: Based on data collected by the National Hospital Discharge Survey conducted by the National Center for Health Statistics and published in **Statistical Abstract of the United States**, 1991 and "1989 Summary: National Hospital Discharge Survey," Advance Data, No. 199, Hyatteville, MD: National Center for Health Statistics, 1991.

Methodology: The National Hospital Discharge Survey is used by NCHS to collect data annually on the characteristics of patients hospitalized in "short-stay" hospitals. Data collection is based on a sample of approximately 200,000 medical records each year. Information is collected on patient demographics, circumstances of the hospitalization, diagnosis and treatment and characteristics of the facility. Data from the sample are weighted up to produce national estimates.

Definitions: "Hospitals" refers to non-federal short-stay hospitals. Rates are age adjusted.

Qualifications: Since the survey is based on a sample of administrative records, all of the drawbacks related to sample surveys apply. In addition, the quality of the dt a also depend heavily on the completeness and accuracy of the medical records examined.

Interpretation: Hospital discharge and average length of stay have declined since 1980.

V-8. HOSPITALS
REGIONAL DIFFERENCES IN HOSPITAL UTILIZATION
1990

Region	Average Length Discharge Rate*	Days of Care**	of Stay (Days)
Northeast	121.5	887.2	7.3
Midwest	114.7	715.7	6.2
South	119.1	707.2	5.9
West	92.6	513.3	5.5

*Discharge rate is reported as discharged patients per 1,000 population.
**Number of days of hospital care per 1,000 population.

Source: Based on data from the National Hospital Discharge Survey conducted by the National Center for Health Statistics (NCHS) and published in **Health, United States, 1991.** Additional data, including some unpublished data, are available from NCHS (Rockville, MD).

Methodology: The National Hospital Discharge Survey is used by NCHS to collect data annually on the characteristics of patients hospitalized in "short-stay" hospitals. Data collection is based on a sample of approximately 200,000 medical records each year. Information is collected on patient demographics, circumstances of the hospitalization, diagnosis and treatment and characteristics of the facility. Data from the sample are weighted up to produce national estimates.

Definitions: "Hospitals" refers to non-federal short-stay hospitals. Rates are age adjusted.

Qualifications: Since the survey is based on a sample of administrative records, all of the drawbacks related to sample surveys apply. In addition, the quality of the dt a also depend heavily on the completeness and accuracy of the medical records examined.

Interpretation: Considerable regional variation exists in hospital utilization. This variation reflects differences in health behavior, practice patterns and insurance coverage.

V-9. HOSPITALS
AVERAGE LENGTH OF STAY FOR HOSPITAL PATIENTS
BY FIRST-LISTED DIAGNOSIS AND AGE
1988

Category of First-Listed Diagnosis	Average Days Stayed by Age Category			
	Under 15	15-44	45-64	65 and over
All Conditions	5.0	4.7	6.8	8.9
Infectious and Parasitic Diseases	4.1	7.5	10.9	11.3
Neoplasms	6.5	5.8	8.1	9.9
Endocrine, Nutritional and Metabolic Diseases, and Immunity Diseases	4.6	5.4	7.2	9.4
Diseases of Blood and Blood Forming Organs	4.2	5.5	6.5	7.4
Mental Disorders	25.0	12.6	11.9	13.3
Diseases of Nervous System and Sense Organs	3.7	5.4	5.5	6.4
Diseases of the Circulatory System	6.8	5.7	6.4	8.4
Diseases of the Respiratory System	3.2	4.5	7.1	9.4
Diseases of the Digestive System	3.6	4.6	6.3	8.0
Diseases of the Genitourinary System	3.9	4.0	5.1	7.2
Complications of Pregnancy, Childbirth and Puerperium	2.4[a]	2.7	[a]	NA
Diseases of the Skin and Subcutaneous Tissue	4.0	5.6	8.2	11.8
Disease of the Musculoskeletal System and Connective Tissues	4.8	4.6	5.9	9.2
Congenital Anomalies	5.9	4.5	8.6	7.2[a]
Certain Conditions Originating in the Perinatal Period	12.4	[a]	[a]	[a]
Symptoms, Signs and Ill-Defined Conditions	2.7	2.9	3.5	4.7
Injury and Poisoning	4.1	5.3	7.1	10.2

Source: Based on data collected by the National Center for Health Statistics and published in Graves, Edmund J. "1988 Summary: National Hospital Discharge Survey." **Advance Data**, No. 185. Hyattsville, MD: National Center for Health Statistics, 1990.

Methodology: The data came from the National Hospital Discharge Survey conducted by the National Center for Health Statistics (NCHS). A sample of hospitals is chosen and hospital records are collected, coded, edited, and weighted in order to form the dataset.

Definitions: A "short stay hospital" is one where the average length of stay for all patients is less than 30 days with the exception of some general hospitals that are also included.

Qualifications: Since these figures are based on a sample, the data are subject to sampling and nonsampling error. A superscript[a] without a corresponding number means that the sample size for that category was less than 30. If the superscript[a] appears with a number, the figure is assumed to be unreliable. NA refers to a non-applicable category.

Interpretation: Average length of stay varies considerably by age. Age-specific length of stay figures differ markedly by first diagnosis.

V-10. HOSPITALS
DISCHARGE RATE FOR HOSPITAL PATIENTS BY FIRST-LISTED DIAGNOSIS AND AGE
1988

| Category of First-Listed Diagnosis | Average Days Stayed by Age Category | | | |
	Under 15	15-44	45-64	65 and over
All Conditions	491.5	1,040.5	1,404.9	3,341.2
Infectious and Parasitic Diseases	35.9	18.4	22.6	61.6
Neoplasms	10.0	33.0	154.1	315.6
Endocrine, Nutritional and Metabolic Diseases, and Immunity Diseases	19.2	20.0	54.4	150.3
Diseases of Blood and Blood Forming Organs	8.9	7.5	11.3	36.2
Mental Disorders	10.9	83.9	62.7	82.5
Diseases of Nervous System and Sense Organs	36.5	19.3	41.3	104.3
Diseases of the Circulatory System	4.7	36.5	354.4	1,061.6
Diseases of the Respiratory System	131.7	47.1	114.2	386.0
Diseases of the Digestive System	51.5	86.5	180.8	385.7
Diseases of the Genitourinary System	13.3	80.3	111.4	230.5
Complications of Pregnancy, Childbirth and Puerperium	0.6[a]	72.6	[a]	NA
Diseases of the Skin and Subcutaneous Tissue	8.6	13.5	23.4	50.1
Disease of the Musculoskeletal System and Connective Tissues	10.1	54.1	107.8	156.9
Congenital Anomalies	28.2	3.9	5.2	2.5[a]
Certain Conditions Originating in the Perinatal Period	29.8	[a]	[a]	[a]
Symptoms, Signs and Ill-Defined Conditions	9.3	15.2	22.8	22.7
Injury and Poisoning	65.6	106.0	108.3	248.6

*Discharge rate is reported as discharges per 100,000 population.

Source: Based on data collected by the National Center for Health Statistics and published in "1988 Summary: National Hospital Discharge Survey." **Advance Data**, No. 185. Hyattsville, MD: National Center for Health Statistics, 1990.

Methodology: The data came from the National Hospital Discharge Survey conducted by the National Center for Health Statistics (NCHS). A sample of hospitals is chosen and hospital records are collected, coded, edited, and weighted in order to form the dataset.

Definitions: A "short stay hospital" is one where the average length of stay for all persons is less than 30 days with the exception of some general hospitals that are also included. A "discharge" is the formal release of a patient by a hospital. The discharge rate is the ratio of the number of discharges in a particular age or other category in a given year to the number of persons in the civilian population in that same category on July 1 of that year.

Qualifications: Since these figures are based on a sample, the data are subject to sampling and nonsampling error. A superscript[a] without a corresponding number means that the sample size for that category was less than 30. If the superscript[a] appears with a number, the figure is assumed to be unreliable. NA refers to a non-applicable category.

Interpretation: There are wide variation in discharge rates by age. Age-first-listed diagnosis rates also vary considerably.

V-11. HOSPITALS
HOSPITAL ADMISSIONS, AVERAGE LENGTH OF STAY, AND INPATIENT DAYS BY STATE
1990-1991

State	Admission Rate*	Average Length of Stay (Days)	Inpatient Days*
Alabama	99.0	5.8	574
Alaska	56.0	6.5	363
Arizona	63.5	6.3	399
Arkansas	95.0	5.7	545
California	62.0	5.6	345
Colorado	59.7	5.0	299
Connecticut	**	*	*
Delaware	89.2	4.8	426
District of Columbia	**	*	*
Florida	83.8	7.0	587
Georgia	98.6	5.5	542
Hawaii	**	*	*
Idaho	58.9	4.8	283
Illinois	76.1	6.2	469
Indiana	90.4	6.2	565
Iowa	74.5	6.6	491
Kansas	52.5	9.2	485
Kentucky	87.4	7.0	609
Louisiana	130.8	5.1	665
Maine	**	*	*
Maryland	58.6	6.6	384
Massachusetts	61.3	6.5	398
Michigan	70.7	5.2	366
Minnesota	68.6	6.7	458
Mississippi	125.3	4.7	587
Missouri	81.6	6.2	502
Montana	80.5	5.3	428
Nebraska	68.8	6.1	422
Nevada	63.1	5.6	355
New Hampshire	**	*	*
New Jersey	80.0	5.5	439
New Mexico	63.8	6.8	431
New York	68.0	7.1	483
North Carolina	61.7	8.4	513
North Dakota	74.4	7.3	543
Ohio	72.8	5.5	402
Oklahoma	49.2	5.0	245
Oregon	49.3	4.6	227
Pennsylvania	54.0	7.3	396
Rhode Island	**	*	*
South Carolina	86.7	7.0	603
South Dakota	71.5	5.1	367
Tennessee	91.8	5.6	513

(Continued on next page)

V-11. HOSPITALS
HOSPITAL ADMISSIONS, AVERAGE LENGTH OF STAY,
AND INPATIENT DAYS BY STATE
1990-1991 *(Continued from previous page)*

State	Admission Rate*	Average Length of Stay (Days)	Inpatient Days*
Texas	94.2	6.4	604
Utah	86.3	8.7	753
Vermont	**	*	*
Virginia	60.0	7.3	440
Washington	50.2	5.1	255
West Virginia	63.5	5.2	331
Wisconsin	61.3	5.4	329
Wyoming	52.5	3.5	186
National Average	72.5	6.0	435

* Admission rate and inpatient days are per 1,000 persons.
** Not enough cases for statistical validity.

Source: Based on data collected by the Mutual of Omaha Companies and published in their report, **Current Trends in Health Care Costs and Utilization** (1991 edition). Mutual of Omaha (Omaha) is a leading health insurer and, as such, generates a large amount of data on the health care of its employees.

Methodology: Utilizing a sample of records from enrollees in Mutual of Omaha group health plans, the company develops statistics related to the cost and utilization of health care for this population. Statistical tests are utilized to assure the validity of the data.

Qualifications: Since these data are based on a sample of records they are subject to sampling error. The accuracy of the data is also a function of the accuracy of the codes applied to the records. These statistics refer only to Mutual of Omaha enrollees in group health plans and may not be entirely representative of the total U.S. population.

V-12. HOSPITALS
HOSPITAL OUTPATIENT VISITS
1965-1989

Year	Number of Visits*
1989	352,248,000
1985	282,140,000
1980	262,951,000
1975	254,844,000
1970	181,370,000
1965	125,793,000

*Rounded to nearest thousand

Source: Data collected by the American Hospital Association (AHA) and published in **Hospital Statistics.** The AHA is the national association of hospitals and, based on data collected from the nation's hospitals, annually publishes **Hospital Statistics** and the **AHA Guide to the Health Care Field.** Although hospital-oriented, these publications contain some information on other facilities. The AHA maintains the nation's most extensive data base on hospitals and maintains information beyond that published in its annual guides. Additional, and sometimes unpublished, data can be obtained from the AHA's data office (Chicago).

Methodology: Data in AHA publications are collected through annual surveys of AHA member hospitals.

Definitions: "Outpatient visits" include all hospital utilization for tests or treatment that does not involve an overnight stay. Most hospitals count emergency room visits in this total.

Qualifications: Although most hospitals are members of the AHA, some are not and are not, therefore, likely to participate in the survey. Some members fail to participate (and are listed as nonresponding). The AHA may obtain some of the missing data from other sources, but this does mean there is some slippage in the data quality. In addition, the AHA must rely on self-reports from the hospitals and this raising the question of the completeness and the accuracy of the data. There is also the problem of timeliness of the data. The magnitude of the data collection, processing and publishing effort means there is a certain time lag between the data can be disseminated (e.g., the 1990 guide contains data for the 1989 fiscal year). Outpatient records historically have not been as carefully maintained as inpatient records so there tends to be some variability in both definitions and the quality of the data. Outpatient statistics are not available for periods prior to 1965.

Interpretation: The utilization of hospitals for outpatient services has increased steadily since 1965. This increase has continued even as inpatient utilization declined during the 1980s.

V-13. HOSPITAL DIAGNOSES
MOST FREQUENT INPATIENT DIAGNOSES
1990

Diagnosis
Normal Newborn
Vaginal Delivery with Complications
Medical Back Problems
Caesarian Section without Complications
Heart Failure and Shock
Angina Pectoris
Esophagitis, Gastroenteritis, Miscellaneous Digestive Disorders
Simple Pneumonia and Pleurisy (Age > 70)
Psychosis
Nonradical Hysterectomy (Age < 70)

Source: Based on data collected through the National Hospital Discharge Survey conducted by the National Center for Health Statistics. The National Center for Health Statistics (NCHS) conducts a variety of surveys from which health-related data are drawn. Additional data, including some unpublished data, on this topic is available from NCHS (Hyattsville, MD).

Definitions: Includes all patients discharged (whether dead or alive) from all non-federal hospitals.

Methodology: The National Hospital Discharge Survey is used by NCHS to collect data annually on the characteristics of patients hospitalized in "short-stay" hospitals. Data collection is based on a sample of approximately 200,000 medical records each year. Information is collected on patient demographics, circumstances of the hospitalization, diagnosis and treatment and characteristics of the facility. Data from the sample are weighted up to produce national estimates.

Qualifications: Since the survey is based on a sample of administrative records, all of the drawbacks related to sample surveys apply. In addition, quality of the data also depends heavily on the completeness and accuracy of the medical records examined. Note that the manner in which conditions are grouped can influence the reported frequency of conditions.

Interpretation: Four of the ten most common diagnoses involve conditions related to female reproductive activities.

V-14. PROCEDURES
MOST FREQUENT PROCEDURES
1990

Procedure
Circumcision
Episiotomy
Low Cervical Caesarian Section
Diagnostic Ultrasound
X-Ray of Head, Face or Neck
Manually-Assisted Delivery
Heart and Pericardium Diagnostic Procedures
Cholecystectomy
Total Abdominal Hysterectomy
Cardiac Function Tests

Source: Based on data collected through the National Hospital Discharge Survey conducted by the National Center for Health Statistics. The National Center for Health Statistics (NCHS) conducts a variety of surveys from which health-related data are drawn. Additional data, including some unpublished data, on this topic is available from NCHS (Hyattsville, MD).

Definitions: Includes all patients discharged (whether dead or alive) from all non-federal hospitals.

Methodology: The National Hospital Discharge Survey is used by NCHS to collect data annually on the characteristics of patients hospitalized in "short-stay" hospitals. Data collection is based on a sample of approximately 200,000 medical records each year. Information is collected on patient demographics, circumstances of the hospitalization, diagnosis and treatment and characteristics of the facility. Data from the sample are weighted up to produce national estimates.

Qualifications: Since the survey is based on a sample of administrative records, all of the drawbacks related to sample surveys apply. In addition, quality of the data also depends heavily on the completeness and accuracy of the medical records examined. Note that the manner in which conditions are grouped can influence the reported frequency of conditions.

Interpretation: Four of the ten most common diagnoses involve conditions related to female reproductive activities.

V-15. HOSPITALS
THE 25 MOST FREQUENT DIAGNOSES AMONG MEDICARE DISCHARGES
1988

Diagnosis	Number of Discharges	Percent of All Medicare Discharges
Heart Failure and Shock	500,766	5.3%
Angina Pectoris	348,682	3.7
Psychosis	310,000	3.3
Certain Cardiovascular Disorders	309,455	3.3
Simple Pneumonia and Pleurisy*	292,265	3.1
Esophagitis, Gastroenteritis and Related*	228,956	2.4
Bronchitis and Asthma*	203,430	2.1
Major Joint/Limb Reattachment Procedures	200,127	2.1
Nutritional and Misc. Metabolic Disorders*	179,992	1.9
Cardiac Arrhythmia and Conduction Disorders*	165,888	1.8
Transient Ischemic Attacks/Precebral Occlusions	142,347	1.5
Kidney and Urinary Tract Infections*	136,916	1.4
Circulatory Disorders with Complications	132,104	1.4
Gastrointestinal Hemorrhage*	128,520	1.3
Medical Back Problems	126,181	1.3
Chemotherapy	125,779	1.3
Circulatory Disorders without complications	118,739	1.3
Major Small/Large Bowel Procedures*	107,653	1.1
Transurethral Prostatectomy**	102,036	1.1
Circulatory Disorders with Cardiac Catherization	101,603	1.1
Septicemia	101,086	1.1
Vascular Procedures (exc. major reconstruction)	100,264	1.1
Transurethral Prostatectomy*	97,022	1.0
Respiratory Infections and Inflammations*	95,381	1.0
Diabetes	95,220	1.0
Total Medicare Discharges	9,471,636	

*Age over 69 with complicating conditions.
**Age under 70 without complicating conditions.

Source: Based on data collected by the Bureau of Data Management and Strategy, Health Care Financing Administration (HCFA), within the Department of Health and Human Services (DHHS). HCFA, as the organization responsible for the administration of the Medicare program, is the primary source of Medicare statistics. Additional data are available directly from HCFA (Washington, D.C.) or through its publications such as **Health Care Financing Review.**

Methodology: The data on Medicare discharges are obtained from the records of HCFA based on claims made on behalf of Medicare beneficiaries.

Definitions: Under the Medicare reimbursement program (referred to as "prospective payment") over 400 conditions (e.g., diagnoses) have been assigned a DRG (Diagnostic Related Category) code. The reporting year is the fiscal year. Payment is made for claims under the Medicare program based on the DRG. Many patients have more than one condition and this may not be reflected in the table. The DRG assigned relates to what is determined to be the primary diagnosis.

Qualifications: Each of the DRGs has a very detailed and often highly qualified description. Since this table can accommodate limited detail, more complete descriptions of each of the DRGs listed should be obtained prior to use of these data.

Interpretation: Of the over 400 DRGs, these 25 account for over 45% of all Medicare discharges.

V-16. HOSPITALS
AVERAGE LENGTH OF HOSPITAL STAY FOR THE 25 MOST FREQUENT DIAGNOSES AMONG MEDICARE DISCHARGES
1988

Diagnosis	Average Days Stay
Heart Failure and Shock	8.0
Angina Pectoris	4.8
Psychosis	21.5
Certain Cardiovascular Disorders	10.6
Simple Pneumonia and Pleurisy*	9.2
Esophagitis, Gastroenteritis and Related*	6.4
Bronchitis and Asthma*	7.3
Major Joint/Limb Reattachment Procedures	12.6
Nutritional and Misc. Metabolic Disorders*	8.6
Cardiac Arrhythmia and Conduction Disorders*	6.3
Transient Ischemic Attacks/Precebral Occlusions	5.5
Kidney and Urinary Tract Infections*	8.8
Circulatory Disorders with Complications	10.5
Gastrointestinal Hemorrhage*	7.2
Medical Back Problems	6.8
Chemotherapy	3.4
Circulatory Disorders without complications	7.5
Major Small/Large Bowel Procedures*	17.4
Transurethral Prostatectomy**	4.6
Circulatory Disorders with Cardiac Catherization	3.1
Septicemia	10.5
Vascular Procedures (exc. major reconstruction)	7.5
Transurethral Prostatectomy*	6.9
Respiratory Infections and Inflammations*	12.5
Diabetes	7.5
Total Medicare Discharges	8.5

*Age over 69 with complicating conditions.
**Age under 70 without complicating conditions.

Source: Based on data collected by the Bureau of Data Management and Strategy, Health Care Financing Administration (HCFA), within the Department of Health and Human Services (DHHS). HCFA, as the organization responsible for the administration of the Medicare program, is the primary source of Medicare statistics. Additional data are available directly from HCFA (Washington, D.C.) or through its publications such as **Health Care Financing Review.**

Methodology: The data on Medicare discharges are obtained from the records of HCFA based on claims made on behalf of Medicare beneficiaries.

Definitions: Under the Medicare reimbursement program (referred to as "prospective payment") over 400 conditions (e.g., diagnoses) have been assigned a DRG (Diagnostic Related Category) code. Payment is made for claims under the Medicare program based on the DRG. Many patients have more than one condition and this may not be reflected in the table. The DRG assigned relates to what is determined to be the primary diagnosis. The reporting year is the fiscal year.

Qualifications: Each of the DRGs has a very detailed and often highly qualified description. Since this table can accommodate limited detail, more complete descriptions of each of the DRGs listed should be obtained prior to use of these data.

Interpretation: The average length of hospital stay varies widely by diagnosis. Length of stay is a crucial measure since reimbursement under Medicare significantly reflects the length of stay for a particular diagnosis.

V-17. HOSPITALS
AVERAGE HOSPITAL CHARGES FOR 25 MOST FREQUENTLY OCCURRING DIAGNOSES AMONG MEDICARE PATIENTS
FY1988

DRG Description	Average Charge Per Bill
Heart failure and shock	$5,800
Angina pectoris	3,502
Psychoses	4,550
Specific cerebral vascular disorders except transient ischemic attack	7,224
Simple pneumonia and pleurisy (age greater than 17)	6,739
Esophagitis, gastrointestinal and miscellaneous digestive disorders (age greater than 17)	4,189
Bronchitis and asthma (age greater than 17)	5,269
Major joint and limb reattachment procedures	13,268
Nutritional and miscellaneous metabolic disorders (age greater than 17, with complications	5,452
Cardiac arrhythmia and conduction disorders with complications	4,910
Transient ischemic attack and precerebral occlusions	3,590
Kidney and urinary tract infections (age greater than 17, with complications	5,894
Circulatory disorders with acute myocardial infarction and cardio-vascular complications, patient discharged alive.	9,058
Chemotherapy	2,938
Gastrointestinal hemorrhage with complications	5,521
Medical back problems	3,711
Circulatory disorders with acute myocardial infarction without cardio-vascular complications; patient discharged alive.	6,125
Extensive operating room procedure unrelated to principal diagnosis	15,620
Major small and large bowel procedures with complications	19,058
Transurethral prostatectomy without complications	3,594
Septicemia (age greater than 17)	8,697

(Continued on next page)

V-17. HOSPITALS
AVERAGE HOSPITAL CHARGES FOR 25 MOST FREQUENTLY OCCURRING
DIAGNOSES AMONG MEDICARE PATIENTS
FY1988 *(Continued from previous page)*

DRG Description	Average Charge Per Bill
Circulatory disorders except acute myocardial infarction with cardiac catheterization (without complex diagnosis)	3,939
Vascular procedures except major reconstruction, without vascular pump	11,299
Transurethral prostatectomy with complications	5,513
Diabetes (age greater than 35)	4,381

Source: Based on data collected by the Health Care Financing Administration (HCFA) within the U.S. Department of Health and Human Services. HCFA, as the organization responsible for the administration of the Medicare program, is the primary source of Medicare statistics. Additional data are available directly from HCFA (Washington, D.C.) or through its publications such as Health Care Financing Review.

Methodology: These data are drawn from the universe of hospitals participating in the Medicare program representing 99% of all short-term non-federal hospitals.

Definition: "Medicare" is the federally-sponsored health insurance program that covers the elderly and the disabled. Participation is mandatory for individuals 65 and over. "DRGs" are diagnostic related groups. Payment for health care claims under the Medicare program are based on the DRG. The DRG assigned reflects what is considered to be the primary diagnosis. "Average charge" refers to the total amount charged on average by the hospital for a patient in these categories.

V-18. SURGICAL PROCEDURES
SURGICAL PROCEDURE RATE FOR INPATIENT, OUTPATIENT, AND OFFICE SURGERY BY STATE
1990-1991

| State | Surgery Utilization Rate* | | |
	Inpatient	Outpatient	Office
Alabama	105	89	239
Alaska	52	48	240
Arizona	82	67	323
Arkansas	97	72	137
California	78	68	341
Colorado	70	68	243
Connecticut	**	**	198
Delaware	72	46	140
District of Columbia	**	**	205
Florida	102	88	292
Georgia	79	69	184
Hawaii	**	**	**
Idaho	72	48	192
Illinois	76	80	224
Indiana	90	103	159
Iowa	65	65	201
Kansas	56	64	161
Kentucky	83	96	170
Louisiana	145	81	135
Maine	**	**	135
Maryland	70	63	215
Massachusetts	67	70	167
Michigan	61	80	265
Minnesota	64	53	184
Mississippi	113	83	124
Missouri	89	79	219
Montana	76	53	250
Nebraska	81	73	283
New Hampshire	**	**	**
New Jersey	86	51	236
New Mexico	**	**	179
New York	74	38	300
North Carolina	60	60	167
North Dakota	79	**	253
Ohio	85	118	268
Oklahoma	51	69	106
Oregon	63	52	206
Pennsylvania	58	60	151
Rhode Island	**	**	**
South Carolina	**	**	159
South Dakota	65	50	161

(Continued on next page)

V-18. SURGICAL PROCEDURES
SURGICAL PROCEDURE RATE FOR INPATIENT, OUTPATIENT,
AND OFFICE SURGERY BY STATE
1990-1991 *(Continued from previous page)*

State	Inpatient	Surgery Utilization Rate* Outpatient	Office
Tennessee	95	89	198
Texas	106	83	261
Utah	77	66	143
Vermont	**	**	**
Virginia	54	57	233
Washington	57	45	208
West Virginia	70	79	181
Wisconsin	57	50	151
Wyoming	56	42	134
National Average	80	69	242

* The surgery rate is based on the number of procedures per 1,000 persons.
** Not enough cases for statistical validity.

Source: Based on data collected by the Mutual of Omaha Companies and published in their report, **Current Trends in Health Care Costs and Utilization** (1991 edition). Mutual of Omaha (Omaha) is a leading health insurer and, as such, generates a large amount of data on the health care of its employees.

Methodology: Utilizing a sample of records from enrollees in Mutual of Omaha group health plans, the company develops statistics related to the cost and utilization of health care for this population. Statistical tests are utilized to assure the validity of the data.

Definitions: The time period refers to the one-year period ending in June of 1991.

Qualifications: Since these data are based on a sample of records they are subject to sampling error. The accuracy of the data is also a function of the accuracy of the codes applied to the records. These statistics refer only to Mutual of Omaha enrollees in group health plans and may not be entirely representative of the total U.S. population.

V-19. SURGICAL PROCEDURES
MOST FREQUENTLY PERFORMED SURGICAL PROCEDURES
(EXCLUDING CHILDBIRTH-RELATED)
1987

Procedure	Surgeries Performed (in 1,000s)
Biopsy	1,378
Caesarean section	953
Cardiac catheterization	866
Hysterectomy	656
Spinal surgery (such as spinal taps, repair of broken vertebrae)	588
Treating skin (such as draining cysts, laser surgery on skin lesions)	588
Joint replacement	556
Removing gallbladder	538
Removing fallopian tubes and/or ovaries	490
Surgically resetting broken bones	481
Tubal ligation	415
Removing prostate	410
Dilation and curettage (non-abortion)	379
Removing disk, fusing vertebrae	362
Removing scar tissue inside abdomen	339
Coronary bypass	332
Repairing groin hernia	329
Repairing muscle, tendons, connective tissue, bursa	322
Repairing part of stomach	308
Appendectomy	303
Tonsillectomy, with or without adenoidectomy	244

Source: Based on data collected through the National Hospital Discharge Survey conducted by the National Center for Health Statistics. The National Center for Health Statistics (NCHS) conducts a variety of surveys from which health-related data are drawn. Additional data, including some unpublished data, on this topic is available from NCHS (Hyattsville, MD). Published in **U.S. News and World Report** (April 30, 1990).

Methodology: The National Hospital Discharge Survey is used by NCHS to collect data annually on the characteristics of patients hospitalized in "short-stay" hospitals. Data collection is based on a sample of approximately 200,000 medical records each year. Information is collected on patient demographics, circumstances of the hospitalization, diagnosis and treatment and characteristics of the facility. Data from the sample are weighted up to produce national estimates.

Definitions: Includes all patients discharged (whether dead or alive) from all non-federal hospitals except for newborn babies. Figures were rounded to the nearest thousand. This table excludes the various procedures related to childbirth.

Qualifications: Since the survey is based on a sample of administrative records, all of the drawbacks related to sample surveys apply. In addition, the quality of the data also depend heavily on the completeness and accuracy of the medical records examined. The age breakdown shown is commonly utilized for comparing utilization rates. It should be noted, however, that major variations exist within each age cohort.

Interpretation: Very few of the most frequently performed surgeries are related to life threatening conditions. A large proportion are childbirth related.

V-20. SURGICAL PROCEDURES
TOP 25 SURGICAL PROCEDURES BY AGE OF PATIENT
1989

Surgical Procedure	Surgical Procedures by Age Group		
	0-17	18-64	65 +
Low cervical caesarean section	31,831	918,986	0
Total cholecystectomy (gall bladder removal)	3,382	352,083	139,574
Total abdominal hysterectomy	239	410,341	34,528
Left heart cardiac catheterization	608	246,405	161,248
Repair of obstetric laceration	15,828	345,464	0
Transurethral prostatectomy	28	63,302	237,338
Intervertebral disc excision	1,093	229,635	31,564
Appendectomy	79,032	148,628	13,121
Low forceps delivery with episiotomy	11,974	192,264	0
Balloon angioplasty	100	97,750	62,521
Biopsy of esophagus, stomach and/or duodenum	2,154	71,716	85,899
Open reduction of femur fracture	3,508	29,682	121,524
Combined right/left heart cardiac catheterization	7,570	76,697	67,829
Cystoscopy (examination of bladder with cystoscope)	2,697	73,691	62,853
Vacuum extraction delivery with episiotomy	6,652	129,938	0
Debridement wound (removal of foreign material)	9,890	73,538	51,923
Vaginal hysterectomy	35	109,039	23,630
Open reduction of tibia/fibula fracture	9,697	90,208	21,467
Venous catheterization	8,344	60,196	50,481
Total knee replacement	110	31,567	86,990
Unilateral simply mastectomy	13	57,170	53,913
Contrast myelogram	800	84,124	19,025
Dilation and curettage post delivery	4,551	91,283	0
Fetal monitoring intrauterine	4,429	88,819	0
Closed biopsy of large bowel	1,759	42,297	43,821

Source: Based on data collected by the National Center for Health Services Research and published in **HealthWeek** (February 25, 1991). The National Center for Health Statistics (NCHS) conducts a variety of surveys from which health-related data are drawn. Additional data, including some unpublished data, on this topic are available from NCHS (Hyattsville, MD). (**HealthWeek** ceased publication at the end of 1991.)

Definitions: "Procedure" refers to the principal procedure in cases where more than one procedure is involved. These procedures are calculated from non-federal, short-stay general hospitals only.

Interpretation: The number of procedures performed by age group varies widely from procedure to procedure. The large number of obstetrical procedures performed increases the size of the 18-64 population. A surprising number of procedures are performed on patients under 18.

V-21. SURGICAL PROCEDURES
TOP 25 SURGICAL PROCEDURES AND AVERAGE LENGTH OF STAY
1989

Surgical Procedure	Procedures Performed	Average Stay (Days)
Low cervical caesarean section	950,817	4.6
Total cholecystectomy (gall bladder removal)	495,038	6.6
Total abdominal hysterectomy	445,109	5.1
Left heart cardiac catheterization	408,261	4.5
Repair of obstetric laceration	361,292	2.2
Transurethral prostatectomy	300,669	5.7
Intervertebral disc excision	262,293	5.3
Appendectomy	240,780	4.6
Low forceps delivery with episiotomy	204,238	2.6
Balloon angioplasty	160,372	5.0
Biopsy of esophagus, stomach and/or duodenum	159,769	7.6
Open reduction of fracture with internal fixation femur	154,713	13.7
Combined right/left heart cardiac catheterization	152,097	5.2
Cystoscopy (examination of bladder with cystoscope)	139,242	6.7
Vacuum extraction delivery with episiotomy	136,591	2.4
Debridement wound (removal of foreign material)	135,350	14.0
Vaginal hysterectomy	132,705	4.3
Open reduction of fracture with internal fixation tibia/fibula	121,372	5.5
Venous catheterization	119,021	13.2
Total knee replacement	117,666	10.6
Unilateral simply mastectomy	111,097	4.6
Contrast myelogram	103,949	3.5
Dilation and curettage post delivery	95,834	1.6
Fetal monitoring intrauterine	93,249	2.0
Closed biopsy of large bowel	87,877	8.1

Source: Based on data collected by the National Center for Health Services Research and published in **HealthWeek** (February 25, 1991). The National Center for Health Statistics (NCHS) conducts a variety of surveys from which health-related data are drawn. Additional data, including some unpublished data, on this topic are available from NCHS (Hyattsville, MD). (**HealthWeek** ceased publication at the end of 1991.)

Definitions: "Procedure" refers to the principal procedure in cases where more than one procedure is involved. These procedures are calculated from non-federal, short-stay general hospitals only.

Qualifications: The number of procedures does not necessarily equal the number of patients involved, since one patient may undergo two or more procedures.

Interpretation: A small number of procedures account for a large proportion of the total. A small fraction of the procedures performed are related to life-threatening situations. In fact, the list is heavily weighted toward obstetrical procedures, since this is the most frequent reason for hospital admission and may involve more than one procedure. The most frequent procedures generally involve short hospital stays. Only a few of the top 25 involve an average stay higher than the overall average (6-7 days in 1989).

V-22. SURGICAL PROCEDURES
TRENDS IN HYSTERECTOMY PROCEDURES
1965-1987

Year	Hysterectomies Performed*	Rate**
1987	653,000	6.7
1985	670,000	6.9
1983	673,000	7.1
1981	674,000	7.3
1979	639,000	7.1
1975	724,000	8.6
1971	569,000	7.3
1965	428,000	6.1

*Rounded to nearest 1,000.
**Rate is based on the number of procedures per 1,000 women of all ages.

Source: Based on data from the National Hospital Discharge Survey conducted by the National Center for Health Statistics. Additional data, including some unpublished data, on this topic are available from NCHS (Hyattsville, MD). Reprinted in the Metropolitan Life **Statistical Bulletin**, April-June 1990. The **Statistical Bulletin** published by Metropolitan Life Insurance Company reprints data from a variety of sources.

Methodology: The National Hospital Discharge Survey is used by NCHS to collect data annually on the characteristics of patients hospitalized in "short-stay" hospitals. Data collection is based on a sample of approximately 200,000 medical records each year. Information is collected on patient demographics, circumstances of the hospitalization, diagnosis and treatment and characteristics of the facility. Data from the sample are weighted up to produce national estimates.

Definitions: A "hysterectomy" refers to the surgical removal of the womb or uterus.

Qualifications: Since the survey is based on a sample of administrative records, all of the drawbacks related to sample surveys apply. In addition, the quality of the data also depends heavily on the completeness and accuracy of the medical records examined.

Interpretation: The rate of hysterectomy procedures performed varies depending on the region of the country in which one resides. The frequency of the performance of this procedure has been demonstrated to be as much a function of practice patterns as it is a medical necessity. The decline since the mid-1970s can probably be attributed to evidence as to the lack of necessity for it in many cases and to the adverse publicity surrounding alleged excessive unnecessary procedures.

V-23. SURGICAL PROCEDURES
REGIONAL DIFFERENCES IN THE RATE OF HYSTERECTOMY PROCEDURES
1987

| Region | Rate by Age Category* | | | |
	15 and over	15-44	45-64	65 and over
Northeast	4.1	3.5	6.2	3.3
Midwest	6.5	6.7	6.5	3.5
South	7.4	8.4	7.9	3.4
West	8.1	8.7	9.7	3.7
Total U.S.	6.6	7.9	8.0	3.4

*Procedure rates are based on the procedures per 1,000 women in each age category.

Source: Based on data from the National Hospital Discharge Survey conducted by the National Center for Health Statistics. Additional data, including some unpublished data, on this topic are available from NCHS (Hyattsville, MD). Reprinted in the Metropolitan Life **Statistical Bulletin**, April-June 1990. The **Statistical Bulletin** published by Metropolitan Life Insurance Company reprints data from a variety of sources.

Methodology: The National Hospital Discharge Survey is used by NCHS to collect data annually on the characteristics of patients hospitalized in "short-stay" hospitals. Data collection is based on a sample of approximately 200,000 medical records each year. Information is collected on patient demographics, circumstances of the hospitalization, diagnosis and treatment and characteristics of the facility. Data from the sample are weighted up to produce national estimates.

Definitions: A "hysterectomy" refers to the surgical removal of the womb or uterus. "Regions" are the official subdivisions of the United States utilized by various government agencies for statistical reporting.

Qualifications: Since the survey is based on a sample of administrative records, all of the drawbacks related to sample surveys apply. In addition, the quality of the data also depend heavily on the completeness and accuracy of the medical records examined.

Interpretation: The rate of hysterectomy procedures performed varies depending on the region of the country in which one resides. The frequency of the performance of this procedure has been demonstrated to be as much a function of practice patterns as it is a medical necessity. Regional variations in practice patterns are thought to account for the differences reported.

V-24. NURSING HOMES
SELECTED CHARACTERISTICS OF NURSING HOME RESIDENTS
1985

Characteristic	Percent
Sex:	
Male	28.4
Female	71.6
Race:	
White	92.2
Nonwhite	7.8
Age:	
Under 65	11.6
65-74	14.2
75-84	34.1
85 and over	40.0

Source: Based on data complied by the National Institute of Mental Health (NIMH). Published in **Mental Health, United States, 1990** (U.S. Government Printing Office, 1990). The National Institute of Mental Health (Washington) is part of the Federally-funded National Institutes of Health (NIH) and is the main source of research funding and statistics on mental health in the United States.

Methodology: Based on data collected from the records of a sample of the nation's nursing homes.

Definitions: "Average length of care" refers to the number of days on average a patient was under treatment at any of the institutions identified by NIMH as a provider of mental health outpatient services.

Qualifications: Since these data have been collected by means of a sample survey, they are subject to sampling error. The national totals reported are extrapolated from these sampled records and could possibly vary from actual figures by a few percentage points either plus or minus. The data are also subject to nonsampling errors due to inaccurate and/or incomplete reporting of the data. Since these data were collected in 1985, significant changes have occurred in health care in general and mental health care in particular.

Interpretation: Among the 1985 nursing home population, whites, females, and those over 85 were disproportionately represented

V-25. NURSING HOMES
AVERAGE LENGTH OF STAY FOR NURSING HOME PATIENTS BY AGE
1985

Length of Stay Since Admission	Under 65 Years	65 to 74 Years	75 to 84 Years	85 Years & Over
Less than 3 months	14.2	15.1	12.7	11.9
3 months to less than 6 months	12.7	10.0	9.6	8.2
6 months to less than 12 months	12.1	14.3	15.8	13.1
1 year to less than 3 years	24.0	31.1	33.2	32.4
3 years to less than 5 years	13.0	12.3	13.6	15.0
5 years or more	24.0	17.1	15.0	19.4
Average length of stay since admission	1,311	1,055	948	1,081
Median length of stay since admission	654	528	554	677

Source: Data collected by the National Center for Health Statistics and published in "Nursing Home Utilization by Current Residents." **Vital and Health Statistics**, Series 13, No. 102. Hyattsville, MD: Public Health Service, 1989. The National Center for Health Statistics (NCHS) conducts a variety of surveys from which health-related data are drawn. Additional data, including some unpublished data, on this topic is available from NCHS (Hyattsville, MD).

Methodology: These data are collected by NCHS through the National Nursing Home Survey, which is a sample survey of nursing homes, their residents, discharges, and staffs in the coterminous U.S. Nurses at the institution referred to medical records in order to provide the information needed.

Definitions: Nursing homes include all types of nursing and related care homes with three or more beds set up and staffed for use by residents and routinely providing nursing and personal care services. Facilities are either freestanding establishments or nursing care units of hospitals, retirement centers, or similar institutions maintaining financial and employee records separate from those of the larger institution. Residential care facilities are excluded. These include community care facilities in California, adult congregate living facilities in Florida, family care homes in Kentucky, and adult foster care homes in Michigan.

Qualifications: Since the National Nursing Home Survey is a sample survey, the data are subject to sampling and nonsampling error. The sample frame consisted of 20,479 nursing and related care facilities of which 1,079 were included in the survey. The response rate was 93 percent. Percentages may not total 100 because of rounding.

V-26. PHYSICIAN VISITS
ANNUAL PHYSICIAN VISITS BY SPECIALTY
1989

Specialty	Estimated Number of Visits*	Percent of Total
General/Family Practice	206,301,000	29.8%
Pediatrics	87,411,000	12.6
Internal Medicine	78,816,000	11.4
Obstetrics/Gynecology	58,381,000	8.4
Ophthalmology	38,761,000	5.6
Orthopedic Surgery	35,148,000	5.1
Dermatology	26,319,000	3.8
General Surgery	25,379,000	3.7
Psychiatry	16,616,000	2.4
Otolaryngology	15,956,000	2.3
Cardiovascular Disease	10,840,000	1.6
Urological Surgery	10,157,000	1.5
Neurology	6,105,000	0.9
All other specialists	76,511,000	11.0
Total Visits	692,702,000	100.0

*Visits are rounded to nearest thousand.

Source: Data collected by the National Center for Health Statistics (NCHS) through its National Ambulatory Medical Care Survey and published by NCHS in **Advance Data**, Number 203, July 1, 1991. NCHS conducts a variety of surveys from which health-related data are drawn. Additional data, including some unpublished data, on this topic are available from NCHS (Hyattsville, MD).

Methodology: These data were collected by NCHS by means of the 1989 National Ambulatory Medical Care Survey (NAMCS). Date are collected from a sample of patient records from a sample of the practices of non-federal office-based physicians. The 1989 survey involved over 38,384 patient records from 2,535 physician practices. The figures obtained through this procedure were extrapolated to apply to the entire U.S. population.

Definitions: An "ambulatory patient" is an individual seeking personal health service who is not currently admitted to any health care institution on the premises. "Physicians" in this study includes doctors of osteopathy (D.O.s). A "visit" is a direct personal exchange between an ambulatory care patient and a physician or a staff member working under the physician's supervision, for the purpose of seeking care and rending personal health services. Visits in this study exclude telephone consultation.

Qualifications: The National Ambulatory Medical Care Survey is faced with the same drawbacks that characterize all sample surveys. The size and representativeness of the sample, questionnaire design, and a variety of other factors may affect the quality of the data. Since the survey is based on a sample of medical records, the quality of data also depends heavily on the completeness and accuracy of the medical records examined. Since these data are extrapolated from a sample to the entire population, they should be considered as estimates.

Interpretation: These estimates yield an average of nearly three visits annually per resident in the United States. General and family practitioners account for the largest share (30%) of physician office visits. Visits to "primary care" physicians (general and family practitioners, internists, OB/GYNs and pediatricians) accounted for over half of all visits.

V-27. PHYSICIAN VISITS
MOST FREQUENT DIAGNOSTIC TESTS PERFORMED IN PHYSICIANS OFFICES
1989

Diagnostic Test	Estimated Number of Visits Involving Test*
Blood pressure check	241,899,000
Other blood test	88,210,000
Urinalysis	87,716,000
Pelvic examination	51,965,000
Visual acuity	45,192,000
Breast palpation	37,929,000
Pap test	32,766,000
Digital rectal examination	25,071,000
Cholesterol measure	24,828,000
Chest x-ray	18,419,000
Stool blood examination	15,576,000
Mammogram	10,655,000
Proctoscopy/sigmoidoscopy	5,134,000
Oral glucose tolerance	5,056,000

*Visits rounded to nearest thousand.

Source: Data collected by the National Center for Health Statistics (NCHS) through its National Ambulatory Medical Care Survey and published by NCHS in **Advance Data,** Number 203, July 1, 1991. NCHS conducts a variety of surveys from which health-related data are drawn. Additional data, including some unpublished data, on this topic are available from NCHS (Hyattsville, MD).

Methodology: These data were collected by NCHS by means of the 1989 National Ambulatory Medical Care Survey (NAMCS). Date are collected from a sample of patient records from a sample of the practices of non-federal office-based physicians. The 1989 survey involved over 38,384 patient records from 2,535 physician practices. The figures obtained through this procedure were extrapolated to apply to the entire U.S. population.

Definitions: An "ambulatory patient" is an individual seeking personal health service who is not currently admitted to any health care institution on the premises. "Physicians" in this study includes doctors of osteopathy (D.O.s). A "visit" is a direct personal exchange between an ambulatory care patient and a physician or a staff member working under the physician's supervision, for the purpose of seeking care and rending personal health services (excluding telephone consultation).

Qualifications: The National Ambulatory Medical Care Survey is faced with the same drawbacks that characterize all sample surveys. The size and representativeness of the sample, questionnaire design, and a variety of other factors may affect the quality of the data. Since the survey is based on a sample of medical records, the quality of data also depends heavily on the completeness and accuracy of the medical records examined. Since these data are extrapolated from a sample to the entire population, they should be considered as estimates.

V-28. PHYSICIAN VISITS
SELECTED CHARACTERISTICS OF PATIENTS VISITING PHYSICIANS
1989

Characteristic	Estimated Percent
Total Office Visits	100.0%
Referred to another physician	5.4
Not referred to another physician	94.6
New patient	16.8
Old patient	83.4
Old patient with new problem	22.5
Old patient with old problem	61.0
Total with new problems	39.3
Total with old problems	60.7

Source: Data collected by the National Center for Health Statistics (NCHS) through its National Ambulatory Medical Care Survey and published by NCHS in **Advance Data**, Number 203, July 1, 1991. NCHS conducts a variety of surveys from which health-related data are drawn. Additional data, including some unpublished data, on this topic are available from NCHS (Hyattsville, MD).

Methodology: These data were collected by NCHS by means of the 1989 National Ambulatory Medical Care Survey (NAMCS). Date are collected from a sample of patient records from a sample of the practices of non-federal office-based physicians. The 1989 survey involved over 38,384 patient records from 2,535 physician practices. The figures obtained through this procedure were extrapolated to apply to the entire U.S. population.

Definitions: An "ambulatory patient" is an individual seeking personal health service who is not currently admitted to any health care institution on the premises. "Physicians" in this study includes doctors of osteopathy (D.O.s). A "visit" is a direct personal exchange between an ambulatory care patient and a physician or a staff member working under the physician's supervision, for the purpose of seeking care and rending personal health services. Visits in this study exclude telephone consultation.

Qualifications: The National Ambulatory Medical Care Survey is faced with the same drawbacks that characterize all sample surveys. The size and representativeness of the sample, questionnaire design, and a variety of other factors may affect the quality of the data. Since the survey is based on a sample of medical records, the quality of data also depends heavily on the completeness and accuracy of the medical records examined. Since these data are extrapolated from a sample to the entire population, they should be considered as estimates.

Interpretation: The overwhelming majority of visits to physicians are for existing patients or patients who were self-referred or referred by someone other than a physician. The bulk of office visits are by "old" patients with previously identified problems.

V-29. PHYSICIAN VISITS
DISPOSITION OF PHYSICIAN OFFICE VISITS
1989

Disposition	Estimated Number	Estimated Percent
Total Office Visits	592,702,000	100.0%
No follow required	66,377,000	9.6
Return at a specified time	424,583,000	61.3
Return if needed	160,282,000	23.1
Telephone follow-up	24,962,000	3.6
Refer to another physician	20,071,000	2.9
Return to referring physician	6,139,000	0.9
Admit to hospital	15,536,000	2.2

Source: Data collected by the National Center for Health Statistics (NCHS) through its National Ambulatory Medical Care Survey and published by NCHS in **Advance Data**, Number 203, July 1, 1991. NCHS conducts a variety of surveys from which health-related data are drawn. Additional data, including some unpublished data, on this topic are available from NCHS (Hyattsville, MD).

Methodology: These data were collected by NCHS by means of the 1989 National Ambulatory Medical Care Survey (NAMCS). Date are collected from a sample of patient records from a sample of the practices of non-federal office-based physicians. The 1989 survey involved over 38,384 patient records from 2,535 physician practices. The figures obtained through this procedure were extrapolated to apply to the entire U.S. population.

Definitions: An "ambulatory patient" is an individual seeking personal health service who is not currently admitted to any health care institution on the premises. "Physicians" in this study includes doctors of osteopathy (D.O.s). A "visit" is a direct personal exchange between an ambulatory care patient and a physician or a staff member working under the physician's supervision, for the purpose of seeking care and rending personal health services. Visits in this study exclude telephone consultation.

Qualifications: The National Ambulatory Medical Care Survey is faced with the same drawbacks that characterize all sample surveys. The size and representativeness of the sample, questionnaire design, and a variety of other factors may affect the quality of the data. Since the survey is based on a sample of medical records, the quality of data also depends heavily on the completeness and accuracy of the medical records examined. Since these data are extrapolated from a sample to the entire population, they should be considered as estimates.

Interpretation: The overwhelming majority of visits to physicians require some type of followup. Approximately three percent of visits result in a referral to another physician and one percent in hospital admittance.

V-30. PHYSICIAN VISITS
ANNUAL PHYSICIAN VISITS BY AGE OF PATIENT
1989

Age Group	Estimated Number of Visits*	Percent of Total	Visits Per Person
Under 15	137,502,000	19.9%	2.6
15-24	66,868,000	9.7	1.9
25-44	192,593,000	27.8	2.4
45-64	145,160,000	21.0	3.1
65-74	83,692,000	12.1	4.7
75 and over	66,888,000	9.7	5.9
Total Visits	692,702,000	100.0	2.8

*Visits are rounded to nearest thousand.

Source: Data collected by the National Center for Health Statistics (NCHS) through its National Ambulatory Medical Care Survey and published by NCHS in **Advance Data,** Number 203, July 1, 1991. NCHS conducts a variety of surveys from which health-related data are drawn. Additional data, including some unpublished data, on this topic are available from NCHS (Hyattsville, MD).

Methodology: These data were collected by NCHS by means of the 1989 National Ambulatory Medical Care Survey (NAMCS). Date are collected from a sample of patient records from a sample of the practices of non-federal office-based physicians. The 1989 survey involved over 38,384 patient records from 2,535 physician practices. The figures obtained through this procedure were extrapolated to apply to the entire U.S. population.

Definitions: An "ambulatory patient" is an individual seeking personal health service who is not currently admitted to any health care institution on the premises. "Physicians" in this study includes doctors of osteopathy (D.O.s). A "visit" is a direct personal exchange between an ambulatory care patient and a physician or a staff member working under the physician's supervision, for the purpose of seeking care and rending personal health services. Visits in this study exclude telephone consultation.

Qualifications: The National Ambulatory Medical Care Survey is faced with the same drawbacks that characterize all sample surveys. The size and representativeness of the sample, questionnaire design, and a variety of other factors may affect the quality of the data. Since the survey is based on a sample of medical records, the quality of data also depends heavily on the completeness and accuracy of the medical records examined. Since these data are extrapolated from a sample to the entire population, they should be considered as estimates.

Interpretation: The average number of physician visits increases steadily with age beginning with the 15-24 age cohort. The higher average visits for those under 15 reflects treatment for pediatric problems.

V-31. PHYSICIAN VISITS
ANNUAL PHYSICIAN VISITS BY SEX AND AGE OF PATIENT
1989

| Age Group | Males | | Females | |
	Estimated Number of Visits*	Visits Per Person	Estimated Number of Visits*	Visits Per Person
Under 15	72,364,000	2.6	65,138,000	2.5
15-24	23,803,000	1.4	43,065,000	2.4
25-44	62,370,000	1.6	130,222,000	3.2
45-64	58,084,000	2.6	87,076,000	3.6
65-74	34,133,000	4.3	49,560,000	5.0
75 and over	24,453,000	5.8	42,435,000	5.9
Total Visits	276,206,000	2.3	417,496,000	3.3

*Visits are rounded to nearest thousand.

Source: Data collected by the National Center for Health Statistics (NCHS) through its National Ambulatory Medical Care Survey and published by NCHS in **Advance Data**, Number 203, July 1, 1991. NCHS conducts a variety of surveys from which health-related data are drawn. Additional data, including some unpublished data, on this topic are available from NCHS (Hyattsville, MD).

Methodology: These data were collected by NCHS by means of the 1989 National Ambulatory Medical Care Survey (NAMCS). Date are collected from a sample of patient records from a sample of the practices of non-federal office-based physicians. The 1989 survey involved over 38,384 patient records from 2,535 physician practices. The figures obtained through this procedure were extrapolated to apply to the entire U.S. population.

Definitions: An "ambulatory patient" is an individual seeking personal health service who is not currently admitted to any health care institution on the premises. "Physicians" in this study includes doctors of osteopathy (D.O.s). A "visit" is a direct personal exchange between an ambulatory care patient and a physician or a staff member working under the physician's supervision, for the purpose of seeking care and rending personal health services (excluding telephone consultation).

Qualifications: The National Ambulatory Medical Care Survey is faced with the same drawbacks that characterize all sample surveys. The size and representativeness of the sample, questionnaire design, and a variety of other factors may affect the quality of the data. Since the survey is based on a sample of medical records, the quality of data also depends heavily on the completeness and accuracy of the medical records examined. Since these data are extrapolated from a sample to the entire population, they should be considered as estimates.

Interpretation: The average number of annual physician visits by age category displays a similar pattern for males and females. However, for every age group except for those under 15, the average number of visits for females is higher than that for males. As a result, females average nearly one and one-half as many physician office visits as males.

V-32. PHYSICIAN VISITS
ANNUAL PHYSICIAN VISITS BY RACE
1989

Race	Estimated Number of Visits*	Percent of Total
White	587,976,000	84.9%
All Nonwhite	83,327,000	12.0
Black	62,146,000	9.0
Asian/Pacific Islander	18,948,000	2.7
American Indian/Alaskan Native	2,233,000	0.3
Unspecified race	21,399,000	3.1
Total Visits	692,702,000	100.0

*Visits are rounded to nearest thousand.

Source: Data collected by the National Center for Health Statistics (NCHS) through its National Ambulatory Medical Care Survey and published by NCHS in **Advance Data**, Number 203, July 1, 1991. NCHS conducts a variety of surveys from which health-related data are drawn. Additional data, including some unpublished data, on this topic are available from NCHS (Hyattsville, MD).

Methodology: These data were collected by NCHS by means of the 1989 National Ambulatory Medical Care Survey (NAMCS). Date are collected from a sample of patient records from a sample of the practices of non-federal office-based physicians. The 1989 survey involved over 38,384 patient records from 2,535 physician practices. The figures obtained through this procedure were extrapolated to apply to the entire U.S. population.

Definitions: An "ambulatory patient" is an individual seeking personal health service who is not currently admitted to any health care institution on the premises. "Physicians" in this study includes doctors of osteopathy (D.O.s). A "visit" is a direct personal exchange between an ambulatory care patient and a physician or a staff member working under the physician's supervision, for the purpose of seeking care and rending personal health services. Visits in this study exclude telephone consultation.

Qualifications: The National Ambulatory Medical Care Survey is faced with the same drawbacks that characterize all sample surveys. The size and representativeness of the sample, questionnaire design, and a variety of other factors may affect the quality of the data. Since the survey is based on a sample of medical records, the quality of data also depends heavily on the completeness and accuracy of the medical records examined. Since these data are extrapolated from a sample to the entire population, they should be considered as estimates.

V-33. PHYSICIAN VISITS
20 MOST COMMON REASONS FOR PHYSICIAN OFFICE VISITS
1989

Reason	Estimated Number of Visits	Percent of Total
Total Office Visits	692,702,000	100.0%
General examination	27,909,000	4.0
Cough	24,997,000	3.6
Prenatal examination (routine)	24,056,000	3.5
Throat symptoms	16,972,000	2.5
Postoperative visit	16,660,000	2.4
Well baby examination	14,831,000	2.1
Earache/ear infection	14,468,000	2.1
Back symptoms	13,744,000	2.0
Skin rash	12,325,000	1.8
Stomach pain/cramps/spasms	12,313,000	1.8
Fever	11,634,000	1.7
Vision dysfunctions	10,253,000	1.5
Hypertension	10,055,000	1.5
Knee symptoms	9,816,000	1.4
Blood pressure test	9,792,000	1.4
Headache/pain in head	9,609,000	1.4
Head cold/upper respiratory infection	8,669,000	1.3
Nasal congestion	8,647,000	1.2
Chest pain and related symptoms	8,339,000	1.2
Neck symptoms	8,112,000	1.2
All other reasons	419,439,000	60.6

*Visits are rounded to nearest thousand.

Source: Data collected by the National Center for Health Statistics (NCHS) through its National Ambulatory Medical Care Survey and published by NCHS in **Advance Data**, Number 203, July 1, 1991. NCHS conducts a variety of surveys from which health-related data are drawn. Additional data, including some unpublished data, on this topic are available from NCHS (Hyattsville, MD).

Methodology: These data were collected by NCHS by means of the 1989 National Ambulatory Medical Care Survey (NAMCS). Date are collected from a sample of patient records from a sample of the practices of non-federal office-based physicians. The 1989 survey involved over 38,384 patient records from 2,535 physician practices. The figures obtained through this procedure were extrapolated to apply to the entire U.S. population.

Definitions: An "ambulatory patient" is an individual seeking personal health service who is not currently admitted to any health care institution on the premises. "Physicians" in this study includes doctors of osteopathy (D.O.s). A "visit" is a direct personal exchange between an ambulatory care patient and a physician or a staff member working under the physician's supervision, for the purpose of seeking care and rending personal health services. Visits in this study exclude telephone consultation.

Qualifications: The National Ambulatory Medical Care Survey is faced with the same drawbacks that characterize all sample surveys. The size and representativeness of the sample, questionnaire design, and a variety of other factors may affect the quality of the data. Since the survey is based on a sample of medical records, the quality of data also depends heavily on the completeness and accuracy of the medical records examined. Since these data are extrapolated from a sample to the entire population, they should be considered as estimates.

Interpretation: Relatively routine problems dominate among the most frequent reasons for visiting a physician. As can be seen, however, no reason accounted for more than four percent.

V-34. PHYSICIAN VISITS
MOST COMMON PRINCIPAL DIAGNOSIS FOR PHYSICIAN OFFICE VISITS
1989

Reason	Estimated Number of Visits*	Percent of Total
Total Office Visits	692,702,000	100.0%
Essential hypertension	27,708,000	4.0
Normal pregnancy	23,578,000	3.4
General medical examination	20,166,000	2.9
Otitis media	20,033,000	2.9
Acute respiratory infections	15,765,000	2.3
Health supervision of infant/child	15,669,000	2.3
Diabetes mellitus	13,237,000	1.9
Allergic rhinitis	11,631,000	1.7
Bronchitis	11,160,000	1.6
Acute pharyngitis	10,958,000	1.6
Chronic sinusitis	8,700,000	1.3
Neurotic disorders	8,511,000	1.2
Diseases of sebaceous glands	8,146,000	1.2
Selected vision disorders	7,686,000	1.1
Sprains/strains of back	7,614,000	1.1
Asthma	6,822,000	1.0
Dermatitis and other eczema	6,542,000	0.9
Cataracts	6,335,000	0.9
Osteoarthrosis and allied disorders	6,259,000	0.9
All other diagnoses	450,469,000	65.0

*Visits are rounded to nearest thousand.

Source: Based on data collected by the National Center for Health Statistics (NCHS) through its National Ambulatory Medical Care Survey and published by NCHS in **Advance Data**, Number 203, July 1, 1991. NCHS conducts a variety of surveys from which health-related data are drawn. Additional data, including some unpublished data, on this topic are available from NCHS (Hyattsville, MD).

Methodology: These data were collected by NCHS by means of the 1989 National Ambulatory Medical Care Survey (NAMCS). Date are collected from a sample of patient records from a sample of the practices of non-federal office-based physicians. The 1989 survey involved over 38,384 patient records from 2,535 physician practices. The figures obtained through this procedure were extrapolated to apply to the entire U.S. population.

Definitions: An "ambulatory patient" is an individual seeking personal health service who is not currently admitted to any health care institution on the premises. "Physicians" in this study includes doctors of osteopathy (D.O.s). A "visit" is a direct personal exchange between an ambulatory care patient and a physician or a staff member working under the physician's supervision, for the purpose of seeking care and rending personal health services. Visits in this study exclude telephone consultation. "Chronic ischemic heart disease" exclude angina pectoris.

Qualifications: The National Ambulatory Medical Care Survey is faced with the same drawbacks that characterize all sample surveys. The size and representativeness of the sample, questionnaire design, and a variety of other factors may affect the quality of the data. Since the survey is based on a sample of medical records, the quality of data also depends heavily on the completeness and accuracy of the medical records examined. Since these data are extrapolated from a sample to the entire population, they should be considered as estimates.

Interpretation: Chronic conditions dominate the list of the top 20 diagnoses for patients visiting a physician. As can be seen, however, no diagnosis accounted for more than four percent.

V-35. PHYSICIAN VISITS
REASONS FOR PHYSICIAN VISIT BY ADOLESCENTS
1985

Reason	Estimated Number of Visits
Total Office Visits	58,996,000
General examination	5,439,431
Symptoms related to throat	4,277,210
Prenatal examination (routine)	3,433,567
Acne or pimples	2,454,234
Cough	1,457,201
Earache to ear infection	1,356,908
Skin rash	1,297,912
Knee symptoms	1,073,727
Allergy medication	1,067,828
Headache	949,836
Warts (not otherwise specified)	943,936
Abdominal pains, cramps, spasms	861,342
Allergy (not otherwise specified)	814,145
Postoperative visit	772,848
Eye examination	725,651
Head cold, upper respiratory infection	719,751
Vision dysfunctions	672,554
Suture insertion, removal	607,659
Fever	572,261
Back symptoms	566,362
All other reasons	28,931,638

Source: Based on data collected by the National Center for Health Statistics and published in **Advance Data,** Number 196, April 11, 1991. The National Center for Health Statistics (NCHS) conducts a variety of surveys from which health-relayed data are drawn. Additional data, including some unpublished data, on this topic is available from NCHS (Hyattsville, MD).

Definitions: "Adolescents" refers to individuals 11-20 years of age.

Methodology: These data were collected by NCHS by means of the 1985 National Ambulatory Medical Care Survey (NAMCS). Data are collected from a sample of patient records from a sample of the practices of non-federal office-based physicians. The 1985 survey involved over 70,000 patient records from over 4,000 physician practices. (The 1985 survey is the latest for which data are available. Another survey is currently underway and those results should be available soon.)

Qualifications: The National Ambulatory Medical Care Survey is faced with the same drawbacks that characterize all sample surveys. The size and representativeness of the sample, questionnaire design, and a variety of other factors may affect the quality of the data. Since the survey is based on a sample of medical records, the quality of the data also depends heavily on the completeness and accuracy of the medical records examined.

V-36. PHYSICIAN VISITS
CHILDREN WITH HEALTH INSURANCE AND CHILDREN WHO VISITED A DOCTOR FOR ROUTINE HEALTH CARE
1988

Age	Percent With Health Insurance	Percent with Routine Physician Visit
All Ages	83.1%	63.9%
Under 1 year	80.1	93.8
1 to 4 years	83.7	81.5
5 to 7 years	83.3	66.0
8 to 11 years	83.8	49.6
12 to 14 years	83.0	54.8
15 to 17 years	82.3	53.9

Source: Based on data collected by the National Center for Health Statistics and published in "Health Insurance and Medical Care." **Advance Data**, No. 188. Hyattsville, MD: National Center for Health Statistics, 1990. The National Center for Health Statistics (NCHS) conducts a variety of surveys from which health-relayed data are drawn. Additional data, including some unpublished data, on this topic is available from NCHS (Hyattsville, MD).

Definitions: "Health insurance" coverage includes all public and private plans including Medicaid. A routine physician visit includes checkups and immunizations when nothing is wrong. The time frame for the visit is during the previous three months.

Qualifications: The data come from the 1988 National Health Interview Survey and are subject to sampling and nonsampling error. In 1988, there were 47,487 households, or 122,310 persons, the sample. The overall response rate to the survey was 91 percent.

V-37. DENTAL VISITS
DENTAL VISIT RATE BY STATE
1990-1991

State	Visit Rate*
Alabama	673
Alaska	449
Arizona	656
Arkansas	429
California	299
Colorado	612
Connecticut	714
Delaware	408
District of Columbia	**
Florida	588
Georgia	649
Hawaii	**
Idaho	705
Illinois	640
Indiana	621
Iowa	652
Kansas	657
Kentucky	421
Louisiana	520
Maine	588
Maryland	637
Massachusetts	519
Michigan	697
Minnesota	708
Mississippi	526
Missouri	680
Montana	505
Nebraska	736
Nevada	488
New Hampshire	677
New Jersey	662
New Mexico	659
New York	643
North Carolina	739
North Dakota	635
Ohio	681
Oklahoma	609
Oregon	696
Pennsylvania	712
Rhode Island	609
South Carolina	628
South Dakota	562
Tennessee	566

(Continued on next page)

V-37. DENTAL VISITS
DENTAL VISIT RATE BY STATE
1990-1991 *(Continued from previous page)*

State	Visit Rate*
Texas	524
Utah	577
Vermont	**
Virginia	757
Washington	709
West Virginia	720
Wisconsin	698
Wyoming	559
National Average	641

 * Visit rate is based on the number of dentist visits per 1,000 persons
** Not enough cases for statistical validity.

Source: Based on data collected by the Mutual of Omaha Companies and published in their report, **Current Trends in Health Care Costs and Utilization** (1991 edition). Mutual of Omaha (Omaha) is a leading health insurer and, as such, generates a large amount of data on the health care of its employees.

Methodology: Utilizing a sample of records from enrollees in Mutual of Omaha group health plans, the company develops statistics related to the cost and utilization of health care for this population. Statistical tests are utilized to assure the validity of the data.

Definitions: A "dental visit" refers to a record which was coded for any type of dental visit. The time period refers to the year ending June 1991.

Qualifications: Since these data are based on a sample of records they are subject to sampling error. The accuracy of the data is also a function of the accuracy of the codes applied to the records. These statistics refer only to Mutual of Omaha enrollees in group health plans and may not be entirely representative of the total U.S. population.

V-38. DRUG PRESCRIPTIONS

FREQUENCY OF DRUG PRESCRIPTIONS BY SELECTED MEDICAL SPECIALTY
1989

Specialty	Percent of Visits Involving Drug Prescription
Cardiovascular disease	82.0%
Internal medicine	75.4
General/family practice	70.7
Pediatrics	67.1
Dermatology	65.6
Neurology	62.0
Otolarynogology	49.3
Psychiatry	48.9
Obstetrics/Gynecology	44.5
Urology	42.6
Ophthalmology	39.9
General surgery	33.2
Orthopedic surgery	27.4
All other specialties	56.4

Source: Based on data collected by the National Center for Health Statistics (NCHS) through its National Ambulatory Medical Care Survey and published by NCHS in Advance Data, Number 203, July 1, 1991. NCHS conducts a variety of surveys from which health-related data are drawn. Additional data, including some unpublished data, on this topic are available from NCHS (Hyattsville, MD).

Methodology: These data were collected by NCHS by means of the 1989 National Ambulatory Medical Care Survey (NAMCS). Date are collected from a sample of patient records from a sample of the practices of non-federal office-based physicians. The 1989 survey involved over 38,384 patient records from 2,535 physician practices.

Definitions: An "ambulatory patient" is an individual seeking personal health service who is not currently admitted to any health care institution on the premises. "Physicians" in this study includes doctors of osteopathy (D.O.s). A "visit" is a direct personal exchange between an ambulatory care patient and a physician or a staff member working under the physician's supervision, for the purpose of seeking care and rending personal health services. Visits in this study exclude telephone consultation.

Qualifications: The National Ambulatory Medical Care Survey is faced with the same drawbacks that characterize all sample surveys. The size and representativeness of the sample, questionnaire design, and a variety of other factors may affect the quality of the data. Since the survey is based on a sample of medical records, the quality of data also depends heavily on the completeness and accuracy of the medical records examined. Since these data are extrapolated from a sample to the entire population, they should be considered as estimates.

Interpretation: Approximately 60% of physician office visits involve the prescribing of at least one drug. The likelihood of receiving a prescription varies widely among the specialties on which data were collected, ranging from a high of 82% for cardiovascular disease specialists to a low of 27% for orthopedic surgeons.

V-39. DRUG PRESCRIPTIONS
MOST COMMON CATEGORIES OF DRUGS PRESCRIBED
DURING PHYSICIAN OFFICE VISITS
1989

Drug Category	Percent Distribution of Prescriptions
Antimicrobial	16.7%
Cardiovascular-renal	14.9
Pain relief	10.7
Respiratory tract	9.8
Hormones and related agents	8.7
Dermatologic	6.6
Psychopharmacologic	5.2
Metabolic and nutrient	4.3
Gastrointestinal	4.1
Ophthalmic	3.5
Immunologic	2.7
Neurologic	1.9
Hemotologic	1.4
Other and unclassified drugs	9.4

Source: Based on data collected by the National Center for Health Statistics (NCHS) through its National Ambulatory Medical Care Survey and published by NCHS in Advance Data, Number 203, July 1, 1991. NCHS conducts a variety of surveys from which health-related data are drawn. Additional data, including some unpublished data, on this topic are available from NCHS (Hyattsville, MD).

Methodology: These data were collected by NCHS by means of the 1989 National Ambulatory Medical Care Survey (NAMCS). Date are collected from a sample of patient records from a sample of the practices of non-federal office-based physicians. The 1989 survey involved over 38,384 patient records from 2,535 physician practices.

Definitions: "Physicians" in this study includes doctors of osteopathy (D.O.s). A "visit" is a direct personal exchange between an ambulatory care patient and a physician or a staff member working under the physician's supervision, for the purpose of seeking care and rending personal health services. Visits in this study exclude telephone consultation. "Drug category" refers to the therapeutic class listed in the National Drug Code Directory. A drug may be assigned to more than one of the categories. For these purposes, it was assigned to the category to which it is most frequently prescribed.

Qualifications: The National Ambulatory Medical Care Survey is faced with the same drawbacks that characterize all sample surveys. The size and representativeness of the sample, questionnaire design, and a variety of other factors may affect the quality of the data. Since the survey is based on a sample of medical records, the quality of data also depends heavily on the completeness and accuracy of the medical records examined. Since these data are extrapolated from a sample to the entire population, they should be considered as estimates.

Interpretation: Three categories of drugs account for over 40% of all prescriptions identified by the NACMS.

V-40. DRUG PRESCRIPTIONS
20 MOST FREQUENTLY PRESCRIBED GENERIC SUBSTANCES
DURING PHYSICIAN OFFICE VISITS
1989

Drug Category	Percent Distribution of Prescriptions
Amoxicillin	4.8%
Acetaminophen	3.3
Erythromycin	2.7
Hydrochlorothiazide	2.2
Codeine	1.7
Phenylephrine	1.6
Ibuprofen	1.6
Aspirin	1.5
Phenylpropanolamine	1.5
Trimethoprim	1.4
Naproxen	1.4
Sulfamethoxazole	1.4
Furosemide	1.4
Digoxin	1.3
Estradiol	1.2
Chlorpheniramine	1.2
Riboflavin	1.2
Vitamin A	1.2
Theophylline	1.2
Ergocalciferol	1.1

Source: Based on data collected by the National Center for Health Statistics (NCHS) through its National Ambulatory Medical Care Survey and published by NCHS in **Advance Data,** Number 203, July 1, 1991. NCHS conducts a variety of surveys from which health-related data are drawn. Additional data, including some unpublished data, on this topic are available from NCHS (Hyattsville, MD).

Methodology: These data were collected by NCHS by means of the 1989 National Ambulatory Medical Care Survey (NAMCS). Date are collected from a sample of patient records from a sample of the practices of non-federal office-based physicians. The 1989 survey involved over 38,384 patient records from 2,535 physician practices.

Definitions: "Physicians" in this study includes doctors of osteopathy (D.O.s). A "visit" is a direct personal exchange between an ambulatory care patient and a physician or a staff member working under the physician's supervision, for the purpose of seeking care and rending personal health services. Visits in this study exclude telephone consultation. Prescriptions involving a combination of two or more of the listed drugs were counted in all relevant categories.

Qualifications: The National Ambulatory Medical Care Survey is faced with the same drawbacks that characterize all sample surveys. The size and representativeness of the sample, questionnaire design, and a variety of other factors may affect the quality of the data. Since the survey is based on a sample of medical records, the quality of data also depends heavily on the completeness and accuracy of the medical records examined.

Interpretation: No drug accounted for as much as five percent of the prescriptions written. The top 20 drugs mentioned on the patient records account for only 35% of the total.

V-41. ORGAN TRANSPLANTS
UNITED STATES ACTIVITY ORGAN TRANSPLANT FOR SPECIFIC ORGANS
1982-1990

Year	Heart	Heart/Lung	Lung	Kidney	Liver	Pancreas
1990	2,085	50	265	9,560	2,656	549
1989	1,673	66	84	8,905	2,162	412
1988	1,650	74	32	8,986	1,705	245
1987	1,438	49	-	9,094	1,199	142
1986	1,368	45	-	8,976	924	149
1985	719	30	-	7,695	602	130
1984	346	17	-	6,968	308	87
1983	172	13	-	6,112	164	35
1982	103	8	-	5,358	82	38

Source: Based on data collected from the nation's transplant centers by the United Network for Organ Sharing (UNOS) and published in **UNOS Annual Reports.**

Methodology: Transplant centers nationwide submit data on transplant activity to UNOS. UNOS compiles and disseminates these data.

Interpretation: The number and type of transplants continues to grow. The advances in pharmaceutical agents to help prevent rejection of the transplanted organ contribute to growth in this area. The number of hospital centers offering transplant is approximately 200. The limiting factors are available organs and financial resources. A transplant center may not transplant all organs.

V-42. ORGAN TRANSPLANTS
PERSONS WAITING FOR ORGAN TRANSPLANTS
JULY, 1990

Organ	Persons Waiting
Kidney	17,445
Heart	1,686
Liver	996
Pancreas	387
Heart-Lung	258
Lung	186
Total	20,958

Source: Based on statistics compiled by the United Network for Organ Sharing (UNOS) and reprinted in the **Source Book of Health Insurance Data** published by the Health Insurance Association of America (HIAA), 1990.

Methodology: Transplant centers nationwide submit data on transplant activity to UNOS. UNOS compiles and disseminates these data.

Definitions: These figures include only those patients who are aware that they need an organ transplant, have been determined as eligible, and have been registered with UNOS.

Interpretation: The number of persons awaiting transplants continues to grow. The number of candidates for transplant far exceeds the number of organs available.

V-43. AIDS TESTING
AIDS TESTING EXPERIENCE BY SELECTED CHARACTERISTICS
1990

Characteristics	Percent With AIDS Test Since 1985
Age cohort:	
18-29	16 %
30-49	14
50 and over	4
Sex:	
Male	13
Female	10
Race:	
White	10
Black	15
Hispanic	16
Education:	
Less than 12 years	11
12 years	9
More than 12 years	13
Total	11

Source: Based on data collected through the National Health Interview Survey conducted by the National Center for Health Statistics (NCHS) and published in **Advance Data**, No. 204, July 1, 1991. **Advance Data** is a regular publication of NCHS that presents data from the organization's various surveys. Additional data, including some unpublished data, on this topic is available from NCHS (Hyattsville, MD).

Methodology: These data were collected by the NCHS by means of the October/November, 1990, National Health Interview Survey. These figures are based on data collected by means of personal interviews conducted annually of a national sample of between 36,000 and 46,000 households. This question was asked only of those 18 and over and excludes AIDS tests conducted at the time of a blood donation.

Definition: "White" and "black" includes only non-Hispanic whites and blacks.

Qualifications: The National Health Interview Survey is faced with the same drawbacks that characterize all sample surveys. The size and representativeness of the sample, questionnaire design, interviewer skills and a variety of other factors may affect the quality of the data. The NCHS is the major health data collection agency in the United States and has a reputation for rigorous research methodology. Since respondents were asked to report their health insurance coverage, some misreporting is possible.

Interpretation: The likelihood of being tested for AIDS varies based on the age, sex, race/ethnicity and educational level of the individual.

V-44. AIDS TESTING
MOST FREQUENT SETTINGS FOR AIDS TESTS
1990

Test Setting	Percent Tested There
Doctor's office/HMO	33%
Hospital emergency room/outpatient clinic	24
Military induction site	10
Public health department	7
Other clinic	6
Clinic run by employer	4
AIDS clinic or related facility	3
Family planning clinic	2
STD clinic	0
Drug treatment facility	0
All other	10

Source: Based on data collected through the National Health Interview Survey conducted by the National Center for Health Statistics (NCHS) and published in **Advance Data**, No. 204, July 1, 1991. **Advance Data** is a regular publication of NCHS that presents data from the organization's various surveys. Additional data, including some unpublished data, on this topic is available from NCHS (Hyattsville, MD).

Methodology: These data were collected by the NCHS by means of the October/November, 1990, National Health Interview Survey. These figures are based on data collected by means of personal interviews conducted annually of a national sample of between 36,000 and 46,000 households. This question was asked only of those 18 and over and excludes AIDS tests conducted at the time of a blood donation.

Definition: "White" and "black" includes only non-Hispanic whites and blacks.

Qualifications: The National Health Interview Survey is faced with the same drawbacks that characterize all sample surveys. The size and representativeness of the sample, questionnaire design, interviewer skills and a variety of other factors may affect the quality of the data. The NCHS is the major health data collection agency in the United States and has a reputation for rigorous research methodology. Since respondents were asked to report their health insurance coverage, some misreporting is possible.

Interpretation: The likelihood of being tested for AIDS varies based on the age, sex, race/ethnicity and educational level of the individual.

V-45. BLOOD DONATION
BLOOD DONATION HISTORY BY SELECTED CHARACTERISTICS
1990

Characteristic	Percent Ever Donating Blood
Age cohort:	
18-29	32%
30-49	43
50 and over	42
Sex:	
Male	51
Female	30
Race:	
White	43
Black	32
Hispanic	26
Education:	
Less than 12 years	28
12 years	35
More than 12 years	50
Total	40

Source: Based on data collected through the National Health Interview Survey conducted by the National Center for Health Statistics (NCHS) and published in **Advance Data**, No. 204, July 1, 1991. **Advance Data** is a regular publication of NCHS that presents data from the organization's various surveys. Additional data, including some unpublished data, on this topic is available from NCHS (Hyattsville, MD).

Methodology: These data were collected by the NCHS by means of the October/November, 1990, National Health Interview Survey. These figures are based on data collected by means of personal interviews conducted annually of a national sample of between 36,000 and 46,000 households. This question was asked only of those 18 and over.

Definition: "White" and "black" includes only non-Hispanic whites and blacks.

Qualifications: The National Health Interview Survey is faced with the same drawbacks that characterize all sample surveys. The size and representativeness of the sample, questionnaire design, interviewer skills and a variety of other factors may affect the quality of the data. The NCHS is the major health data collection agency in the United States and has a reputation for rigorous research methodology. Since respondents were asked to report their health insurance coverage, some misreporting is possible.

Interpretation: The likelihood of donating blood varies based on the age, sex, race/ethnicity and educational level of the individual.

DATA ON HEALTH CARE EXPENDITURES

The demand for health care expenditure data has grown incredibly faster over the past decade. Policy-setters, decision-makers, planners and researchers both inside and outside of health care have created an almost insatiable demand for data on all aspects of health care spending. In fact, concerns over what health services are being purchased, what is being charged for them and who is paying for them have become a national obsession. Without a doubt, the major changes that have occurred in health care over the past several years have been more a function of the financial dimension than of the clinical dimension. For the foreseeable future, it is going to be health care expenditure patterns that influence the course of the U.S. health care system and these patterns will continue to fuel the demand for data on health care spending.

The growth in the demand for health expenditure data has been triggered by pressure from a variety of powerful groups that have an interest in where health care dollars are coming from and where they are going. Demand for such data on the part of the Federal government has been a major driving force behind this surge in interest. The Federal government, primarily through such programs as Medicare, Medicaid, and the Veterans Administration, is a major purchaser of health care, accounting for over one-third of the nation's personal health care expenditures. The amounts spent by the Federal government on health care have been rapidly escalating and drastic measures have been instituted in an attempt to contain these costs. At the state level, while the dollar amounts are insignificant relative to Federal expenditures, health care is often one of the largest items in a state's budget. The growing significance of the Medicaid budget alone for a state's expenditures has brought the issue of health care spending to the forefront.

The Federal push to obtain health care data has been joined by insurance companies and other organizations (such as health maintenance organizations and managed care programs) that are involved in the financing of health care. Following in the footsteps of Federal agencies, these organizations are finding accurate, current and detailed financial data on health care utilization critical to their success. By the late 1980s, the influence of major employers and business coalitions was being felt as the entities that ultimately pay for most private health care began demanding accountability, and this further boosted the need for expenditure data.

Finally, health care consumers have begun to demand information on all aspects of health care including costs and charges. While the interests of the health care consumer are somewhat different from those of the entities listed above, their demands for health expenditure data seem to be insatiable. Formerly docile patients are now demanding detailed information on insurance costs, physicians' fees, and hospital charges.

Historically, it has been difficult to obtain data on health care expenditures. Although some entities, such as Federal agencies, have always provided some information as a matter of public record, this has offered only a superficial view of health care expenditures. Since most health care is actually provided by private hospitals, physicians and other organizations, little information on the costs and charges traditionally has been made public. Private health care providers were reluctant to furnish information on their finances and, even when required to do so by various regulations, typically made public as little information as possible. Thus, even when available from these sources in the past, the data were of limited accessibility, timeliness and detail. Even the data that were available tended to be fragmented, since no clearinghouse existed for the national compilation and dissemination of such data.

At the institutional level, hospitals and other health care organizations historically failed to maintain the types of financial data that would be common in other industries. There was no reason for hospitals to maintain that sort of information, since they were generally reimbursed on a cost-plus basis. This required only a general view of the costs involved in delivering services and cost accounting techniques were poorly developed. Organizations that one would think had a vested interest in tracking costs (e.g., insurance companies) typically accepted provider data at face value and, for all practical purposes, rubberstamped the charges that were passed on to them.

In response to the explosion in the demand for expenditure data, the sources of such data have multiplied. Government organizations, insurers, business coalitions, public interest groups and private data vendors have all gotten into the business of collecting, manipulating and disseminating health care expenditure data. The Federal government has perhaps become the biggest single processor of such data. The Health Care Financing Administration (HCFA), which manages the Medicare program, and other Federal agencies now maintain huge databases of patients who receive Federally-subsidized health services and the providers who serve them. Statistical arms of the Federal government, like the National Center for Health Statistics (NCHS), collect information on personal health care expenditures. Insurance companies and other third-party payers are also now demanding accountability from the providers with which they deal and they require detailed financial information. As managed care organizations have proliferated, these entities have demanded extensive financial data in order to intelligently negotiate with the providers of care.

For these and other reasons the providers themselves are now forced to develop better accounting systems. As reimbursement has become squeezed for hospitals, they have had to develop a better understanding of the costs involved in their operations. For them to objectively negotiate with third-party payers they require detailed information on their own costs and charges. Many hospitals, nursing homes, and other organizations have developed statewide databanks for collecting and analyzing financial data on their own institutions. Professional associations (such as the Medical Group Management Association for physician groups) collect expenditure data that they disseminate back to their members. Some not-for-profit providers have had their tax-exempt status questioned and this has forced many of them to develop a better understanding of their costs and charges. Major employers and business coalitions have not only begun demanding more data from the providers they are tied to, but have begun to collect expenditure data on their covered employees.

As a result of this activity, the industry is now flooded with financial data. The two major sources of expenditure data are the Federal government and private data vendors. HCFA, NCHS and other agencies have made an effort to make expenditure data available to the public inexpensively and in easily-accessible forms. Private vendors have gotten into the health expenditure data business by assisting in the establishment of state databanks or by obtaining Federal or state data, repackaging it and selling if back to the public. Various associations of providers now also make this information available. Public interest groups have also begun to compile information and disseminate it to the nation's consumers.

Expenditures allocated for medical and health research are also reported in this section. The data on medical and health research include information on who is conducting research and who is paying for it. The major sources of these data are the Federal government and various private organizations.

Despite this recent outpouring of data, there are some limitations to its usefulness. Much of these data are at the national level, although health care organizations are often local operations that require local data which is much more difficult to obtain. There is still no central clearinghouse for health expenditure data and many sources of data are obscure. Much expenditure data is still considered proprietary and may not, therefore, be available to the public. Even when the provision of financial data is required by state agencies (e.g., state hospital reports) or is voluntarily offered, the data must be interpreted with caution. The industry is a long way from establishing uniform accounting and reporting procedures; comparing financial statistics for two hospitals, for example, may be like comparing apples and oranges. Because of the complexity of the health care industry, interpretation of any financial data is problematic.

VI-1. EXPENDITURE CATEGORIES.
NATIONAL HEALTH EXPENDITURES BY CATEGORY
(In $ Millions)
1965-1990

Type of Expenditure	1965	1975	1985	1990
Total health expenditures	$41.6	$132.9	$420.1	$666.3
Health services and supplies	38.2	124.7	404.7	643.4
Personal health care	35.6	116.6	367.2	585.3
Hospital care	14.0	52.4	167.9	256.0
Physician services	8.2	23.3	74.0	125.7
Dental services	2.8	8.2	23.3	34.0
Other professional services	0.9	3.5	16.6	31.6
Home health care	0.1	0.4	3.8	6.9
Drugs and other medical nondurables	5.9	13.0	32.3	54.6
Vision products & other medical nondurables	1.2	3.1	8.4	12.1
Nursing home care	1.7	9.9	34.1	53.1
Other personal health care	0.8	2.7	6.8	11.3
Program administration & net cost of private health insurance	1.9	5.1	25.2	38.7
Government public health activities	0.6	3.0	12.3	19.3
Research and construction	3.5	8.3	15.4	22.8
Research	1.5	3.3	7.8	12.4
Construction	1.9	5.0	7.6	10.4

Note: Numbers may not add up to totals because of rounding.

Source: Based on data collected and published by the Health Care Financing Administration within the U.S. Department of Health and Human Services. The Health Care Financing Administration (HCFA) administers the Medicare program and is a major federal source of health data.

Methodology: Compiled by HCFA from various sources.

Qualifications: Research and development expenditures of drug companies and other manufacturers and providers of medical equipment and supplies are excluded from research expenditures, but they are included in the expenditure class in which the product falls.

VI-2. EXPENDITURE TRENDS
NATIONAL HEALTH EXPENDITURES
1970-1990

	Total Expenditures (in $ billion)	Per Capita Expenditures	Percent of GNP
1990	$666.2	$2,566	12.4%
1985	419.0	1,696	10.4
1980	248.1	1,055	9.1
1975	132.7	591	8.3
1970	75.0	349	7.4

Source: Based on data collected by the Health Care Financing Administration and published in "National Health Expenditures, 1990," **Health Care Financing Review** 13 (Winter), 1991. The Health Care Financing Administration (HCFA) within the U.S. Department of Health and Human Services administers the Medicare program and is a major federal source of health data.

Methodology: Compiled by HCFA from various sources

Definitions: "Health expenditures" include money spent on health services and supplies (e.g., insurance premiums, Medicare, and public health activities), medical research, and medical facilities construction. "Total expenditures" include medical research and medical facilities construction. "GNP," or Gross National Product, represents the value of all goods and services produced for sale by the nation plus the estimated value of certain imputed outputs. Per capita expenditures are calculated by taking total national health expenditures and dividing by the total population.

Qualifications: The data appearing in this table are estimates and are therefore subject to error. The data for the federal component of health care expenditures are taken from administrative sources. Non-federal sources are varied, including data from the American Hospital Association, the U.S. Bureau of the Census, and the National Nursing Home study.

VI-3. EXPENDITURE TRENDS
NATIONAL HEALTH EXPENDITURES BY TYPE OF EXPENDITURE
(In $ Billions)
1970-1990

	1970	1975	1980	1985	1990
Total Expenditures	$74.4	$132.9	$249.1	$420.1	$666.2
Private Expenditures	46.7	77.8	143.9	245.0	383.6
Public Expenditures	27.7	55.1	105.2	175.1	282.6
Federal	17.7	36.4	72.0	123.6	195.4
State and Local	9.9	18.7	33.2	51.5	87.3
Percent Change from Previous Year	12.3	12.3	13.4	11.0	10.5

Source: Based on data collected by the Health Care Financing Administration and published in **Health Care Financing Review**. The Health Care Financing Administration (HCFA) administers the Medicare program and is a major federal source of health data.

Methodology: Compiled by HCFA from various sources

Definitions: "Health expenditures" include money spent on health services and supplies (e.g., insurance premiums, Medicare, and public health activities), medical research, and medical facilities construction. "Total expenditures" include medical research and medical facilities construction. "GNP," or Gross National Product, represents the value of all goods and services produced for sale by the nation plus the estimated value of certain imputed outputs (i.e., goods and services that are neither bought nor sold).

Qualifications: The data appearing in the table are estimates and are therefore subject to error. The data for the federal component of health care expenditures are taken from administrative sources. Non-federal sources are varied, including data from the American Hospital Association, the U.S. Bureau of the Census, and the National Nursing Home Study.

VI-4. CONSUMER PRICE INDEX
CONSUMER PRICE INDEX FOR SELECTED ITEMS
1950-1990

Category	1950	1960	1970	1980	1985	1990
Medical Care	15.1	22.3	34.0	74.9	113.5	162.8
Energy	11.3	13.8	17.0	86.1	95.9	102.1
Food	25.4	30.0	39.2	86.8	105.6	132.4
Housing	NA	NA	36.4	81.1	107.7	128.5
All Items	24.1	29.6	38.8	82.4	107.6	130.7

NA = Not Available

Source: Data collected by the U.S. Department of Labor, Bureau of Labor Statistics and published in **Health, United States, 1991.** The Bureau of Labor Statistics is a major federal source of consumer expenditure data.

Methodology: The "Consumer Price Index" (CPI) measures the purchasing power of consumers' dollars by comparing what a sample of a "market basket" of goods and services costs today with what it cost at an earlier date. The base reference year is 1982-84, which means that the price of a specific item in 1982-84 is entered as 100, and changes are indicated in relation to that figure.

Definitions: "Energy" refers to expenditures for household fuel.

Interpretation: The price index for medical care has increased much faster than the index for other categories of consumption.

VI-5. CONSUMER PRICE INDEX
TRENDS IN CONSUMER PRICE INDICES
1960/61 - 1989/1990

Item	Annual Percentage Change in the Annual Average CPI				
	1960-1961	1970-1971	1980-1981	1985-1986	1989-1990
All Items	1.0%	4.4%	10.3%	1.9%	5.4%
Excluding Medical care	1.0	4.1	10.4	1.5	4.7
Medical care	2.7	6.2	10.7	7.5	9.0
Food	1.3	3.1	7.8	3.2	5.8
Apparel and upkeep	0.9	3.2	4.8	0.9	4.6
Housing	NA	4.4	11.5	3.0	4.5
Transportation	1.0	5.3	12.2	-3.9	5.6
Entertainment	NA	5.3	7.8	3.4	4.7
Other goods/services	NA	4.9	9.8	6	7.7

NA = Not Available

Source: Data collected by the U.S. Department of Labor, Bureau of Labor Statistics and published in **Statistical Abstract of the U.S., 1991.** The Bureau of Labor Statistics is a major federal source of consumer expenditure data.

Methodology: The "Consumer Price Index" (CPI) measures the purchasing power of consumers' dollars by comparing what a sample of a "market basket" of goods and services costs today with what it cost at an earlier date. The base reference year is 1982-84, which means that the price of a specific item in 1982-84 is entered as 100, and changes are indicated in relation to that figure.

Definitions: "Energy" refers to expenditures for household fuel.

Qualifications: With the release of the January 1988 CPI, the CPI reference base was changed from 1967 = 100 to 1982-84 = 100. For this reason, indices differ from those previously published.

Interpretation: The price index for medical care has increased much faster than the index for other categories of consumption.

VI-6. CONSUMER PRICE INDEX
CONSUMER PRICE INDEX FOR MEDICAL EXPENDITURES
1950-1990

Year	Total Medical Care	Prescription Drugs	Physicians' Fees	Dentists' Fees	Hospital Room Charges
1990	162.7	181.7	160.8	155.8	175.4
1985	113.5	120.1	113.3	114.2	115.4
1980	74.9	72.5	76.5	78.9	68.0
1975	47.5	51.2	48.1	53.2	38.3
1970	34.0	47.4	34.5	39.2	23.6
1965	25.2	47.8	25.1	30.3	12.3
1960	22.3	54.9	21.9	27.0	9.3
1955	18.2	47.6	18.6	24.0	6.9
1950	15.1	43.4	15.7	21.0	4.9

Source: Data collected by the U.S. Department of Labor, Bureau of Labor Statistics and published in **Health, United States, 1991.** The Bureau of Labor Statistics is a major federal source of consumer expenditure data.

Methodology: The "Consumer Price Index" (CPI) measures the purchasing power of consumers' dollars by comparing what a sample of a "market basket" of goods and services costs today with what it cost at an earlier date. The base reference year is 1982-84, which means that the price of a specific item in 1982-84 is entered as 100, and changes are indicated in relation to that figure.

Definitions: The "hospital room charge" component was changed in January 1978 from semiprivate rooms to include all types of accommodations, including private and intensive care rooms.

Qualifications: With the release of the January 1988 CPI, the CPI reference base was changed from 1967 = 100 to 1982-84 = 100. For this reason, indices differ from those previously published.

Interpretation: The indices for physicians' fees and hospital room charges increased faster than other components of the medical care index.

VI-7. MEDICAL CPI
TRENDS IN MEDICAL CARE CONSUMER PRICE INDEX (CPI)
1981-1991

Year	Overall CPI	Medical Care: All Items	Annual Percent Change Prescription Drugs	Physician Services	Hospital Rooms	Dental Services
1991	4.2%	8.7%	9.9%	6.0%	9.4%	7.5%
1990	5.4	9.1	9.9	7.2	10.9	6.8
1989	4.8	7.7	8.7	7.4	10.3	6.3
1988	4.1	6.5	8.0	7.2	9.3	6.8
1987	3.6	6.6	8.0	7.3	7.2	6.8
1986	1.9	7.5	8.6	7.2	6.0	5.6
1985	3.6	6.3	9.5	5.9	5.9	6.2
1984	4.3	6.2	9.6	6.9	8.3	8.1
1983	3.2	8.8	11.0	7.8	11.3	6.8
1982	6.2	11.6	11.6	9.4	15.7	7.6
1981	10.3	10.7	11.4	11.0	14.9	9.6

Source: Data collected by the U.S. Department of Labor, Bureau of Labor Statistics and published in **Health Care Financing Review.** The Bureau of Labor Statistics is a major federal source of consumer expenditure data.

Methodology: The "Consumer Price Index" (CPI) measures the purchasing power of consumers' dollars by comparing what a sample of a "market basket" of goods and services costs today with what it cost at an earlier date. The base reference year is 1982-84, which means that the price of a specific item in 1982-84 is entered as 100, and changes are indicated in relation to that figure.

Qualifications: Figures for 1990 and 1991 are estimates.

Interpretation: The price index for medical care has increased much faster than the index for other categories of consumption.

VI-8. CONSUMER PRICE INDEX
PERSONAL CONSUMPTION BY TYPE OF EXPENDITURE
1950-1989

	1950	1960	1970	1980	1989
Total personal consumption (in $ billions)	$192.1	$330.7	$640.0	$1,732.6	$3,450.1
Category	**Percent Distribution**				
Food, beverages, and tobacco	34.4%	30.4%	27.0%	24.0%	18.5%
Housing and household operations	26.4	28.7	27.9	28.5	27.2
Transportation	13.2	13.0	12.7	13.8	12.3
Clothing, accessories, and jewelry	12.3	9.9	9.0	7.8	7.4
Recreation	5.8	5.6	5.7	6.6	7.7
Medical care	4.8	6.4	8.8	10.8	14.0
Other	3.0	6.2	8.0	8.5	12.9

Note: Percentages may not add to 100 due to rounding.

Source: Based on data collected by the U.S. Department of Commerce, Bureau of Economic Analysis and published in **Survey of Current Business.**

Methodology: The "Consumer Price Index (CPI's) measures the purchasing power of consumers' dollars by comparing what a sample of a "market basket" of goods and services costs today with what it cost at an earlier date. The base reference year is 1982-84, which means that the price of a specific item in 1982-84 is entered as 100, and changes are indicated in relation to that figure.

Qualifications: With the release of the January 1988 CPI, the CPI reference base was changed from 1967 = 100 to 1982-84 = 100. For this reason, indices differ from those previously published.

Interpretation: Since 1950 medical care expenditures have accounted for a growing share of personal expenditures. Food and clothing costs, on the other hand, have decreased in terms of their significance.

VI-9. PERSONAL HEALTH CARE
TOTAL EXPENDITURES ON PERSONAL HEALTH CARE BY CATEGORY
(In $ Billions)
1980-1990

Year	Total Personal Health Care	Hospital Care	Physicians' Services	Dentists' Services	Other Prof'l. Services	Home Health Care	Drugs & Medical Nondurables	Vision & Other Durables	Nursing Home Care	Other Health Services
1990	$578.4	$258.5	$126.5	$34.4	$28.2	$5.1	$49.4	$13.4	$51.4	$11.5
1989	524.5	233.6	114.8	31.7	25.0	4.7	45.3	12.1	47.0	10.3
1988	478.3	211.8	105.1	29.4	22.5	4.4	41.9	10.8	43.1	9.3
1987	434.7	193.7	93.0	27.1	20.2	4.2	38.6	9.8	39.7	8.4
1986	397.7	179.3	82.1	24.7	18.3	4.0	35.6	9.5	36.7	7.6
1985	367.2	167.9	74.0	23.3	16.6	3.8	32.3	8.4	34.1	6.8
1980	218.3	102.4	41.9	14.4	8.7	1.3	20.1	5.0	20.0	4.6

Sources: Based on the data compiled by the Health Care Financing Administration and the Metropolitan Life Insurance Company. Published in Metropolitan Life's **Statistical Bulletin** (January-March, 1991). HCFA, as the organization responsible for the administration of the Medicare program, is the primary source of Medicare statistics. The **Statistical Bulletin** published by Metropolitan Life Insurance Company reprints data from a variety of sources, including statistics on the experiences of the large Metropolitan Life insured population, data not available elsewhere.

Methodology: Extrapolated to the total population based on the experience of Metropolitan Life Insurance enrollees.

Qualifications: The figures for 1989 and 1990 are estimates prepared by Metropolitan Life and not actual data.

Interpretation: Hospital care accounts for the largest share of personal health care expenditures, followed by physician's services. Although the relative distribution of expenditures among the categories did not change much during the 1980s "nontraditional" health services grew disproportionately.

VI-10. PERSONAL HEALTH CARE
PERSONAL HEALTH CARE EXPENDITURES BY CATEGORY
(In $ Billions)
1990

	Expenditures	
	Amount	Percent
Total	$578.4	100.0%
Hospital care	258.5	44.7
Physician's services	126.5	21.9
Dentists' services	34.4	5.9
Other professional services	28.2	4.9
Home health care	5.1	0.9
Drugs and medical nondurables	49.4	8.5
Vision and other durables	13.4	2.3
Nursing home care	51.4	8.9
Other health services	11.5	2.0

Source: Based on estimates prepared by the Metropolitan Life Insurance Company. Published in Metropolitan Life's **Statistical Bulletin** (Jan.-March 1991). The Statistical Bulletin published by Metropolitan Life Insurance Company reprints data from a variety of sources, including statistics on the experiences of the large Metropolitan Life insured population, data not available elsewhere.

Methodology: Extrapolated to the total population based on the experience of Metropolitan Life Insurance enrollees.

Interpretation: Hospital care and physicians' services accounted for nearly two-thirds of the personal health care expenditures in 1990.

VI-11. HOSPITAL CARE
EXPENDITURES ON HOSPITAL CARE
1960-1990

Year	Expenditures (in $ billions)
1990	$232.6
1985	167.9
1980	102.4
1975	52.4
1970	27.9
1965	14.0
1960	9.3

Source: Based on data collected by the Health Care Financing Administration and published in **Health, United States, 1991.** The Health Care Financing Administration (HCFA) within the U.S. Department of Health and Human Services administers the medicare program and is a major source of health data.

Methodology: Estimates of expenditures were made by the federal Office of National Cost Estimates and HCFA and compiled by HCFA.

Interpretation: Expenditures for hospital care increased much more rapidly than for most other categories of consumer expenditures between 1960 and 1988.

VI-12. PER CAPITA EXPENDITURES
PER CAPITA HEALTH EXPENDITURES
1935-1990

Year	Per Capita Expenditure
1990	$2,566
1985	1,700
1980	1,059
1975	592
1970	346
1965	204
1960	143
1955	101
1950	80
1945	29
1935	23

Source: Based on data collected by the Health Care Financing Administration and published in **Health, United States, 1991.** The Health Care Financing Administration (HCFA) within the U.S. Department of Health and Human Services administers the medicare program and is a major source of health data.

Methodology: Estimates of expenditures were made by the federal Office of National Cost Estimates and HCFA and compiled by HCFA. Per capita expenditures are calculated by taking total national health expenditures and dividing by the total population.

Qualifications: The Bureau of Economic Analysis (Department of Commerce) has made periodic revisions of both the level of historic expenditures and the population counts for years in question.

VI-13. INTERNATIONAL COMPARISONS
PER CAPITA HEALTH CARE EXPENDITURES FOR
SELECTED INDUSTRIALIZED COUNTRIES
1990

Country	Per Capita Expenditures
Australia	$1,151
Canada	1,795
France	1,379
Italy	1,138
Japan	1,145
Netherlands	1,182
Sweden	1,421
United Kingdom	932
United States	2,566
West Germany	1,287

Source: Based on data collected through various surveys and reported by the Organization for Economic Cooperation and Development (OECD) and published in the **Health Care Financing Review.**

Methodology: Data collected by means of separate international opinion studies.

Definitions: "Per capita expenditures" are calculated by dividing the total amount of health care expenditures of all types by the total relevant population. Expenditures are in U.S. dollars and are estimates for 1990.

Interpretation: Per capita health care expenditures in the U.S. exceed those of other industrialized nations, most of which have some form of socialized medicine.

VI-14. FUNDING SOURCES
SOURCES OF FUNDS FOR PERSONAL HEALTH EXPENDITURES
1950-1990

Source	1950	1960	1970	1980	1990
Out-of-pocket payments by consumers	65.5%	55.9%	39.5%	26.8%	23.3%
Insurance benefits	9.1	21.0	23.4	29.9	31.84
Public programs	22.4	21.4	34.6	39.9	41.86
Other	2.9	1.7	2.6	3.5	3.1

Source: Based on data collected by the Health Care Financing Administration within the U.S. Department of Health and Human Services. The Health Care Financing Administration (HCFA) administers the Medicare program and is a major federal source of health data.

Methodology: Compiled by HCFA from various sources.

Definitions: "Public" includes Federal, state, and local government funds.

Qualifications: Data for 1960, 1970, and 1980 differ from previously published data for those years because of revisions made by HCFA. Data for 1950 have not been revised.

Interpretation: The share of health care expenditures that patients pay "out of pocket" has declined dramatically since 1950. Insurers and public programs (e.g., Medicare and Medicaid) has significantly increased their shares of the expenditures.

VI-15. SOURCE OF PAYMENT
DISTRIBUTION OF SOURCES OF PAYMENT FOR HOSPITAL,
NURSING HOME, AND PHYSICIANS
1988

Source	Hospital Care	Nursing Home Care	Physician Services
Private health insurance	35.4%	1.1%	47.6%
Medicare	27.5	1.9	23.6
Medicaid	9.5	44.4	3.6
Other government	17.4	2.3	6.2
Out-of-pocket	5.3	48.4	18.9
Other private funds	4.9	1.9	0.0

Source: Based on data collected by the Health Care Financing Administration and published in **Health, United States, 1990.** The Health Care Financing Administration (HCFA) administers the Medicare program and is a major federal source of health data.

Methodology: Estimates of expenditures were made by the Federal Office of National Cost Estimates and HCFA and compiled by HCFA.

Definitions: "Other government" refers to any other outlays by any level of government (e.g., Veterans Administration expenditures or local government subsidies of hospitals). "Out-of-pocket" refers to payments made directly by patients for their care.

Interpretation: The sources of payment for these three categories of services vary widely, reflecting the lack of uniformity in the financing of health care.

VI-16. DISTRIBUTION OF CHARGES
DISTRIBUTION OF MEDICAL CHARGES BY CATEGORY
1990-1991

Category	Percent of Charges
Hospital Room and Board	12.7%
Hospital Ancillary	26.5
Hospital Outpatient	13.4
Physician	11.2
Inpatient Surgery	7.3
Outpatient Surgery	3.3
Office Surgery	2.5
Anesthesia	2.2
X-ray and Lab	8.5
Drugs	7.1
Psychotherapy	2.1
Other	3.2

Source: Based on data collected by the Mutual of Omaha Companies and published in their report, **Current Trends in Health Care Costs and Utilization** (1991 edition). Mutual of Omaha (Omaha) is a leading health insurer and, as such, generates a large amount of data on the health care of its employees.

Methodology: Utilizing a sample of records from enrollees in Mutual of Omaha group health plans, the company develops statistics related to the cost and utilization of health care for this population. Statistical tests are utilized to assure the validity of the data.

Definitions: The time period refers to the one-year period ending in June of 1991.

Qualifications: Since these data are based on a sample of records they are subject to sampling error. The accuracy of the data is also a function of the accuracy of the codes applied to the records. These statistics refer only to Mutual of Omaha enrollees in group health plans and may not be entirely representative of the total U.S. population.

VI-17. MEDICARE
MEDICARE PART B EXPENDITURES BY PROVIDER TYPE
1970-1990

Type of Provider	1970	1975	1985	1990
	Expenditures (in millions)			
Total	$1,975	$4,273	$22,947	$43,987
Physicians and suppliers	1,801	3,454	17,869	29,628
Outpatient facilities	117	652	4,304	8,475
All other	57	167	774	5,884
	Percent distribution			
Total	100.0%	100.0%	100.0%	100.0%
Physicians and suppliers	80.9	72.1	72.5	67.4
Outpatient facilities	5.2	13.8	18.0	19.3
All other	13.9	14.1	9.5	13.3

Source: Based on data collected by the Health Care Financing Administration within the U.S. Department of Health and Human Services. The Health Care Financing Administration (HCFA) administers the Medicare program and is a major federal source of health data.

Methodology: Compiled by HCFA from Medicare records.

Definitions: "Medicare" is the federally-sponsored health insurance program that covers the elderly and disabled. "Part B" refers to the Medicare program component that pays for physician, suppliers, and outpatient services. "Outpatient facilities" includes outpatient hospital facilities, end stage renal disease freestanding facilities, rural health clinics, and outpatient rehabilitation facilities. "All other" includes health maintenance organizations, competitive medical plans and other prepaid health plans, and home health agency services.

Qualifications: 1990 figures are preliminary.

Interpretation: The Medicare costs for physician and outpatient services have risen each year since the program's inception.

VI-18. MEDICARE
MEDICARE EXPENDITURES FOR PHYSICIAN SERVICES
1970-1988

Year	Amount (in billions)	Percent of Medicare Expenditures
1988	$24.2	26.7%
1987	21.6	26.1
1986	18.8	24.4
1985	16.6	23.7
1984	14.7	22.8
1983	13.4	22.8
1982	11.4	21.8
1981	9.7	21.7
1980	7.9	21.7
1975	3.4	20.9
1970	1.6	21.3

Source: Based on data collected by the Health Care Financing Administration within the U.S. Department of Health and Human Services. The Health Care Financing Administration (HCFA) administers the Medicare program and is a major federal source of health data.

Methodology: Estimates of expenditures were made by the Federal Office of National Cost Estimates and HCFA and compiled by HCFA.

Definitions: "Medicare" is the federally-sponsored health insurance program that covers the elderly and disabled.

Interpretation: The Gross National Product (GNP) grew consistently between 1970 and 1988 but expenditures for health care, and specifically Medicare expenditures for physician services, increased much faster. Physician expenditures under Medicare have grown at nearly twice the rate of total health care expenditures. The GNP grew in the period 1970-1988 to average a doubling each eight years. The Medicare expenditures for physician services doubled every four years during the same period.

VI-19. MEDICARE
MOST FREQUENTLY OCCURRING MEDICARE CHARGES
1988

Type of Charge	Medicare Patients with Charges	Median Total Charge
Laboratory	30.6%	$35
Radiology	14.5	113
Emergency room	13.7	150
Clinic	11.6	57
Surgery	5.9	796
Other	3.7	125
Therapy	3.4	201
Medical	2.8	110
Radiology & laboratory	2.4	188
Dialysis	1.4	1,134
Supplies	1.3	38

Source: Based on an analysis by the Prospective Payment Assessment Commission (ProPAC). ProPAC monitors the operation of the Medicare prospective payment system and makes recommendations for modifications to the Health Care Financing Administration.

Methodology: Data were compiled by ProPAC from the 1988 Medicare file.

Definitions: "Medicare" is the federally-sponsored health insurance program that covers the elderly and disabled. "Emergency room" refers to direct ER charges only and does not include other departments that may provide services to the ER.

VI-20. MEDICARE
MOST FREQUENTLY OCCURRING DIAGNOSIS CODES ON OUTPATIENT MEDICARE BILLS
1988

Diagnosis	Percent of Bills	Median Total Charge
Diabetes, uncomplicated adult	4.1%	$ 34
Hypertension, NOS	4.1	65
Chronic renal failure	2.8	1,064
Urinary tract infection, NOS	2.1	60
Abdominal pain	1.9	169
Congestive heart failure	1.8	80
Coronary atherosclerosis	1.7	72
Chest pain	1.6	154
Anemia, NOS	1.6	83

Source: Based on an analysis by the Prospective Payment Assessment Commission (ProPAC). ProPAC monitors the operation of the Medicare prospective payment system and makes recommendations for modifications to the Health Care Financing Administration.

Methodology: Data were compiled by ProPAC from the 1988 Medicare file.

Definitions: "Medicare" is the federally-sponsored health insurance program that covers the elderly and the disabled. "NOS" = not otherwise specified.

VI-21. HOSPITAL CHARGES
CHARGE FOR THE 25 MOST FREQUENT DRGs FOR MEDICARE PATIENTS
1989

DRG Name	Average Charge per Discharge
Heart failure and shock	$6,373
Angina pectoris	3,854
Simple pneumonia and pleurisy with complications, age greater than 17	7,194
Specific cerebrovascular disorders except transient ischemic attack	8,167
Psychoses	9,279
Esophagitis, gastroenteritis and miscellaneous digestive disorders with complications, age greater than 17	4,691
Bronchitis and asthma with complications, age greater than 17	5,757
Major joint and limb reattachment procedures	14,857
Nutritional and miscellaneous metabolic disorders with complications, age greater than 17	6,058
Cardia arrhythmia and conduction disorders with complications	5,323
Circulatory disorders with acute myocardial infarction and cardiovascular complications; patient discharged alive	9,850
Kidney and urinary tract infections with complications, age greater than 17	6,419
Gastrointestinal hemorrhage with complications	6,036
Chemotherapy	3,440
Transient ischemic attack and precerebral occlusions	4,022
Major small and large bowel procedures with complications	21,213
Medical back problems	4,228
Circulatory disorders with acute myocardial infarction without cardiovascular complications; patient discharged alive	6,760
Vascular procedures except major reconstruction without vascular pump	12,639
Septicemia, age greater than 17	9,771
Respiratory infections and inflammations with complications, age greater than 17	11,376
Transurethral prostatectomy with complications	5,822
Chest pain	3,186
Hip and femur procedures except minor joint, with complications, age greater than 17	12,955
Circulatory disorders except acute myocardial infarctions with cardiac catheterization without complex diagnoses	4,458

Source: Based on data collected by the Health Care Financing Agency and published in **HealthWeek** (April 22, 1991). The Health Care Financing Administration (HCFA) administers the Medicare program and is a major federal source of health data. (**HealthWeek** ceased publication at the end of 1991.)

Methodology: Compiled by HCFA from Medicare records.

Definitions: "Medicare" is the federally-sponsored health insurance program that covers the elderly and disabled.

Interpretation: Of the most frequent discharge diagnosis for Medicare patients, major digestive system, cardiology and orthopedic conditions accrue the most costs.

VI-22. HOSPITAL CHARGES
AVERAGE CHARGE FOR SELECTED HOSPITAL SERVICES
FOR THE 25 MOST FREQUENT DIAGNOSTIC RELATED GROUPS
FOR MEDICARE PATIENTS
1989

DRG Name	Average Charge Per Service			
	Laboratory	Radiology	Supplies	Pharmacy
Heart failure and shock	$1,307	$352	$343	$715
Angina pectoris	974	235	186	301
Simple pneumonia and pleurisy with complications, age greater than 17	1,058	356	405	1,518
Specific cerebrovascular disorders except transient ischemic attack	1,149	786	502	901
Psychoses	443	166	61	384
Esophagitis, gastroenteritis and miscellaneous digestive disorders with complications, age greater than 17	870	424	267	803
Bronchitis and asthma with complications, age greater than 17	836	218	272	1,091
Major joint and limb reattachment procedures	1,035	345	4,365	1,228
Nutritional and miscellaneous metabolic disorders with complications, age greater than 17	1,071	376	418	944
Cardia arrhythmia and conduction disorders with complications	1,285	312	356	469
Circulatory disorders with acute myocardial infarction and cardiovascular complications	2,177	469	587	1,169
Kidney and urinary tract infections with complications, age greater than 17	1,036	347	468	1,397
Gastrointestinal hemorrhage with complications	1,233	338	392	888
Chemotherapy	316	227	195	1,484
Transient ischemic attack and precerebral occlusions	823	684	188	283
Major small and large bowel procedures with complications	2,593	861	2,366	4,612
Medical back problems	435	671	209	361
Circulatory disorders with acute myocardial infarction without cardiovascular complications	1,683	321	363	792
Vascular procedures except major reconstruction without vascular pump	4,252	853	1,697	1,150
Septicemia, age greater than 17	1,604	508	734	2,337
Respiratory infections and inflammations with complications, age greater than 17	1,536	478	857	2,629

(Continued on next page)

VI-22. HOSPITAL CHARGES
AVERAGE CHARGE FOR SELECTED HOSPITAL SERVICES
FOR THE 25 MOST FREQUENT DIAGNOSTIC RELATED GROUPS
FOR MEDICARE PATIENTS
1989 *(Continued from previous page)*

DRG Name	Average Charge Per Service			
	Laboratory	Radiology	Supplies	Pharmacy
Transurethral prostatectomy with complications	$723	$247	$634	$785
Chest pain	870	296	144	211
Hip and femur procedures except minor joint, with complications, age greater than 17	1,356	702	1,703	1,449
Circulatory disorders except acute myocardial infarctions with cardiac catheterization without complex diagnoses	2,050	390	363	278

Source: Based on data collected by the Health Care Financing Agency and published in **HealthWeek** (April 22, 1991). The Health Care Financing Administration (HCFA) administers the Medicare program and is a major federal source of health data. (**HealthWeek** ceased publication at the end of 1991.)

Methodology: Compiled by HCFA from Medicare records.

Definitions: "Medicare" is the federally-sponsored health insurance program that covers the elderly and disabled.

Interpretation: Of the four ancillary services analyzed, laboratory tests accounted for the most costs for the majority of procedures.

VI-23. INPATIENT CHARGES
AVERAGE CHARGES PER ADMISSION FOR INPATIENT SERVICES
BY STATE
1990-1991

State	Average Inpatient Charges Per Admission
Alabama	$6,786
Alaska	6,510
Arizona	8,654
Arkansas	6,137
California	9,814
Colorado	*
Connecticut	6,607
Delaware	*
District of Columbia	4,989
Florida	*
Georgia	8,228
Hawaii	5,982
Idaho	*
Illinois	5,089
Indiana	7,423
Iowa	7,054
Kansas	5,745
Kentucky	7,428
Louisiana	9,499
Maine	5,335
Maryland	*
Massachusetts	4,970
Michigan	8,560
Minnesota	6,457
Mississippi	6,722
Missouri	3,716
Montana	6,950
Nebraska	5,539
Nevada	6,485
New Hampshire	9,496
New Jersey	6,293
New Mexico	6,082
New York	6,554
North Carolina	7,443
North Dakota	5,249
Ohio	6,424
Oklahoma	5,195
Oregon	5,730
Pennsylvania	7,620
Rhode Island	*
South Carolina	5,505

(Continued on next page)

VI-23. INPATIENT CHARGES
AVERAGE CHARGES PER ADMISSION FOR INPATIENT SERVICES
BY STATE
1990-1991 *(Continued from previous page)*

State	Average Inpatient Charges Per Admission
South Dakota	4,328
Tennessee	6,118
Texas	7,641
Utah	9,571
Vermont	*
Virginia	6,412
Washington	6,452
West Virginia	5,081
Wisconsin	4,679
Wyoming	3,579
National Average	$6,972

* Not enough cases for statistical validity.

Source: Based on data collected by the Mutual of Omaha Companies and published in their report, **Current Trends in Health Care Costs and Utilization** (1991 edition). Mutual of Omaha (Omaha) is a leading health insurer and, as such, generates a large amount of data on the health care of its employees.

Methodology: Utilizing a sample of records from enrollees in Mutual of Omaha group health plans, the company develops statistics related to the cost and utilization of health care for this population. Statistical tests are utilized to assure the validity of the data.

Definitions: The time period refers to the one-year period ending in June of 1991.

Qualifications: Since these data are based on a sample of records they are subject to sampling error. The accuracy of the data is also a function of the accuracy of the codes applied to the records. These statistics refer only to Mutual of Omaha enrollees in group health plans and may not be entirely representative of the total U.S. population.

VI-24. ACCIDENTS/INJURIES
COST OF ACCIDENTS AND UNINTENTIONAL INJURIES
1989

Cost Component	Cost (In $ billions)
Wage loss	$37.1
Medical expenses	23.6
Insurance administration	28.7
Motor vehicle damage	23.6
Fire loss	8.4
Indirect loss from work accidents	22.0
Total Cost	$143.4

Source: Based on data collected by the National Safety Council (Chicago) and published in **Accident Facts**, 1989 edition. The National Safety Council is an independent non-profit education and service organization.

Definitions: "Indirect loss" includes money value of time lost by noninjured workers, including time spent filling out accident reports, time spent giving first aid to injured workers, and time lost due to production slowdowns. The figures do not consider the "cost" of emotional damage resulting from accident and injury.

Interpretation: The cost of accidents and unintentional injuries equals 4% of the gross national product of the U.S. The costs associated with accidents and unintentional injuries are larger than the GNPs of many countries.

VI-25. VETERANS MEDICAL CARE
EXPENDITURES ON VETERANS MEDICAL CARE
1965-1990

Year	Total Expenditures (in $ billions)
1990	$11,500
1985	8,936
1980	5,981
1975	3,328
1970	1,689
1965	1,150

Source: Unpublished data compiled by the Budget Office of the Veterans Administration (VA) and published in **Health, United States, 1991.** The VA is the federal agency providing medical services to former military servicemen.

Methodology: Data were compiled from the records of the Veterans Administration.

Definitions: "Expenditures" refers solely to outlays of the Veterans Administration. These figures exclude construction, medical administration, and miscellaneous operation expenses.

Qualifications: Figures for 1965, 1970, and 1975 reflect a fiscal year ending June 30. All other figures are for fiscal years ending September 30.

VI-26. VETERANS MEDICAL CARE
DISTRIBUTION OF EXPENDITURES ON VETERANS MEDICAL CARE BY CATEGORY
1990

Category	Percent
Inpatient hospital care	57.5%
Outpatient care	25.3
VA nursing homes and related	7.1
Community nursing homes	2.4
All other	7.7

Source: Unpublished data compiled by the Budget Office of the Veterans Administration (VA) and published in **Health, United States, 1991.** The VA is the federal agency providing medical services to former military servicemen.

Methodology: Data were compiled from the records of the Veterans Administration.

Definitions: "Expenditures" refers solely to outlays of the Veterans Administration. These figures exclude construction, medical administration, and miscellaneous operation expenses. "All other" refers to miscellaneous benefits and services, contract hospitals, education and training, subsidies to state veterans hospitals, nursing homes and domiciliaries, and the Civilian Health and Medical Program.

Interpretation: The proportion of VA expenditures devoted to inpatient care has declined dramatically over the past three decades, while the proportion devoted to outpatient care has increased dramatically.

VI-27. VETERANS MEDICAL CARE
PATIENTS SERVED BY THE VETERANS ADMINISTRATION
ON AN INPATIENT AND OUTPATIENT BASIS
1965-1990

| Year | Veterans Treated (in 1,000s) | |
	Inpatient	Outpatient
1990	1,029	22,602
1985	1,306	19,586
1980	1,235	18,206
1975	1,065	13,799
1970	787	7,312
1965	730	5,987

Source: Unpublished data compiled by the Budget Office of the Veterans Administration (VA) and published in **Health, United States, 1991.** The VA is the federal agency providing medical services to former military servicemen.

Methodology: Data were compiled from the records of the Veterans Administration.

Qualifications: Figures for 1965, 1970, and 1975 reflect a fiscal year ending June 30. All other figures are for fiscal years ending September 30.

Interpretation: The proportion of VA expenditures devoted to inpatient care declined dramatically over the past three decades, while the proportion devoted to outpatient care has increased dramatically.

VI-28. PUBLIC HEALTH
PUBLIC HEALTH EXPENDITURES BY STATE AND
TERRITORIAL HEALTH AGENCIES
1976-1989

Year	Total Expenditures (in $ millions)
1989	$9,669
1986	7,491
1984	6,242
1982	5,145
1980	4,451
1978	3,256
1976	2,540

Source: Based on unpublished data compiled by the Public Health Foundation and published in **Health, United States, 1991.** The Public Health Foundation (Washington) is a nonprofit organization established by the Association of State and Territorial Health Officials. Additional data are available through the foundation's publication, **Public Health Macroview.**

Methodology: Based on data compiled by the Public Health Foundation from Federal sources and agencies in 50 states, the District of Columbia, and four U.S. territories.

Definitions: "Public health expenditures" refers to money spent by public health agencies at the state and territorial levels of government.

VI-29. PUBLIC HEALTH
STATE PUBLIC HEALTH EXPENDITURES BY SOURCE OF FUNDS
1989

Source	Expenditures (in $ millions)	Percent
Federal grants and contracts	$3,503	36.7%
State	5,184	53.6
Local	154	1.6
All other	829	8.6

Source: Based on unpublished data compiled by the Public Health Foundation and published in **Health, United States, 1991.** The Public Health Foundation (Washington) is a nonprofit organization established by the Association of State and Territorial Health Officials. Additional data are available through the foundation's publication **Public Health Macroview.**

Methodology: Based on data compiled by the Public Health Foundation from Federal sources and agencies in 50 states, the District of Columbia, and four U.S. territories.

Definitions: "Public health expenditures" refers to money spent by public health agencies at the state and territorial levels of government.

VI-30. PUBLIC HEALTH
STATE PUBLIC HEALTH EXPENDITURES BY PROGRAM
1989

Program	Expenditures (in $ millions)	Percent
WIC	$1,938	20.0%
Personal health	3,972	41.1
Health institutions	1,459	15.1
Environmental health	520	5.4
Health resources	824	8.5
Laboratory	308	3.2
Other	649	6.7

Source: Based on unpublished data compiled by the Public Health Foundation and published in **Health United States, 1990.** The Public Health Foundation (Washington) is a nonprofit organization established by the Association of State and Territorial Health Officials. Additional data are available through the foundation's publication **Public Health Macroview.**

Methodology: Based on data compiled by the Public Health Foundation from Federal sources and agencies in 50 states, the District of Columbia, and four U.S. territories.

Definitions: "Public health expenditures" refers to money spent by public health agencies at the state and territorial levels of government. "WIC" is a supplemental food program for women, infants, and children. "Personal health" refers to noninstitutional services for maternal and child health (other than WIC), handicapped children's services, communicable disease control, dental health, chronic disease control, mental health, alcohol and drug abuse and supporting personal health programs. "Health institutions" refers to facilities operated by state agencies.

VI-31. WORKER'S COMPENSATION
HEALTH SERVICES EXPENDITURES UNDER THE
WORKER'S COMPENSATION PROGRAM
1965-1988

Year	Expenditures (in $ millions)
1988	$9,968
1985	7,000
1980	5,151
1975	2,436
1970	1,409
1965	799

Source: Based on data compiled by the Health Care Financing Administration (HCFA) with the U.S. Department of Health and Human Services and published in the **Source Book of Health Insurance Data** published by the Health Insurance Association of America (HIAA).

Methodology: Compiled from reports submitted by the state and Federal agencies involved in worker's compensation.

Definitions: The "Worker's Compensation Program" is the state-administered program for compensating the costs to workers injured or becoming ill as a result of their work.

Interpretation: Expenditures under the Worker's Compensation Program have increased steadily since its inception, although not as rapidly as expenditures for other health programs.

VI-32. AIDS-RELATED ACTIVITIES
FEDERAL SPENDING ON AIDS-RELATED ACTIVITIES
(In $ Millions)
1982-1990

Year	Total	Research	Education/ Prevention	Medical Care	Cash Assistance
1990	$2,973	$1,164	$470	$1,120	$219
1988	1,594	722	282	492	96
1987	926	394	160	312	60
1986	507	203	75	195	33
1985	207	86	25	83	13
1984	104	59	4	35	6
1983	44	22	7	15	0
1982	6	4	2	2	0

Source: Based on data compiled by the Budget Office of the U.S. Public Health Service. Published in **Health, United States, 1991.**

Methodology: Data were collected from the relevant federal agencies by the Budget Office of the U.S. Public Health Service.

Definitions: "Health Care Financing Administration" refers to the Federal agency that administers the Medicare and Medicaid programs.

Qualifications: These figures refer only to Federal expenditures for AIDS-related activities and do not include funds from other sources.

VI-33. AIDS-RELATED ACTIVITIES
FEDERAL SPENDING ON AIDS-RELATED ACTIVITIES BY FEDERAL AGENCY
1990

Agency	Expenditures (in $ millions)
Department of Health and Human Services	$2,529
Public Health Service	1,590
National Institute of Health	744
Alcohol, Drug Abuse and Mental Health Administration	215
Center for Disease Control	443
Food and Drug Administration	57
Health Resources and Services Administration	113
Social Security Administration	219
Other DHHS agencies	3
Department of Veterans Affairs	208
Department of Defense	125
Agency for International Development	41
Other Departments	7

Source: Based on data compiled by the Budget Office of the U.S. Public Health Service and published in **Health, United States, 1991.**

Methodology: Data were collected from the relevant Federal agencies by the Budget Office of the U.S. Public Health Service.

Qualifications: These figures refer only to Federal expenditures for AIDS-related activities and do not include funds from other sources.

Interpretation: The Department of Health and Human Services has been responsible for the bulk of federal expenditures related to AIDS.

VI-34. NURSING HOME CARE
EXPENDITURES FOR NURSING HOME CARE
1960-1990

Year	Expenditures (in $ billions)
1990	$53.1
1985	34.1
1980	20.0
1975	9.9
1970	4.9
1965	1.7
1960	1.0

Source: Based on data collected by the Health Care Financing Administration and published in **Health, United States, 1991**. The Health Care Financing Administration (HCFA) within the U.S. Department of Health and Human Services administers the Medicare program and is a major source of health data.

Methodology: Estimates of expenditures were made by the Federal Office of National Cost Estimates and HCFA and compiled by HCFA.

Interpretation: Expenditures for nursing home care grew faster than expenditures for other categories of health care between 1960 and 1988. During this period nursing care expenditures came to account for an increasing share of overall health expenditures.

VI-35. NURSING CARE
EXPENDITURES FOR NURSING HOME CARE BY SOURCE
(In $ Millions)
1960-1990

	Percent Paid By:	
Year	Third Parties	Out-of-Pocket
1990	55.1%	44.9%
1988	52.0	48.0
1987	52.0	48.0
1986	50.9	49.1
1985	51.4	48.6
1980	56.7	43.3
1975	57.9	42.1
1970	51.8	48.2
1965	35.4	64.5
1960	20.0	80.0

Source: Based on data collected by the Health Care Financing Administration within the U.S. Department of Health and Human Services. The Health Care Financing Administration (HCFA) administers the Medicare program and is a major federal source of health data.

Methodology: Compiled by Health Care Financing Administration (HCFA) from various sources.

Definitions: "Third-parties" refers to insurers such as private insurance companies or the government. "Out-of-pocket" refers to expenditures for care made directly by the patient or his family.

Interpretation: Nursing home care has historically been paid for out of pocket by individuals. Since the 1960s, however, an increasing proportion has been covered by third-party insurers, especially the Medicaid program.

VI-36. PHYSICIAN SERVICES
EXPENDITURES FOR PHYSICIANS SERVICES
1960-1990

Year	Expenditures (in $ billions)
1990	$125.7
1985	74.0
1980	41.9
1975	23.3
1970	13.6
1965	8.2
1960	5.3

Source: Based on data collected by the Health Care Financing Administration and published in **Health, United States, 1991.** The Health Care Financing Administration (HCFA) within the U.S. Department of Health and Human Services administers the Medicare program and is a major source of health data.

Methodology: Estimates of expenditures were made by the Federal Office of National Cost Estimates and HCFA and compiled by HCFA.

Interpretation: Expenditures for physician services nearly tripled during the 1980s, making them one of the fastest growing components of health care expenditures.

VI-37. RESEARCH FUNDING
DISTRIBUTION OF FEDERAL HEALTH RESEARCH FUNDING
WITHIN THE DEPARTMENT OF HEALTH AND HUMAN SERVICES
1990

Agency	Percent of Department Research Funding
National Institutes of Health	85.1%
Centers for Disease Control	1.2
Other Public Health Service	13.3
Other DHHS	0.4

Source: Based on data collected from the National Institutes of Health (NIH) and the U.S. Public Health Service (PHS) and published in **Health, United States, 1991.** The National Institutes of Health (NIH) is the major agency for federal health research.

Methodology: Compiled by NIH and the PHS from various sources.

Qualifications: The distribution of funding within agency is estimated.

VI-38. RESEARCH FUNDING
DISTRIBUTION OF FEDERAL HEALTH RESEARCH FUNDING BY AGENCY
1990

Agency	Percent of Federal Health Research Funding
Department of Health and Human Services	85.2%
Department of Agriculture	1.1
Department of Defense	4.1
Department of Education	0.6
Department of Energy	2.8
Department of the Interior	0.4
Environmental Protection Agency	0.3
International Development Cooperation Agency	0.2
National Aeronautics and Space Administration	1.6
National Science Foundation	0.9
Veterans Administration	2.4
All Others	0.3

Source: Based on data collected from the National Institutes of Health and the U.S. Public Health Service (PHS) and published in **Health, United States, 1991.** The National Institutes of Health (NIH) is the major agency for federal health research.

Definitions: "Department of Energy" includes the Atomic Energy Commission and the Energy Research and Development Administration. "International Development Cooperation Agency" includes the Department of State and the Agency for International Development.

Qualifications: Distribution of funding by agency is estimated.

VI-39. HEALTH BENEFITS COSTS
AVERAGE MONTHLY COST FOR HEALTH CARE
FOR SELECTED LARGE EMPLOYERS
1990

Beneficiary Category	Average Medical Cost per Month	Average Dental Cost per Month
Active employees		
Employee only	$137	$15
Employee plus one dependent	278	32
Employee plus two or more dependents	374	44
Retirees under age 65		
Retiree only	156	16
Retiree plus one dependent	298	32
Retiree plus two or more dependents	390	44
Retirees age 65 or over		
Retiree only	79	15
Retiree plus one dependent	161	31
Retiree plus two or more dependents	229	31

Source: Based on data collected by Towers Perrin and published in **Medical Benefits** (September 15, 1990). **Medical Benefits** is a semi-monthly publication devoted to health care costs. For additional information, contact Towers Perrin (Valhalla, NY).

Methodology: Based on data collected through surveys administered by Towers Perrin to 123 of the nation's largest employers. The sample was chosen from the national employer database maintained by the Employee Benefits Information Center.

Definitions: "Average cost per month" includes both employee premium expenditures and employer contributions.

Qualifications: Since these figures are based on data drawn from a sample of the nation's large employers, they suffer from all of the potential drawbacks of sample survey data. Estimates for average monthly cost were necessary for those companies that are self-insured.

Interpretation: The cost of employee health care has continued to grow as a proportion of employer costs. Not only have increases continued for current employees, but retirees and their dependents are creating a financial burden on employers unanticipated at the time the benefits were put into place.

VI-40. HEALTH INSURANCE
MEDICAL PLAN COSTS PER EMPLOYEE BY SIZE OF COMPANY
1987-1989

Number of Employees	1987	1988	1989 (est.)
Less than 500	$2,021	$2,358	$2,552
500-999	1,972	2,193	2,498
1,000-2,499	1,879	2,177	2,457
2,500-4,999	1,930	2,201	2,474
5,000-9,999	1,924	2,208	2,553
10,000-14,999	2,064	2,363	2,766
15,000 or more	2,056	2,449	2,727

Source: Based on data collected by Hewitt Associates and published in **Medical Benefits** (February 28, 1990). **Medical Benefits** is a semi-monthly publication devoted to health care costs.

Methodology: Based on data collected by Hewitt Associates from a sample of the nation's employers.

Qualifications: Since these figures are based on data drawn from a sample of the nation's employers, they suffer from all of the potential drawbacks of sample survey data.

VI-41. RESEARCH FUNDING
SOURCES OF FUNDING FOR HEALTH RESEARCH AND DEVELOPMENT
1960-1990
(In $ Millions)

Year	Total Funding	Federal Funding	State and Local Funding	Industry Funding	Private Nonprofit Funding
1990	$22,584	$9,856	$1,517	$10,368	$843
1989	20,781	9,230	1,339	9,433	779
1988	18,729	8,454	1,272	8,260	744
1987	16,827	7,827	1,146	7,130	725
1986	14,801	6,895	1,096	6,166	714
1985	13,408	6,791	874	5,244	500
1984	12,014	6,087	793	4,643	491
1983	10,634	5,399	712	4,145	377
1982	9,483	4,970	634	3,561	318
1981	8,703	4,848	564	2,998	292
1980	7,935	4,723	480	2,459	274
1975	4,701	2,832	465	2,093	254
1970	2,847	1,667	170	795	215
1965	1,890	1,174	90	450	176
1960	886	448	46	253	139

Source: Based on data collected from the National Institutes of Health (NIH) and the U.S. Public Health Service (PHS) and published in **Health, United States, 1991.** The National Institutes of Health (NIH) is the major agency for federal health research.

Methodology: Compiled by NIH and the PHS from various sources.

Qualifications: The 1990 figures are estimates.

Interpretation: The growth rate for funding for health-related research has been fairly constant throughout the 1980s. However, the amount of private industry funding has been growing faster than government funding for health-related research.

VI-42. COMPARATIVE COSTS
HIGHEST COST LARGE CITIES FOR HEALTH CARE
1990

City	Index
Miami/Fort Lauderdale	138
Los Angeles/Anaheim	136
Philadelphia	135
New York	131
Detroit	131
Boston	123
San Francisco/Oakland	121
San Diego	118
Washington	118
Houston	113
Chicago	111
Baltimore	109
Dallas	101

Source: Based on data collected by Milliman & Robertson (Seattle). Published in **HealthWeek** (July 1, 1991). Milliman & Robertson is an actuarial consulting firm. (**HealthWeek** ceased publication at the end of 1991.)

Definition: "Index" is a measure of the extent to which the city's average health care costs vary from the national average. The national average = 100.

Methodology: Based on data collected in a study of local health care costs that factored in statistics on admissions, average length of stay, outpatient visits, hospital and physician charges and other indicators of health care utilization and cost. Data were collected for only the non-Medicare population.

Qualifications: Health statistics are compiled differently in different areas and, for this reason, city to city comparisons are sometimes difficult.

Interpretation: A number of factors contribute to the differences noted between city in health care costs. Local economic factors (e.g., wage rates, cost of loving) and health-related factors (e.g., Medicare population, managed care penetration) influence costs as do local physician practice patterns.

Section VII

DATA ON INSURANCE AND OTHER FINANCING MECHANISMS

Historically, the greatest interest in insurance statistics has been shown by the state agencies that have the responsibility for regulating the industry. Even for them, information on premium rates has been the primary interest. By the 1970s, however, certain consumer groups began expressing an interest in insurance statistics as the consumerism movement demanded more access to industry data. These groups were joined by employers during the 1980s who, when faced with the accelerating costs of health benefits, began to require a better understanding of the insurance industry and its implications for their employees.

At the same time, the federal government began to take an interest in the nature of enrollment in its Medicare and Medicaid programs and the relationship between these federally-sponsored programs and the private insurance industry. By the late 1970s the interests of the federal government became urgent as it was obvious that spending in the Medicare and Medicaid programs was going to exceed all previous projections, and in fact, exceed the amount of funds available.

These trends characterizing the financing of health care also resulted in the development of organizations that offered alternative forms of financing for health insurance. During the 1970s, the health maintenance organization (HMO) movement emerged, followed in the 1980s by the development of preferred provider organizations (PPOs) and other varieties of "managed" care programs. These alternative forms of financing were all directed toward holding down the costs of health services.

This growing interest in insurance-related data resulted in the development of new and better sources of information. The data on health insurance and other financing mechanisms falls roughly into three categories. The first category is data related to the private insurance industry, which includes commercial for-profit firms as well as not-for-profit insurors such as Blue Cross. Although considered proprietary in the past, pressure for accountability has led to the widespread dissemination of data on the private health insurance industry. Much of this information is available at the state level, since this is the level of government at which insurors are regulated. The quality and availability of these data improved as national organizations became involved in its compilation and dissemination. Organizations such as the Health Insurance Association of America (HIAA) and the Employee Benefits Research Institute (ERBI) became involved. In addition, various consumer groups took advantage of this new availability to data to step up their repackaging and dissemination activities. By the mid-1980s certain data vendors had also begun to collect data on insurance characteristics and develop models for estimating the extent of insurance coverage.

The second category of insurance data is that compiled by the federal government. Not only do the administrators of the Medicare and Medicaid programs require an accurate accounting of program activities–in fact, it is legally mandated–but they have an interest in controlling the costs of these programs. This has led the involved federal agencies to not only collect data on federal programs but on private insurors and alternative financing programs as well. The major source of such data is the Health Care Financing Administration (HCFA) which, as administrator of the Medicare and Medicaid programs, compiles and disseminates extensive data on these programs. HCFA also sponsors research that generates data on non-federal insurance programs. The Census Bureau and the National Center for Health Statistics also collect information on insurance coverage through the various surveys they conduct.

The third category of data relates to alternative forms of financing such as HMOs and PPOs. Data on HMOs have been relatively accessible since the inception of the HMO movement due to the fact that early HMOs were subsidized by the federal government. As government-funded entities, they were required to report on their activities. As PPOs developed and HMOs gradually lost their federal subsidy, public sources of data on these organizations became less readily available. However, the federal government continues to track the development of alternative forms of financing and maintains extensive databases. Associations of HMOs, PPOs and other managed care programs also began to maintain data on their member organizations. For example, the American Managed Care and Review Association maintains data on preferred provider organizations. Some private organizations, including commercial data vendors, also began to maintain databases of these organizations. InterStudy has long maintained a database of HMOs, and SMG, Inc., is a commercial vendor of such data. Other commercial data vendors have begun to collect data on health insurance coverage and the characteristics of the insured and the uninsured. Some also maintain, or at least disseminate, data on insurance companies and alternative forms of financing.

VII-1. PRIVATE INSURANCE
PRIVATE HEALTH INSURANCE CLAIMS PAYMENTS
(In $ Billions)
1950-1989

Year	Commercial Insurance	Blue Cross-Blue Shield	Self-insured and HMO Plans	Total Payments
1989	$89.4	$50.7	$79.8	$185.3
1988	83.0	48.2	62.8	171.1
1987	72.5	44.5	56.5	151.7
1986	64.3	40.6	36.8	128.5
1985	60.0	37.5	32.5	117.6
1984	56.0	35.7	26.1	107.5
1983	51.7	34.4	24.1	104.1
1982	49.2	32.2	21.6	97.1
1981	41.6	29.2	18.9	85.9
1980	37.0	25.5	16.2	76.3
1975	16.5	16.9	NA	32.1
1970	9.1	8.1	NA	17.2
1965	5.2	4.5	NA	9.6
1960	3.0	2.6	NA	5.7
1955	1.8	1.4	NA	3.1
1950	0.8	0.6	NA	1.3

Source: Based on data collected by the Health Insurance Association of America (HIAA) and published in the **Source Book of Health Insurance Data.** Additional data are available from HIAA (Washington, DC).

Methodology: Compiled from data collected by HIAA from its annual member survey.

Definitions: "Commercial" insurance refers to health coverage provided by private for-profit insurance companies. "Blue Cross-Blue Shield" insurance refers to health coverage provided by members of the not-for-profit Blue Cross Association. The data have been adjusted to eliminate dual coverage. "Self-Insured Plans" are those in which an employer chooses to fund insurance coverage for its employees rather than utilizing the commercial insurance market. "HMOs" are health maintenance organizations which involve a prepayment financing mechanism rather than the "indemnity" approach utilized by commercial insurance and Blue Cross plans.

Interpretation: Prior to World War II the health insurance industry had been poorly developed. Formed during the Depression, the Blue Cross plans were the first plans to be widely accepted. However, by the mid-1950s commercial, for-profit plans become dominant. Coverage under both types of insurance increased steadily until the 1980s when alternate forms of insurance coverage became available.

VII-2. PRIVATE INSURANCE
PRIVATE HEALTH INSURANCE CLAIMS PAYMENTS BY TYPES OF COVERAGE
(In $ Billions)
1950-1989

Year	Total Payments	Hospital/ Medical	Dental	Medicare Supplement	Loss of Income
1090	$82.2	$68.6	$6.5	$2.1	$5.0
1988	76.4	63.3	6.3	2.2	4.6
1987	66.5	54.6	5.9	1.5	4.6
1986	58.9	48.1	5.3	1.5	4.0
1985	53.7	43.9	5.3	0.5	4.0
1984	50.3	41.1	4.9	0.4	3.9
1983	46.9	38.6	4.4	0.1	3.9
1982	44.2	35.9	4.0	0.1	4.1
1981	37.7	30.0	3.5	0.2	4.2
1980	33.0	25.8	2.8	0.1	4.3
1975	14.2	11.6	0.6	NA	2.7
1970	7.5	6.0	0.1	NA	1.8
1965	4.0	3.3	NA	NA	1.0
1960	2.4	1.8	NA	NA	0.8
1955	1.3	NA	NA	NA	NA
1950	0.4	NA	NA	NA	NA

NA = Not applicable

Source: Based on data collected by the Health Insurance Association of America (HIAA) and published in the **Source Book of Health Insurance Data.** Additional data are available from HIAA (Washington, DC).

Methodology: Compiled from data collected by HIAA from its annual member survey.

Definitions: "Hospital/Medical" refers to payments to hospitals and physicians.

Interpretation: Payments for health insurance claims have grown steadily in all categories. Dental coverage and Medicare supplemental coverage did not become widespread until the 1970s.

VII-3. PRIVATE INSURANCE
HEALTH INSURANCE PREMIUMS
(In $ Billions)
1950-1989

Year	Net Total Premiums	Commercial Insurance	Self-Insured and HMO Plans	Blue-Cross/ Blue Shield
1989	$215.6	$108.0	$89.2	$56.0
1988	192.3	98.2	73.7	51.2
1987	168.6	84.1	61.7	46.3
1986	143.4	75.5	40.6	43.5
1985	139.5	75.2	36.7	41.5
1984	127.6	70.4	28.6	40.0
1983	119.9	63.2	25.6	37.6
1982	109.5	58.3	22.9	34.3
1981	95.1	49.0	20.0	30.4
1980	84.7	43.7	17.3	26.3
1975	37.0	20.8	NA	17.6
1970	20.0	11.5	NA	8.4
1965	12.1	7.4	NA	4.8
1960	7.5	4.7	NA	2.8
1955	4.3	2.7	NA	1.5
1950	2.0	1.3	NA	0.7

NA = Not applicable

Source: Based on data collected by the Health Insurance Association of America (HIAA) and published in the **Source Book of Health Insurance Data**. Additional data are available from HIAA (Washington, DC).

Methodology: Compiled from data collected by HIAA from its annual member survey.

Definitions: "Commercial" insurance refers to health coverage provided by private for-profit insurance companies. "Blue Cross-Blue Shield" insurance refers to health coverage provided by members of the not-for-profit Blue Cross Association. The data have been adjusted to eliminate dual coverage. "Self-Insured Plans" are those in which an employer chooses to fund insurance coverage for its employees rather than utilizing the commercial insurance market. "HMOs" are health maintenance organizations which involve a prepayment financing mechanism rather than the "indemnity" approach utilized by commercial insurance and Blue Cross plans. "Net total" refers to total after member distributions.

Qualifications: The 1989 figure for total premiums is an estimate.

Interpretation: Prior to World War II the health insurance industry had been poorly developed. Formed during the depression, the Blue Cross plans were the first plans to be widely accepted. However, by the mid-1950s commercial, for-profit plans became dominant. Coverage under both types of insurance increased steadily until the 1980s when alternate forms of insurance coverage became available. Premiums paid for all three types of insurance have continued to rise through the 1980s.

VII-4. UNINSURED POPULATION
PERSONS WITHOUT HEALTH INSURANCE
BY SELECTED CHARACTERISTICS
1990

Characteristic	Number (millions)	Percent
Total Not Covered	33.6	13.6%
Sex:		
Male	18.1	13.6
Female	15.5	15.1
Race/Ethnicity:		
White	26.4	12.7
Black	5.6	18.4
Hispanic Origin	6.5	31.4
Age:		
Under Age 16	8.5	14.7
16-24 years	7.0	21.9
25-34 years	8.1	18.7
35-44 years	4.8	12.9
45-54 years	3.0	11.9
55-64 years	2.1	9.9
65 years and over	0.1	0.3

Source: Based on data collected in the Current Population Survey and published in the **Statistical Abstract of the United States, 1992,** table 153.

Methodology: The Current Population Survey (CPS) is part of the Census Bureau's intercensal data gathering activities. Albeit large, because it is a sample, some sampling error is contained in the data.

Definition: Persons not covered by health insurance are those not covered at the time of the survey. A much larger number of individuals are without health insurance at some time during any given year.

Interpretation: Almost 14 percent of the total population was without health insurance at the time of the survey. However, non-coverage is much higher for blacks, Hispanics, and the young.

VII-5. HEALTH MAINTENANCE ORGANIZATIONS
AVERAGE MONTHLY PREMIUM RATES FOR HMOs BY STATE
1989

State	Average Monthly Family Premium	Average Monthly Individual Premium
Alabama	$242.69	$90.62
Arizona	265.93	95.98
Arkansas	237.67	77.74
California	271.89	132.99
Colorado	256.20	95.45
Connecticut	320.75	124.32
Delaware	313.29	123.33
District of Columbia	286.73	109.74
Florida	235.44	93.80
Georgia	250.15	98.67
Hawaii	230.71	80.65
Idaho	215.00	104.75
Illinois	242.05	93.12
Indiana	266.44	88.53
Iowa	255.21	89.36
Kansas	251.34	94.20
Kentucky	252.50	85.83
Louisiana	293.43	101.71
Maine	298.83	115.86
Maryland	288.57	94.58
Massachusetts	333.13	126.64
Michigan	259.81	98.75
Minnesota	263.05	97.08
Missouri	260.74	94.16
Montana	205.00	80.00
Nebraska	258.90	97.77
Nevada	309.00	127.50
New Hampshire	281.50	100.50
New Jersey	240.74	95.33
New Mexico	263.81	110.67
New York	262.37	100.85
North Carolina	251.85	95.62
North Dakota	234.00	93.00
Ohio	283.45	106.54
Oklahoma	237.74	87.36
Oregon	234.63	80.76
Pennsylvania	243.54	91.73
Rhode Island	249.92	107.97
South Carolina	240.00	89.33
South Dakota	262.26	93.89
Tennessee	261.91	103.72
Texas	281.83	100.94

(Continued on next page)

VII-5. HEALTH MAINTENANCE ORGANIZATIONS
AVERAGE MONTHLY PREMIUM RATES FOR HMOs BY STATE

1989 *(Continued from previous page)*

State	Average Monthly Family Premium	Average Monthly Individual Premium
Utah	279.29	90.58
Vermont	243.71	92.87
Virginia	271.26	102.02
Washington	272.17	87.29
Wisconsin	280.30	106.56
U.S. Average	265.50	101.79

Source: Based on data collected by SMG Marketing Group, Inc., and published in **Medical Benefits**, September 30, 1990. SMG is a private data vendor that specializes in data on HMOs and other health-related organizations. **Medical Benefits** is a semi-monthly publication devoted to health care costs. For additional information on available data, contact SMG (Chicago).

Methodology: Based on data collected by means of surveys conducted by SMG on the nation's HMOs.

Definitions: "HMOs" are health maintenance organizations which involve a prepayment financing mechanisms rather than the "indemnity" approach utilized by commercial insurance and Blue Cross plans.

Qualifications: Not all organizations calculate their rates in the same manner. Presumably these differences have been accounted for by SMG in processing the data. Nevertheless, such figures should be used with caution. Since these are averages for the HMOs in the various states, caution should be used in applying these rates to a particular HMO. Some states have no HMOs headquartered within their boundaries and, thus, do not appear on this table. Some residents of these states, however, may be enrolled in one or more HMOs headquartered in another state.

VII-6. INSURANCE COVERAGE
POPULATION UNDER 65 COVERED BY PRIVATE HEALTH INSURANCE AND POPULATION WITHOUT INSURANCE BY DEMOGRAPHIC CHARACTERISTICS
1989

| | Percent With: | |
Characteristic	Private Insurance Coverage	No Insurance Coverage
Total	76.6%	15.7%
Age:		
Under 15	71.7	15.9
15-44	76.6	18.1
45-64	83.3	10.6
Race:		
White	79.7	14.5
Black	59.2	22.0
Family Income:		
Less than $14,000	34.6	37.3
$14,000-$24,999	71.4	21.4
$25,000-$34,999	87.9	9.3
$35,000-$49,999	92.4	5.6
$50,000 or more	95.7	3.2

Source: Based on data collected by the National Center for Health Statistics and published in **Health, United States, 1991.** National Center for Health Statistics (NCHS) conducts a variety of surveys from which health-related data are drawn. Additional data, including some unpublished data, on this topic are available from NCHS (Hyattsville, MD).

Methodology: These data were collected by the NCHS by means of the 1989 National Health Interview Survey. These figures are based on data collected annually from a nationwide sample of between 36,000 and 46,000 households.

Definitions: "Family income" refers to the household's (i.e., related individuals) total annual income.

Qualifications: Figures are age-adjusted.

Interpretation: During the late 1980s there was a decline in health insurance coverage for the U.S. population. While the majority of individuals have private insurance, the level of coverage varies by demographic characteristic. Segments of the population that are older, white, and affluent have higher levels of insurance coverage than those that are younger, black and less affluent.

VII-7. INSURANCE COVERAGE
INSURANCE COVERAGE FOR THE POPULATION 65 AND OVER
BY DEMOGRAPHIC CHARACTERISTICS
1989

| | Percent With Insurance Coverage | | |
Characteristic	Medicare Only	Medicare and Private Insurance	Medicare and Medicaid
Total	16.8%	73.5%	5.7%
Age:			
65-74	15.5	74.2	5.0
75-84	17.4	74.1	6.4
85 and over	26.1	64.8	8.5
Race:			
White	14.7	77.3	4.0
Black	37.9	39.3	19.9
Family Income:			
Less than $14,000	21.5	64.8	11.4
$14,000-$24,999	13.4	81.2	2.6
$25,000-$34,999	12.5	80.0	2.4
$35,000-$49,999	10.2	80.3	1.9*
$50,000 or more	12.6	76.5	1.1*

*High standard error due to small number of cases.

Source: Based on data collected by the National Center for Health Statistics and published in **Health, United States, 1991**. National Center for Health Statistics (NCHS) conducts a variety of surveys from which health-related data are drawn. Additional data, including some unpublished data, on this topic are available from NCHS (Hyattsville, MD).

Methodology: These data were collected by the NCHS by means of the 1989 National Health Interview Survey. These figures are based on data collected annually from a nationwide sample of between 36,000 and 46,000 households.

Definitions: "Medicare" is the federally-sponsored health insurance program that covers the elderly and disabled. "Medicaid" is the joint federal-state program of health insurance for the poor. "Family income" refers to the household's (i.e., related individuals) total annual income.

Qualifications: Figures are age-adjusted.

Interpretation: Since virtually all Americans age 65 and over are eligible for Medicare benefits, there is near universal participation. Most Medicare enrollees also maintain private insurance to supplement Medicare reimbursement, although this differs based on race and income. Blacks and low-income individuals are more likely to be covered under the Medicaid Program as well due to their higher levels of poverty.

VII-8. MEDICARE
MEDICARE AS A PERCENTAGE OF FEDERAL BUDGET OUTLAYS
1970-1990

Year	Total Budget Outlays (in billions)	Medicare Outlays (in billions)	Medicare as Percentage of Total Budget
1990	$1,251.8	$111.2	8.9%
1980	946.4	72.1	7.6
1975	590.9	37.5	6.3
1970	195.6	7.6	3.9

Source: Data gathered by the U.S. Office of Management and Budget and published in **Statistical Abstract of the United States, 1992,** table 136 and 491.

Methodology: These data are compiled as part of the cyclical information gathering activities performed at the Office of Management and Budget.

Definitions: "Medicare" is the federally-sponsored health insurance program that covers the elderly and the disabled.

Interpretation: The percentage of federal budget outlays allocated for Medicare has more than doubled since 1970.

VII-9. MEDICARE/MEDICAID
MEDICARE AND MEDICAID EXPENDITURES ON PERSONAL HEALTH CARE
(In $ Billions)
1966-1990

Year	Medicare and Medicaid	Medicare	Medicaid
1990	$180	$108.9	$71.3
1985	110	70.3	39.7
1980	61	36.4	24.8
1975	29	15.7	12.9
1970	12	7.2	5.1
1966	3	1.6	1.3

Source: Based on data collected by the Health Care Financing Administration (HCFA) within the U.S. Department of Health and Human Services. HCFA, as the organization responsible for the administration of the Medicare program, is the primary source of Medicare statistics. Additional data are available directly from HCFA (Washington, D.C.) or through its publications such as **Health Care Financing Review.**

Methodology: Based on records maintained by HCFA.

Definitions: "Medicare" is the federally-sponsored health insurance program that covers the elderly and the disabled. Participation is mandatory for individuals 65 and over. "Medicaid" is the joint federal-state program of health insurance for the poor. "SMI" is supplementary medical insurance.

Qualifications: Excludes "buy-in" premiums paid by Medicaid for SMI coverage of aged and disabled Medicaid recipients eligible for coverage.

Interpretation: Federal expenditures for both Medicare and Medicaid tripled between 1980 and 1990.

VII-10. MEDICARE
MEDICARE ENROLLEES AND USERS
(In Millions)
1966-1990

Year	Medicare Enrollees	Medicare Users
1990	34.2	26.6
1985	31.1	22.3
1980	28.5	18.0
1975	25.0	13.0
1970	20.5	NA
1966	19.1	3.7

NA = Not applicable

Source: Based on data collected by the Health Care Financing Administration (HCFA) within the U.S. Department of Health and Human Services. HCFA, as the organization responsible for the administration of the Medicare program, is the primary source of Medicare statistics. Additional data are available directly from HCFA (Washington, D.C.) or through its publications such as **Health Care Financing Review**.

Methodology: Based on records maintained by HCFA.

Definitions: "Medicare" is the federally-sponsored health insurance program that covers the elderly and the disabled. Participation is mandatory for individuals 65 and over. "Medicare enrollees" include all individuals covered by Medicare hospital insurance and/or supplementary medical insurance. Enrollees are counted as of July 1 of specified year. "Medicare users" includes enrollees who actually utilized health services under the Medicare program. Data through 1973 reflect aged users only. Data for 1974 and later includes aged and disabled users.

Qualifications: The 1990 figure for Medicare users is an estimate.

Interpretation: The number of Medicare enrollees has increased by more than one and one-half times since 1966 and the number of users by over six times.

VII-11. MEDICAID
MEDICAID RECIPIENTS AND PAYMENTS
1970-1990

Year	Number of Recipients (in millions)	Medicaid Payments (in $ billions)
1990	25.2	$64.9
1985	21.8	37.5
1980	21.6	23.3
1975	22.0	12.2
1970	14.5	5.1

Source: Based on data collected by the Health Care Financing Administration (HCFA) within the U.S. Department of Health and Human Services. HCFA, as the organization responsible for the administration of the Medicare program, is the primary source of Medicare statistics. Additional data are available directly from HCFA (Washington, D.C.) or through its publications such as **Health Care Financing Review.**

Methodology: Based on records maintained by HCFA.

Definitions: "Medicaid" is the joint federal-state program of health insurance for the poor.

Interpretation: Although the number of Medicaid recipients increased less than 60% between 1970 and 1988, the payments made increased more than nine fold. This reflects the increased use of Medicaid funds for nursing home care.

VII-12. MEDICAID
MEDICAID RECIPIENTS BY ELIGIBILITY GROUP AND TYPE OF SERVICE
(In 1,000s)
1975-89

| Year | Total | Type of Service | | Intermediate Nursing Facility | Physician | Skilled Outpatient Hospital | Home Health | Prescription Drugs |
		Inpatient Hospital	Care Facility					
1989	23,511	4,170	1,036	564	15,686	11,344	609	15,916
1985	21,814	3,434	975	547	14,387	10,072	535	13,921
1980	21,605	3,680	910	606	13,765	9,705	392	13,707
1975	22,007	3,432	751	630	15,198	7,437	343	14,155

Source: Based on data collected by the Health Care Financing Administration (HCFA) within the U.S. Department of Health and Human Services. HCFA, as the organization responsible for the administration of the Medicaid program, is the primary source of Medicaid statistics. Additional data are available directly from HCFA (Washington, D.C.) or through its publications such as **Health Care Financing Review.**

Methodology: Based on records maintained by HCFA.

Definitions: "Medicaid" is the joint federal-state program of health insurance for the poor.

Qualifications: Total by type of service is greater than grand total since many recipients use more than one service.

Interpretation: The total number of Medicaid recipients grew relatively slowly between 1975 and 1989 and drops in enrollment were actually recorded at times during the interim period.

VII-13. MEDICAID
MEDICAID PAYMENTS BY ELIGIBILITY GROUP AND TYPE OF SERVICE:
(In $ MILLIONS)
1975-89

				Type of Service				
Year	Total	Inpatient Hospital	Imediate Care Facility	Skilled Nursing Facility	Physician	Outpatient Hospital	Home Health	Prescription Drugs
1989	$54,500	$13,378	$15,520	$6,660	$3,408	$2,837	$2,572	$3,689
1985	37,508	9,453	11,247	5,071	2,346	1,789	1,120	2,315
1980	23,311	6,412	6,191	3,685	1,875	1,101	332	1,318
1975	12,242	3,374	2,265	2,434	1,225	373	70	815

Source: Based on data collected by the Health Care Financing Administration (HCFA) within the U.S. Department of Health and Human Services. HCFA, as the organization responsible for the administration of the Medicaid program, is the primary source of Medicaid statistics. Additional data are available directly from HCFA (Washington, D.C.) or through its publications such as **Health Care Financing Review**.

Methodology: Based on records maintained by HCFA.

Definitions: "Medicaid" is the joint federal-state program of health insurance for the poor.

Interpretation: Although the number of Medicaid recipients only increased marginally between 1975 and 1989, Medicaid expenditures increased more than four fold. Expenditures for physician and inpatient hospital services deceased in importance relative to the other categories of expenditures.

VII-14. MEDICAID
MEDICAID PAYMENT PER RECIPIENT BY ELIGIBILITY GROUP
AND TYPE OF SERVICE:
1975-89

Year	Total	Inpatient Hospital	Immediate Care Facility	Skilled Nursing Facility	Physician	Outpatient Hospital	Home Health	Prescription Drugs
				Type of Service				
1989	$2,318	$3,251	$54,993	$11,809	$217	$250	$4,225	$232
1985	1,719	2,753	40,106	9,278	163	178	2,092	166
1980	1,079	1,742	21,761	6,079	136	113	846	96
1975	556	983	8,302	3,865	81	50	204	58

Source: Based on data collected by the Health Care Financing Administration (HCFA) within the U.S. Department of Health and Human Services. HCFA, as the organization responsible for the administration of the Medicaid program, is the primary source of Medicaid statistics. Additional data are available directly from HCFA (Washington, D.C.) or through its publications such as **Health Care Financing Review.**

Methodology: Based on records maintained by HCFA.

Definitions: "Medicaid" is the joint federal-state program of health insurance for the poor.

Interpretation: Per capita Medicaid expenditures increased significantly for all categories. Home health care recorded the greatest growth, with a twenty fold increase in expenditures per eligible recipient.

VII-15. MEDICARE/MEDICAID
DISABLED MEDICARE ENROLLEES UNDER AGE 65 AND
DISABLED MEDICAID RECIPIENTS
1975-1988

Year	Disabled Medicare Enrollees		Disabled Medicaid Recipients	
	Number	Percent Change	Number	Percent Change
1988	3,101,000	2.3%	3,345,345	3.7%
1987	3,031,000	2.4	3,225,726	7.0
1986	2,959,000	1.8	3,013,521	5.1
1985	2,907,000	0.8	2,867,539	3.3
1984	2,884,000	-1.2	2,776,640	-0.1
1983	2,918,000	-1.2	2,779,692	0.9
1982	2,954,000	-1.5	2,754,378	-2.6
1981	2,999,000	1.2	2,828,533	1.6
1980	2,963,000	1.8	2,783,048	5.3
1979	2,911,000	4.2	2,642,217	1.8
1978	2,793,000	6.6	2,595,938	-2.1
1977	2,619,000	9.5	2,652,740	4.2
1976	2,392,000	10.3	2,546,664	9.1
1975	2,168,000	-	2,333,681	-

Note: Medicare enrollees rounded to the nearest 1,000.

Source: Based on data collected by the Health Care Financing Administration (HCFA) within the U.S. Department of Health and Human Services. HCFA, as the organization responsible for the administration of the Medicare program, is the primary source of Medicare statistics. Additional data are available directly from HCFA (Washington, D.C.) or through its publications such as **Health Care Financing Review**.

Methodology: Based on records maintained by HCFA.

Definitions: "Disabled Medicare enrollees" are the number of persons enrolled as of July 1. "Disabled Medicaid recipients" are the total unduplicated number receiving Medicaid-covered services during the federal fiscal year.

VII-16. MEDICARE
MEDICARE EXPENDITURES FOR SELECTED CATEGORIES OF CARE
(In $ Millions)
1967-1990

Year	Inpatient Hospital	Physician	Outpatient Hospital	Home Health	Skilled Nursing	Hospice
1990	$59,301	$29,268	$8,475	$3,517	$2,876	$356
1985	44,698	17,311	4,304	2,148	578	20
1980	24,082	8,188	1,935	568	401	0
1975	10,877	3,415	652	160	278	0
1970	4,827	1,790	117	51	246	0
1967	3,034	1,128	26	29	282	0

Source: Based on data collected by the Health Care Financing Administration (HCFA) within the U.S. Department of Health and Human Services. HCFA, as the organization responsible for the administration of the Medicare program, is the primary source of Medicare statistics. Additional data are available directly from HCFA (Washington, D.C.) or through its publications such as **Health Care Financing Review.**

Definition: "Medicare" is the federally-sponsored health insurance program that cover the elderly and the disabled. Participation is mandatory for individuals 65 of age and older.

Interpretation: Most components of the Medicare program have experienced steady increases since the program's inception in 1967. The variations noted in the figures above reflect changing demand for various services and changing emphasis at HCFA concerning the types of services that are appropriate under the program.

VII-17. MEDICARE
MEDICARE EXPENDITURES BY PROGRAM COMPONENT
(In $ Millions)
1967-1990

	Benefits Under:	
Year	Hospital Insurance	Supplementary Medical Insurance
1990	$66,997	$43,987
1989	$60,803	$39,783
1988	53,331	35,229
1987	50,289	22,618
1986	50,422	19,212
1985	48,414	17,311
1980	25,577	11,245
1975	11,581	3,415
1970	5,281	1,790
1967	3,430	1,128

Source: Based on data collected by the Health Care Financing Administration (HCFA) within the U.S. Department of Health and Human Services. HCFA, as the organization responsible for the administration of the Medicare program, is the primary source of Medicare statistics. Additional data are available directly from HCFA (Washington, D.C.) or through its publications such as **Health Care Financing Review**.

Methodology: Based on records maintained by HCFA.

Definition: "Medicare" is the federally-sponsored health insurance program that covers the elderly and the disabled. "Hospital Insurance" covers the hospital expenses of Medicare enrollees and is also referred to as Part A. "Supplementary medical insurance" covers physician expenses and other non-hospital expenses and is also referred to as Part B. Part A of Medicare is mandatory, while Part B participation is voluntary.

Interpretation: At its inception, Medicare involved primarily hospital coverage. During the 1980s the portion of Medicare covering physician services grew in importance.

VII-18. MEDICARE
SELECTED MEDICARE STATISTICS BY AGE CATEGORY
FOR ENROLLEES 65 AND OLDER
1989

Age	Enrollment (in millions)	Persons served per 1,000 Enrollees	Payments per Person Served	Payments per Enrollee
65-66 years	3.9	703	$2,381	$1,737
67-68 years	3.9	703	2,964	2,015
69-70 years	3.5	732	3,029	2,271
71-72 years	3.2	764	3,204	2,449
73-74 years	2.9	795	3,486	2,772
75-79 years	5.9	820	3,755	3,079
80-84 years	3.9	857	4,074	3,493
85 years & over	3.2	869	4,384	3,809
Total	30.4	785	3,445	2,704

Source: Based on unpublished data from the Bureau of Data Management and Strategy of the Health Care Financing Administration (HCFA) and published in **Health, United States, 1990.** HCFA, as the organization responsible for the administration of the Medicare program, is the primary source of Medicare statistics. **Health United States** is an annual collection of statistics published by the Department of Health and Human Services.

Methodology: Based on records maintained by HCFA.

Definition: "Medicare" is the federally-sponsored health insurance program that covers the elderly and the disabled. Participation is mandatory for individuals 65 of age and older. The enrollment figure includes the U.S. population living in various U.S. territories and in foreign countries.

Interpretation: Although the number of Medicare enrollees decreases with each increasing age cohort, the participation rate and the amount of payment per enrollee increases with each advancing age cohort.

VII-19. MEDICARE
MEDICARE ENROLLEES BY AGE CATEGORY FOR ENROLLEES 65 AND OLDER
(In Millions)
1967, 1977 AND 1989

Age	Enrollees		
	1967	1977	1989
65-66 years	2.8	3.3	3.9
67-68 years	2.6	3.2	3.9
69-70 years	2.4	2.9	3.5
71-72 years	2.3	2.6	3.2
73-74 years	2.1	2.3	2.9
75-79 years	3.9	4.5	5.9
80-84 years	2.2	3.0	3.9
85 years and over	1.3	2.1	3.2
Total	19.5	23.8	30.4

Source: Based on unpublished data from the Bureau of Data Management and Strategy of the Health Care Financing Administration (HCFA) and published in **Health, United States, 1991.** HCFA, as the organization responsible for the administration of the Medicare program, is the primary source of Medicare statistics. **Health, United States** is an annual collection of statistics published by the Department of Health and Human Services.

Methodology: Based on records maintained by HCFA.

Definition: "Medicare" is the federally-sponsored health insurance program that covers the elderly and the disabled. Participation is mandatory for individuals 65 of age and older. The enrollment figure includes the U.S. population living in various U.S. territories and in foreign countries.

Interpretation: Although the number of Medicare enrollees increased over the three time periods for each age cohort, the increases among the oldest cohorts were proportionately much larger.

DATA ON MEDICAL AND HEALTH PERSONNEL

Health care is a highly labor-intensive industry involving a myriad of occupations. There is probably no other industry that surpasses health care in terms of the variety of occupational categories and the complexity of its occupational structure. From the perspective of the national economy, employment in health care is not inconsequential, since this industry employs more workers than nearly any other industry. Because of the need to efficiently allocate health care training resources and effectively meet future health care needs, there has been growing demand for data related to the medical and health professions. Increasingly, decision-makers are faced with the need for such data for decision support purposes, especially in view of the controversy that often surrounds the issue of manpower adequacy.

Demand for information on medical and health education is driven by forces at two different levels–the system level and the institutional level. At the system level, federal and state agencies require information for policy setting and funding decisions. Much of the medical and health education that is provided is subsidized by government funds. Therefore, the existing manpower pool (and its adequacy) must be assessed for a variety of medical and health professions as a basis for funding decisions. Other issues that require decision-support data include the controversies surrounding the adequacy of the health professional manpower pool (e.g., physicians and nurses) and problems related to the (mal)distribution of health professionals by area of training and geographic location.

At the institutional level, health care organizations require increasingly accurate data for planning purposes. Not only do budget constraints require that more attention be paid to planning, but shortages of some health professionals mean that greater effort must be expended for both recruiting and training by these health care organizations. As health care organizations, especially hospitals, become more competitive, accurate information on the number and characteristics of medical manpower becomes critical.

There is also growing interest on the part of the general public with regard to data on medical and health education. Today there is much more interest among prospective students in the numbers and characteristics of existing educational programs and their current students. Chronic shortages of nurses and/or physicians in some communities have contributed to the demand for information on the supply of health workers on the part of those involved in acquiring services for these communities.

The two main types of information available are aggregate data related to each medical and health profession and detailed listings of the existing personnel in specific fields. Aggregate data are most useful at the system level for planning purposes, but they are often used at the institutional level (e.g., by hospitals) to evaluate the organization's existing manpower supply.

The major sources of aggregate data on medical and health professionals are various government agencies. Since the 1970s the federal government has collected information on many categories of health professionals. The Bureau of Health Professions comes closest within the federal government to an agency that systematically collects such information. Other health-related federal agencies (e.g., the National Institutes of Health) may assemble such information incidental to other data collection activities.

Data on medical and health professionals are available from the various state agencies that accredit, monitor and/or fund such programs. Since most educational programs are accredited at the state level, each state has licensure boards and other organizations whose functions include the maintenance of such information. The drawback to these data at both the federal and state level are their less than optimum accessibility. Even when computerized databases are maintained, the information may be available to users only in printed form. At the state level, there is considerable variability in the form of the data and in its availability. Note that these sources only include occupations that are involved in patient care and/or require state licensure or registration.

Professional associations also maintain data on their members and, in some cases, on non-members as well. Associations supported by organized medicine maintain often extensive data files on physicians, medical students, residents, fellows, and other trainees. Individual medical specialty associations maintain data on professionals in their specialty areas. More than one nursing association maintains data on nurse manpower. Similarly, associations formed by other "independent" practitioners (e.g., dentists, podiatrists, optometrists) and by other health and paramedical personnel (e.g., clinical psychologists, medical librarians, medical records clerks) typically maintain records on the workers in their respective fields. Sometimes the best sources of these data are the databooks and/or journals of the respective associations. For example, each year the Journal of the American Medical Association presents detailed data on medical training programs and the medical students, residents and fellow involved in them.

Although the federal government generally does not provide lists of the members of various professions, many state agencies do. In addition to generating aggregate data, state agencies often make their databases available to the public, most often in paper form but increasingly in some computerized format. State medical licensure boards, for example, typically publish directories of those licensed to practice in the state (e.g., physicians). Similar information may also be available for other occupations that require state registration. Professional associations may also be a source of lists of health professionals. The American Medical Association maintains a master file on all physicians known to be practicing in the United States, whether they are AMA members or not. Increasingly, private data vendors are developing lists that they sell to the public.

In many ways, the data on medical and health professionals are among the most fragmented in the health care field. The degree of specialization and the plethora of medical and health professions make the systematic collection, maintenance and dissemination of these data problematic. The federal government comes the closest to maintaining a national database, at least for selected professions. If only state level data are required, the individual states become the best sources. In either case, the data are not likely to be available in particularly user-friendly form. If the user only requires a particular fact (e.g., the number of nurses now in practice), the information is probably available at a local library. However, if a policy setter or researcher requires comprehensive data or data that can be analyzed on a computer, the situation is not very favorable. As yet, private vendors have expressed limited interest in establishing such databases or repackaging existing data.

VIII-1. HEALTH PROFESSIONALS
NUMBER AND RATE OF PRACTITIONERS FOR
SELECTED HEALTH PROFESSIONS
(In 1,000s)
1989

Profession	Number	Rate*
Physicians	563	231
Dentists	144	58
Optometrists	26	11
Pharmacists	160	64
Podiatrists	12	5
Registered nurses	1,666	67
Veterinarians	49	20

*Rates are based on number of professionals per 100,000 population.

Source: Based on data collected by the Bureau of Health Professions within the Department of Health and Human Services. Published in **Health, United States, 1991.** The Bureau of Health Professions is charged by Congress with monitoring the supply of medical health personnel.

Methodology: Compiled from a variety of industry sources by the Bureau of Health Professions.

Definitions: "Physicians" includes osteopaths but excludes physicians whose activity status was unknown.

Interpretation: Physicians are by far the most numerous of "independent" practitioners. Nurses are the most numerous of other health professionals.

VIII-2. HOSPITAL EMPLOYMENT
EMPLOYMENT IN COMMUNITY HOSPITALS
1981-1988

Occupation	1981	1985	1988
All hospital personnel	3,069,955	3,024,929	3,231,745
Administrators	26,734	30,174	35,715
Registered nurses	629,354	709,253	770,613
Licensed practical nurses	234,226	186,780	170,637
Ancillary nursing personnel	280,614	235,853	244,297
Medical record administrators & technicians	38,186	41,199	46,937
Pharmacists and pharmacy technicians	47,053	52,973	58,759
Technologists and other laboratory personnel	147,451	144,831	148,635
Dietitians and dietetic technicians	40,192	33,305	35,126
Radiologic service personnel	90,738	91,353	101,098
Occupational and recreational therapists	8,481	10,030	13,133
Physical therapists, assistants and aids	27,675	29,064	32,680
Speech pathologists and audiologists	2,463	3,253	4,346
Respiratory therapists and technicians	47,312	51,056	55,690
Medical social workers	13,915	15,192	18,685
Total trainee personnel	66,906	63,367	67,587

Source: Based on data collected by the American Hospital Association and published in **Health, United States, 1990.** The AHA is the national association of hospitals and, based on data collected from the nation's hospitals, annually publishes **AHA Hospital Statistics** and the **AHA Guide to the Health Care Field.**

Methodology: Data in AHA publications are collected through annual surveys of U.S. hospitals.

Definitions: "Community hospitals" include all nonfederal short-term general and other special hospitals, whose facilities and services are available to the public. Employees are reported in terms of full-time equivalents (FTEs). Payroll amounts are adjusted for inflation. "Trainee personnel" are primarily medical residents.

Qualifications: The data published here are based on voluntary replies to an annual survey that seeks a variety of information. The information gathered by the survey includes specific services.

VIII-3. HOSPITAL EMPLOYMENT
CHANGE IN HOSPITAL EMPLOYMENT
1981-1989

| | Percent Change from Previous Year | | |
Year	Full-Time Personnel	Part-Time Personnel	Full-Time Equivalent
1989	2.6%	5.7%	3.0%
1988	2.6	5.3	2.8
1987	2.8	3.0	2.9
1986	1.1	0.7	1.0
1985	-1.2	2.0	-0.8
1984	-2.2	-4.1	-2.5
1983	0.7	1.8	-0.2
1982	1.9	3.5	2.2
1981	3.6	10.4	4.5

Source: Based on data compiled by the Bureau of Labor Statistics (BLS). The BLS within the U.S. Department of Labor is the federal agency responsible for monitoring employment trends.

Methodology: The BLS compiles data from a variety of sources in order to track employment trends in the U.S.

Definitions: "Community hospitals" includes all nonfederal short-term general and other special hospitals, whose facilities and services are available to the public.

Interpretation: Staffing at the nation's hospitals was generally reduced during the mid-1980s in response to declining admissions resulting from changes in reimbursement procedures. By the late 1980s, however, the severity level of admitted patients had generally become worse and staffing levels were raised. By the late 1980s, part-time personnel were accounting for a larger share of all personnel.

VIII-4. HOSPITAL EMPLOYMENT
COMMUNITY HOSPITAL EMPLOYEES AND PAYROLLS
1950-1989

Year	Number of Employees*	Payroll ($ billions)
1989	3,937,000	99.3
1985	3,625,000	74.4
1980	3,492,000	47.0
1975	3,023,000	27.1
1970	2,537,000	15.7
1965	1,952,000	8.6
1960	1,598,000	5.6
1955	1,301,000	3.6
1950	1,058,000	2.2

*Rounded to nearest 1,000.

Source: Based on calculations made by the Health Care Financing Administration (HCFA) from data collected by the American Hospital Association through its national panel survey. HCFA is the Federal Agency responsible for the administration of the Medicare program and regularly publishes statistics on community hospitals in **Health Care Financing Review**.

Methodology: The AHA collects data from hospitals on a monthly basis. These monthly figures have been utilized by HCFA to calculate annual totals.

Definitions: "Community hospitals" include all nonfederal short-term general and other special hospitals, whose facilities and services are available to the public. Employees are reported in terms of full-time equivalents (FTEs). Payroll amounts are adjusted for inflation.

Qualifications: The data published here are based on voluntary replies to an annual survey that seeks a variety of information. The information gathered by the survey includes specific services.

Interpretation: The hospital industry has always been labor intensive and became more so during the 1950-1989 period. Even more dramatic than the growth in employees has been the nearly 50-fold jump in unadjusted payroll expenditures.

VIII-5. HOSPITAL EMPLOYMENT
DISTRIBUTION OF HOURS WORKED IN THE HOSPITAL INDUSTRY
BY EMPLOYEE CATEGORY
1980-1989

Occupation and Type of Hospital	Distribution of Hours by Occupation		
	1980	1985	1989
All hospitals:			
All occupations	100.0%	100.0%	100.0%
Registered nurses	21.3	23.2	22.8
Licensed practical nurses	5.5	5.0	4.3
Technicians	8.4	10.1	9.9
Therapists	2.5	3.1	3.2
Nursing aides	12.1	8.7	8.4
Other health occupations	9.3	10.6	10.8
Nonhealth occupations	41.0	39.5	40.6
Private Hospitals:			
All occupations	100.0%	100.0%	100.0%
Registered nurses	23.5	24.6	24.7
Licensed practical nurses	5.7	4.9	4.3
Technicians	9.1	10.7	10.4
Therapists	2.6	3.4	3.1
Nursing aides	10.1	7.7	7.6
Other health occupations	8.7	9.5	9.4
Nonhealth occupations	40.3	39.3	40.4

*Column values may not sum to 100 percent due to rounding.

Source: Based on data collected by the Bureau of Labor Statistics (BLS) within the U.S. Department of Commerce and published in **Statistical Abstract of the United States, 1990.** The BLS is the federal agency responsible for employment statistics.

Methodology: Compiled from a variety of industry sources by the Bureau of Labor Statistics.

Interpretation: The technological advances, malpractice concerns and the emphasis on quality are changing employee composition. The industry is demanding more registered nurses relative to other categories of nursing personnel. Technicians and therapists are also in increased demand.

VIII-6. GROWTH OCCUPATIONS
HEALTH CARE PROFESSIONS AMONG THE FASTEST GROWING OCCUPATIONS
1988-2000 PROJECTIONS

Occupation	Employment		Expected Change in Employment 1988-2000	
	1988	Projected 2000	Number	Percent
Paralegals	83,000	145,000	62,000	+75.3
Medical assistants	149,000	253,000	104,000	+70.0
Home health aides	236,000	397,000	160,000	+67.9
Radiologic technologists & technicians	132,000	218,000	87,000	+66.0
Data processing equipment repairers	71,000	115,000	44,000	+61.2
Medical record technicians	47,000	75,000	28,000	+59.9
Medical secretaries	207,000	327,000	120,000	+58.0
Physical therapists	68,000	107,000	39,000	+57.0
Surgical technologists	35,000	55,000	20,000	+56.4
Operations research analysts	55,000	85,000	30,000	+55.4
Securities & financial services sales workers	200,000	309,000	109,000	+54.8
Travel agents	142,000	219,000	77,000	+54.1
Computer systems analysts	403,000	617,000	214,000	+53.3
Physical & corrective therapy assistants	39,000	60,000	21,000	+52.5
Social welfare service aides	91,000	138,000	47,000	+51.5
Occupational therapists	33,000	48,000	16,000	+48.8
Computer programmers	519,000	769,000	250,000	+48.1
Human services workers	118,000	171,000	53,000	+44.9
Respiratory therapists	56,000	79,000	23,000	+41.3
Correction officers and jailers	186,000	262,000	76,000	+40.8

Source: Based on calculations made by the U.S. Department of Labor and published in **Occupational Outlook Quarterly**. The Department of Labor (DOL) maintains data and projects occupational demand for all occupations including health care occupations. For more information contact the DOL (Washington, D.C.). The **Occupational Outlook Quarterly** is published four times per year by the DOL's Bureau of Labor Statistics.

Methodology: Every two years the Bureau of Labor Statistics prepares occupational supply and demand projections for hundreds of individual occupations. Over 200 variables are utilized in calculations that consider population forecasts, economic trends and anticipated policy decisions. Three sets of projections are developed to provide low, middle and high estimates.

Interpretation: Ten of the twenty fastest growing (in terms of percent) occupations are in health care. It is likely that some of the other fast growing occupations also include health-related positions (e.g., operations research analysts). The fast growing health care occupations are generally in the technical and allied health areas.

VIII-7. PHYSICIANS
NUMBER OF NONFEDERAL PHYSICIANS
AND PHYSICIAN-TO-POPULATION RATIO
BY STATE
1990

	Total Physicians	Physicians Per 100,000 Population
Total	584,921	237
Alabama	6,964	170
Alaska	777	155
Arizona	8,226	233
Arkansas	3,966	165
California	78,285	272
Colorado	7,606	232
Connecticut	10,699	332
Delaware	1,449	217
Dist. of Columbia	3,929	658
Florida	31,483	251
Georgia	11,929	187
Hawaii	2,809	266
Idaho	1,435	142
Illinois	26,603	229
Indiana	9,558	171
Iowa	4,728	167
Kansas	4,861	195
Kentucky	6,701	181
Louisiana	8,689	200
Maine	2,522	208
Maryland	16,716	360
Massachusetts	21,475	364
Michigan	18,620	201
Minnesota	10,458	240
Mississippi	3,753	144
Missouri	10,759	209
Montana	1,452	181
Nebraska	2,955	185
Nevada	1,921	175
New Hampshire	2,507	227
New Jersey	20,579	267
New Mexico	3,114	206
New York	60,744	339
North Carolina	13,492	209
North Dakota	1,195	184
Ohio	23,239	213
Oklahoma	5,095	160
Oregon	6,562	233

(Continued on next page)

VIII-7. PHYSICIANS
NUMBER OF NONFEDERAL PHYSICIANS AND
PHYSICIAN-TO-POPULATION RATIO BY STATE

1990 *(Continued from previous page)*

	Total Physicians	Physicians Per 100,000 Population
Pennsylvania	30,824	256
Rhode Island	2,744	277
South Carolina	6,096	177
South Dakota	1,093	154
Tennessee	10,334	210
Texas	31,647	188
Utah	3,406	200
Vermont	1,631	288
Virginia	13,795	233
Washington	11,325	241
West Virginia	3,388	183
Wisconsin	10,049	207
Wyoming	734	156

Source: Based on data collected by the American Medical Association (AMA) and published in **Physician Characteristics and Distribution in the U.S.**

Methodology: The AMA maintains a file of all physicians practicing in the U.S. and compiles statistics such as these from that database. Population estimates by the U.S. Census Bureau are used to calculate the rates.

Definitions: "Physicians" excludes osteopaths.

Interpretation: The number and rate of physicians varies widely from state to state. Some states–mostly on the East Coast–have physician supplies much higher than the average. Others–mostly Southern and Western states–have a physician rate well below average.

VIII-8. PHYSICIANS
ACTIVE PHYSICIANS PER 10,000 POPULATION
1950-2000

Year	Active Physicians Per 10,000 Population
2000 (Projected)	27
1990	24
1985	22
1980	20
1975	17
1970	16
1960	14
1950	14

Source: Based on data compiled by the Bureau of Health Professions within the U.S. Department of Health and Human Services (DHHS) and published in **Health, United States, 1991**. The Bureau of Health Professions is the federal agency charged with monitoring the supply of medical and health personnel.

Methodology: The Bureau of Health Professions compiles data from various state sources and the American Medical Association.

Definitions: "Physician" includes osteopaths.

Interpretation: The middle of the century witnessed a drop in the physician to population ratio. Efforts initiated during the 1970s resulted in an increase in the physician supply leading to historical highs in the ratio. The trend toward more physicians per 10,000 residents is expected to continue through the end of the decade but level off thereafter.

VIII-9. MEDICAL LICENSURE
INITIAL MEDICAL LICENSES ISSUED BY STATE
1990

State	Number of Licenses Issued
Alabama*	222
Alaska*	16
Arizona	156
Arkansas	153
California	2,089
Colorado*	221
Connecticut	246
Delaware*	35
District of Columbia*	160
Florida	588
Georgia	396
Hawaii	113
Idaho*	19
Illinois*	1,013
Indiana	309
Iowa	236
Kansas	155
Kentucky*	216
Louisiana*	444
Maine	197
Maryland*	676
Massachusetts*	986
Michigan	581
Minnesota*	483
Mississippi*	105
Missouri*	342
Montana*	14
Nebraska*	211
Nevada	8
New Hampshire	41
New Jersey*	705
New Mexico	97
New York*	2,691
North Carolina*	440
North Dakota*	19
Ohio	1,335
Oklahoma	149
Oregon*	166
Pennsylvania	1,107
Rhode Island*	84
South Carolina*	211
South Dakota*	46

(Continued on next page)

VIII-9. MEDICAL LICENSURE
INITIAL MEDICAL LICENSES ISSUED BY STATE

1990 *(Continued from previous page)*

State	Number of Licenses Issued
Tennessee	688
Texas*	1,072
Utah	140
Vermont	42
Virginia	433
Washington	291
West Virginia	110
Wisconsin*	477
Wyoming	12
Total	20,853

*Figure includes doctors of osteopathy (D.O.s).

Source: Data collected by the Federation of State Medical Boards and published annually in **U.S. Medical Licensure Statistics/Licensure Requirements** (American Medical Association). Unpublished data on licensure may also be available from the Federation (Fort Worth, Texas) or from individual state medical licensure boards.

Definitions: Licenses to practice medicine are issued by the state medical boards of each state and various U.S. territories. Once licensed in one state, it is possible for a physician to obtain licenses in other states without the complicated process of an initial licensure. These figures are for "initial" licenses only.

Interpretation: The variation in licensure of physicians by state is a function of population size, population composition, health care needs, preferences of physicians, and differences in licensure requirements in the various states.

VIII-10. MEDICAL LICENSURE

TOTAL MEDICAL LICENSES ISSUED BY STATE
1990

State	Number of Licenses Issued
Alabama*	631
Alaska*	141
Arizona	606
Arkansas	318
California	4,174
Colorado*	720
Connecticut	768
Delaware*	177
District of Columbia*	482
Florida	2,041
Georgia*	1,206
Hawaii	352
Idaho*	183
Illinois*	2,027
Indiana	912
Iowa	562
Kansas	425
Kentucky*	736
Louisiana	741
Maine	197
Maryland*	1,259
Massachusetts*	1,645
Michigan	1,237
Minnesota*	936
Mississippi*	335
Missouri*	943
Montana*	120
Nebraska*	246
Nevada	204
New Hampshire	204
New Jersey*	1,573
New Mexico	388
New York*	3,403
North Carolina*	1,330
North Dakota*	110
Ohio	1,730
Oklahoma*	358
Oregon*	587
Pennsylvania	2,351
Rhode Island*	131
South Carolina*	507
South Dakota*	102
Tennessee	880

(Continued on next page)

VIII-10. MEDICAL LICENSURE
TOTAL MEDICAL LICENSES ISSUED BY STATE
1990 *(Continued from previous page)*

State	Number of Licenses Issued
Texas*	1,908
Utah	319
Vermont	137
Virginia	1,341
Washington	955
West Virginia	353
Wisconsin*	923
Wyoming	168
Total	44,341

*Figure includes doctors of osteopathy (D.O.s)

Source: Data collected by the Federation of State Medical Boards and published annually in **U.S. Medical Licensure Statistics/Licensure Requirements** (American Medical Association). Unpublished data on licensure may also be available from the Federation (Fort Worth, Texas) or from individual state medical licensure boards.

Definitions: Licenses to practice medicine are issued by the state medical boards of each state and various U.S. territories. Once licensed in one state, it is possible for a physician to obtain licenses in other states without the complicated process of an initial licensure. These figures are for total licenses issued and include "initial" licenses and subsequent licenses issued by "endorsement" to physicians already licensed to practice in another state. Less than one-third of the licenses issued in this year were initial licenses; the overwhelming majority were issued to physicians already licensed to practice in some other state.

Interpretation: The variation in licensure of physicians by state is a function of population size, population composition, health care needs, preferences of physicians, and differences in licensure requirements in the various states.

VIII-11. MEDICAL LICENSURE

INITIAL MEDICAL LICENSES ISSUED
1935-1990

Year	Number of Licenses Issued
1990	20,853
1989	20,115
1988	21,235
1987	20,324
1986	19,528
1985	18,288
1984	18,340
1983	20,601
1982	17,605
1981	18,831
1980	18,172
1975	16,859
1970	11,032
1965	9,147
1960	8,030
1955	7,737
1950	6,002
1945	5,748
1940	5,887
1935	5,510

Source: Data collected by the Federation of State Medical Boards and published annually in **U.S. Medical Licensure Statistics/Licensure Requirements** (American Medical Association). Unpublished data on licensure may also be available from the Federation (Fort Worth, Texas) or from individual state medical licensure boards.

Definitions: Licenses to practice medicine are issued by the state medical boards of each state and various U.S. territories. Once licensed in one state, it is possible for a physician to obtain licenses in other states without the complicated process of an initial licensure. These figures are for "initial" licenses only.

Interpretation: The variation in licensure of physicians over time reflects the number of new physicians entering practice, including graduates of American medical schools and foreign-trained physicians who have entered the United States to practice. The increase in annual licenses issued during the 1970s reflects both an increase in domestic production of M.D.s and a jump in the number of foreign-trained physicians applying for licensure.

VIII-12. FOREIGN MEDICAL GRADUATES

INITIAL MEDICAL LICENSES ISSUED TO FOREIGN MEDICAL GRADUATES BY STATE
1990

State	Number of Licenses Issued
Alabama	11
Alaska	1
Arizona	14
Arkansas	13
California	355
Colorado	29
Connecticut	23
Delaware	9
District of Columbia	19
Florida	156
Georgia	38
Hawaii	15
Idaho	0
Illinois	369
Indiana	50
Iowa	49
Kansas	31
Kentucky	20
Louisiana	3
Maine	14
Maryland	239
Massachusetts	151
Michigan	31
Minnesota	38
Mississippi	5
Missouri	16
Montana	0
Nebraska	35
Nevada	1
New Hampshire	4
New Jersey	318
New Mexico	26
New York	975
North Carolina	18
North Dakota	0
Ohio	43
Oklahoma	20
Oregon	6
Pennsylvania	107
Rhode Island	11
South Carolina	2
South Dakota	0

(Continued on next page)

VIII-12. FOREIGN MEDICAL GRADUATES
INITIAL MEDICAL LICENSES ISSUED TO FOREIGN MEDICAL
GRADUATES BY STATE

1990 *(Continued from previous page)*

State	Number of Licenses Issued
Tennessee	25
Texas	54
Utah	36
Vermont	3
Virginia	49
Washington	30
West Virginia	35
Wisconsin	75
Wyoming	2
Total	3,599

Source: Data collected by the Federation of State Medical Boards and published annually in **U.S. Medical Licensure Statistics/Licensure Requirements** (American Medical Association). Unpublished data on licensure may also be available from the Federation (Fort Worth, Texas) or from individual state medical licensure boards.

Definitions: Foreign medical graduates (FMGs) are physicians who receive their "undergraduate" medical training (the M.D. degree) from a medical school outside the United States or Canada. Most FMGs are foreign nationals although during the 1970s and 1980s many American citizens enrolled in foreign schools for medical training. Licenses to practice medicine are issued by the state medical boards of each state and various U.S. territories. "Initial" license refers to the first medical license received. Once licensed in one state, it is possible for a physician to obtain licenses in other states without the complicated process of an initial licensure.

Interpretation: The variation in licensure of foreign medical graduates by state is a function of population size, population composition, health care needs, preferences of foreign physicians, and differences in licensure requirements for FMGs in the various states.

VIII-13. FOREIGN MEDICAL GRADUATES

INITIAL MEDICAL LICENSES ISSUED TO FOREIGN MEDICAL GRADUATES
1950-1990

Year	Number of Licenses Issued
1990	3,599
1989	2,749
1988	3,230
1987	3,228
1986	2,926
1985	3,049
1984	4,094
1983	4,753
1982	4,196
1981	3,131
1980	3,310
1979	3,566
1978	4,578
1977	5,851
1976	6,436
1975	5,851
1974	6,436
1973	7,419
1972	6,661
1971	4,314
1970	3,016
1965	1,528
1960	1,419
1955	907
1950	308

Source: Data collected by the Federation of State Medical Boards and published annually in **U.S. Medical Licensure Statistics/Licensure Requirements** (American Medical Association). Unpublished data on licensure may also be available from the Federation (Fort Worth, Texas) or from individual state medical licensure boards.

Definitions: Foreign medical graduates (FMGs) are physicians who receive their "undergraduate" medical training (the M.D. degree) from a medical school outside the United States or Canada. Most FMGs are foreign nationals although during the 1970s and 1980s many American citizens enrolled in foreign schools for medical training. Licenses to practice medicine are issued by the state medical boards of each state and various U.S. territories. "Initial" license refers to the first medical license received. Once licensed in one state, it is possible for a physician to obtain licenses in other states without the complicated process of an initial licensure.

Interpretation: The trend in licenses issued to foreign medical graduates reflects the extent to which licensure for physicians not trained in the United States (or Canada) is facilitated. The high levels in the 1970s are a function of efforts to reduce the physician shortage, while the declining figures in the mid-1980s reflect restrictions being placed on foreign-trained physicians in the face of an alleged surplus of physicians.

VIII-14. PHYSICIAN SHORTAGES

COUNTIES WITHOUT AN ACTIVE PHYSICIAN IN PATIENT CARE BY STATE
JANUARY 1, 1990

State	Number of Counties
Alabama	0
Alaska	0
Arizona	0
Arkansas	1
California	1
Colorado	5
Connecticut	0
Delaware	0
Florida	0
Georgia	12
Hawaii	0
Idaho	4
Illinois	1
Indiana	1
Iowa	0
Kansas	4
Kentucky	2
Louisiana	0
Maine	0
Maryland	0
Massachusetts	0
Michigan	0
Minnesota	0
Mississippi	2
Missouri	10
Montana	8
Nebraska	17
Nevada	2
New Hampshire	0
New Jersey	0
New Mexico	1
New York	0
North Carolina	0
North Dakota	11
Ohio	1
Oklahoma	0
Oregon	3
Pennsylvania	0
Rhode Island	0
South Carolina	0
South Dakota	15
Tennessee	1
Texas	19
Utah	3
Vermont	0

(Continued on next page)

VIII-14. PHYSICIAN SHORTAGES
COUNTIES WITHOUT AN ACTIVE PHYSICIAN IN PATIENT CARE BY STATE
JANUARY 1, 1990 *(Continued from previous page)*

State	Number of Counties
Virginia	1
Washington	0
West Virginia	0
Wisconsin	0
Wyoming	0
Total	126

Source: Based on data collected by the U.S. Public Health Service (PHS) within the Department of Health and Human Services. The PHS is the federal organization responsible for the administration of the nation's public health programs and is a primary source of data on the distribution of physicians. Additional data are available directly from the PHS (Washington, D.C.) or through its publications.

Methodology: The Public Health Service maintains a registry of all counties and the number of physicians serving them.

Definitions: "Active physicians" excludes physicians who are licensed to practice in a community but are not actively treating patients.

Qualifications: The various states have used differing criteria for subdividing into counties. As a result the size of counties varies from state to state and this has implications for the calculation of physician supply.

Interpretation: Twenty-four states contain at least one county without an active patient care physician. Most of these counties are in sparsely-populated states (e.g., North Dakota and South Dakota), although some states with high numbers of unserved counties (e.g., Missouri and Georgia) are densely populated and include pockets of sparse population.

VIII-15. NURSES

CHARACTERISTICS OF NEWLY LICENSED NURSES
1980-1987

	1980	1982	1987
Sex:			
Female	94.4%	94.5%	94.2%
Male	5.6	5.5	5.8
Racial/Ethnic Background:			
White	90.7	N/A	91.7
Black	4.3	N/A	4.5
Hispanic	1.4	N/A	2.0
Asian	3.3	N/A	1.5
Native American	0.3	N/A	0.4
Marital Status:			
Never Married	46.7	44.6	40.8
Married	44.6	45.9	48.9
Divorced/Separated	8.0	8.9	9.5
Widowed	0.7	0.6	0.8

Source: Peri Rosenfeld, **Profiles of the Newly Licensed Nurse**, published by the National League of Nursing (NLN) 1989. Additional information is available from the NLN's Division of Research (New York).

Methodology: Based on data collected through a February, 1988, mailout survey to over 53,000 recently licensed nurses. The overall response rate was 71%, with no state recording a rate less than 68%. Follow-up studies indicated that nonrespondents were not significantly different from respondents.

Definitions: "Newly licensed" refers to nurses who passed their qualifying examination and were licensed by the respective states during the year prior to the survey.

Qualifications: American territories are excluded from these figures.

Interpretation: The characteristics of the nurse population are gradually changing. Between 1980 and 1987 there were slight increases in the proportions that were male, black, married, and divorced. While the young, white female is still the typical nurse, nurses with "nontraditional" characteristics are becoming more common.

VIII-16. NURSE SALARIES

AVERAGE SALARIES OF NEWLY LICENSED NURSES RANKED BY STATE
1987

State	Average Salary
Connecticut	$27,190
California	26,274
Delaware	24,943
Massachusetts	24,921
New Jersey	24,910
District of Columbia	24,881
Alaska	24,832
New York	24,699
Louisiana	23,981
Pennsylvania	23,364
Nevada	23,241
Maryland	23,107
Michigan	23,040
Georgia	22,920
Rhode Island	22,865
Ohio	22,759
Arizona	22,447
Texas	22,287
Washington	22,077
North Carolina	21,826
Oregon	21,762
Minnesota	21,684
New Hampshire	21,640
Illinois	21,560
Florida	21,522
Oklahoma	21,375
Vermont	21,375
South Carolina	21,335
Hawaii	21,331
Colorado	21,296
Indiana	21,272
Tennessee	21,184
Virginia	21,128
Mississippi	20,984
Missouri	20,801
Wisconsin	20,769
New Mexico	20,760
Wyoming	20,658
Kentucky	20,603
Alabama	20,365
West Virginia	20,098
Kansas	20,091
Arkansas	19,852
Utah	19,829

(Continued on next page)

VIII-16. NURSE SALARIES
AVERAGE SALARIES OF NEWLY LICENSED NURSES RANKED BY STATE
1987 *(Continued from previous page)*

State	Average Salary
Montana	19,722
Idaho	19,712
Maine	19,614
Iowa	19,085
Nebraska	18,968

Source: Peri Rosenfeld, **Profiles of the Newly Licensed Nurse**, published by the National League of Nursing (NLN) 1989. Additional information is available from the NLN's Division of Research (New York).

Methodology: Based on data collected through a February, 1988, mailout survey to over 53,000 recently licensed nurses. The overall response rate was 71%, with no state recording a rate less than 68%. Follow-up studies indicated that nonrespondents were not significantly different from respondents.

Definitions: "Newly licensed" refers to nurses who passed their qualifying examination and were licensed by the respective states during the year prior to the survey. Salaries are for full-time employment only.

Qualifications: In many areas salaries have been raised since 1987. The relative order of the salaries is therefore a more useful indicator than the absolute number.

VIII-17. HOSPITAL SALARIES

AVERAGE SALARY AND TOTAL COMPENSATION
FOR SELECTED HOSPITAL POSITIONS
JULY, 1991

Position	Base Salary	Compensation Total
Chief Executive Officer/Administrator	$125,400	$136,400
Chief Operating Officer	107,500	114,500
Chief Financial Officer	81,700	85,500
Top Human Resources Executive	65,300	67,100
Head of Nursing Services	64,300	66,600
Head of Marketing	59,400	61,000
Head of Medical Affairs (M.D.)	134,800	137,700
Head of Public Relations	45,700	46,300

Source: Based on data conducted in the 1991 Hay Hospital Management/Professional Compensation Survey and published in **Hospitals** (9/5/91). The survey is co-sponsored by The Hay Group and the American Society for Healthcare Resources Administration. The Hay Group administers a variety of health-related surveys; additional information can be obtained from their Health Care Client Services (Philadelphia). **Hospitals** magazine is a publication of the American Hospital Association (Chicago).

Methodology: The Hay Group annually surveys a sample of the nation's hospitals, representing the for-profit, not-for-profit, religious and government-owned sectors. The 1991 survey included 1,211 hospitals. A variety of compensation data were collected for (or as of) 7/1/91 on 61 executive/management positions, 11 nursing positions, and 15 professional/technical positions.

Definitions: "Total compensation" refers to total cash compensation. It is assumed that "average" refers to the mean, but that information is not provided.

Qualifications: Since the Hay Corporation survey is based on a sample of institutions, it is characterized by the shortcomings of any sample survey. However, the size of the sample and its representativeness give this survey considerable credibility. Note that salary levels vary substantially by hospital size and other characteristics and averages should be used with caution. Some other figures that are available indicate higher salaries for these positions.

DATA ON PHYSICIAN PRACTICE CHARACTERISTICS

There has been a great deal of interest in recent years in the characteristics of physician practices in the United States. Our society has displayed a fascination with the lifestyles and activities of this elite group, and there appears to be an insatiable demand for data on physicians and their practices. Over the past couple of decades, a more practical interest in physician practice patterns has developed on the part of government policy-makers, health care regulators, and third-party payers. As questions have been raised concerning the appropriateness of certain patterns of care, the appropriateness of charges for health services and the level of equity in the provision of care, the physician has become an object of intense scrutiny. This interest reflects not only the fact that physicians benefit economically from the provision of health services but also from the fact that physicians, through the clinical decisions they make, influence most of the expenditures made for health care. The interest in physician practice characteristics was ultimately, although belatedly, been pursued by physicians themselves, who are now being forced to carefully evaluate their practices and to incorporate sound business principles.

Although some information is collected on physicians and their practices by government agencies at different levels of government, most of the information generated concerning physicians is compiled by private organizations. The primary collectors of such data are the associations that represent organized medicine. The American Medical Association (AMA) has been in the forefront of the collection of data on physicians and is joined by other "official" medical organizations such as the American Association of Medical Colleges (AAMC) and those representing the various medical specialties. Other private sources of data are the federations of those involved in the management of medical practices (rather than physicians themselves), including the Medical Group Management Association (MGMA) and the American Group Practice Association (AGPA).

There are a few other private sources of data on physicians and their practices beyond those officially linked to physicians or practice managers. Medical Economics, Inc., maintains a database on physicians that includes information on their practice patterns, and a few private vendors have begun collecting such information. In addition, *some* information on *some* medical groups is maintained in such business databases as the Dun & Bradstreet registry. These sources of data tend to be less complete than the industry sources mentioned above. They are, however, sometimes more accessible.

Little of the information on physician practice characteristics is available as computerized databases, although some organizations are beginning to disseminate their data in machine-readable form. For the most part, printed reports must be relied upon. Publications of the AMA and some of the other representatives of organized medicine are made available to organizational members and may or may not be available to the general public. When they are available, they tend to be expensive. Some of these publications may be available, however, at medical school libraries.

The only other sources of data on physician practices are sample surveys that are conducted periodically either by private vendors or by quasi-public research institutes. While some of these survey findings may be available in report form (and generally expensive), findings are occasionally published in various health care publications.

IX-1. PHYSICIAN ACTIVITY
MAJOR PROFESSIONAL ACTIVITIES FOR ALL PHYSICIANS
1965-1990

Activity	1965	1975	1985	1990
Total Physicians	292,088	393,742	552,716	615,421
Patient Care	259,418	311,937	448,820	503,870
Office Based Practice	185,338	215,429	330,197	366,995
Hospital Based Practice	74,080	96,508	118,623	142,875
Residents	43,506	57,802	75,411	83,389
Clinical Fellows	-	-	-	8,691
Full-time Staff	30,574	38,706	43,212	50,795
Other Professional Activity	18,157	28,343	48,320	43,440
Medical Teaching	9,794	6,445	7,832	8,090
Administration	4,057	11,161	13,810	14,819
Research	4,306	7,944	23,268	16,930
Other	-	2,793	3,410	3,601
Not Classified	-	26,145	13,950	12,678
Inactive	13,279	21,449	38,646	52,653

Source: Based on data collected by the American Medical Association (AMA) and published in **Physician Distribution and Licensure in the United States** (1973 through 1979 editions); **Physician Characteristics and Distribution in the U.S.** (1992 edition).

Methodology: The AMA conducts an annual survey of the practice patterns of a sample of the nation's physicians. The surveys include responses from approximately 3,000 physicians.

Definitions: "Physicians" includes all federal and non-federal physicians with an active license. "Residents" in 1965 includes residents, interns, and fellows; in all other years it includes residents only.

Qualifications: "Other" was not established as a category until 1968. "Not classified" was added as a category in 1970.

IX-2. GROUP SIZE
DISTRIBUTION OF PHYSICIAN GROUPS
BY SIZE
1988

Number in Group	Groups		Physicians	
	Number	Percent	Number	Percent
3	4,547	28.0	13,641	8.8
4	3,618	22.3	14,472	9.3
5-6	3,569	22.0	19,166	12.3
7-9	1,850	11.4	14,385	9.2
10-15	1,266	7.8	15,098	9.7
16-25	672	4.1	13,109	8.4
26-49	403	2.5	13,872	8.9
50-75	147	0.9	8,915	5.7
76-99	51	0.3	4,367	2.8
100 or more	118	0.7	38,603	24.8

Source: Based on data collected by the American Medical Association (AMA) and published in the AMA publication **Medical Groups in the U.S.**

Methodology: Based on a survey of all physician groups maintained on the AMA master list. The survey involved a mailout with telephone follow up. Nearly 90% of the eligible groups responded.

Definitions: "Group" refers to an arrangement by three or more physicians to practice jointly, share facilities, and to divide income based on some prearranged agreement.

Interpretation: The majority of physicians now practice in groups of three or more. The median size of groups is 4-5 physicians, with more physicians practicing in 5-6 man groups than any other size.

IX-3. GROUP AFFILIATION
LEVEL OF GROUP AFFILIATION FOR SELECTED SPECIALTIES
1988

Specialty	Percent of Physicians in Group Practices
Anesthesiology	43%
Cardiovascular Diseases	36
Emergency Medicine	91
Family/General Practice	26
General Surgery	20
Internal Medicine	24
Neurology	33
Obstetrics/Gynecology	30
Ophthalmology	26
Orthopedic Surgery	38
Pathology	33
Pediatrics	31
Psychiatry	15
Radiology	64
All specialties	30

Source: Based on data collected by the American Medical Association (AMA) and published in the AMA publication **Medical Groups in the U.S.**

Methodology: Based on a survey of all physician groups maintained on the AMA master list. The survey involved a mailout with telephone follow up. Nearly 90% of the eligible groups responded.

Definitions: "Group" refers to an arrangement by three or more physicians to practice jointly, share facilities, and to divide income based on some prearranged agreement.

Interpretation: The proportion of physicians involved in group practice varies widely among the specialties, ranging from a low of 15% for psychiatry to a high of 91% for emergency medicine. In general, physicians in hospital-based specialties are more likely to be involved in groups than are those in office-based practices.

IX-4. PRACTICE ORGANIZATION
FORM OF ORGANIZATION FOR MEDICAL GROUPS
1988

Form of Organization	Percent of Groups
Professional corporation	71.2%
Investor-owned for-profit corporation	2.4
Not-for-profit corporation	3.4
Sole proprietorship	0.7
Partnership	16.4
Association	3.6
Foundation	0.4
Other	1.9

Source: Based on data collected by the American Medical Association (AMA) and published in the AMA publication **Medical Groups in the U.S.**

Methodology: Based on a survey of all physician groups maintained on the AMA master list. The survey involved a mailout with telephone follow up. Nearly 90% of the eligible groups responded.

Definitions: "Group" refers to an arrangement by three or more physicians to practice jointly, share facilities, and to divide income based on some prearranged agreement.

IX-5. PRACTICE REVENUE
MEDIAN PRACTICE REVENUES FOR SELECTED SPECIALTIES
1988

Specialty	Total Practice Revenue
General/Family Practice	$197,000
Internal Medicine (All)	237,000
General Internal Medicine	221,000
Surgery (All)	370,000
General Surgery	301,000
Orthopedic Surgery	460,000
Ophthalmology	400,000
Pediatrics	200,000
Obstetrics/Gynecology	341,000
Radiology	345,000
Psychiatry	156,000
Anesthesiology	266,000

Note: Revenues rounded to the nearest $1,000.

Source: American Medical Association (AMA) Socioeconomic Monitoring System. Reprinted in **Physician Marketplace Statistics**, 1990, published by the AMA.

Methodology: The AMA conducts an annual survey of the practice patterns of a sample of the nation's physicians. The 1989 survey included responses from approximately 3,000 physicians.

Definitions: These figures refer to self-employed physicians only and does not include those employed in an organizational setting. "Revenue" refers to total charges per physician generated by the practice and not to the actual income of the physicians.

Qualifications: Since these data are based on a sample they suffer from the drawbacks of any sample data. Due to the sample size some specialties are not included in the table. Note that revenue figures are based on self-report by physicians and should be interpreted with caution.

Interpretation: Average practice revenues for physicians varies from specialty to specialty.

IX-6. PHYSICIAN INCOME
AVERAGE ANNUAL PHYSICIAN COMPENSATION
BY SPECIALTY
1991

Specialty	Average Compensation
Anesthesiologists	$220,800
Cardiologists (invasive)	258,875
Cardiovascular Surgeons	420,090
Dermatologists	145,092
Emergency Medicine	123,942
Family Practitioners	101,876
Gastroenterologists	188,133
General Surgeons	172,952
Internists	110,606
Neurologists	132,000
Neurosurgeons	338,692
Obstetrics/Gynecology	197,745
Orthopedic Surgeons	274,255
Pediatricians	104,937
Psychiatrists	110,143
Pulmonologists	154,795
Radiologists	246,462
Urologists	195,715

Source: Based on data collected by Center for Research in Ambulatory Health Care Administration and the Medicaid Group Management Association (MGMA) and republished in **MGM Update** (January, 1992). For additional information contact MGMA (Denver).

Methodology: Survey forms were mailed to a sample of physicians and allied health professionals. Over 15,000 responses were received and these provided the basis for these figures. Funding for the survey was provided by Cijka & Company, a St. Louis physician recruiting team.

Definitions: "Average compensation" refers to direct compensation and does not include fringe benefits.

Qualifications: Since these figures are based on a sample, they are subject to sampling error and should be interpreted with caution. These figures refer to compensation for physicians "employed" by groups and not to self-employed physicians in solo practices or partnerships.

Interpretation: Average compensation for physicians varies widely from specialty to specialty. The lowest average compensation, however, is several times higher than that of the average worker.

IX-7. INCOME
MEDIAN NET INCOME FOR SELECTED SPECIALTIES
1978-1988

Specialty	Net Income		
	1978	1985	1988
All Physicians	$60,000	$94,000	$120,000
General/Family Practice	50,000	70,000	85,000
Internal Medicine	58,000	90,000	156,000
Surgery	71,000	129,000	180,000
Pediatrics	48,000	70,000	85,000
Obstetrics/Gynecology	68,000	120,000	150,000
Radiology	80,000	135,000	158,000
Psychiatry	48,000	80,000	97,000
Anesthesiology	70,000	133,000	180,000

Note: Incomes rounded to the nearest $1,000.

Source: Based on data collected through the American Medical Association (AMA) socioeconomic monitoring system. Reprinted in **Socioeconomic Characteristics of Medical Practice**, 1989, published by the AMA.

Methodology: The AMA conducts an annual survey of the practice patterns of a sample of the nation's physicians. The 1989 survey included responses from approximately 3,000 physicians.

Definitions: "Net income" refers to income after expenses but before taxes.

Qualifications: Since these data are based on a sample they suffer from the drawbacks of any sample data. Due to the sample size some specialties are not included in the table. Note that revenue figures are based on self-reports by physicians and should be interpreted with caution.

Interpretation: Median net income for physicians varies widely from specialty to specialty.

IX-8. PHYSICIAN FEES
COMPARATIVE PHYSICIAN OFFICE VISIT CHARGES
BY SPECIALTY
1989

| Specialty | Median Office Visit Charge | |
	First Visit	Return Visit
General Practice	$35	$26
Family Practice	34	26
General Internal Medicine	51	34
Obstetrics/Gynecology	60	30
Pediatrics	40	30
General Surgery	41	29
Orthopedic Surgery	51	31
Cardiovascular Surgery	75	31
Neurosurgery	120	37
Plastic Surgery	46	27
Thoracic Surgery	75	33
Cardiology	101	37
Dermatology	45	31
Gastroenterology	80	35
Neurology	136	45
All surgical specialists	51	31
All non-surgical specialists	51	33

Source: Data collected annually by the Medical Economics Company and published in **Medical Economics** (October 2, 1989). Medical Economics Company is a major publisher of medical information, including the **Physicians Desk Reference.** Medical Economics is published semimonthly and is devoted to issues related to physician financial and practice matters.

Methodology: These data were collected by the Medical Economic Company through its 1989 Continuing Survey of medical practice patterns. The survey involves data collection from a sample of physician practices in eleven specialties.

Definitions: "Office visit" refers only to charges for the visit itself and does not include any charges for tests, medications or treatment that might be performed at the time of the visit. "Non-surgical specialists" excludes general practitioners and family practitioners.

Qualifications: Any sample survey is faced with the drawbacks that characterize all sample surveys. The size and representativeness of the sample, questionnaire design, interviewer skills, and a variety of other factors may affect the quality of the data. It should also be noted that physician self-reports sometimes suffer from problems of completeness, reliability, and accuracy.

Interpretation: Office-visit charges vary widely by specialty. There is a general tendency for medical and surgical specialists to charge more for office-visits than do primary care physicians.

IX-9. PHYSICIAN FEES
COMPARATIVE PHYSICIAN OFFICE VISIT CHARGES
BY REGION
1989

First Visit:

	Region			
	West	Midwest	South	East
General Practice	$43	$30	$31	$36
Family Practice	40	30	31	35
General Internal Medicine	56	41	56	55
Obstetrics/Gynecology	70	49	55	73
Pediatrics	46	35	36	41
General Surgery	51	35	41	46
Orthopedic Surgery	58	45	50	70
Cardiovascular Surgery	*	51	65	*
Neurosurgery	153	100	202	*
Plastic Surgery	50	*	41	*
Thoracic Surgery	*	*	75	*
Cardiology	*	*	100	*
Dermatology	49	*	40	*
Gastroenterology	75	*	80	96
Neurology	158	122	131	130
All surgical specialists	62	45	50	61
All non-surgical specialists	60	45	51	55

Revisit:

	Region			
	West	Midwest	South	East
General Practice	$33	$25	$25	$30
Family Practice	31	25	26	29
General Internal Medicine	36	29	31	36
Obstetrics/Gynecology	40	31	35	41
Pediatrics	35	27	28	33
General Surgery	31	26	28	31
Orthopedic Surgery	36	29	30	41
Cardiovascular Surgery	*	*	31	*
Neurosurgery	41	31	36	*
Plastic Surgery	*	*	26	*
Thoracic Surgery	*	*	31	*
Cardiology	41	*	35	41
Dermatology	35	*	29	*
Gastroenterology	36	*	35	40
Neurology	50	41	41	51
All surgical specialists	35	29	30	40
All non-surgical specialists	36	29	31	36

*Too few cases to be statistically reliable.

Source: Data collected annually by the Medical Economics Company by means of their Continuing Survey of medical practice patterns. Published in **Medical Economics** (October 2, 1989). Medical Economics Company is a major publisher of medical information, including the **Physicians Desk Reference**. **Medical Economics** is published semimonthly and is devoted to issues related to physician financial and practice matters.

Methodology: These data are collected by the Medical Economic Company through its 1989 Continuing Survey of medical practice patterns. It involves data collection from a sample of physician practices in eleven specialties.

Definitions: "Office visit" refers only to charges for the visit itself and does not include any charges for tests, medications or treatment that might be performed at the time of the visit.

Qualifications: Any sample survey is faced with the drawbacks that characterize all sample surveys. The size and representativeness of the sample, questionnaire design, interviewer skills, and a variety of other factors may affect the quality of the data. It should also be noted that physician self-reports sometimes suffer from problems of completeness, reliability, and accuracy.

Interpretation: Office-visit charges vary widely by region of the country. Charges are generally higher in the West than in any other region, although there is considerable variation from specialty to specialty.

IX-10. HOSPITAL ADMISSIONS
AVERAGE ANNUAL HOSPITAL REVENUE GENERATED
PER PHYSICIAN AND PER ADMISSION
1991

Specialty	Average Revenue Per Physician	Average Revenue Per Admission
All Physicians	$566,000	$ 7,400
Primary Care	536,000	5,100
Internal Medicine	840,000	7,000
General/Family Practice	512,000	5,000
Obstetrics/Gynecology	504,000	4,200
Pediatrics	236,000	3,500
Specialties	581,000	8,100
Thoracic Surgery	934,000	14,200
Pulmonology	880,000	9,800
Oncology	862,000	8,000
Neurosurgery	845,000	8,800
Cardiology	803,000	8,000
General Surgery	793,000	7,100
Hematology	792,000	8,100
Nephrology	721,000	9,400
Psychiatry	706,000	11,000
Orthopaedic Surgery	699,000	7,700
Cardiovascular Surgery	604,000*	10,942*
Urology	375,000	5,200
Gastroenterology	356,000	7,700
Rheumatology	262,000	7,841
Neurology	252,000	6,700
Plastic Surgery	168,000	6,200
Otolaryngology	153,000	4,800
Ophthalmology	59,000	9,100

*1990 figures.

Source: Based on data collected through a nationwide survey of hospitals conducted by Ernst & Young and Jackson and Coker. These data were published in their booklet 1991 **Physician Revenue Survey.** Ernst & Young is a national consulting firm and Jackson and Coker is a physician recruitment and medical staff development firm.

Methodology: The Ernst & Young/Jackson and Coker physician revenue survey is conducted annually. The figures are based on responses from "more than 800" of the nation's 6,000+ relevant hospitals. The figures are calculated by weighting responses according to bed size, type and ownership of the reporting hospitals.

Definitions: An "admission" refers to the entry of a patient by a physician for at least an overnight stay. "Revenue" refers to hospital charges generated as a result of the physician's admitting a patient.

Qualifications: Since the survey is based on an unrepresentative sample of community hospitals, the drawbacks related to sample surveys apply. In addition, responding hospitals may be characterized by differences in record-keeping or by greater or lesser precision in reporting their figures. Although statistical adjustments have been made to override defects in the sample, the figures should be used with caution. These figures represent averages and as such should be used cautiously as a measure of appropriate physician activity. There appears to be a slight bias toward patterns displayed at smaller hospitals. Some specialties are not included in the study. These figures are subject to substantial year-to-year fluctuations.

Interpretation: The amount of revenue generated for a hospital by its admitting physicians varies widely by specialty. Revenues generated per physician and per admission are typically higher for specialists (especially for surgical specialists) than for primary care physicians. Many specialists perform their procedures primarily on an outpatient basis and, if done at the hospital, may contributed as much as an inpatient admission.

IX-11. HOSPITAL ADMISSIONS
AVERAGE ANNUAL HOSPITAL INPATIENT ADMISSIONS
BY PHYSICIAN SPECIALTY
1991

Specialty	Average Annual Admissions
Overall Average	90
Primary Care	134
Obstetrics/Gynecology	164
General/Family Practice	129
Internal Medicine	121
Pediatrics	121
Specialties	75
General Surgery	119
Hematology	98
Oncology	113
Pulmonology	110
Cardiology	98
Orthopaedic Surgery	96
Thoracic Surgery	61
Neurosurgery	103
Urology	75
Psychiatry	98
Gastroenterology	47
Cardiovascular Surgery	105
Nephrology	75
Rheumatology	31
Plastic Surgery	26
Neurology	38
Otolaryngology	44
Ophthalmology	12

Source: Based on data collected through a nationwide survey of hospitals conducted by Ernst & Young and Jackson and Coker. These data were published in their booklet 1991 **Physician Revenue Survey.** Ernst & Young is a national consulting firm and Jackson and Coker is a physician recruitment and medical staff development firm.

Methodology: The Ernst & Young/Jackson and Coker physician revenue survey is conducted annually. The figures are based on responses from an unspecified number of the nation's 6,000+ relevant hospitals. The figures are calculated by weighting responses according to bed size, type and ownership of the reporting hospital.

Definitions: An "admission" refers to the entry of a patient by a physician for at least an overnight stay.

Qualifications: Since the survey is based on an unrepresentative sample of community hospitals, the drawbacks related to sample surveys apply. In addition, responding hospitals may be characterized by differences in record-keeping or by greater or lesser precision in reporting their figures. Although statistical adjustments have been made to override defects in the sample, the figures should be used with caution. These figures represent averages and as such should be used cautiously as a measure of appropriate physician activity. There appears to be a slight bias toward patterns displayed at smaller hospitals. Some specialties are not included in the study. These figures are subject to substantial year-to-year fluctuations.

Interpretation: The number of average annual admissions varies widely by specialty. Annual reported admissions are higher for primary care physicians than for specialists; this is more typically the case for smaller hospitals than for larger ones. The volume of admissions does not necessarily reflect the specialty's contribution to the financial viability of the hospital. The contribution made by an admission varies widely among the specialties.

IX-12. MEDICARE PARTICIPATION
PHYSICIAN PARTICIPATION RATES FOR MEDICARE BY STATE
1989

State	Percent of Physicians Participating
Alabama	75.9%
Alaska	38.8
Arizona	41.2
Arkansas	53.1
California	54.0
Colorado	28.1
Connecticut	29.3
Delaware	37.5
District of Columbia	34.4
Florida	32.8
Georgia	49.7
Hawaii	53.7
Idaho	16.0
Illinois	40.0
Indiana	40.0
Iowa	45.3
Kansas	61.6
Kentucky	50.5
Louisiana	32.6
Maine	51.2
Maryland	42.8
Massachusetts	46.9
Michigan	41.7
Minnesota	25.4
Mississippi	33.4
Missouri	39.6
Montana	21.5
Nebraska	42.5
Nevada	57.0
New Hampshire	28.0
New Jersey	26.0
New Mexico	36.3
New York	29.8
North Carolina	54.2
North Dakota	31.7
Ohio	46.8
Oklahoma	31.6
Oregon	36.9
Pennsylvania	39.0
Rhode Island	58.8
South Carolina	42.1
South Dakota	20.0

(Continued on next page)

IX-12. MEDICARE PARTICIPATION
PHYSICIAN PARTICIPATION RATES FOR MEDICAREBY STATE
1989 *(Continued from previous page)*

State	Percent of Physicians Participating
Tennessee	57.6
Texas	28.9
Utah	54.7
Vermont	40.5
Virginia	40.9
Washington	31.4
West Virginia	59.1
Wisconsin	40.0
Wyoming	19.3

Source: Data on records maintained by the Health Care Financing Administration (HCFA) within the U.S. Department of Health and Human Services. HCFA, as the organization responsible for the administration of the Medicare program, is the primary source of Medicare statistics. Additional data are available directly from HCFA (Washington, D.C.) or through its publications such as **Health Care Financing Review.**

Definitions: "Participating" physicians are those who enter an agreement with HCFA indicating that they will accept Medicare reimbursement as full payment for care rendered (i.e., charge no additional fees to the patient) in exchange for expeditious processing of Medicare claims by HCFA. Figures include M.D.s, osteopaths, and physicians with limited licenses.

Methodology: The data on participating physicians are obtained from the records of HCFA.

Qualifications: If a physician practices in more than one setting and is both a participating and non-participating, the physician is listed as participating for these purposes.

Interpretation: Medicare participation rates for physicians vary widely by state. The variation is partly a function of differences in practice patterns among physicians from state to state, as well as to the level of marketing knowledge among physicians as to the benefits of participating or non-participating.

IX-13. MEDICARE PARTICIPATION
MEDICARE PARTICIPATION RATES BY MEDICAL SPECIALTY
1985-86 - 1988-1990

Specialty	Percent of Physicians		
	1985-86	1988	1990
All physicians	28.4%	37.3%	44.1%
Cardiovascular Disease	35.6	52.8	60.6
General Surgery	33.9	48.5	55.8
Ophthalmology	27.3	46.3	55.6
Radiology	41.3	46.3	55.6
Orthopedic Surgery	29.0	44.0	53.7
Dermatology	34.0	45.7	53.4
Pathology	39.6	48.1	53.4
Neurology	34.8	44.1	53.1
Urology	27.8	41.7	49.6
Internal Medicine	32.5	41.2	48.8
Obstetrics-Gynecology	29.1	40.4	48.8
Family Practice	25.5	35.6	47.2
Otorhinolaryngology	24.6	36.9	45.2
Psychiatry	30.0	34.4	41.6
General Practice	27.3	32.3	39.7
Anesthesiology	21.1	25.0	30.8

Source: Based on data collected by the Health Care Financing Administration (HCFA) within the U.S. Department of Health and Human Services. HCFA, as the organization responsible for the administration of the Medicare program, is the primary source of Medicare statistics. Additional data are available directly from HCFA (Washington, D.C.) or through its publications such as **Health Care Financing Review.**

Methodology: Based on records maintained by HCFA.

Definitions: "Medicare" is the federally-sponsored health insurance program that covers the elderly and the disabled. "All physicians" include all practitioners defined as physicians under the Medicare statute. "Participation" in Medicare refers to physicians who are willing to accept Medicare patients and the Medicare allowable reimbursement as the full charge.

IX-14. MALPRACTICE PREMIUMS
ANNUAL MALPRACTICE PREMIUMS FOR ALL PHYSICIANS
1983-1990

Year	Average Annual Premium
1990	$14,500
1989	15,500
1988	15,900
1987	15,000
1986	12,800
1985	10,500
1984	8,400
1983	6,900

Source: Based on data collected annually by the American Medical Association (AMA) by means of its Socioeconomic Monitoring System. The AMA maintains records on all licensed physicians in the U.S. (maintained in the AMA Physician Master File) and makes this information available through various publications that can be purchased from the organization (Chicago).

Methodology: The data collected by the AMA are based on a mail survey conducted of a sample of the physicians in its Master File. These data were collected in 1989.

Qualifications: Any sample survey is faced with the drawbacks that characterize all sample surveys. The size and representativeness of the sample, questionnaire design, interviewer skills and a variety of other factors may affect the quality of the data. The size of the AMA annual sample is large enough to be statistically valid for the total physician population; however, it loses some of its usefulness when applied to subgroups of physicians who may be represented by a relatively small sample. It should also be noted that physician self-reports suffer from problems of completeness, reliability, and accuracy.

Interpretation: Malpractice insurance premiums for physicians were not a major issue until the 1980s. However, during that decade the escalating premiums resulted in something of a crisis, forcing many physicians to retire from practice. Malpractice premiums vary widely by specialty.

IX-15. MALPRACTICE PREMIUMS
COMPARATIVE ANNUAL MALPRACTICE PREMIUMS FOR SPECIALTIES
1988

Specialty	Average Annual Premium
All Physicians	$15,900
General/Family Practice	9,400
General Internal Medicine	8,500
Obstetrics/Gynecology	35,300
Pediatrics	9,300
General Surgery	27,300
Orthopedic Surgery	38,200
Ophthalmology	16,700
Otolaryngology (ENT)	22,400
Urology	16,700
Psychiatry	4,400
Radiology	12,400
Anesthesiology	23,600

Source: Based on data collected annually by the American Medical Association (AMA) by means of its Socioeconomic Monitoring System. The AMA maintains records on all licensed physicians in the U.S. (maintained in the AMA Physician Master File) and makes this information available through various publications that can be purchased from the organization (Chicago).

Methodology: The data collected by the AMA are based on a mail survey conducted of a sample of the physicians in its Master File. These data were collected in 1989.

Definitions: Refers only to physicians who are self-employed. "General Internal Medicine" refers to internists with a general rather than specialty practice.

Qualifications: Any sample survey is faced with the drawbacks that characterize all sample surveys. The size and representativeness of the sample, questionnaire design, interviewer skills and a variety of other factors may affect the quality of the data. The size of the AMA annual sample is large enough to be statistically valid for the total physician population; however, it loses some of its usefulness when applied to subgroups of physicians who may be represented by a relatively small sample. It should also be noted that physician self-reports suffer from problems of completeness, reliability, and accuracy.

Interpretation: Malpractice premiums vary widely by specialty. These variations partially reflect the risk inherent in the procedures performed (e.g., the surgical specialties) and partially the degree of patient reaction to negligence (e.g., obstetrics/gynecology).

IX-16. MALPRACTICE AWARDS
MALPRACTICE SUIT AWARDS
1975-1988

| Year | Average Award | |
	Mean	Median
1988	$ 993,450	$400,000
1985	1,179,095	400,000
1980	404,726	200,000
1975	220,018	126,750

Source: Published in **Current Award Trends** (Solon, Ohio) based on data collected by Jury Verdict Research.

Qualifications: Both the mean award and the median award are presented since a small number of unusually large awards could distort the average.

Interpretation: During the 1980s the sums awarded in medical malpractice suit verdicts increased dramatically. This probably reflects a nationwide trend for jury awards in all types of cases. It also reflects declining public support for physicians. Some leveling off of award levels was experienced during the late 1980s, partly as a result of tort reforms and limitations on awards introduced in some states.

IX-17. MALPRACTICE CLAIMS
TEN MOST FREQUENT ALLEGATIONS RESULTING IN MALPRACTICE CLAIMS
1987-88

Type of Allegation	Number of Claims
Postoperative complications from surgery	1,474
Improper treatment (birth related)	661
Failure to diagnose cancer	607
Inadvertent act during surgery	375
Failure to diagnose fracture/dislocation	304
Improper treatment (based on drug side-effects)	288
Improper treatment (based on insufficient therapy)	277
Improper treatment of a fracture/dislocation	272
Death resulting from surgery	258
Inappropriate procedure performed during surgery	233

Source: Based on data collected by the St. Paul Companies (St. Paul, Minnesota) and published in **Physicians and Surgeons' Update** (1988). St. Paul is the major national insurer of physicians.

Methodology: Based on an analysis of 9,947 medical professional liability claims submitted to St. Paul on behalf of their 31,000 covered physicians during 1987-88.

Definitions: These data reflect claims submitted and do not necessarily reflect the extent to which awards were made or settlements reached.

Interpretation: During the 1980s the number of medical malpractice suits filed increased dramatically. This probably reflects a nationwide trend toward more litigation as well as an increased willingness of patients to sue their physicians. It also reflects declining public support for physicians.

IX-18. MALPRACTICE CLAIMS
AVERAGE ANNUAL CLAIMS PER 100 PHYSICIANS
IN SELECTED SPECIALTIES
1990

Specialty	Claims per 100 Physicians
All Physicians	7.7
General/Family Practice	5.9
Internal Medicine	6.2
Obstetrics/Gynecology	11.9
Pediatrics	9.7
All Surgery Specialties	11.5
Psychiatry	2.4
Radiology	8.7
Anesthesiology	5.3
Pathology	1.5
All Other Specialties	7.0

Source: Data collected annually by the American Medical Association (AMA) by means of their Socioeconomic Monitoring System. The AMA maintains records on all licensed physicians in the U.S. (maintained in the AMA Physician Master File) and makes this information available through various publications that can be purchased from the organization (Chicago).

Methodology: The data collected by the AMA are based on a mail survey conducted of a sample of the physicians in its Master File. These data were collected in 1989.

Qualifications: Any sample survey is faced with the drawbacks that characterize all sample surveys. The size and representativeness of the sample, questionnaire design, interviewer skills and a variety of other factors may affect the quality of the data. The size of the AMA annual sample is large enough to be statistically valid for the total physician population; however, it loses some of its usefulness when applied to subgroups of physicians who may be represented by a relatively small sample. It should also be noted that physician self-reports suffer from problems of completeness, reliability, and accuracy. The number of claims does not necessarily indicate the incidence of negligence characterizing the physicians in a particular specialty; it may reflect the volume of cases seen or procedures performed or the nature of the patients treated (e.g., newborns).

Interpretation: Obstetricians and surgeons have the highest rates of malpractice claims among the specialties analyzed.

IX-19. PHYSICIAN ACTIVITY
CAREER ACTIVITY CHOICES FOR GRADUATING M.D.s
1981-1989

Activity	Percent Choosing:			
	1981	1985	1987	1989
Full-Time Faculty Appointment				
Basic science	1.0%	1.2%	1.1%	1.3%
Clinical science	21.5	26.4	27.2	28.8
Salaried Research Scientist				
Basic medical sciences	0.2	0.2	0.2	0.1
Clinical sciences	0.5	0.3	0.3	0.3
Private Clinical Practice				
Solo	5.0	3.3	3.1	3.1
In partnership with one other physician	11.3	9.3	8.9	7.2
In a group of three or more physicians	35.2	35.2	37.1	35.8
Undecided among options	12.0	10.1	9.0	9.9
Salaried Clinical Practice, Employed by				
Hospital	6.4	6.1	6.1	7.0
Prepaid group clinic	2.9	2.7	2.2	1.2
State or federal agency	3.0	3.2	2.8	3.0
Administration - No Practice	0.2	0.2	0.2	0.3
Other	-	1.3	1.5	1.2
No Response	0.7	0.6	0.5	0.7

Source: Based on data collected by the American Association of Medical Colleges, Section for Student and Educational Programs. The American Association of Medical Colleges (AAMC) is an organization of all U.S. colleges of medicine.

Methodology: Data collected by means of the AAMC's annual survey of graduating M.D.s.

Qualifications: These data are obtained by means of a questionnaire. Since significant numbers of medical school graduating seniors do not respond, these data must be interpreted with caution. The original specialty choice may not be pursued.

Interpretation: The structure of medicine is shifting dramatically from solo/small practice to group practice. Also, it facilitated the recruitment of faculty for academic practices.

IX-20. PHYSICIAN SPECIALTIES
SPECIALTY SELECTED BY GRADUATING M.D.s
1981-1989

Specialty	Percent Choosing:			
	1981	1985	1987	1989
Family Medicine/Practice	17.3%	15.9%	18.3%	13.7%
General Internal medicine	12.7	10.3	6.8	5.3
General Pediatrics	8.8	6.3	6.7	6.4
Total Primary Care	38.8	32.5	31.8	25.4
Allergy and immunology	0.2	0.2	0.2	0.7
Anesthesiology and Critical Care	4.2	6.6	6.6	7.1
Dermatology	1.2	1.6	1.7	2.7
Emergency Medicine	2.6	3.0	3.7	4.1
Internal Medicine Subspecialties	5.9	4.6	5.3	8.6
Neurology and Child Neurology	1.4	2.3	2.0	2.5
Nuclear Medicine	0.1	0.0	0.0	0.3
OB/GYN and Subspecialties	7.9	7.2	6.7	6.9
Ophthalmology	3.8	4.0	4.1	3.9
Pathology	2.5	2.1	2.4	2.4
Physical Medicine and Rehabilitation	0.6	1.3	1.8	2.1
Preventive Medicine	0.2	0.2	0.2	0.4
Psychiatry and Child Psychiatry	4.8	6.0	6.6	6.4
Radiology and Subspecialties	5.3	6.6	6.9	7.4
General Surgery	6.3	6.1	5.9	5.0
Neurological Surgery	1.3	1.1	1.2	1.1
Orthopaedic Surgery	6.0	6.6	5.8	5.9
Otolaryngology	2.0	2.6	2.4	2.6
Urology	1.3	2.4	2.3	1.8
Other Surgical Subspecialties*	3.1	2.8	3.2	3.3
Total Non-Primary Care	60.7	67.3	69.0	75.2
No Response to Specialty Question	0.6	0.6	0.1	0.4
Total Number of Students Who Responded to Questionnaire	10,795	11,048	11,307	11,175
Percent of All Final Year Students Who Responded to Questionnaire	68.8	66.3	71.4	71.5

*Includes critical care, colon and rectal, pediatric, plastic and thoracic subspecialties.

Source: Based on data collected by the American Association of Medical Colleges, Section for Student and Educational Programs. The American Association of Medical Colleges (AAMC) is an organization of all U.S. colleges of medicine.

Methodology: Data collected by means of the AAMC's annual survey of graduating M.D.s.

Qualifications: These data are obtained by means of a questionnaire. Since significant numbers of medical school graduating seniors do not respond, these data must be interpreted with caution. The original specialty choice may not be pursued.

Interpretation: There has been a trend over the past two decades away from primary care practices and toward specialty practices. This trend has resulted in "surpluses" in some subspecialties and "shortages" in primary care. However, there are no universally-accepted standards for the appropriate level of physical manpower, making it difficult to determine the appropriateness of the existing pool.

IX-21. PRACTICE LOCATION
PRACTICE SETTING CHOICE OF GRADUATING M.D.s
1981-1989

	Percent of Graduates		
	1981	1985	1989
Large city (pop. 500,000 or more)	20.6%	21.8%	23.7%
Suburb of a large city	10.3	14.1	17.4
City of moderate size (pop. 50,0000-500,000)	27.3	29.1	29.9
Suburb of moderate size city	7.1	7.8	8.5
Small city (pop. 10,000-50,000 - other than suburb)	16.9	12.5	9.1
Town (pop. 2,500-10,000 - other than suburb)			
Small town (pop. less than 2500)	1.3	1.1	0.7
Rural/unincorporated area	1.1	0.8	0.8
Undecided or no preference	8.2	7.5	6.5
No response	0.4	0.5	0.4

Source: Based on data collected by the American Association of Medical Colleges, Section for Student and Educational Programs. The American Association of Medical Colleges (AAMC) is an organization of all U.S. colleges of medicine.

Methodology: Data collected by means of the AAMC's annual survey of graduating M.D.s.

Qualifications: The initial choice of practice location is not a permanent location decision. The undecided or no preference is a relatively large percentage of a scarce resource.

Interpretation: The average physician will change practice location and/or organizational affiliation four times during his career.

Section X

DATA ON MEDICAL AND HEALTH EDUCATION

Education is a major component of the health care field. Training for medical and health care professionals is relatively long and complex and the costs for this training are relatively high. Issues such as the cost of medical education, the adequacy of the supply of health professionals, and the quality of medical and health education being received have driven the demand for these data. Increasingly, decision-makers are faced with the need for such data for decision support purposes.

There has been growing demand for data related to medical and health education for a variety of reasons. Yet, data on this topic are often more difficult to find than those for other health-related issues. There is no one source of data related to medical and health education. A variety of sources do exist, but they tend to be uncoordinated. Many of them involve proprietary data and therefore are not available to the public. At the same time there has been little interest in making such data more accessible and usable.

The demand for information on medical and health education is driven by forces at two different levels–the system level and the institutional level. At the system level, federal and state government agencies require information for policy setting and funding decisions. Much of the medical and health education that is provided is subsidized with government funds, and, in a period of tighter budgets, an increasing amount of such information is required as a basis for informed decisions. Other factors facing policy setters are the controversies surrounding the adequacy of the health professional manpower pool (e.g., physicians and nurses) and problems related to the (mal)distribution of health professions by area of training and geographic location.

At the institutional level, health care organizations require better data today for planning purposes. Not only do budget constraints require more attention to planning, but shortages of some health professionals mean that greater emphasis must be placed on both recruiting and training by these health care organizations.

There is also growing interest among the general public with regard to data on medical and health education. In the past, students casually chose careers in the health professionals. They often had little background information on their chosen field and its future manpower needs. Today there is much more interest among prospective students in the numbers and characteristics of the existing educational programs and their students.

The two main categories of data are those on training programs and those on students being trained. While some information is usually available on both of these topics for most medical and health training programs, it is often not very systematic or accessible. Further, this information is likely to take the form of simple lists. These typically offer no interpretation although there are often factors of which the user should be aware that are not very obvious.

The major sources of data on medical and health education are various government agencies and the professional associations for the professions to which educational programs relate. The federal government has historically collected information on both educational programs and on students trained or in training. The Bureau of Health Professions within the U.S. Department of Health and Human Services comes closest within the federal government to an agency that systematically collects such information. Other health-related federal agencies (e.g., the National Institutes of Health) may compile such information incidental to other data collection activities.

Data on both educational programs and their trainees are available from the various state agencies that accredit, monitor and/or fund such programs. Since most educational programs are accredited at the state level, each state has licensure boards and other organizations whose function it is to maintain such information. The drawback to these data at both the federal and state levels is their less than optimum accessibility. Even when computerized databases are maintained, the information may only be available to users in printed form. At the state level, there is considerable variability in the form of the data and in its availability.

Professional associations often maintain data on both the educational programs in operation in their respective fields and the trainees involved in these programs. There are some organizations that are formed of educational programs, such as the Association of American Medical Colleges. Associations supported by organized medicine maintain often extensive data files on medical students, residents, fellows and other trainees. Individual medical specialty associations maintain data on residents in training programs and their characteristics. Similarly, associations formed by other "independent" practitioners (e.g., dentists, podiatrists, optometrists) and by other health and paramedical personnel (e.g., clinical psychologists, medical librarians, medical records clerks) typically maintain records on the relevant programs and trainees. Sometimes the best sources of these data are the databooks and/or journals of the respective associations. For example, each year the Journal of the American Medical Association presents detailed data on medical training programs and the medical students, residents and fellows involved in them.

In many ways, the data on medical and health education are among the most fragmented in the health care field. The degree of specialization and the plethora of medical and health professions make the systematic collection, maintenance and dissemination of these data problematic. The federal government comes the closest to maintaining a national database, at least for selected professions. If only state level data are required, the individual states become the best sources. In either case, the data are not likely to be available in particularly user-friendly form. If the user only requires a specific fact (e.g., the number of nurses now in training), the information is probably available at a local library. However, if a policy setter or a researcher requires comprehensive data or data that can be analyzed on a computer, the situation is not very favorable. As yet, private vendors have expressed limited interest in establishing such databases or repackaging existing data.

X-1. HEALTH PROFESSIONS SCHOOLS
NUMBER OF SCHOOLS FOR SELECTED HEALTH PROFESSIONS
1990

Profession	Number of Schools
Medicine	126
Osteopathy	15
Nursing	1,457
Dentistry	58
Optometry	16
Pharmacy	74
Chiropractic	17

Source: Based on data compiled by the Bureau of Health Professions within the Department of Health and Human Services and data provided by the respective professional associations. Published in **Health, United States, 1991.** The Bureau of Health Professions has responsibility at the federal level for monitoring the nation's health manpower pool.

Methodology: The Bureau of Health Professions routinely collects data on educational programs from a variety of associations of health professionals.

Definitions: "Nursing" refers to registered nurses only.

Qualifications: The figure for nursing schools refers to 1988.

X-2. STUDENT ENROLLMENT
ENROLLMENT AND GRADUATION FOR SELECTED HEALTH PROFESSIONS
1990

Profession	First-Year Enrollment	Graduates
Medicine	16,749	15,774
Osteopathy	1,844	1,557
Nursing	108,580	61,660
Dentistry	3,979	4,312
Optometry	1,258	1,115
Pharmacy	8,088	6,557
Chiropractic	NA	2,400

NA = Not available

Source: Based on data compiled by the Bureau of Health Professions within the Department of Health and Human Services and data provided by the respective professional associations. Published in **Health, United States, 1991.** The Bureau of Health Professions has responsibility at the federal level for monitoring the nation's health manpower pool.

Methodology: The Bureau of Health Professions routinely collects data on educational programs from a variety of associations of health professionals.

Definitions: "Nursing" refers to registered nurses only.

Qualifications: The figure for nursing refers to 1988. The figure for medicine is an estimate.

X-3. STUDENT ENROLLMENT
TRENDS IN GRADUATION FOR SELECTED HEALTH PROFESSIONS
1975-1990

Profession	Number of Graduates			
	1975	1980	1985	1990
Medicine	12,714	15,135	16,319	15,433
Osteopathy	702	1,059	1,474	1,520
Nursing	73,915	75,523	82,075	61,660
Dentistry	4,969	5,256	5,353	4,312
Optometry	806	1,073	1,114	1,112
Pharmacy	6,712	7,278	5,724	6,557
Chiropractic	1,093	2,049	NA	2,400

Source: Based on data compiled by the Bureau of Health Professions within the Department of Health and Human Services and data provided by the respective professional associations. Published in **Health, United States, 1991.** The Bureau of Health Professions has responsibility at the federal level for monitoring the nation's health manpower pool.

Methodology: The Bureau of Health Professions routinely collects data on educational programs from a variety of associations of health professionals.

Definitions: "Nursing" refers to registered nurses only.

Qualifications: The 1990 figures are estimates.

Interpretation: Health professions education has been a growth industry since World War II. However, by the mid-1980s certain professions were experiencing a downturn in graduate production, although for differing reasons. It was felt that dentistry had produced a surplus, medicine had become less attractive as a profession, and females were choosing professions other than nursing.

X-4. PROFESSIONAL SCHOOL ENROLLMENT
ENROLLMENT IN SELECTED PROFESSIONAL SCHOOLS
BY RACE AND ETHNICITY
1988-89

Race/Ethnic Group	Osteopathy No.	Percent	Podiatry No.	Percent	School Dentistry No.	Percent	Optometry No.	Percent	Pharmacy No.	Percent
White	5,801	87.7	2,102	80.6	12,683	74.2	3,821	84.7	16,589	77.5
Black	159	2.4	236	9.0	984	5.8	117	2.6	1,729	8.1
Hispanic	240	3.6	95	3.6	1,038	6.1	139	3.1	1,055	4.9
Native American	33	0.5	5	0.2	63	0.4	22	0.5	45	0.2
Asian	381	5.8	156	6.0	2,326	13.6	410	9.1	2,000	9.3
Total	6,614		2,608		17,094		4,509		21,418	

Source: Based on data compiled by the Bureau of Health Professions within the Department of Health and Human Services and data provided by the respective professional associations. Published in **Health, United States, 1990.** The Bureau of Health Professions has responsibility at the federal level for monitoring the nation's health manpower pool.

Methodology: The Bureau of Health Professions routinely collects data from a variety of associations of health professionals.

Definitions: "White" and "black" groupings include only non-Hispanic whites and blacks.

Qualifications: Figures for optometry and pharmacy students are for 1987-88. Pharmacy students only include those in the last three years of pharmacy school.

Interpretation: While all health-related professional schools continue to be dominated by white students, minorities (particularly Asian-Americans) have become increasingly common among the students.

X-5. MEDICAL SCHOOLS
NUMBER OF U.S. MEDICAL SCHOOLS, STUDENTS AND GRADUATES
1965/66 TO 1989/90

Academic Year	Total Schools	Total Students	Total Graduates
1989/90	127	65,016	15,398
1985/86	126	66,585	16,117
1980/81	115	65,189	15,673
1975/76	109	55,818	13,634
1970/71	103	40,487	8,974
1965/66	84	32,835	7,574

Source: Based on data collected by the American Association Medical Colleges, Section of Student Services and published in **AAMC Data Book** (May 1990).

Methodology: The AAMC compiles data from its members which include all U.S. medical schools.

Interpretation: The number of medical schools and students increased by nearly 50% in the twenty-five years between 1965 and 1990. However, by the late 1980s the number of students entering medical school had dropped to the lowest level in years.

X-6. MEDICAL SCHOOL ENROLLMENT
ENROLLMENT IN MEDICAL SCHOOL BY RACE AND ETHNICITY
1978-79, 1988-89 AND 1991-92

| | Enrollment | | | | | |
| | 1978-79 | | 1988-89 | | 1991-92 | |
Race/Ethnic Group	Number	Percent	Number	Percent	Number	Percent
White	53,720	87.6%	50,366	77.7%	47,971	73.2%
Black	3,537	5.8	3,995	6.2	4,293	6.5
Hispanic	2,265	3.7	3,566	5.5	3,623	5.6
American Indian	202	0.3	237	0.4	299	0.4
Asian	1,592	2.6	6,595	10.2	9,353	14.3

Source: Based on data compiled by the Bureau of Health Professions within the Department of Health and Human Services and data provided by the respective professional associations and published in **Health, United States, 1990.** The data for the 1991-92 year were published in the **Journal of the American Medical Association.** The Bureau of Health Professions has responsibility at the federal level for monitoring the nation's health manpower pool.

Methodology: The Bureau of Health Professions routinely collects data on educational programs from a variety of associations of health professionals.

Definitions: "White" and "black" groupings include only non-Hispanic whites and blacks.

Qualifications: The "white" category includes a few non-U.S. citizen foreign students of various race and ethnic backgrounds.

Interpretation: Whites have been steadily declining as a proportion of medical students. The greatest gains in representation among medical students has been by Asian-Americans.

X-7. MEDICAL SCHOOL GRADUATES
MINORITY GROUP STATUS OF GRADUATING MEDICAL DOCTORS
1971-72 TO 1988-89

			Minority Group Status			
Year	Total Graduates	Black American	American Indian	Mexican American	Puerto Rican	Percent Minority
1988-89	15,630	821	57	245	124	8.0%
1985-86	16,117	824	49	233	89	7.4
1980-81	15,673	766	43	201	76	7.0
1975-76	13,634	743	31	130	19	6.9
1971-72	9,558	229	2	19	14	2.8

Source: Based on data collected by the American Association Medical Colleges, Section of Student Services, and published in **AAMC Data Book**.

Methodology: The AAMC compiles data from its members which include all U.S. medical schools.

Interpretation: The 1970s began the Affirmative Action period that increased the enrollment of minority groups in medical school. However, the growth rate for physicians in these minority categories is much slower than that for the minority populations themselves.

X-8. MEDICAL SCHOOLS
WOMEN APPLICANTS AND FIRST-YEAR ENTRANTS TO
U.S. MEDICAL SCHOOLS
1960-61 TO 1989-90

First-Year Class	Applicants			New First-Year Entrants		
	Total	Women	Percent Women	Total	Women	Percent Women
1989-90	26,915	10,546	39.2%	15,867	6,025	38.0%
1988-89	26,721	10,264	38.4	15,969	5,878	36.8
1987-88	28,123	10,411	37.0	15,927	5,767	36.2
1986-87	31,323	11,267	36.0	16,103	5,574	34.6
1980-81	36,100	10,664	29.5	16,590	4,747	28.7
1975-76	42,303	9,617	22.7	14,898	3,534	23.7
1970-71	24,987	2,734	10.9	11,169	1,228	11.0
1965-66	18,703	1,676	9.0	8.554	799	9.3
1960-61	14,397	1,044	7.3	7,845	-	-

Source: Based on data collected by the American Association Medical Colleges, Section of Student Services, and published in **AAMC Data Book**.

Methodology: The AAMC compiles data from its members which include all U.S. medical schools.

Qualifications: Data for 1974-75 through 1977-78 were revised to eliminate missing information based on AP, MCAT and other data in the AAMC Student and Applicant Information Management system (SAIMS).

Interpretation: The proportion of medical school applicants and enrollees that are women has increased steadily since the 1950s.

X-9. FOREIGN MEDICAL GRADUATES
ECFMG CERTIFICATES ISSUED TO FOREIGN MEDICAL GRADUATES
BY NATIONALITY AND LOCATION OF MEDICAL SCHOOL
1990

	Nationality		School Location	
	Number	Percent	Number	Percent
Australia	142	3.0%	164	3.5%
Dominican Republic	27	0.6	157	3.3
Egypt	105	2.2	113	2.4
Germany	104	2.2	110	2.3
Greece	44	0.9	58	0.1
Grenada	2	0.0	72	1.5
Hong Kong	63	0.1	75	0.1
India	758	16.1	778	16.5
Iran	62	1.3	34	0.7
Ireland	45	1.0	79	1.7
Israel	106	2.3	136	2.9
Italy	59	1.3	89	1.9
Lebanon	100	2.1	91	1.9
Mexico	45	1.0	106	2.3
Montserrat	0	0.0	63	1.3
Nigeria	150	3.2	156	3.3
Pakistan	299	6.3	292	6.2
Philippines	300	6.4	363	7.7
Poland	83	1.8	88	1.9
South Africa	50	1.1	64	1.4
Switzerland	57	1.2	63	0.1
Syria	146	3.1	147	3.1
Taiwan	51	1.1	54	1.1
Turkey	54	1.1	57	0.1
United Kingdom	160	3.4	163	3.5
United States	543	11.5	0	0.0
Other countries	1,299	27.6	1,138	24.2
Total	4,710		4,710	

Note: Percentages may not add due to rounding.

Source: Based on data collected by the Educational Commission for Foreign Medical Graduates (ECFMG) and published annually in **U.S. Medical Licensure Statistics/Licensure Requirements** (American Medical Association). Unpublished data on licensure may also be available from the ECFMG (Washington, DC).

Methodology: The ECFMG maintains data on all FMGs who apply for residency training.

Definitions: "Foreign medical graduates" (FMGs) are physicians who receive their "undergraduate" medical training (the M.D. degree) from a medical school outside the United States or Canada. Most FMGs are foreign nationals although during the 1970s and 1980s many American citizens enrolled in foreign schools for medical training. Licenses to practice medicine are issued by the state medical boards of each state and various U.S. territories. In order to be licensed to practice all physicians must complete a certain residency training. In order to be eligible for residency training, foreign medical graduates must receive a certificate from the Educational Commission for Foreign Medical Graduates verifying that they have met the necessary requirements.

Interpretation: The figures on national origin indicate the sources of foreign-trained physicians who seek to enter residency training in the United States. The origin of FMGs reflects such factors as world events, quality of foreign medical schools and the political climate in the United Sates. The sources have tended to change dramatically over the years. This table also reflects the phenomenon of foreign-trained American citizens. The numbers of certificatees attending medical school in Dominica, the Dominican Republic, Grenada, Montserrat and some other countries are a function of Americans attending these "offshore" medical schools. Note the 543 United States citizens who received certificates after being trained outside of the U.S.

X-10. MEDICAL RESIDENTS
FIRST-YEAR MEDICAL RESIDENTS ON DUTY BY MAJOR SPECIALTY
1980-1991

Specialty	1980	1985	1989	1991
Anesthesiology	523	423	348	265
Dermatology	7	9	26	9
Emergency Medicine	-	257	344	425
Family Practice	2,371	2,521	2,588	2,058
Internal Medicine	5,941	7,047	7,168	7,012
Neurological Surgery	20	49	47	21
Neurology	81	81	82	29
Obstetrics/Gynecology	1,220	1,113	1,112	1,104
Ophthalmology	31	30	38	3
Orthopaedic Surgery	218	323	286	285
Otolaryngology	48	119	59	30
Pathology	642	603	489	606
Pediatrics	1,864	2,089	2,130	1,860
Physical Medicine and Rehab	129	111	80	76
Preventive Medicine	27	32	13	8
Psychiatry	1,063	1,038	1,147	1,112
Radiology, Diagnostic	409	370	292	460
Surgery	2,539	2,765	2,597	2,506
Urology	65	78	63	25
Flexible	1,407	1,463	-	-
Transitional Year	-	-	1,475	1,349
Total	18,702	20,583	20,399	19,497

Source: Based on data collected by the American Medical Association (AMA) and published in the **Journal of the American Medical Association.** The AMA maintains extensive data on physicians in the U.S. including those who are in residency training.

Methodology: The AMA annually surveys residency programs to determine the level of postgraduate training being carried out.

Definitions: 1980 through 1983 data for "Preventive Medicine" includes Occupational Medicine and Public Health. Beginning in 1984 the specialty term "Flexible" was replaced with "Transitional Year". In 1988 the specialty term Radiology, Therapeutic" was replaced with "Radiation Oncology".

X-11. MEDICAL RESIDENTS
MEDICAL RESIDENTS IN TRAINING BY SPECIALTY
1980-1991

Specialty	1980	1985	1988	1991
Allergy and Immunology	192	276	281	298
Anesthesiology	2,490	4,025	4,480	5,213
Colon and Rectal Surgery	37	45	42	66
Dermatology	755	745	771	859
Dermatopathology	30	27	27	33
Emergency Medicine	-	1,122	1,311	1,876
Family Practice	6,344	7,276	7,175	6,610
Internal Medicine	15,964	17,832	18,074	18,662
Cardiovascular Disease	-	-	1,659	1,925
Endocrinology & Metabolism	-	-	370	342
Gastroenterology	-	-	870	803
Hematology	-	-	425	438
Infectious Diseases	-	-	493	595
Medical Oncology	-	-	513	642
Nephrology	-	-	468	482
Pulmonary Diseases	-	-	735	881
Rheumatology	-	-	308	337
Neurological Surgery	511	704	631	711
Neurology	1,114	1,386	1,326	1,362
Nuclear Medicine	176	191	173	199
Obstetrics/Gynecology	4,221	4,630	4,426	4,526
Ophthalmology	1,480	1,561	1,479	1,537
Orthopaedic Surgery	2,418	2,817	2,758	2,740
Otolaryngology	923	1,094	1,036	1,061
Pathology	2,186	2,358	2,054	2,437
Blood Banking	23	32	32	31
Chemical Pathology	-	-	5	1
Forensic Pathology	22	49	42	38
Hematology	-	8	21	17
Medical Microbiology	-	-	0	1
Neuropathology	52	41	53	42
Pediatrics	5,171	6,088	6,231	6,233
Pediatric Cardiology	130	140	174	210
Pediatric Endocrinology	-	-	75	112
Pediatric Hematology-Oncology	-	-	174	158
Pediatric nephrology	-	-	55	74
Neonatal-perinatal Medicine	-	325	395	392
Physical Medicine & Rehab	592	763	893	915
Plastic Surgery	367	405	407	414
Preventive Medicine, General	157	196	215	273
Aerospace Medicine	25	62	51	42
Occupational Medicine	71	106	113	130
Public Health	31	26	17	28

(Continued on next page)

X-11. MEDICAL RESIDENTS
MEDICAL RESIDENTS IN TRAINING BY SPECIALTY

1980-1991 *(Continued from previous page)*

Specialty	1980	1985	1988	1991
Combined General Preventive Medicine/Public Health	-	58	53	73
Psychiatry	3,911	4,809	5,097	4,905
Child Psychiatry	426	480	667	664
Radiology, Diagnostic	2,766	3,132	3,322	3,847
Radiology, Diagnostic (nuclear)	48	74	35	26
Radiology Oncology	288	524	470	451
Surgery	7,794	8,070	7,739	7,712
Pediatric Surgery	29	24	34	38
Vascular Surgery	-	51	76	109
Thoracic Surgery	256	285	277	305
Urology	917	1,057	972	1,012
Transitional year	-	1,520	1,423	1,440
Total	61,817	74,514	81,003	84,328

Source: Based on data collected by the American Medical Association (AMA) and published in the **Journal of the American Medical Association.** The AMA maintains extensive data on physicians in the U.S. including those who are in residency training.

Methodology: The AMA annually surveys residency programs to determine the level of postgraduate training being carried out.

Interpretation: Subspecialties of Internal Medicine were first accredited by the ACGME in 1986. The number of programs reporting residents on duty in these subspecialties increased steadily in the next two years.

X-12. NURSING SCHOOL
GRADUATIONS FROM REGISTERED NURSING PROGRAMS
1969-70 TO 1988-89

Academic Year	Number of Graduations	Percent Change from Previous Year
1988-89	61,660	-4.9%
1987-88	64,839	-8.0
1986-87	70,561	-8.4
1985-86	77,027	-6.2
1984-85	82,075	+2.2
1983-84	80,312	+3.8
1982-83	77,408	+4.5
1981-82	74,052	+0.1
1980-81	73,985	-2.0
1979-80	75,523	-2.1
1978-79	77,132	-1.0
1977-78	77,874	+0.1
1976-77	77,755	+0.9
1975-76	77,065	+4.3
1974-75	73,915	+10.2
1973-74	67,061	+13.9
1972-73	58,881	+14.8
1971-72	51,304	+10.4
1970-71	46,466	+7.8
1969-70	43,103	+3.1

Source: Based on data collected by the National League of Nursing (NLN) and published in the NLN's **Nursing Data Review**, 1990. Additional information is available from the NLN's Division of Research (New York).

Methodology: Data are collected from the various programs that offer degrees, associate degrees or diplomas in nursing.

Definitions: "Nursing" refers to registered nurses.

Qualifications: American territories are excluded from these figures.

Interpretation: The number of nurses receiving various nursing degrees and diplomas peaked during the early 1980s and has declined since then.

X-13. NURSING SCHOOL
GRADUATES FROM REGISTERED NURSING SCHOOLS
OFFERING DEGREES, ASSOCIATE DEGREES, AND DIPLOMAS
1969-70 TO 1988-89

Year	Baccalaureate Programs	Associate Degree Programs	Diploma Programs
1988-89	18,997	37,837	4,826
1987-88	21,504	37,397	5,938
1986-87	23,761	38,528	8,272
1985-86	25,170	41,333	10,524
1984-85	24,975	45,208	11,892
1983-84	23,718	44,394	12,200
1982-83	23,855	41,849	11,704
1981-82	24,081	38,289	11,682
1980-81	24,370	36,712	12,903
1979-80	24,994	36,034	14,495
1978-79	25,048	36,264	15,820
1977-78	24,187	36,556	17,131
1976-77	23,452	36,289	18,014
1975-76	22,579	34,625	19,861
1974-75	20,170	32,183	21,562
1973-74	16,957	28,919	21,185
1972-73	13,055	24,497	21,329
1971-72	10,968	18,926	21,410
1970-71	9,856	14,534	22,065
1969-70	9,069	11,483	22,551

Source: Based on data collected by the National League of Nursing (NLN) and published in the NLN's **Nursing Data Review**, 1990. Additional information is available from the NLN's Division of Research (New York).

Methodology: Data are collected from the various programs that offer degrees, associate degrees or diplomas in nursing.

Definitions: "Nursing" refers to registered nurses.

Qualifications: American territories are excluded from these figures.

Interpretation: Since the mid-1980s, the number of graduates has decreased for all types of nursing programs. Diploma programs have become less common.

X-14. NURSING SCHOOL
ENROLLMENT IN REGISTERED NURSING PROGRAMS
1970-1989

Year	Number of Enrollment	Percent Change from Previous Year
1989	201,458	+8.9
1988	184,924	+1.1
1987	182,947	-5.6
1986	193,712	-11.1
1985	217,955	-8.1
1984	237,232	-5.3
1983	250,553	+3.5
1982	242,035	+3.0
1981	234,995	+1.7
1980	230,966	-1.6
1979	234,659	-2.0
1978	239,486	-2.4
1977	245,390	-0.7
1976	247,044	-0.4
1975	248,171	+2.3
1974	242,551	+5.1
1973	230,803	+9.3
1972	211,239	+13.6
1971	185,869	+14.1
1970	162,924	+9.2

Source: Based on data collected by the National League of Nursing (NLN) and published in the NLN's **Nursing Data Review**, 1990. Additional information is available from the NLN's Division of Research (New York).

Methodology: Data are collected from the various programs that offer degrees, associate degrees or diplomas in nursing.

Definitions: "Nursing" refers to registered nurses.

Qualifications: American territories are excluded from these figures.

Interpretation: Total enrollment in nursing schools peaked in the early 1980s then declined until 1989 when a slight upswing was recorded.

X-15. NURSING SCHOOL
ENROLLMENT IN REGISTERED NURSING PROGRAMS BY TYPE OF PROGRAM
1970-1989

Year	Baccalaureate Programs	Associate Degree Programs	Diploma Programs
1989	74,865	106,175	20,418
1988	70,078	95,986	18,860
1987	73,621	90,399	18,927
1986	81,602	89,469	22,641
1985	91,020	96,756	30,179
1984	95,008	104,968	37,256
1983	98,941	109,605	42,007
1982	94,363	105,324	42,348
1981	93,967	100,019	41,009
1980	95,858	94,060	41,048
1979	98,939	92,069	43,651
1978	99,900	91,527	48,059
1977	101,430	91,102	52,828
1976	99,494	91,004	56,091
1975	99,837	88,121	60,213
1974	94,413	84,166	63,972
1973	84,738	77,508	68,557
1972	73,499	66,402	71,338
1971	59,454	55,425	70,990
1970	48,657	43,855	70,412

Source: Based on data collected by the National League of Nursing (NLN) and published in the NLN's **Nursing Data Review**, 1990. Additional information is available from the NLN's Division of Research (New York).

Methodology: Data are collected from the various programs that offer degrees, associate degrees or diplomas in nursing.

Definitions: "Nursing" refers to registered nurses.

Qualifications: American territories are excluded from these figures.

Interpretation: Enrollment in all types of nursing programs peaked in the early 1980s, then all experienced declines until the slight upturn recorded in 1989. Growth in baccalaureate and associate degree enrollment has been achieved at the expense of diploma programs.

X-16. NURSING SCHOOL
BASIC REGISTERED NURSING PROGRAMS BY TYPE OF PROGRAM
1970-1989

Year	Number of Schools	Total RN Programs	Baccalaureate Programs	Associate Degree Programs	Diploma Programs
1989	1,429	1,457	488	812	157
1988	1,391	1,442	479	792	171
1987	1,406	1,465	467	789	209
1986	1,426	1,469	455	776	238
1985	1,434	1,473	441	776	256
1984	1,445	1,477	427	777	273
1983	1,432	1,466	421	764	281
1982	1,406	1,432	402	742	288
1981	1,377	1,401	383	715	303
1980	1,360	1,385	377	697	311
1979	1,354	1,374	363	678	333
1978	1,340	1,358	348	666	344
1977	1,339	1,362	344	645	367
1976	1,337	1,358	336	632	390
1975	1,349	1,362	326	608	428
1974	1,347	1,358	310	588	460
1973	1,348	1,360	302	565	493
1972	1,350	1,362	290	532	540
1971	1,338	1,349	282	484	583
1970	1,330	1,340	267	437	636

Source: Based on data collected by the National League of Nursing (NLN) and published in the NLN's **Nursing Data Review**, 1990. Additional information is available from the NLN's Division of Research (New York).

Methodology: Data are collected from the various programs that offer degrees, associate degrees or diplomas in nursing.

Definitions: "Nursing" refers to registered nurses.

Qualifications: American territories are excluded from these figures.

Interpretation: The number of nursing schools (and programs) increased slowly but steadily between 1970 and 1989. However, the number of baccalaureate and associate degree programs essentially doubled, while three-fourths of the diploma programs were closed down during this time period.

X-17. NURSING SCHOOLS
NUMBER OF REGISTERED NURSING PROGRAMS BY STATE
1980-1989

	1980	1985	1989
United States	1,385	1,473	1,457
Alabama	34	36	35
Alaska	2	2	2
Arizona	16	16	15
Arkansas	19	20	21
California	87	92	91
Colorado	12	14	12
Connecticut	19	18	18
Delaware	7	6	7
Dist. of Columbia	7	6	5
Florida	34	39	40
Georgia	35	34	33
Hawaii	5	6	7
Idaho	6	6	7
Illinois	80	76	70
Indiana	30	37	44
Iowa	36	39	37
Kansas	27	30	32
Kentucky	26	28	29
Louisiana	16	22	21
Maine	9	10	14
Maryland	22	25	23
Massachusetts	51	47	41
Michigan	45	50	49
Minnesota	25	25	20
Mississippi	23	22	21
Missouri	37	41	44
Montana	4	4	5
Nebraska	11	14	13
Nevada	4	5	6
New Hampshire	7	11	9
New Jersey	40	39	38
New Mexico	11	12	14
New York	98	105	101
North Carolina	50	57	59
North Dakota	9	9	7
Ohio	72	70	68
Oklahoma	22	27	27
Oregon	16	17	18
Pennsylvania	95	98	90
Rhode Island	7	7	7
South Carolina	15	20	20

(Continued on next page)

X-17. NURSING SCHOOLS
NUMBER OF REGISTERED NURSING PROGRAMS BY STATE
1980-1989 *(Continued from previous page)*

	1980	1985	1989
South Dakota	8	9	10
Tennessee	33	33	34
Texas	56	65	68
Utah	5	4	7
Vermont	4	5	5
Virginia	38	37	34
Washington	21	22	24
West Virginia	17	18	18
Wisconsin	29	33	29
Wyoming	3	5	7
American Samoa	0	1	1
Guam	1	1	1
Puerto Rico	16	20	22
Virgin Islands	1	2	2

Source: Based on data collected by the National League of Nursing (NLN) and published in the NLN's **Nursing Data Review**, 1990. Additional information is available from the NLN's Division of Research (New York).

Methodology: Data are collected from the various programs that offer degrees, associate degrees or diplomas in nursing.

Definitions: "Nursing" refers to registered nurses.

Qualifications: American territories are excluded from these figures.

Section XI

DATA ON MENTAL HEALTH AND ILLNESS

Among the various topics under the heading of health care, mental health is one of the most difficult on which to find information. The problems characterizing data on other health topics appear to be magnified when it comes to mental health and illness. The topic itself has certain characteristics that create barriers to the collection, analysis, and dissemination of data. In addition, the subject of mental illness faces more problems in terms of definition and uniformity of data than does the subject of physical illness.

In the area of physical health/illness, there are numerous agencies charged with maintaining registries, monitoring utilization and conducting surveys on a wide variety of topics. Not only are numerous government agencies involved in this process but, with the growing demand for health statistics, a number of private sector organizations have become involved in the collection and dissemination of health data. Standards for data collection are well developed and most definitional issues have been resolved. Participation in data collection is strongly encouraged, even by non-public health care providers, so that the coverage of the population is very extensive. In fact, various government agencies (e.g., the Health Care Financing Administration) mandate the provision of complete and accurate data from many providers of care.

While a parallel system has developed in the United States for the treatment of mental illness, the highly-developed data collection mechanisms available for physical illness are generally not applicable. Further, much of the care of the mentally ill is provided by private practitioners and institutions who have generally not been willing to participate in data collection activities. Perhaps most important, the federal government plays a limited role in the provision of mental health services and, in particular, does not play a major part in the financing of these services. Thus, unlike the case with physical illness where the federal government provides significant subsidization, there is little government pressure for participation in monitoring systems or other data collection activities. Although during the 1960s and 1970s the federal government did play a role in the development and funding of community mental health centers, these funds have now essentially been eliminated. This major force for the collection of outpatient data was removed along with that funding. Since there is limited interest in mental health services, private sector vendors have not developed the databases as they have done for physical illness.

As with physical illness, there are two primary sources of mental health/illness data. These are official records and community surveys. Official records are maintained by various institutions in order to monitor operations, develop budgets, and to meet mandated reporting requirements. While official records have numerous drawbacks (e.g., they only include "known" cases), they are often the only statistics available. Unfortunately, in the area of mental health/illness such records are extremely limited. Perhaps the only consistent source of such data that could be considered "public record" are figures maintained by state mental health programs. These data for state-operated mental hospitals are generally available but involve only a fraction of the patients under treatment and, in fact, encompass a source of care that is quickly dwindling in importance. The only other category of mental health data has been figures compiled in the past by state-operated, federally-subsidized mental health centers. With the decline of the federal role, these data have become less available.

The other primary source of health-related data is sample surveys. Surveys may be conducted on either the general public or on known mental health patients. The latter type of survey (like the official records approach) has the drawback of including data on only the mentally ill who have already been diagnosed and/or treated. However, sample surveys do add a data dimension not currently available using official records and compile data from sources otherwise untapped. Sample surveys may suffer from both sampling and nonsampling errors. Extrapolations made for the entire population based on sample surveys, of course, need to be interpreted with caution.

Community surveys generally involve the total population and not simply those identified as having a mental disorder. In some cases, a nationwide sample is utilized. More often, a localized survey is conducted. Community surveys focusing on mental health/illness date back to the early years of this century. It has only been in the past two decades, however, that the methodological precision required for such work has been developed. Even now, few organizations attempt to undertake massive community surveys on this topic. The major exception involves some federally-funded research in various localities across the nation.

The major source of data on mental illness in the United States has been historically the National Institute of Mental Health (NIMH), one of the federally-funded National Institutes of Health (NIH). This has been the one organization charged with the systematic collection, analysis and dissemination of data on mental health/illness. Through monitoring programs and sample surveys of mental health personnel, NIMH has compiled and published information on many aspects of mental health and illness. It has also funded community surveys on general mental health/illness issues and research on specific aspects of mental illness (e.g., drug abuse, the mental health of various population groups). The most extensive of the community surveys is the Epidemiological Catchment Areas Program initiated by NIMH in the 1980s for research in communities across the U.S. The most visible source of NIMH data is its publication entitled **Mental Health, United States**. Published periodically, the last issue was released in 1992 and the previous one was printed in 1990. (As this book goes to press NIMH is being reorganized and is likely to take a quite different form in the future.)

Other sources of data on mental health/illness include statistics maintained by the individual states on their inpatient and outpatient services and statistics compiled by comprehensive community mental health centers. None of these data, of course, can be extrapolated to the national population. Similarly, localized community surveys also result in data that are published (sometimes in government reports but more often in scholarly journals). These also suffer from limitations on generalizability although, if the samples are properly drawn, they do have their uses.

For the foreseeable future data on mental health/illness are going to be relatively difficult to obtain. A limited number of organizations are involved in compiling such data and funding for these activities is limited. Just as mental illness has been something of the "black sheep" of health care, the same could be said of mental health/illness statistics.

XI-1. ORGANIZATIONS
ORGANIZATIONS PROVIDING MENTAL HEALTH CARE
1970-1988

Type of Organization	Number of Organizations		
	1970	1980	1988
All organizations	3,005	3,727	4,930
State and county mental hospitals	310	280	285
Private psychiatric hospitals	150	184	444
Non-federal general hospitals with separate psychiatric services	797	923	1,484
VA medical centers	115	136	138
Federally funded community mental health centers	196	691	-
Residential treatment centers for emotionally disturbed children	261	368	440
Freestanding psychiatric outpatient clinics	1,109	1,053	751
All other organizations	67	92	1,388

Type of Organization	Percent Distribution of Organizations		
	1970	1980	1988
All organizations	100.0%	100.0%	100.0%
State and county mental hospitals	10.3	7.5	5.8
Private psychiatric hospitals	5.0	4.9	9.0
Non-federal general hospitals with separate psychiatric services	26.5	24.8	30.1
VA medical centers	3.8	3.6	2.8
Federally funded community mental health centers	6.5	18.5	-
Residential treatment centers for emotionally disturbed children	8.7	9.9	8.9
Freestanding psychiatric outpatient clinics	36.9	28.3	15.2
All other organizations	2.3	2.5	28.2

Source: Based on data compiled by the National Institute of Mental Health (NIMH) and published in **Mental Health, United States**, 1992. The National Institute of Mental Health (Washington) was part of the federally-funded National Institutes of Health (NIH) and the main source of research funding and statistics on mental health in the United States. NIMH was reorganized in 1993; for additional information contact NIH (Bethesda, MD).

Methodology: Based on data collected in 1988 through a sampling of client/patient records at a sample of institutions providing mental health services. The survey covered inpatient, outpatient and partial care programs operated by eight different categories of health organizations. Data were collected from over 1,500 institutions providing mental health care. Some figures are based on data provided by cooperating agencies such as state mental health agencies and the American Hospital Association.

Definitions: "All other organizations" includes freestanding psychiatric partial care organizations and multi-service mental health organizations with inpatient services not elsewhere classified.

Qualifications: Since these data have been collected by means of a sample survey, they are subject to sampling error. The national totals reported are extrapolated from these sampled records and could possibly vary from actual figures by a few percentage points either plus or minus. The data are also subject to nonsampling errors due to inaccurate and/or incomplete reporting of the data. Since these data were collected in 1988, significant changes have occurred in health care in general and mental health care in particular.

Interpretation: Significant changes have occurred in the number and distribution of organizations providing mental health care since 1970. The numbers of private psychiatric hospitals and general hospitals offering inpatient psychiatric care have increased dramatically, as have residential treatment centers for children. The most significant increase has been for the "all other organizations" category. There are no longer federally-funded community health centers, although some of these centers have continued to operate and account for some of the increase in the "other" category. By the 1970s, "public" (i.e., state and county) mental hospitals have ceased to be the major source of care for mental patients.

XI-2. INPATIENT FACILITIES
HEALTH CARE ORGANIZATIONS PROVIDING INPATIENT
MENTAL HEALTH CARE
1970-1988

Type of Organization	Number of Organizations		
	1970	1980	1988
All organizations	1,734	2,526	3,231
State and county mental hospitals	310	280	285
Private psychiatric hospitals	150	184	444
Non-federal general hospitals with separate psychiatric services	664	843	1,425
VA medical centers	110	121	125
Federally funded community mental health centers	196	691	-
Residential treatment centers for emotionally disturbed children	261	368	440
All other organizations	43	39	512

Type of Organization	Percent Distribution of Organizations		
	1970	1980	1986
All organizations	100.0%	100.0%	100.0%
State and county mental hospitals	17.9	11.0	8.8
Private psychiatric hospitals	8.6	7.3	13.7
Non-federal general hospitals with separate psychiatric services	38.3	33.4	44.1
VA medical centers	6.3	4.8	3.9
Federally funded community mental health centers	11.3	27.4	-
Residential treatment centers for emotionally disturbed children	15.1	14.6	13.6
All other organizations	2.5	1.5	15.9

Source: Based on data compiled by the National Institute of Mental Health (NIMH) and published in **Mental Health, United States**, 1992. The National Institute of Mental Health (Washington) was part of the federally-funded National Institutes of Health (NIH) and the main source of research funding and statistics on mental health in the United States. NIMH was reorganized in 1993; for additional information contact NIH (Bethesda, MD).

Methodology: Based on data collected in 1988 through a sampling of client/patient records at a sample of institutions providing mental health services. The survey covered inpatient, outpatient and partial care programs operated by eight different categories of health organizations. Data were collected from over 1,500 institutions providing mental health care. Some figures are based on data provided by cooperating agencies such as state mental health agencies and the American Hospital Association.

Definitions: "Inpatient services" includes care received as a "resident" of a health care institution. These figures include residential treatment centers. "All other organizations" includes freestanding psychiatric partial care organizations and multiservice mental health organizations with inpatient services not elsewhere classified.

Qualifications: Since these data have been collected by means of a sample survey, they are subject to sampling error. The national totals reported are extrapolated from these sampled records and could possibly vary from actual figures by a few percentage points either plus or minus. The data are also subject to nonsampling errors due to inaccurate and/or incomplete reporting of the data. Since these data were collected in 1988, significant changes have occurred in health care in general and mental health care in particular.

Interpretation: Significant changes have occurred in the number and distribution of organizations providing mental health care since 1970. The numbers of private psychiatric hospitals and general hospitals offering inpatient psychiatric have increased dramatically, as have residential treatment centers for children. The most significant increase is for the "all other organizations" category. There are no longer federally-funded community health centers, although some of these centers have continued to operate and account for some of the increase in the "other" category. By the 1970s, "public" (i.e., state and county) mental hospitals had ceased to be the major source of care for mental patients.

XI-3. INPATIENT FACILITIES
HOSPITALS PROVIDING INPATIENT MENTAL HEALTH CARE BY STATE
1986

State	State and County Mental Hospitals	Private Psychiatric Hospitals	Non-Federal General Hospital Psychiatric Services
Total United States	285	314	1,351
Alabama	5	4	23
Alaska	1	1	2
Arizona	1	3	15
Arkansas	1	1	9
California	6	37	99
Colorado	2	5	17
Connecticut	8	6	28
Delaware	2	1	4
District of Columbia	1	1	8
Florida	7	22	55
Georgia	8	13	25
Hawaii	1	1	7
Idaho	2	7	3
Illinois	12	6	69
Indiana	7	14	32
Iowa	5	-	28
Kansas	4	6	19
Kentucky	5	6	19
Louisiana	6	11	13
Maine	2	1	10
Maryland	9	6	27
Massachusetts	9	10	52
Michigan	15	8	56
Minnesota	5	1	35
Mississippi	2	2	9
Missouri	10	5	41
Montana	2	1	5
Nebraska	3	1	11
Nevada	2	2	3
New Hampshire	1	3	8
New Jersey	11	4	51
New Mexico	1	3	7
New York	32	12	104
North Carolina	4	9	30
North Dakota	1	-	4
Ohio	17	9	71
Oklahoma	4	3	14
Oregon	3	2	11
Pennsylvania	15	16	93

(Continued on next page)

XI-3.INPATIENT FACILITIES
HOSPITALS PROVIDING INPATIENT MENTAL HEALTH CARE BY STATE
1986 *(Continued from previous page)*

State	State and County Mental Hospitals	Private Psychiatric Hospitals	Non-Federal General Hospital Psychiatric Services
Rhode Island	1	2	4
South Carolina	5	3	12
South Dakota	1	-	4
Tennessee	5	6	27
Texas	10	33	65
Utah	1	4	16
Vermont	1	1	4
Virginia	10	15	28
Washington	3	2	23
West Virginia	3	1	12
Wisconsin	12	2	36
Wyoming	1	2	3

Source: Based on data complied by the National Institute of Mental Health (NIMH) and published in **Mental Health, United States,** 1990. The National Institute of Mental Health (Washington) was part of the federally-funded National Institutes of Health (NIH) and the main sources of research funding and statistics on mental health in the United States. NIMH was reorganized in 1993; for additional information contact NIH (Bethesda, MD).

Methodology: Based on facility data maintained by NIMH (Survey and Reports Branch) on institutions providing mental health services.

Definitions: "Hospitals" includes only the three types of facilities inventories above. There are some other types of inpatient mental health facilities but they account for small portion of the mental patient population.

XI-4. INPATIENT TREATMENT
DISTRIBUTION OF INPATIENT TREATMENT BEDS AMONG ORGANIZATIONS
OFFERING MENTAL HEALTH CARE
1970-1988

Type of organization	Number of Inpatient Beds		
	1970	1980	1988
All organizations	524,878	274,713	271,997
State and county mental hospitals	413,066	156,482	106,705
Private psychiatric hospitals	14,295	17,157	42,340
Non-federal general hospitals with separate psychiatric services	22,394	29,384	48,499
VA medical centers	50,688	33,796	25,742
Federally-funded community mental health centers	8,108	16,264	-
Residential treatment centers for emotionally disturbed children	15,129	20,197	25,271
All other organizations	1,198	1,433	23,440

Type of organization	Percent Distribution of Inpatient Beds		
	1970	1980	1988
All organizations	100.0%	100.0%	100.0%
State and county mental hospitals	78.7	57.0	39.2
Private psychiatric hospitals	2.7	6.6	15.6
Non-federal general hospitals with separate psychiatric services	4.3	10.7	17.8
VA medical centers	9.7	12.3	9.5
Federally funded community mental health centers	1.5	5.5	-
Residential treatment centers for emotionally disturbed children	2.9	7.4	9.3
All other organizations	0.2	0.5	8.6

Type of organization	Inpatient Beds per 100,000 Civilian Population		
	1970	1980	1988
All organizations	263.6	124.3	111.5
State and county mental hospitals	207.4	70.2	43.8
Private psychiatric hospitals	7.2	7.7	17.3
Non-federal general hospitals with separate psychiatric services	11.2	13.7	19.9
VA medical centers	25.5	15.7	10.5
Federally funded community mental health centers	4.1	7.3	-
Residential treatment centers for emotionally disturbed children	7.6	9.1	10.4
All other organizations	0.6	0.6	9.6

Source: Based on data compiled by the National Institute of Mental Health (NIMH) and published in **Health, United States, 1991.** The National Institute of Mental Health (Washington) was part of the federally-funded National Institutes of Health (NIH) and the main source of research funding and statistics on mental health in the United States. NIMH was reorganized in 1993; for additional information contact NIH (Bethesda, MD).

Methodology: Based on data collected in 1988 through a sampling of client/patient records at a sample of institutions providing mental health services. The survey covered inpatient, outpatient and partial care programs operated by eight different categories of health organizations. Data were collected from over 1,500 institutions providing mental health care. Some figures are based on data provided by cooperating agencies such as state mental health agencies and the American Hospital Association.

Definitions: "Inpatient services" includes care received as a "resident" of a health care institution. These figures include residential treatment centers. "All other organizations" includes freestanding psychiatric partial care organizations and multiservice mental health organizations with inpatient services not elsewhere classified.

Qualifications: Since these data have been collected by means of a sample survey, they are subject to sampling error. The national totals reported are extrapolated from these sampled records and could possibly vary from actual figures by a few percentage points either plus or minus. The data are also subject to nonsampling errors due to inaccurate and/or incomplete reporting of the data.

Interpretation: Significant changes have occurred in the number and distribution of organizations providing mental health care since 1970. The numbers of private psychiatric hospitals and general hospitals offering inpatient psychiatric have increased dramatically, as have residential treatment centers for children. The most significant increase is for the "all other organizations" category. There are no longer federally-funded community health centers, although some of these centers have continued to operate and account for some of the increase in the "other" category. By the 1970s, "public" (i.e., state and county) mental hospitals had ceased to be the major source of care for mental patients and the number of beds decreased dramatically between 1970 and 1988.

XI-5. HOSPITALS
CHARACTERISTICS OF PSYCHIATRIC HOSPITALS BY OWNERSHIP TYPE
1989

Type of Hospital	Number	Beds	Admissions
Nongovernment not-for-profit	77	7,082	94,688
Investor-owned (for-profit)	260	22,166	245,768
Local government	8	2,206	12,686
State government	31	5,873	68,340
Total	376	37,327	421,482

Source: Collected by the American Hospital Association (AHA) and published in **Hospital Statistics.** The AHA is the national association of hospitals and, based on data collected from the nation's hospitals, annually publishes **Hospital Statistics** and the **AHA Guide to the Health Care Field.** Although hospital-oriented, these publications contain some information on other facilities. The AHA maintains the nation's most extensive data base on hospitals and maintains information beyond that published in its annual guides. Additional, and sometimes unpublished, data can be obtained from the AHA's data office (Chicago).

Methodology: Data in AHA publications are collected through annual surveys of AHA member hospitals.

Definitions: "Nongovernment not-for-profit" hospitals are usually religious-affiliated institutions.

Qualifications: Although most hospitals are members of the AHA, some are not and are not, therefore, likely to participate in the survey. Some members fail to participate (and are listed as nonresponding). The AHA may obtain some of the missing data from other sources, but this does mean there is some slippage in the data quality. In addition, the AHA must rely on self-reports from the hospitals and this raising the question of the completeness and the accuracy of the data. There is also the problem of timeliness of the data. The magnitude of the data collection, processing and publishing effort means there is a certain time lag between the data can be disseminated (e.g., the 1990 guide contains data for the 1989 fiscal year).

XI-6. INPATIENT ADMISSIONS
INPATIENT "ADDITIONS" AMONG ORGANIZATIONS OFFERING
MENTAL HEALTH CARE
1969-1988

Type of Organization	Number of Inpatient Additions			
	1969	1979	1981	1988
All organizations	1,282,698	1,541,659	1,482,589	2,002,000
State and county mental hospitals	486,661	383,323	370,693	304,000
Private psychiatric hospitals	92,056	140,831	162,034	382,000
Non-federal general hospitals with separate psychiatric services	478,000	551,190	648,205	879,000
VA medical centers	135,217	180,416	162,884	246,000
Federally funded community mental health centers	59,730	246,409	-	-
Residential treatment centers for emotionally disturbed children	7,596	15,453	17,703	23,000
All other organizations	23,438	24,037	121,070	168,000

Type of Organization	Percent Distribution of Inpatient Additions			
	1969	1979	1981	1988
All organizations	100.0%	100.0%	100.0%	100.0%
State and county mental hospitals	37.9	24.8	25.0	15.2
Private psychiatric hospitals	7.2	9.1	10.9	19.1
Non-federal general hospitals with separate psychiatric services	37.3	35.8	43.7	43.9
VA medical centers	10.5	11.7	11.0	12.3
Federally funded community mental health centers	4.7	16.0	-	-
Residential treatment centers for emotionally disturbed children	0.6	1.0	1.2	1.1
All other organizations	1.8	1.6	8.2	8.4

Type of Organization	Inpatient Beds per 100,000 Civilian Population			
	1969	1979	1981	1988
All organizations	644.2	704.2	651.2	759.9
State and county mental hospitals	244.4	172.0	162.8	139.1
Private psychiatric hospitals	46.2	63.2	71.2	98.0
Non-federal general hospitals with separate psychiatric services	240.1	256.7	284.7	354.8
VA medical centers	67.9	84.0	71.5	75.1
Federally funded community mental health centers	30.0	110.6	-	-
Residential treatment centers for emotionally disturbed children	3.8	6.9	7.8	10.2
All other organizations	11.8	11.9	10.8	82.7

Source: Based on data compiled by the National Institute of Mental Health (NIMH) and published in **Health, United States, 1991.** The National Institute of Mental Health (Washington) was part of the federally-funded National Institutes of Health (NIH) and the main source of research funding and statistics on mental health in the United States. NIMH reorganized in 1993; for additional information contact NIH (Bethesda, MD).

Methodology: Based on data collected in 1988 through a sampling of client/patient records at a sample of institutions providing mental health services. The survey covered inpatient, outpatient and partial care programs operated by eight different categories of health organizations. Data were collected from over 1,500 institutions providing mental health care. Some figures are based on data provided by cooperating agencies such as state mental health agencies and the American Hospital Association.

Definitions: "Inpatient additions" refers to the number of admissions to mental health inpatient facilities. These figures include residential treatment centers. "All other organizations" includes freestanding psychiatric partial care organizations and multiservice mental health organizations with inpatient services not elsewhere classified.

Qualifications: Since these data have been collected by means of a sample survey, they are subject to sampling error. The national totals reported are extrapolated from these sampled records and could possibly vary from actual figures by a few percentage points either plus or minus. The data are also subject to nonsampling errors due to inaccurate and/or incomplete reporting of the data.

Interpretation: Significant changes have occurred since 1970 in the number and distribution of beds among organizations providing mental health care, reflecting to a great extent the movement away from inpatient psychiatric care to outpatient care. The numbers of additions to private psychiatric hospitals and general hospitals offering inpatient psychiatric care have increased dramatically, as have those to residential treatment centers for children. The most significant increase is for the "all other organizations" category. There are no longer federally-funded community health centers, although some of these centers have continued to operate and account for some of the increase in the "other" category. By the 1970s, "public" (i.e., state and county) mental hospitals had ceased to be the major source of care for mental patients and the number of beds decreased dramatically between 1970 and 1988.

XI-7. INPATIENT DAYS
INPATIENT DAYS AMONG ORGANIZATIONS OFFERING
MENTAL HEALTH CARE
1969-1988

Type of Organization	Number of Inpatient Days in Thousands			
	1969	1975	1981	1988
All organizations	168,934	104,970	77,053	83,167
State and county mental hospitals	134,185	70,584	44,558	36,310
Private psychiatric hospitals	4,237	4,401	5,578	10,857
Non-federal general hospitals with separate psychiatric services	6,500	8,349	10,727	13,126
VA medical centers	17,206	11,725	7,591	7,155
Federally funded community mental health centers	1,924	3,718	-	-
Residential treatment centers for emotionally disturbed children	4,528	5,900	6,127	8,464
All other organizations	354	293	2,472	7,255

Type of Organization	Percent Distribution of Inpatient Days			
	1969	1975	1981	1988
All organizations	100.0%	100.0%	100.0%	100.0%
State and county mental hospitals	79.4	67.2	58.8	43.7
Private psychiatric hospitals	2.5	4.2	7.2	13.1
Non-federal general hospitals with separate psychiatric services	3.9	8.0	13.9	15.8
VA medical centers	10.2	11.2	9.9	8.6
Federally funded community mental health centers	1.1	3.5	-	-
Residential treatment centers for emotionally disturbed children	2.7	5.6	8.0	10.2
All other organizations	0.2	0.3	3.2	8.7

Source: Based on data compiled by the National Institute of Mental Health (NIMH) and published in **Health, United States, 1991.** The National Institute of Mental Health (Washington) was part of the federally-funded National Institutes of Health (NIH) and the main source of research funding and statistics on mental health in the United States. NIMH was reorganized in 1993; for additional information contact NIH (Bethesda, MD).

Methodology: Based on data collected in 1988 through a sampling of client/patient records at a sample of institutions providing mental health services. The survey covered inpatient, outpatient and partial care programs operated by eight different categories of health organizations. Data were collected from over 1,500 institutions providing mental health care. Some figures are based on data provided by cooperating agencies such as state mental health agencies and the American Hospital Association.

Definitions: "Inpatient days" refers to the number of patient days of care provided to inmates of mental health facilities. These figures include residential treatment centers. "All other organizations" includes freestanding psychiatric partial care organizations and multiservice mental health organizations with inpatient services not elsewhere classified.

Qualifications: Since these data have been collected by means of a sample survey, they are subject to sampling error. The national totals reported are extrapolated from these sampled records and could possibly vary from actual figures by a few percentage points either plus or minus. The data are also subject to nonsampling errors due to inaccurate and/or incomplete reporting of the data. Since these data were collected in 1988, significant changes have occurred in health care in general and mental health care in particular.

Interpretation: Significant changes have occurred since 1970 in the number of inpatient days recorded, reflecting to a great extent the movement away from inpatient psychiatric care to outpatient care and the trend toward shorter average lengths of stay. The numbers of inpatient days attributed to private psychiatric hospitals and general hospitals offering inpatient psychiatric care have increased dramatically, as have those to residential treatment centers for children. The most significant increase has been in the "all other organizations" category. There are no longer federally-funded community health centers, although some of these centers have continued to operate and account for some of the increase in the "other" category. By the 1970s, "public" (i.e., state and county) mental hospitals had ceased to be the major source of care for mental patients and the number of patient days attributable to these institutions decreased dramatically between 1970 and 1988.

XI-8. INPATIENT CENSUS
AVERAGE DAILY CENSUS AMONG ORGANIZATIONS OFFERING MENTAL HEALTH CARE
1969-1988

Type of Organization	Average Daily Inpatient Census			
	1969	1975	1981	1988
All organizations	468,831	287,588	211,024	227,836
State and county mental hospitals	367,629	193,380	122,073	99,869
Private psychiatric hospitals	11,608	12,058	15,281	29,698
Non-federal general hospitals with separate psychiatric services	17,808	22,874	29,307	35,902
VA medical centers	47,140	32,123	20,798	19,602
Federally funded community mental health centers	5,270	10,186	-	-
Residential treatment centers for emotionally disturbed children	12,406	16,164	16,786	23,092
All other organizations	970	803	6,779	19,673

Type of Organization	Percent Occupancy			
	1969	1979	1981	1988
All organizations	88.2%	84.4%	85.3%	83.8%
State and county mental hospitals	89.4	87.0	87.1	93.2
Private psychiatric hospitals	81.2	74.9	80.4	70.3
Non-federal general hospitals with separate psychiatric services	79.5	79.7	80.2	74.1
VA medical centers	93.0	89.4	84.3	76.1
Federally funded community mental health centers	65.0	59.8	-	-
Residential treatment centers for emotionally disturbed children	82.0	89.7	90.9	91.7
All other organizations	81.0	80.9	79.6	84.7

Source: Based on data compiled by the National Institute of Mental Health (NIMH) and published in **Mental Health, United States, 1992.** The National Institute of Mental Health (Washington) was part of the federally-funded National Institutes of Health (NIH) and the main source of research funding and statistics on mental health in the United States. NIMH was reorganized in 1993; for additional information contact NIH (Bethesda, MD).

Methodology: Based on data collected in 1988 through a sampling of client/patient records at a sample of institutions providing mental health services. The survey covered inpatient, outpatient and partial care programs operated by eight different categories of health organizations. Data were collected from over 1,500 institutions providing mental health care. Some figures are based on data provided by cooperating agencies such as state mental health agencies and the American Hospital Association.

Definitions: "Average daily census" refers to the number of patients residing in inpatient mental health facilities on the "average" day. These figures include residential treatment centers. "Occupancy" refers to the proportion of beds that are occupied by a patient on an "average" day. "All other organizations" includes freestanding psychiatric partial care organizations and multiservice mental health organizations with inpatient services not elsewhere classified.

Qualifications: Since these data have been collected by means of a sample survey, they are subject to sampling error. The national totals reported are extrapolated from these sampled records and could possibly vary from actual figures by a few percentage points either plus or minus. The data are also subject to nonsampling errors due to inaccurate and/or incomplete reporting of the data. Since these data were collected in 1988, significant changes have occurred in health care in general and mental health care in particular.

Interpretation: Significant changes have occurred since 1970 in the daily average census among mental health care providers, reflecting to a great extent the movement away from inpatient psychiatric care to outpatient care and the trend toward shorter average lengths of stay. The numbers of inpatient days attributed to private psychiatric hospitals and general hospitals offering inpatient psychiatric care have increased dramatically, as have those to residential treatment centers for children. The most significant increase has been in the "all other organizations" category. There are no longer federally-funded community health centers, although some of these centers have continued to operate and account for some of the increase in the "other" category. By the 1970s, "public" (i.e., state and county) mental hospitals had ceased to be the major source of care for mental patients and the number of patient days attributable to these institutions decreased dramatically between 1970 and 1988.

XI-9. OUTPATIENT SERVICES
HEALTH CARE ORGANIZATIONS PROVIDING OUTPATIENT
MENTAL HEALTH CARE
1970-1988

Type of Organization	Number of Organizations		
	1970	1980	1988
All organizations	2,156	2,431	2,965
State and county mental hospitals	195	100	81
Private psychiatric hospitals	100	54	172
Non-federal general hospitals with separate psychiatric services	376	299	486
VA medical centers	100	127	134
Federally funded community mental health centers	196	691	-
Residential treatment centers for emotionally disturbed children	48	68	130
Freestanding psychiatric outpatient clinics	1,109	1,053	751
All other organizations	32	39	1,211

Type of Organization	Percent Distribution of Organizations		
	1970	1980	1986
All organizations	100.0%	100.0%	100.0%
State and county mental hospitals	9.1	4.1	2.7
Private psychiatric hospitals	4.6	2.2	5.8
Non-federal general hospitals with separate psychiatric services	17.5	12.3	16.4
VA medical centers	4.6	5.2	4.5
Federally funded community mental health centers	9.1	28.5	-
Residential treatment centers for emotionally disturbed children	2.2	2.8	4.4
Freestanding psychiatric outpatient clinics	51.4	43.3	25.3
All other organizations	1.5	1.6	40.9

Source: Based on data compiled by the National Institute of Mental Health (NIMH) and published in **Mental Health, United States, 1990.** The National Institute of Mental Health (Washington) part of the federally-funded National Institutes of Health (NIH) and the main source of research funding and statistics on mental health in the United States. NIMH was reorganized in 1993; for additional information contact NIH (Bethesda, MD).

Methodology: Based on data collected in 1988 through a sampling of client/patient records at a sample of institutions providing mental health services. The survey covered inpatient, outpatient and partial care programs operated by eight different categories of health organizations. Data were collected from over 1,500 institutions providing mental health care. Some figures are based on data provided by cooperating agencies such as state mental health agencies and the American Hospital Association.

Definitions: "Outpatient services" includes care received from a health care institution by ambulatory (i.e., non-admitted) patients or clients. "All other organizations" includes freestanding psychiatric partial care organizations and multiservice mental health organizations with inpatient services not elsewhere classified.

Qualifications: Since these data have been collected by means of a sample survey, they are subject to sampling error. The national totals reported are extrapolated from these sampled records and could possibly vary from actual figures by a few percentage points either plus or minus. The data are also subject to nonsampling errors due to inaccurate and/or incomplete reporting of the data. Since these data were collected in 1988, significant changes have occurred in health care in general and mental health care in particular.

Interpretation: Significant changes have occurred in the number and distribution of organizations providing mental health care since 1970. There was a decline during the 1970s in the number of organizations offering outpatient mental health services, followed by a resurgence in the number of such organizations during the 1980s. There are no longer federally-funded community health centers, although some of these centers have continued to operate and account for some of the increase in the "other" category which demonstrated the greatest increase over this time period.

XI-10. MENTAL HEALTH PERSONNEL
HEALTH PROFESSIONALS IN ORGANIZATIONS PROVIDING MENTAL HEALTH CARE
1972-1988

	Number of FTE Staff			
	1972	1978	1984	1988
All staff	375,984	430,051	440,925	496,630
Patient care staff	241,265	292,699	313,243	382,065
Professional patient care staff	100,886	153,598	202,474	257,382
Psychiatrists	12,938	14,492	18,482	18,114
Psychologists	9,443	16,501	21,052	22,812
Social workers	17,687	28,125	36,397	46,051
Registered nurses	31,110	42,399	54,406	73,429
Other professional staff	25,717	49,047	68,652	96,976
Other mental health workers	140,379	139,101	110,769	124,683
Administrative, clerical, and maintenance staff	134,719	137,352	127,682	150,000

	Percent Distribution of FTE Staff			
	1972	1978	1984	1988
All staff	100.0%	100.0%	100.0%	100.0%
Patient care staff	64.2	68.1	71.0	76.9
Professional patient care staff	26.9	35.8	45.9	51.8
Psychiatrists	3.4	3.4	4.2	3.6
Psychologists	2.5	3.8	4.8	4.6
Social workers	4.7	6.5	8.2	9.3
Registered nurses	8.3	9.9	12.3	14.8
Other professional staff	6.9	11.5	15.6	19.5
Other mental health workers	37.3	32.3	25.1	25.1
Administrative, clerical, and maintenance staff	35.8	31.9	29.0	30.2

Source: Based on data compiled by the National Institute of Mental Health (NIMH) and published in **Mental Health, United States, 1992.** The National Institute of Mental Health (Washington) was part of the federally-funded National Institutes of Health (NIH) and the main source of research funding and statistics on mental health in the United States. NIMH was reorganized in 1993; for additional information contact NIH (Bethesda, MD).

Methodology: The NIMH (Survey and Reports Branch) maintains files on personnel employed by institutions providing mental health services.

Definitions: "FTEs" stands for full-time equivalent. "Other mental health workers" refers to paraprofessionals with less than a bachelor's degree.

Qualifications: Some changes in the definitions of organizations and in the classification of professionals were made during some of the reporting years. These figures only include professionals employed by the categories of mental health organizations on which the NIMH maintains statistics. They do not include mental health professionals who are in private office practice or psychiatrists who treat hospitalized patients but are not employees of the hospital. The number of administrative, clerical, and maintenance staff for 1988 is an estimate.

Interpretation: A steady increase was recorded in the number of mental health personnel between 1972 and 1986. Most of the increase has been in "paraprofessional" categories and in nursing and the number of psychiatrists actually declined between 1984 and 1988.

XI-11. MENTAL HEALTH PERSONNEL
DISTRIBUTION OF HEALTH PROFESSIONALS AMONG ORGANIZATIONS
PROVIDING MENTAL HEALTH CARE
1988

Professional	Percent by Type of Mental Health Organization			
	Public Hospitals	Private Hospitals	General Hospitals	Freestanding Clinics
Patient care staff	65.3%	60.2%	87.1%	66.7%
Professional patient care staff	30.1	46.2	71.6	64.5
Psychiatrists	2.1	2.6	8.6	5.2
Psychologists	1.9	2.6	4.3	13.5
Social workers	3.4	4.9	8.0	30.4
Registered nurses	10.6	17.3	33.4	2.1
Other professional staff	12.1	18.8	17.3	13.3
Other mental health workers	14.0	15.6	2.2	-
Administrative, clerical, and maintenance staff	34.7	29.8	12.9	33.3

Source: Based on data compiled by the National Institute of Mental Health (NIMH) and published in **Mental Health, United States, 1990.** The National Institute of Mental Health (Washington) was part of the federally-funded National Institutes of Health (NIH) and the main source of research funding and statistics on mental health in the United States. NIMH was reorganized in 1993; for additional information contact NIH (Bethesda, MD).

Methodology: Based on personnel data maintained by NIMH (Survey and Reports Branch) on institutions providing mental health services.

Definitions: "FTEs" stands for full-time equivalent. "Public hospital" refers to state and county mental hospitals. "General hospital" refers to non-federal acute care hospitals offering psychiatric services. "Freestanding clinic" refers to outpatient clinics not affiliated with hospitals or other institutions.

Qualifications: Some change in the definitions of organizations and in the classification of professionals were made during some of the reporting years. These figures only include professionals employed by the categories of mental health organizations on which the NIMH maintains statistics. They do not include mental health professionals who are in private office practice or psychiatrists who treat hospitalized patients but are not employees of the hospital. Since these data were compiled in 1988 significant changes have occurred in mental health care.

Interpretation: Staffing patterns for mental health organizations vary depending on the type of organization.

XI-12. MENTAL HEALTH PERSONNEL
PSYCHOLOGISTS AND SOCIAL WORKERS INVOLVED IN MENTAL HEALTH
CARE BY LOCATION OF EMPLOYMENT
1989

Employment Location	Psychologists	Social Workers
Hospital	13.9%	20.5%
Clinic	12.0	16.7
Private practice	48.4	21.1
Nursing home	0.1	1.7
Academic setting	17.4	0.0
Social service agency	NA	30.3
Other/unspecified	8.3	9.7
Total Number	41,269	71,634

Source: Based on data complied by the National Institute of Mental Health (NIMH) and published in **Mental Health, United States, 1990.** The National Institute of Mental Health (Washington) was part of the federally-funded National Institutes of Health (NIH) and the main source of research funding and statistics on mental health in the United States. NIMH was reorganized in 1993; for additional information contact NIH (Bethesda, MD).

Methodology: Based on data collected by NIMH from the respective organizations involved in tracking psychology and social work manpower.

Definitions: "Employment" refers to primary place of employment. Many psychologists and social workers practice in more than one setting.

XI-13. EXPENDITURES
TOTAL EXPENDITURES FOR MENTAL HEALTH CARE
1969-1988

Year	Amount	Per Capita
1988	$23,071,000	$95.00
1983	14,431,943	62.12
1979	8,763,795	39.61
1975	6,564,312	31.05
1969	3,292,563	16.53

Source: Based on data compiled by the National Institute of Mental Health (NIMH) and published in **Mental Health, United States, 1990.** The National Institute of Mental Health (Washington) was part of the federally-funded National Institutes of Health (NIH) and the main source of research funding and statistics on mental health in the United States. NIMH was reorganized in 1993; for additional information contact NIH (Bethesda, MD).

Methodology: Based on personnel data maintained by NIMH (Survey and Reports Branch) on institutions providing mental health services.

Definitions: "Expenditures" are presented in current dollars.

Qualifications: Since the last period for which data are reported is 1988, these figures should be interpreted with caution. The figures for 1988 are preliminary estimates by NIMH and are rounded to nearest $1,000.

Interpretation: Total unadjusted expenditures on mental health care have increased dramatically since 1969. A major increase in expenditures (and the only significant one when the figures are adjusted for inflation) occurred during the early 1970s expenditures as measured by constant dollars primarily reflects decreases in funds allotted for public (i.e., state and county) mental hospitals.

XI-14. EXPENDITURES
DISTRIBUTION OF EXPENDITURES FOR MENTAL HEALTH CARE
1988

Type of Organization	Total Expenditures (in $ millions)
All organizations	$23,071
State and county mental hospitals	6,990
Private psychiatric hospitals	4,604
Non-federal general hospitals with psychiatric services	3,617
VA medical centers	1,290
Residential treatment centers for emotionally disturbed children	1,311
Freestanding psychiatric outpatient clinics	668
All other organizations	4,591

Type of Organization	Distribution Among Organizations
All organizations	100.0%
State and county mental hospitals	30.3
Private psychiatric hospitals	20.0
Non-federal general hospitals with psychiatric services	15.7
VA medical centers	5.6
Residential treatment centers for emotionally disturbed children	5.7
Freestanding psychiatric outpatient clinics	2.9
All other organizations	19.9

Type of Organization	Per Capita per Organization
All organizations	$95
State and county mental hospitals	29
Private psychiatric hospitals	19
Non-federal general hospitals with psychiatric services	15
VA medical centers	5
Residential treatment centers for emotionally disturbed children	5
Freestanding psychiatric outpatient clinics	3
All other organizations	19

Source: Based on data compiled by the National Institute of Mental Health (NIMH) and published in **Health, United States, 1991.** The National Institute of Mental Health (Washington) was part of the federally-funded National Institutes of Health (NIH) and the main source of research funding and statistics on mental health in the United States. NIMH was reorganized in 1993; for additional information contact NIH (Bethesda, MD).

Methodology: Based on personnel data maintained by NIMH (Survey and Reports Branch) on institutions providing mental health services.

Definitions: "All other organizations" includes freestanding psychiatric partial care organizations and multiservice mental health organizations with inpatient services not elsewhere classified.

Qualifications: Since the last period for which data are reported is 1988, these figures should be interpreted with caution. The figures for 1988 are preliminary estimates by NIMH.

Interpretation: Expenditures on mental health care by organizational type reflect both the type of care and the intensity of care provided.

XI-15. REVENUE SOURCES
SOURCES OF REVENUE FOR MENTAL HEALTH SERVICES
1988

Source of Revenue	Type of Mental Health Organizations				
	Public Hospitals	Private Hospitals	VA Hospitals	Outpatient Clinics	Multiservice Organizations
State Funding	77.3%	5.2%	0.0%	28.6%	50.3%
Client Fees	1.7	61.8	0.4	16.7	7.9
Medicaid	10.7	8.9	0.0	9.8	14.5
Medicare	3.8	8.1	0.0	0.5	1.6
Other Federal	0.8	8.7	99.1	1.2	2.8
Local Government	2.3	0.9	0.1	25.5	15.9
Contract Funds	0.1	1.9	0.2	2.2	1.4
All Other Sources					4.5

Source: Based on data compiled by the National Institute of Mental Health (NIMH) and published in **Mental Health, United States, 1992**. The National Institute of Mental Health (Washington) was part of the federally-funded National Institutes of Health (NIH) and the main source of research funding and statistics on mental health in the United States. NIMH was reorganized in 1993; for additional information contact NIH (Bethesda, MD).

Methodology: Based on data maintained by NIMH (Survey and Reports Branch) on institutions providing mental health services.

Definitions: "Public hospitals" refer to state and county mental hospitals. "Private hospital" refers to private psychiatric hospitals; general hospitals with psychiatric services are not included. "State funding" includes all funds provided by states. "All other sources" includes grants, bequests, other charitable contributions and revenue unrelated to patient care (e.g., vending machines, gift shops, rental property and investments).

Qualifications: Since the last period for which data are reported is 1988, these figures should be interpreted with caution. A number of changes have occurred in mental health care since 1988. "State funding" excludes Medicaid funds.

Interpretation: The source of revenue varies widely depending on the type of health care organization, the type of "ownership" and the characteristics of its clientele. Mental health care is the one area in which state funds are provided for direct patient care. While state funding remained in 1988 an important source of revenue for many organizations, funds from states are of declining importance in terms of overall support for mental health services.

XI-16. REVENUE SOURCES
SOURCES OF PAYMENT FOR ADMISSIONS TO PRIVATE PSYCHIATRIC HOSPITALS
1989

Payer	Percent Contributed
Commercial insurers	35.1%
Blue Cross/Blue Shield	24.4
Medicare (65 years and older)	15.4
Medicare (under 65 years)	3.4
Medicaid	6.1
CHAMPUS	3.5
At-risk contracts	2.9
Self-pay	2.7
Other governmental	0.3
Other	6.2
Total	100.0%

Source: Based on data collected by the National Association of Private Psychiatric Hospitals (NAPPH) and published in **Medical Benefits** (September 30, 1990). NAPPH is an association of 317 private psychiatric hospitals in 44 states and the District of Columbia. **Medical Benefits** is a semi-monthly publication devoted to health care costs. For additional information on psychiatric hospitalization contact NAPPH (Washington, D.C.)

Methodology: Based on data collected by means of an annual survey of the 317 private psychiatric hospitals that belong to the NAPPH.

Definitions: "Admissions" refers to all individuals admitted for inpatient treatment by any hospital belonging to NAPPH. "Self-pay" may include charity patients who actually pay very little for the care they receive.

Qualifications: Not all private psychiatric hospitals participate in the NAPPH so these data can only approximately the figures for all such hospitals. These data exclude public psychiatric hospitals, general hospitals with psychiatric wards and other organizations that may admit psychiatric patients. Since these figures represent the aggregate payer mix for all NAPPH members, they should be applied to an individual psychiatric hospital with caution.

Interpretation: Although these data are for "private hospitals", it can be seen that their patient mix is not strictly private pay. Commercial insurance and Blue Cross coverage account for not quite 60% of the admissions.

XI-17. STATE EXPENDITURES
PER CAPITA EXPENDITURE FOR ALL MENTAL HEALTH
ORGANIZATIONS BY STATE
1988

State	Per Capita Expenditure
Total, United States	$94.33
Alabama	70.64
Alaska	83.30
Arizona	83.22
Arkansas	53.47
California	83.48
Colorado	80.96
Connecticut	145.09
Delaware	108.52
District of Columbia	395.91
Florida	71.04
Georgia	96.59
Hawaii	55.41
Idaho	45.49
Illinois	67.66
Indiana	82.25
Iowa	68.05
Kansas	99.85
Kentucky	76.68
Louisiana	78.25
Maine	89.93
Maryland	94.53
Massachusetts	174.44
Michigan	131.19
Minnesota	80.49
Mississippi	49.47
Missouri	82.12
Montana	82.99
Nebraska	55.91
Nevada	83.73
New Hampshire	122.85
New Jersey	92.91
New Mexico	87.58
New York	173.20
North Carolina	85.62
North Dakota	78.69
Ohio	76.34
Oklahoma	73.05
Oregon	68.56
Pennsylvania	125.35
Rhode Island	104.64

(Continued on next page)

XI-17. STATE EXPENDITURES
PER CAPITA EXPENDITURE FOR ALL MENTAL HEALTH
ORGANIZATIONS BY STATE
1988 *(Continued from previous page)*

State	Per Capita Expenditure
South Carolina	59.11
South Dakota	65.91
Tennessee	75.98
Texas	77.72
Utah	91.55
Vermont	165.32
Virginia	96.34
Washington	59.24
West Virginia	56.74
Wisconsin	84.76
Wyoming	121.75

Source: Based on data complied by the National Institute of Mental Health (NIMH) and published in **Mental Health, United States, 1992.** The National Institute of Mental Health (Washington) was part of the federally-funded National Institutes of Health (NIH) and the main source of research funding and statistics on mental health in the United States. NIMH was reorganized in 1993; for additional information contact NIH (Bethesda, MD).

Methodology: Based on facility data maintained by NIMH (Survey and Reports Branch) on institutions providing mental health services.

Definitions: "All Mental Health Organizations" includes all organizations providing either inpatient or outpatient care.

Qualifications: Since the last period for which data are reported is 1988, these figures should be interpreted with caution. A number of changes have occurred in mental health care since 1988.

XI-18. HOSPITAL CHARGES
AVERAGE DAILY ROOM AND BOARD CHARGES AT PRIVATE
PSYCHIATRIC HOSPITALS BY PROGRAM TYPE
1989

Program Type	Average Daily Charge
Child	$534
Adolescent	487
Adult	430
Older adult	434
Alcohol and drug (combined)	422
Alcohol only	448
Drug/chemical dependency only	426
Substance use-adolescent	443

Source: Based on data collected by the National Association of Private Psychiatric Hospitals (NAPPH) and published in **Medical Benefits** (September 30, 1990). NAPPH is an association of 317 private psychiatric hospitals in 44 states and the District of Columbia. **Medical Benefits** is a semi-monthly publication devoted to health care costs. For additional information on psychiatric hospitalization contact NAPPH (Washington, D.C.)

Methodology: Based on data collected by means of an annual survey of the 317 private psychiatric hospitals that belong to the NAPPH.

Qualifications: Not all private psychiatric hospitals participate in the NAPPH so these data can only approximately the figures for all such hospitals. These data exclude public psychiatric hospitals, general hospitals with psychiatric wards and other organizations that may admit psychiatric patients. Since these figures represent the aggregate payer mix for all NAPPH members, they should be applied to an individual psychiatric hospital with caution.

XI-19. STATE FACILITIES
INPATIENT AND RESIDENTIAL TREATMENT BEDS BY STATE
1988

State	Number of Beds	Beds per 1,000 Population
Total United States	273,540	111.4
Alabama	5,248	128.7
Alaska	525	105.0
Arizona	3,682	106.3
Arkansas	1,739	72.9
California	22,239	79.4
Colorado	3,212	98.6
Connecticut	4,450	138.3
Delaware	803	122.6
District of Columbia	2,173	356.2
Florida	13,511	110.4
Georgia	6,974	111.2
Hawaii	526	50.5
Idaho	729	73.1
Illinois	10,604	91.6
Indiana	6,624	119.4
Iowa	3,292	116.2
Kansas	3,612	146.5
Kentucky	3,413	92.4
Louisiana	4,213	96.3
Maine	1,364	114.0
Maryland	4,950	108.3
Massachusetts	10,036	170.8
Michigan	11,653	126.3
Minnesota	4,858	112.8
Mississippi	3,097	119.1
Missouri	6,192	120.8
Montana	805	100.5
Nebraska	1,374	86.5
Nevada	732	70.0
New Hampshire	970	89.8
New Jersey	7,849	101.9
New Mexico	1,511	101.3
New York	32,313	180.8
North Carolina	6,622	103.7
North Dakota	817	124.5
Ohio	10,369	95.6
Oklahoma	2,820	87.8
Oregon	2,139	77.4
Pennsylvania	16,576	138.3
Rhode Island	729	73.9
South Carolina	3,071	90.0

(Continued on next page)

XI-19. STATE FACILITIES
INPATIENT AND RESIDENTIAL TREATMENT BEDS BY STATE
1988 *(Continued from previous page)*

State	Number of Beds	Beds per 1,000 Population
South Dakota	1,091	154.4
Tennessee	4,866	99.8
Texas	16,818	100.7
Utah	1,857	110.3
Vermont	470	84.4
Virginia	7,759	132.7
Washington	3,167	69.0
West Virginia	1,445	77.0
Wisconsin	5,256	108.3
Wyoming	771	162.3

Source: Based on data complied by the National Institute of Mental Health (NIMH) and published in **Mental Health, United States, 1992.** The National Institute of Mental Health (Washington) was part of the federally-funded National Institutes of Health (NIH) and the main source of research funding and statistics on mental health in the United States. NIMH was reorganized in 1993; for additional information contact NIH (Bethesda, MD).

Methodology: Based on facility data maintained by NIMH (Survey and Reports Branch) on institutions providing mental health services.

Qualifications: Since the last period for which data are reported is 1988, these figures should be interpreted with caution. A number of changes have occurred in mental health care since 1988.

XI-20. INPATIENT CENSUS
AVERAGE DAILY CENSUS INPATIENT AND RESIDENTIAL
TREATMENT FACILITIES BY STATE
1988

State	Average Daily Census
Total United States	227,396
Alabama	4,183
Alaska	407
Arizona	3,027
Arkansas	1,262
California	17,953
Colorado	2,665
Connecticut	4,117
Delaware	745
District of Columbia	1,838
Florida	11,097
Georgia	5,942
Hawaii	451
Idaho	456
Illinois	9,278
Indiana	5,333
Iowa	2,736
Kansas	2,752
Kentucky	2,735
Louisiana	3,099
Maine	1,209
Maryland	4,338
Massachusetts	8,979
Michigan	9,984
Minnesota	4,005
Mississippi	2,276
Missouri	4,946
Montana	585
Nebraska	1,122
Nevada	478
New Hampshire	808
New Jersey	6,957
New Mexico	1,064
New York	31,386
North Carolina	5,484
North Dakota	591
Ohio	8,693
Oklahoma	2,143
Oregon	1,892
Pennsylvania	14,088
Rhode Island	623

(Continued on next page)

XI-20. INPATIENT CENSUS
AVERAGE DAILY CENSUS INPATIENT AND RESIDENTIAL
TREATMENT FACILITIES BY STATE
1988 *(Continued from previous page)*

State	Average Daily Census
South Carolina	2,570
South Dakota	920
Tennessee	3,902
Texas	12,043
Utah	1,428
Vermont	416
Virginia	6,439
Washington	2,736
West Virginia	1,158
Wisconsin	3,917
Wyoming	580

Source: Based on data complied by the National Institute of Mental Health (NIMH) and published in **Mental Health, United States, 1990**. The National Institute of Mental Health (Washington) was part of the federally-funded National Institutes of Health (NIH) and the main source of research funding and statistics on mental health in the United States. NIMH was reorganized in 1993; for additional information contact NIH (Bethesda, MD).

Methodology: Based on facility data maintained by NIMH (Survey and Reports Branch) on institutions providing mental health services.

Definitions: "Average Daily Census" refers to the number of patients in hospitals and residential treatment centers on an "average" day during the year.

Qualifications: Since the last period for which data are reported is 1988, these figures should be interpreted with caution. A number of changes have occurred in mental health care since 1988.

XI-21. ADMISSIONS
ADMISSIONS TO ORGANIZATIONS OFFERING MENTAL HEALTH CARE
1986

Nature of Program	All Mental Health Organizations	State and County Mental Hospitals	Private Psychiatric Hospitals	Non-Federal General Hospitals	VA Medical Centers	Free-standing Outpatient Clinics	All Others
Inpatient:							
Number	2,002,000	330,000	235,000	849,000	180,000	NA	408,000
Percent	100.0%	20.4%	13.0%	49.8%	11.2%	NA	20.4%
Outpatient:							
Number	3,014,000	91,000	127,000	460,000	214,000	558,000	1,564,000
Percent	100.0%	3.0%	4.2%	15.3%	7.1%	18.5%	51.9%
Partial Care:							
Number	304,000	5,000	39,000	39,000	16,000	NA	205,000
Percent	100.0%	1.6%	12.8%	12.8%	5.3%	NA	67.4%

Above the type-of-organization columns: **Type of Organization**

Source: Based on data compiled by the National Institute of Mental Health (NIMH) and published in **Mental Health, United States, 1990.** The National Institute of Mental Health (Washington) was part of the federally-funded National Institutes of Health (NIH) and the main source of research funding and statistics on mental health in the United States. NIMH was reorganized in 1993; for additional information contact NIH (Bethesda, MD).

Methodology: Based on data collected in 1986 through a sampling of client/patient records at a sample of institutions providing mental health services. The survey covered inpatient, outpatient and partial care programs operated by eight different categories of health organizations. Data were collected from over 1,500 institutions providing mental health care. Some figures are based on data provided by cooperating agencies such as state mental health agencies and the American Hospital Association.

Definitions: "Admissions" refers to all new cases recorded for inpatient, outpatient or partial treatment basis by any organization providing mental health services. These figures do not include treatment by clinicians, therapists, or counselors in a private practice. Figures are for persons and not treatment episodes. "All others" includes multiservice mental health organizations and miscellaneous other sources of care.

Qualifications: Since these data have been collected by means of a sample survey, they are subject to sampling error. The national totals represent extrapolations from these sampled records and could possibly vary from actual figures by a few percentage points either plus or minus. The data are may suffer from errors due to inaccurate and/or incomplete reporting data. Since these data were collected in 1986, significant changes have occurred in health care in general and mental health care in particular. The 1988 figures are preliminary estimates by NIMH and are rounded to the nearest 1,000.

Interpretation: The distribution of mental health "admissions" varies among mental health organizations based on type of care received. General hospitals record the greatest number of admissions, although they do not have the largest share of persons under care. Mental hospitals record significantly fewer admissions than general hospitals, although they have more persons under care the difference between admissions and persons under care reflect differences in the average length of stay of patients at the respective outpatient. "Admissions" are dominated by multi-service mental health organizations, freestanding outpatient clinics and general hospitals. Psychiatric hospitals and general hospitals have been increasing their share of the outpatient patient pool.

XI-22. ADMISSIONS
RATE OF ADMISSION OF MENTAL PATIENTS TO ORGANIZATIONS
PROVIDING INPATIENT AND RESIDENT TREATMENT BY STATE
1988

State	Admission Rate*
Total, United States	819.1
Alabama	839.6
Alaska	567.4
Arizona	1,704.9
Arkansas	779.5
California	676.2
Colorado	646.7
Connecticut	739.0
Delaware	837.3
District of Columbia	1,819.3
Florida	796.6
Georgia	1,354.0
Hawaii	442.1
Idaho	829.2
Illinois	930.3
Indiana	871.1
Iowa	944.1
Kansas	791.1
Kentucky	895.3
Louisiana	702.5
Maine	721.7
Maryland	600.7
Massachusetts	949.0
Michigan	756.8
Minnesota	806.7
Mississippi	636.5
Missouri	995.4
Montana	1,350.9
Nebraska	694.7
Nevada	808.6
New Hampshire	754.1
New Jersey	541.4
New Mexico	905.0
New York	769.8
North Carolina	898.0
North Dakota	1,056.1
Ohio	812.6
Oklahoma	738.0
Oregon	589.9
Pennsylvania	798.8
Rhode Island	638.8

(Continued on next page)

XI-22. ADMISSIONS
RATE OF ADMISSION OF MENTAL PATIENTS TO ORGANIZATIONS
PROVIDING INPATIENT AND RESIDENT TREATMENT BY STATE
1988 *(Continued from previous page)*

State	Admission Rate*
South Carolina	638.7
South Dakota	1,023.1
Tennessee	885.1
Texas	812.6
Utah	989.5
Vermont	660.5
Virginia	1,019.1
Washington	627.3
West Virginia	800.0
Wisconsin	967.5
Wyoming	892.4

*Rate is based on number of admissions per 100,000 population.

Source: Based on data compiled by the National Institute of Mental Health (NIMH) and published in **Mental Health, United States, 1992.** The National Institute of Mental Health (Washington) was part of the federally-funded National Institutes of Health (NIH) and the main source of research funding and statistics on mental health in the United States. NIMH was reorganized in 1993; for additional information contact NIH (Bethesda, MD).

Methodology: Based on data collected in 1988 through a sampling of client/patient records at a sample of institutions providing mental health services. The survey covered inpatient, outpatient and partial care programs operated by eight different categories of health organizations. Data were collected from over 1,500 institutions providing mental health care. Some figures are based on data provided by cooperating agencies such as state mental health agencies and the American Hospital Association.

Definitions: "Inpatient services" includes care received as a "resident" of a health care institution. These figures include residential treatment centers.

Qualifications: Since these data have been collected by means of a sample survey, they are subject to sampling error. The national totals reported are extrapolated from these sampled records and could possibly vary from actual figures by a few percentage points either plus or minus. The data are also subject to nonsampling errors due to inaccurate and/or incomplete reporting of the data. Since these data were collected in 1988, significant changes have occurred in health care in general and mental health care in particular.

XI-23. PREVALENCE
ADULTS WITH SERIOUS MENTAL ILLNESS BY SELECTED CHARACTERISTICS
1990

Characteristic	Number*	Percent
Age:		
18-24	361,000	14.2%
25-34	707,000	23.9
35-44	744,000	22.8
45-64	919,000	28.2
65-69	244,000	7.5
75 and over	288,000	8.8
Sex:		
Male	1,320,000	40.4
Female	1,944,000	59.6
Race:		
White	2,812,000	86.1
Black	393,000	12.0
Other	59,000	1.8

*Rounded to nearest thousand.

Source: Based on data collected by the National Center for Health Statistics. The National Center for Health Statistics (NCHS) conducts a variety of surveys from which health-related data are drawn. Additional data, including some unpublished data, on this topic is available from NCHS (Hyattsville, MD).

Methodology: NCHS collects data annually on the characteristics of patients. Data from the sample are weighted up to produce national estimates.

Qualifications: Since the survey is based on a sample, all of the drawbacks related to sample surveys apply. There are problems inherent in collecting information on mental illness that require that the data be utilized with caution.

Interpretation: The incidence of serious mental illness appears to be higher among those 25-44 than among other age groups, and higher for females than for males. On the other hand, the distribution by race is fairly even.

XI-24. PREVALENCE
ADULTS WITH SERIOUS MENTAL ILLNESS
WHO HAVE EVER SEEN A MENTAL HEALTH PROFESSIONAL
BY SELECTED CHARACTERISTICS
1990

Characteristic	Number*	Percent
Age:		
18-24	276,000	80.3%
25-34	503,000	75.8
35-44	630,000	87.6
45-64	719,000	82.5
65-69	179,000	69.0
75 and over	93,000	37.0
Sex:		
Male	959,000	77.9
Female	1,421,000	76.8
Race:		
White	2,041,000	76.8
Black	292,000	80.3
Other	46,000	79.7

*Rounded to nearest thousand.

Source: Based on data collected by the National Center for Health Statistics. The National Center for Health Statistics (NCHS) conducts a variety of surveys from which health-related data are drawn. Additional data, including some unpublished data, on this topic is available from NCHS (Hyattsville, MD).

Methodology: NCHS collects data annually on the characteristics of patients. Data from the sample are weighted up to produce national estimates.

Qualifications: Since the survey is based on a sample, all of the drawbacks related to sample surveys apply. There are problems inherent in collecting information on mental illness that require that the data be utilized with caution.

Interpretation: The likelihood of seeking treatment for mental illness varies with age but is less affected by sex and race.

XI-25. PATIENT CHARACTERISTICS
AGE CHARACTERISTICS OF PERSONS ADMITTED TO
INPATIENT MENTAL HEALTH FACILITIES
1986

Age Cohort	Number	Percent	Rate*
Total	1,596,063	100.0	666.8
Under 18	112,215	7.0	177.3
18-24	216,419	13.6	802.5
25-44	838,488	52.5	1118.9
45-64	298,498	18.7	663.3
65 and over	130,443	8.2	447.2

Median Age = 34

*Rate calculated based on persons under care per 100,000 population.

Source: Based on data complied by the National Institute of Mental Health (NIMH) and published in **Mental Health, United States, 1990.** The National Institute of Mental Health (Washington) was part of the federally-funded National Institutes of Health (NIH) and the main source of research funding and statistics on mental health in the United States. NIMH was reorganized in 1993; for additional information contact NIH (Bethesda, MD).

Methodology: Based on data collected in 1986 through a sampling of client/patient records at a sample of institutions providing mental health services. The survey covered inpatient, outpatient and partial care programs operated by eight different categories of health organizations. Data were collected from over 1,500 institutions providing mental health care. Some figures are based on data provided by cooperating agencies such as state mental health agencies and the American Hospital Association.

Definitions: "Admissions" refers to all individuals admitted for inpatient treatment by any organization identified by NIMH as providing inpatient mental health services. These figures are for persons and not treatment episodes.

Qualifications: Since these data have been collected by means of a sample survey, they are subject to sampling error. The national totals reported are extrapolated from these sampled records and could possibly vary from actual figures by a few percentage points either plus or minus. The data are also subject to nonsampling errors due to inaccurate and/or incomplete reporting of the data. Since these data were collected in 1986, significant changes have occurred in health care in general and mental health care in particular.

Interpretation: Individuals aged 25-44 tend to be overrepresented among institutionalized mental patients in numbers, percent, and rate of treatment. This situation is at least partly a function of two trends: a decline in treatment rates for older cohorts and an increase in the treatment for substance abuse, a condition particularly prevalent in this age cohort.

XI-26. PSYCHOTHERAPY VISITS
PSYCHOTHERAPY VISIT RATE BY STATE
1989

State	Psychotherapy Visit Rate*
Total United States	350
Alabama	87
Alaska	322
Arizona	592
Arkansas	100
California	520
Colorado	875
Connecticut	900
Delaware	NA
District of Columbia	1,374
Florida	311
Georgia	172
Hawaii	NA
Idaho	200
Illinois	413
Indiana	134
Iowa	192
Kansas	423
Kentucky	377
Louisiana	96
Maine	65
Maryland	259
Massachusetts	611
Michigan	235
Minnesota	302
Mississippi	NA
Missouri	319
Montana	383
Nebraska	269
Nevada	NA
New Hampshire	743
New Jersey	281
New Mexico	603
New York	1,267
North Carolina	131
North Dakota	NA
Ohio	178
Oklahoma	65
Oregon	644
Pennsylvania	168
Rhode Island	NA
South Carolina	NA

(Continued on next page)

XI-26. PSYCHOTHERAPY VISITS
PSYCHOTHERAPY VISIT RATE BY STATE

1989 *(Continued from previous page)*

State	Psychotherapy Visit Rate*
South Dakota	129
Tennessee	145
Texas	349
Utah	859
Vermont	NA
Virginia	720
Washington	502
West Virginia	205
Wisconsin	285
Wyoming	199

NA = Not available
*The visit rate is calculated based on visits per 1,000 population.

Source: Based on data collected by Mutual of Omaha Insurance Company and published in their **Current Trends in Health Care Costs and Utilization.**

Methodology: Based on data collection by Mutual of Omaha based on the experience of their covered enrollees.

Qualifications: Since these figures are based on the experiences of a certain segment of the population (e.g., Mutual of Omaha enrollees), they may not be generalizable to the total population. For some states figures are not available. The figures for Maine and Wyoming are for 1988.

Interpretation: The psychotherapy visit rate varies widely by state. These differences are probably less of a function of the degree of impairment among the various states' populations as they are a reflection of the availability of resources and the public acceptance of psychotherapy.

XI-27. PATIENT CHARACTERISTICS
SELECTED CHARACTERISTICS OF PATIENTS DISCHARGED
FROM STATE AND COUNTY MENTAL HOSPITALS
1987

Characteristic	Discharges	Percent of: Patients Under Care
Sex:		
Male	61.1%	60.8%
Female	38.9	39.2
Race/Ethnicity:		
White	67.1	77.6
Black	32.4	21.9
American Indian/Alaskan	0.1	0.2
Asian/Pacific Islander	0.2	0.2
Hispanic	2.0	2.6
Age:		
Under 18	6.8	7.5
18-24	14.6	8.4
25-44	56.7	46.8
45-64	17.3	23.1
65 and over	4.6	14.2
Education Level:		
None	10.1	31.0
Less than high school	45.5	39.8
High school graduate	31.4	21.0
More than high school	13.0	8.2
Marital Status:		
Never married	57.1	64.5
Married	11.2	8.1
Separated	7.3	4.1
Divorced	19.0	15.5
Widowed	5.5	7.5

Source: Based on data complied by the National Institute of Mental Health (NIMH) and published in **Mental Health, United States, 1990.** The National Institute of Mental Health (Washington) is part of the federally-funded National Institutes of Health (NIH) and is the main source of research funding and statistics on mental health in the United States.

Methodology: Based on data collected by NIMH for fiscal year 1987 from state and county hospitals in five states.

Definitions: "Discharges" excludes deaths. "Hispanics" are defined in a variety of ways by government agencies and may be of any race. Therefore, the Hispanics included here were probably all counted as white or black in the table as well.

Qualifications: Since these data have been collected by means of a sample survey, they are subject to sampling error. The national totals reported are extrapolated from these sampled records and could possibly vary from actual figures by a few percentage points either plus or minus. The data are also subject to nonsampling errors due to inaccurate and/or incomplete reporting of the data. Since these data were collected in 1987, significant changes have occurred in health care in general and mental health care in particular.

Interpretation: Historically, minority populations have been overrepresented among patients at state and county mental hospitals. Although blacks continue to be overrepresented among those treated at state and county mental hospitals, the figure is lower than in the past. Nevertheless, it could be argued that the typical patient in such institutions is a 25-44 year old unmarried male with limited education.

XI-28. PREVALENCE
MOST COMMON MENTAL DISORDER DIAGNOSES BY REGION
(In Thousands)
1989

Disorder	Region			
	Northeast	Midwest	South	West
Senile/presenile organic psychotic conditions	7	10	15	0
Alcohol psychoses	17	13	13	10
Transient organic psychotic conditions	6	6	10	10
Schizophrenia	87	49	44	24
Affective psychoses	120	98	106	48
Other nonorganic psychoses	16	14	17	8
Neurotic disorders	24	32	35	21
Personality disorders	13	6	0	0
Acute alcoholic intoxication	54	66	71	28
Opioid-type dependence	28	34	37	14
Depression disorders	7	11	13	0
All other disorders	78	74	81	50
Total	457	413	442	203

Source: Based on data collected by the National Center for Health Statistics (NCHS). NCHS conducts a variety of surveys from which health-related data are drawn. Additional data, including some unpublished data, on this topic is available from NCHS (Hyattsville, MD).

Methodology: These data were collected by the NCHS by means of the 1989 National Health Interview Survey. These figures are based on data collected by means of personal interviews conducted annually of a national sample between 36,000 and 46,000 households.

Qualifications: The National Health Interview Survey is faced with the same drawbacks that characterize all sample surveys. The size and representativeness of the sample, questionnaire design, interviewer skills and a variety of other factors may affect the quality of the data. The nature of mental illness makes collecting this type of information especially problematic. The NCHS is the major health data collection agency in the United States, however, and has a reputation for rigorous research methodology.

Interpretation: The prevalence of different types of mental disorder varies by geographic region. The northeast appears to have a disproportionately high amount of mental disorder and the west a disproportionately low amount. These differences partially reflect differences in medical practices from region to region.

XI-29. PREVALENCE
MOST COMMON MENTAL DISORDER DIAGNOSES BY SEX
(In Thousands)
1989

Disorder	Total	Male	Female
Senile/presenile organic psychotic conditions	36	15	21
Alcohol psychoses	53	42	10
Drug psychoses	15	6	8
Transient organic psychotic conditions	24	10	15
Schizophrenia	204	120	84
Affective psychoses	372	128	244
Simple paranoia	9	0	6
Other nonorganic psychoses	55	24	32
Neurotic disorders	112	43	69
Personality disorders	25	11	14
Acute alcoholic intoxication	218	165	53
Opioid-type dependence	113	72	41
Depression disorders	34	10	24
All other disorders	259	142	115
Total	1,514	778	736

Source: Based on data collected by the National Center for Health Statistics (NCHS). NCHS conducts a variety of surveys from which health-related data are drawn. Additional data, including some unpublished data, on this topic is available from NCHS (Hyattsville, MD).

Methodology: These data were collected by the NCHS by means of the 1989 National Health Interview Survey. These figures are based on data collected by means of personal interviews conducted annually of a national sample between 36,000 and 46,000 households.

Qualifications: The National Health Interview Survey is faced with the same drawbacks that characterize all sample surveys. The size and representativeness of the sample, questionnaire design, interviewer skills and a variety of other factors may affect the quality of the data. The nature of mental illness makes collecting this type of information especially problematic. The NCHS is the major health data collection agency in the United States, however, and has a reputation for rigorous research methodology.

Interpretation: The prevalence of different types of mental disorder varies by sex, with certain conditions being more common among males and others among females. In general the prevalence of alcohol- and drug-related conditions is higher among males while the prevalence of affective disorders and depression is higher among females.

XI-30. PREVALENCE
MOST COMMON MENTAL DISORDER DIAGNOSES BY AGE
(In Thousands)
1989

Disorder	Age Category			
	Under 15	15-44	45-64	65 & over
Senile/presenile organic psychotic conditions	0	0	0	35
Alcohol psychoses	0	27	20	6
Drug psychoses	0	8	0	0
Transient organic psychotic conditions	0	6	0	14
Schizophrenia	0	145	47	11
Affective psychoses	9	204	85	75
Simple paranoia	0	0	0	0
Other nonorganic psychoses	0	21	14	20
Neurotic disorders	5	65	25	17
Personality disorders	0	21	14	20
Acute alcoholic intoxication	0	149	55	14
Opioid-type dependence	0	105	0	0
Depression disorders	0	23	5	7
All other disorders	33	163	45	41
Total	47	937	294	239

Source: Based on data collected by the National Center for Health Statistics (NCHS). NCHS conducts a variety of surveys from which health-related data are drawn. Additional data, including some unpublished data, on this topic is available from NCHS (Hyattsville, MD).

Methodology: These data were collected by the NCHS by means of the 1989 National Health Interview Survey. These figures are based on data collected by means of personal interviews conducted annually of a national sample between 36,000 and 46,000 households.

Qualifications: The National Health Interview Survey is faced with the same drawbacks that characterize all sample surveys. The size and representativeness of the sample, questionnaire design, interviewer skills and a variety of other factors may affect the quality of the data. The nature of mental illness makes collecting this type of information especially problematic. The NCHS is the major health data collection agency in the United States, however, and has a reputation for rigorous research methodology.

Interpretation: The prevalence of different types of mental disorder varies by age, with certain conditions being more common among different age groups. For this point in time (1989) the number of diagnosed cases of mental disorders is higher among the 15-44 age group than among other age cohorts. This reflects both the large size of this cohort and the fact that many disorders occur most frequently among members of this age group.

XI-31. DIAGNOSES
LEADING DIAGNOSIS FOR PERSONS ADMITTED TO INPATIENT
MENTAL HEALTH FACILITIES
1986

Diagnosis	Number	Percent
Affective Disorders	490,991	30.8%
Schizophrenia	369,402	23.1
Alcohol-Related Disorders	236,197	14.8
Adjustment Disorders	121,330	7.6
Drug-Related Disorders	105,096	6.6
Organic Disorders	47,796	3.0
Personality Disorders	29,910	1.9

Source: Based on data complied by the National Institute of Mental Health (NIMH) and published in **Mental Health, United States, 1990**. The National Institute of Mental Health (Washington) was part of the federally-funded National Institutes of Health (NIH) and the main source of research funding and statistics on mental health in the United States. NIMH was reorganized in 1993; for additional information contact NIH (Bethesda, MD).

Methodology: Based on data collected in 1986 through a sampling of client/patient records at a sample of institutions providing mental health services. The survey covered inpatient, outpatient and partial care programs operated by eight different categories of health organizations. Data were collected from over 1,500 institutions providing mental health care. Some figures are based on data provided by cooperating agencies such as state mental health agencies and the American Hospital Association.

Definitions: "Admissions" refers to all individuals admitted for inpatient treatment by any organization identified by NIMH as providing inpatient mental health services. These figures are for persons and not treatment episodes. "Affective disorders" include more common mental disorders such as depression and manic-depression.

Qualifications: Since these data have been collected by means of a sample survey, they are subject to sampling error. The national totals reported are extrapolated from these sampled records and could possibly vary from actual figures by a few percentage points either plus or minus. The data are also subject to nonsampling errors due to inaccurate and/or incomplete reporting of the data. Since these data were collected in 1986, significant changes have occurred in health care in general and mental health care in particular.

Interpretation: The more severe types of mental disorder (schizophrenia and certain affective disorders) account for the majority of inpatient admissions. The number of admissions for drug- and alcohol-related disorders has been increasing over time, partly due to an increase in the incidence of these conditions and partly due to a growing tendency to treat such conditions in mental health facilities. However, by the late 1980s there had been a substantial negative reaction toward the inpatient treatment of substance abuse. Thus, the number of such admissions are not likely to continue to increase.

XI-32. DIAGNOSES
LEADING DIAGNOSIS FOR PERSONS UNDER CARE BY INPATIENT MENTAL HEALTH FACILITIES
APRIL 1, 1986

Diagnosis	Number	Percent
Schizophrenia	69,994	43.5%
Affective Disorders	34,772	21.6
Alcohol-Related Disorders	10,008	6.2
Organic Disorders	9,001	5.6
Adjustment Disorders	6,301	3.9
Drug-Related Disorders	4,829	3.0
Personality Disorders	3,898	2.4

Source: Based on data complied by the National Institute of Mental Health (NIMH) and published in **Mental Health, United States, 1990.** The National Institute of Mental Health (Washington) was part of the federally-funded National Institutes of Health (NIH) and the main source of research funding and statistics on mental health in the United States. NIMH was reorganized in 1993; for additional information contact NIH (Bethesda, MD).

Methodology: Based on data collected in 1986 through a sampling of client/patient records at a sample of institutions providing mental health services. The survey covered inpatient, outpatient and partial care programs operated by eight different categories of health organizations. Data were collected from over 1,500 institutions providing mental health care. These data refer to those under care April 1, 1986. Some figures are based on data provided by cooperating agencies such as state mental health agencies and the American Hospital Association.

Definitions: "Admissions" refers to all individuals admitted for inpatient treatment by any organization identified by NIMH as providing inpatient mental health services. These figures are for persons and not treatment episodes. "Affective disorders" include more common mental disorders such as depression and manic-depression.

Qualifications: Since these data have been collected by means of a sample survey, they are subject to sampling error. The national totals reported are extrapolated from these sampled records and could possibly vary from actual figures by a few percentage points either plus or minus. The data are also subject to nonsampling errors due to inaccurate and/or incomplete reporting of the data. Since these data were collected in 1986, significant changes have occurred in health care in general and mental health care in particular.

Interpretation: The more severe types of mental disorder (schizophrenia and certain affective disorders) account for the majority of inpatient admissions. The number of admissions for drug- and alcohol-related disorders has been increasing over time, partly due to an increase in the incidence of these conditions and partly due to a growing tendency to treat such conditions in mental health facilities. However, by the late 1980s there had been a substantial negative reaction toward the inpatient treatment of substance abuse. Thus, the number of such admissions are not likely to continue to increase. Patients with schizophrenia and organic disorders are disproportionately represented among those under care (compared to those admitted) because of their longer lengths of stay.

XI-33. DIAGNOSES
DISTRIBUTION OF PATIENTS BY DIAGNOSIS
UNDER CARE BY INPATIENT MENTAL HEALTH FACILITIES
APRIL 1, 1986

Diagnosis	State/County Mental Hospitals	Private Psychiatric Hospitals	VA Medical Centers	General Hospitals	Multiservice Mental Health Organizations
Schizophrenia	57.5%	13.3%	40.6%	19.0%	44.0%
Affective Disorders	12.4	49.7	16.1	36.8	18.6
Alcohol-Related Disorders	2.9	3.0	18.8	12.5	5.3
Organic Disorders	7.0	2.9	6.0	3.0	3.9
Adjustment Disorders	2.6	4.0	0.9	8.8	*
Drug-Related Disorders	1.5	3.6	4.0	6.1	5.2
Personality Disorders	2.5	3.7	1.9	1.7	*

*Sample size too small to calculate a reliable estimate.

Source: Based on data complied by the National Institute of Mental Health (NIMH) and published in **Mental Health, United States, 1990.** The National Institute of Mental Health (Washington) was part of the federally-funded National Institutes of Health (NIH) and the main source of research funding and statistics on mental health in the United States. NIMH was reorganized in 1993; for additional information contact NIH (Bethesda, MD).

Methodology: Based on data collected in 1986 through a sampling of client/patient records at a sample of institutions providing mental health services. The survey covered inpatient, outpatient and partial care programs operated by eight different categories of health organizations. Data were collected from over 1,500 institutions providing mental health care. These data refer to those under care April 1, 1986. Some figures are based on data provided by cooperating agencies such as state mental health agencies and the American Hospital Association.

Definitions: "Admissions" refers to all individuals admitted for inpatient treatment by any organization identified by NIMH as providing inpatient mental health services. These figures are for persons and not treatment episodes. "Affective disorders" include more common mental disorders such as depression and manic-depression.

Qualifications: Since these data have been collected by means of a sample survey, they are subject to sampling error. The national totals reported are extrapolated from these sampled records and could possibly vary from actual figures by a few percentage points either plus or minus. The data are also subject to nonsampling errors due to inaccurate and/or incomplete reporting of the data. Since these data were collected in 1986, significant changes have occurred in health care in general and mental health care in particular.

Interpretation: The type of mental patient under care varies widely by type of inpatient facility. This variation is partly a result of differences in the types of services offered by the various facilities and partly as a result of the type of individual (e.g., in terms of age or sex) that becomes institutionalized in the various facilities. For example, since VA facilities treat older males primarily, the diagnoses of patients under care there are primarily those of older males.

XI-34. DIAGNOSES
DIAGNOSES OF PATIENTS DISCHARGED FROM
STATE AND COUNTY MENTAL HOSPITALS
1987

| | Percent of Patients | |
Diagnosis	Discharges	Patients Under Care
Mental Retardation	1.4%	3.1%
Alcohol related	5.7	2.4
Substance related	5.4	1.7
Organic disorders	4.0	8.9
Affective disorders	20.8	13.7
Schizophrenia and related	38.2	55.6
Other psychotic conditions	4.1	2.7
Anxiety and related	0.7	0.5
Personality disorders	3.4	2.1
Preadult disorders	3.6	3.2
Other nonpsychotic conditions	11.0	3.4
Social conditions	0.7	0.2
None/other/unknown	1.0	2.3

Source: Based on data complied by the National Institute of Mental Health (NIMH) and published in **Mental Health, United States, 1990.** The National Institute of Mental Health (Washington) was part of the federally-funded National Institutes of Health (NIH) and the main source of research funding and statistics on mental health in the United States. NIMH was reorganized in 1993; for additional information contact NIH (Bethesda, MD).

Methodology: Based on data collected by NIMH for fiscal year 1987 from state and county hospitals in five states.

Definitions: "Discharges" excludes deaths.

Qualifications: Since these data have been collected by means of a sample survey, they are subject to sampling error. The national totals reported are extrapolated from these sampled records and could possibly vary from actual figures by a few percentage points either plus or minus. The data are also subject to nonsampling errors due to inaccurate and/or incomplete reporting of the data. Since these data were collected in 1987, significant changes have occurred in health care in general and mental health care in particular.

Interpretation: Historically, minority populations have been overrepresented among patients at state and county mental hospitals. Although blacks continue to be overrepresented among those treated at state and county mental hospitals, the figure is lower than in the past. Nevertheless, it could be argued that the typical patient in such institutions is a 25-44 year old unmarried male with limited education.

Section XII

DATA ON DEMOGRAPHICS

The collection of demographic data has a long history in the United States as evidenced by the fact that the first decennial census was taken in 1790. Until recently, the use of census data for health care research and planning has been limited primarily to the application of population size figures for the calculation of incidence and prevalence rates. However, as competition in the health care arena has increased and organizations have become more market driven, demographic data have become vital for a wide range of planning activities including site selection, market share calculation, and market estimation. Health care planners have come to view demographic data as a necessity for carrying out their tasks.

Demographic data are generated from a wide variety of sources. For example, community surveys and the internal datasets of health care providers almost always include a demographic dimension (e.g., patient's age). Nevertheless, most national-level demographic data in the United States come from only two federal sources: the decennial census and the Current Population Survey (CPS). While the first census conducted by the U.S. Bureau of the Census was modest in its goals and information collected, recent censuses have been rich in information and potential use. Beside the standard items such as a person's age, race, sex, and marital status, there are data on such factors as housing (e.g., own or rent), commuting patterns, and disability status. These standard items are frequently used by health care planners and marketers to describe market areas. For example, using demographic data to estimate and/or project the number of women in their childbearing years can assist in forecasting the number of births likely to occur in a market area. These birth figures, after factoring in market share, are key items in determining how well a new or expanded obstetrical unit is likely to fare. Additional items can be used to identify atypical or unusual markets. For example, an area with a high incidence of crowded housing (a census derived item) is likely to have a unique set of health care needs.

The second source of demographic data is the CPS. The CPS is part of an ongoing set of Census Bureau data collection activities that occur during the intercensal period. It contains basic demographic items (e.g., age, sex, and race) along with a few questions tailored to current issues (e.g., presence or absence of health care insurance). These data can be used in the same fashion as census data once again allowing for geographic limitations. The health insurance question, for example, has been used to derive estimates of the population without health insurance along with the identifying characteristics of those without coverage. Since these data collection activities involve a national sample, the CPS has limited application at the subnational level.

A nontraditional, but nevertheless demographic, dataset is available from the Immigration and Naturalization Services (INS). These data contain information on the size, country-of-origin, and characteristics of legal immigrants to the U.S. Health care researchers have utilized these data in order to gain insight into the unique needs of market areas that have large concentrations of immigrants.

The data noted above are available directly from the federal government (e.g., Data User Services Division of the Bureau of the Census) in printed form, computer tape, and more recently on compact disk (CD). The 1990 Census data on CD-ROM are proving to be particularly user friendly, allowing ready access to a wide range of data for extremely small geographic units. The CPS is now available on CD, with each CD-ROM containing three consecutive years of data.

In addition, data vendors are taking existing data and repackaging them in a more user-friendly manner such as customized tables and graphs which contain only the variables the user has specified. Vendors are also producing population and economic estimates and projections for a host of large and small geographic units, though the potential user is warned that these data often contain a significant error factor. Vendor-generated data (particularly intercensal estimates and projections) have become so common that users of demographic data have become less directly dependent on census data.

XII-1. POPULATION SIZE
POPULATION OF THE UNITED STATES
(In Millions)
1900-1990

Year	Population
1991	253.6
1990	248.7
1980	226.5
1970	203.3
1960	178.5
1950	150.7
1940	131.7
1930	122.8
1920	105.7
1910	92.0
1900	76.0

Source: Decennial census figures aggregated in the **Statistical Abstract of the United States, 1991**. The 1991 estimate is from **Census and You** (January, 1991).

Methodology: Data collected by the U.S. Census Bureau every ten years. Data for 1991 are an estimate also produced by the U.S. Census Bureau.

Interpretation: While the U.S. population continues to grow, the rate of growth is slowing. The population could well stop increasing in the latter part of the twenty-first century.

XII-2. POPULATION GROWTH/DENSITY
U.S. POPULATION GROWTH AND DENSITY
1950-1990

Year	Population	Population per sq. mile	Increase Over previous decade	Percent change
1990	248,710,000	70.8	23,864,195	9.8
1980	226,545,805	64.0	23,243,774	11.4
1970	203,302,031	57.4	23,978,856	13.4
1960	179,323,175	50.6	27,997,377	18.5
1950	151,325,798	42.6	19,161,229	14.5

Sources: Based on data collected and calculations made by the U.S. Bureau of the Census and published in **Statistical Abstract of the United States, 1992**, tables 1.

Methodology: Data collected by the Census Bureau every ten years.

Definition: Resident population includes Armed Forces stationed overseas.

Qualifications: Decennial population censuses are carried out in the U.S. in years that end in zero. The 1990 census was the twenty-first taken. Recent censuses have inquired about a host of factors (e.g. income, commuting patterns and home ownership) beyond the simple counting of persons by age, race and sex required by the U.S. Constitution. Census population count data are subject to some error. The undercount for 1990 is likely to be less than two percent.

Interpretation: Population growth continues but is slowing in the U.S. Population density steadily increases.

XII-3. AGE STRUCTURE
POPULATION PROJECTIONS BY AGE
(In Thousands)
1990-2010

Age	1990	2000	2010
Under 5	18,408	16,898	16,899
5-17	45,630	48,815	45,747
18-24	26,140	25,231	27,155
25-34	43,925	37,149	37,572
35-44	37,897	43,911	37,502
45-54	25,487	37,223	43,207
55-64	21,364	24,158	35,430
65-74	18,374	18,243	21,039
75 and over	13,187	16,639	18,323
Total	250,410	268,266	282,575

Source: Based on calculations by the U.S. Bureau of the Census and published in "Projections of the Population of the United States, by Age, Sex, and Race: 1988 to 2080." **Current Population Reports,** Series P-25, No. 1018, 1989.

Methodology: As part of its responsibilities the Census Bureau regularly prepares population projections.

Definitions: Data are as of July 1 of the relevant year and include Armed Forces personnel overseas.

Qualifications: These data come from the middle series of the U.S. Census Bureau's population projections. The middle series assumes that fertility rates will remain constant over the projection period, while life expectancy at birth (mortality assumption) will gradually increase from nearly 75 years currently to 81.2 years in 2080. Net annual immigration is assumed to be 500,000. The cohort component method is utilized beginning with the most recent population estimate classified by age, race and sex. Independent rates of fertility and mortality, as stated above, are applied to projected change. A specific number of immigrants, 500,000 per year for the middle series, distributed by age, race, and sex, as stated above, is also added at each iterative step.

Interpretation: While all age cohorts will grow over the next two decades, the cohorts 45 to 54 and 55 to 64 will grow fastest. At the same time, the number of persons age 25 to 44 will decline.

XII-4. AGE, RACE AND ETHNICITY
POPULATION PROJECTIONS BY AGE, RACE AND ETHNICITY
(In Thousands)
1990-2010

| Age | White Population | | |
	1990	Projected 2000	Projected 2010
Under 5	14,893	13,324	13,084
5-13	25,958	26,520	23,855
14-17	10,579	12,049	11,403
18-24	21,154	19,823	21,122
25-34	36,487	29,855	29,453
35-44	32,252	36,519	29,942
45-54	21,944	31,611	35,853
55-64	18,636	20,667	29,912
65-74	16,380	15,811	17,875
75 and over	11,965	14,965	16,108
Total	210,247	221,144	228,608
Median Age	33.9	37.6	40.3

| Age | Black Population | | |
	1990	Projected 2000	Projected 2010
Under 5	2,184	2,748	2,820
5-13	5,063	5,412	5,305
14-17	2,107	2,484	2,504
18-24	3,756	3,867	4,257
25-34	5,633	5,212	5,537
35-44	4,199	5,469	5,065
45-54	2,685	4,105	5,367
55-64	2,156	2,579	3,995
65-74	1,608	1,848	2,277
75 and over	1,004	1,284	1,583
Total	31,026	35,006	38,710
Median Age	28.2	30.8	32.9

(Continued on next page)

XII-4. AGE, RACE AND ETHNICITY
POPULATION PROJECTIONS BY AGE, RACE AND ETHNICITY
(In Thousands)
1990-2010 *(Continued from previous page)*

Age	1990	Hispanic Population Projected 2000	Projected 2010
Under 5	2,282	2,496	2,852
5-13	3,472	4,382	4,776
14-17	1,353	1,825	2,072
18-24	2,737	3,147	4,101
25-34	3,629	3,804	5,204
35-44	2,788	3,803	3,983
45-54	1,668	1,811	3,806
55-64	1,183	1,619	2,704
65-74	707	1,031	1,432
75 and over	419	678	1,045
Total	19,887	25,223	30,795
Median Age	26.3	28.0	29.3

Sources: Based on calculations by the U.S. Bureau of the Census and published in "Population Projections of the United States by Age, Sex and Race: 1988-2010." **Current Population Reports** P-25, No. 1017, 1988, and "Projections of the Hispanic Population: 1983 to 2080." **Current Population Reports** P-25, No. 995, 1986.

Methodology: As part of its responsibilities the Census Bureau regularly prepares population projections.

Definitions: Data are as of July 1 of the relevant year and include Armed Forces personnel overseas. Race and ethnic data are the result of self-identification in a census or survey situation. That is, respondents select the category they deem appropriate. White and black data include Hispanics because Hispanics may be of either race.

Qualifications: These data are derived from the middle series of the U.S. Census Bureau's population projections. The middle series assumes that fertility rates will remain constant over the projection period, while life expectancy at birth (mortality assumption) will gradually increase from nearly 75 years currently to 81.2 years in 2080. Net annual immigration is assumed to be 500,000. The cohort component method is utilized beginning with the most recent population estimate classified by age, race and sex. Independent rates of fertility and mortality, as stated above, are applied to projected change. A specific number of immigrants, 500,000 per year for the middle series, distributed by age, race, and sex, as stated above, is also added at each iterative step.

Interpretation: Of the three groups presented, Hispanics have the youngest age structure followed by blacks and whites. The white population will increase in terms of numbers more than blacks and Hispanics by 2010, although those two groups are growing faster proportionately.

XII-5. POPULATION CHANGE
STATE POPULATIONS TRENDS
(In 1,000s)
1960-1990

State	1960	1970	1980	1990
Alabama	3,267*	3,444	3,894	4,041
Alaska	226	303	402	550
Arizona	1,302	1,775	2,718	3,665
Arkansas	1,786	1,923	2,286	2,351
California	15,717	19,971	23,668	29,760
Colorado	1,754	2,210	2,890	3,294
Connecticut	2,535	3,032	3,108	3,287
Delaware	446	548	594	666
Florida	4,952	6,791	9,746	12,938
Georgia	3,943	4,588	5,463	6,478
Hawaii	633	770	965	1,108
Idaho	667	713	944	1,007
Illinois	10,081	11,110	11,427	11,431
Indiana	4,662	5,195	5,490	5,544
Iowa	2,758	2,825	2,914	2,777
Kansas	2,179	2,249	2,364	2,478
Kentucky	3,038	3,221	3,661	3,685
Louisiana	3,257	3,645	4,206	4,220
Maine	969	994	1,125	1,227
Maryland	3,101	3,924	4,217	4,781
Massachusetts	5,149	5,689	5,737	6,016
Michigan	7,823	8,882	9,262	9,295
Minnesota	3,414	3,806	4,076	4,375
Mississippi	2,178	2,217	2,521	2,573
Missouri	4,320	4,678	4,917	5,117
Montana	675	694	787	799
Nebraska	1,411	1,485	1,570	1,578
Nevada	285	489	800	1,202
New Hampshire	607	738	921	1,109
New Jersey	6,067	6,171	7,365	7,730
New Mexico	951	1,017	1,303	1,515
New York	16,782	18,241	17,558	17,990
North Carolina	4,556	5,084	5,882	6,629
North Dakota	632	618	653	639
Ohio	9,706	10,657	10,798	10,847
Oklahoma	2,328	2,559	3,025	3,146
Oregon	1,769	2,092	2,633	2,842
Pennsylvania	11,319	11,801	11,864	11,882
Rhode Island	859	950	947	1,003
South Carolina	2,383	2,591	3,122	3,487
South Dakota	681	666	690	696
Tennessee	3,567	3,926	4,591	4,877

(Continued on next page)

XII-5. POPULATION CHANGE
STATE POPULATIONS TRENDS
(In 1,000s)
1960-1990 *(Continued from previous page)*

State	1960	1970	1980	1990
Texas	9,580	11,199	14,229	16,987
Utah	891	1,059	1,461	1,723
Vermont	390	445	511	563
Virginia	3,967	4,651	5,347	6,187
Washington	2,853	3,413	4,132	4,867
West Virginia	1,860	1,744	1,950	1,793
Wisconsin	3,952	4,418	4,706	4,892
Wyoming	330	332	470	454
District of Columbia	764	757	638	607
Total	179,323	203,302	226,546	248,710

Source: Decennial census figures aggregated in the **Statistical Abstract of the United States**. The 1990 figure is from **Census and You** (January, 1991).

Methodology: Data collected by the U.S. Census Bureau every ten years.

Definitions: Resident population includes Armed Forces stationed in the state specified.

Qualifications: Decennial population censuses are carried out in the U.S. in years that end in zero. The 1990 census was the twenty-first taken. Recent censuses have inquired about a host of factors (e.g. income, commuting patterns and home ownership) beyond the simple counting of persons by age, race and sex required by the U.S. Constitution. Census population count data are subject to some error. The undercount for 1990 is likely to be less than two percent.

Interpretation: Wide state-to-state variation exists in both size and growth patterns since 1960. Between 1980 and 1990, three states lost population and several others grew very little.

XII-6. POPULATION PROJECTIONS
STATE POPULATION PROJECTIONS
(In Thousands)
2000 AND 2010

State	2000	2010
Alabama	4,410	4,609
Alaska	687	765
Arizona	4,618	5,319
Arkansas	2,529	2,624
California	33,500	37,347
Colorado	3,813	4,098
Connecticut	3,445	3,532
Delaware	734	790
Florida	15,415	17,530
Georgia	7,957	9,045
Hawaii	1,345	1,559
Idaho	1,047	1,079
Illinois	11,580	11,495
Indiana	5,502	5,409
Iowa	2,549	2,382
Kansas	2,529	2,564
Kentucky	3,733	3,710
Louisiana	4,516	4,545
Maine	1,271	1,308
Maryland	5,274	5,688
Massachusetts	6,087	6,255
Michigan	9,250	9,097
Minnesota	4,490	4,578
Mississippi	2,877	3,028
Missouri	5,383	5,521
Montana	794	794
Nebraska	1,556	1,529
Nevada	1,303	1,484
New Hampshire	1,333	1,455
New Jersey	8,546	8,980
New Mexico	1,968	2,248
New York	17,986	18,139
North Carolina	7,483	8,154
North Dakota	629	611
Ohio	10,629	10,397
Oklahoma	3,376	3,511
Oregon	2,877	2,991
Pennsylvania	11,503	11,134
Rhode Island	1,049	1,085
South Carolina	3,906	4,205
South Dakota	714	722
Tennessee	5,266	5,500

(Continued on next page)

XII-6. POPULATION PROJECTIONS
STATE POPULATION PROJECTIONS
(In Thousands)
2000 AND 2010 *(Continued from previous page)*

State	2000	2010
Texas	20,211	22,281
Utah	1,991	2,171
Vermont	591	608
Virginia	6,877	7,410
Washington	4,991	5,282
West Virginia	1,722	1,617
Wisconsin	4,784	4,713
Wyoming	489	487
District of Columbia	634	672
Total	267,747	282,055

Source: Based on calculations by the U.S. Bureau of the Census and published in "Projection of the Population of the United States by Age, Sex, and Race: 1988 to 2010." **Current Population Reports, Series P-25, No. 1017, 1988.**

Methodology: As part of its responsibilities the Census Bureau regularly prepares population projections.

Definitions: Data are as of July 1 of the relevant year and include Armed Forces personnel overseas.

Qualifications: Data come from the middle series of the U.S. Census Bureaus' population projections. The cohort component method is utilized beginning with the most recent population estimate classified by age, race and sex. Independent rates of fertility and mortality are applied to project change. A specific number of immigrants (distributed by age, race, and sex) is also added at each iterative step.

Interpretation: The populations of states in the South and West are increasing much faster than states in the Northeast or Midwest. Several states will experience either no growth or population decline early in the twenty-first century.

XII-7. SEX RATIO
RATIO BY AGE
1990

Age	Sex Ratio
Births	105
Under 5 years	105
5-9 years	105
10-14 years	105
15-19 years	104
20-24 years	102
25-29 years	101
30-34 years	101
35-39 years	99
40-44 years	97
45-49 years	95
50-54 years	94
55-59 years	91
60-64 years	87
65-74 years	78
75 years and over	54

Source: Based on calculations made by the authors. Data from which calculations were made are published in the **Statistical Abstract of the United States, 1991,** tables 13 and 82, 1991.

Methodology: These figures are based on population estimates for the United States produced by the Census Bureau.

Definitions: "Sex ratio" refers to the number of men per 100 women in a population.

Interpretation: The sex ratio at birth is 105 and males are a majority of the population through the age interval 30 to 34. The female majority grows slowly at first, but by the interval 75 and over the ratio is 55, or 182 females for every 100 males.

XII-8. SEX RATIO
SEX RATIO BY AGE
1960-1990

	1960	1970	1980	1990
Births	105	105	105	105
Under 5 years	103	104	105	105
5-9 years	103	104	105	105
10-14 years	103	104	104	105
15-19 years	102	103	104	104
20-24 years	100	101	102	102
25-29 years	98	99	100	101
30-34 years	97	97	99	101
35-39 years	96	96	97	99
40-44 years	96	95	96	97
45-49 years	97	94	95	95
50-54 years	97	93	92	94
55-59 years	96	92	89	91
60-64 years	91	88	86	87
65-74 years	87	78	77	78
75 years and over	75	55	55	54

Source: Based on calculations made by the authors. Data from which calculations were made are published in the **Statistical Abstract of the United States, 1991,** tables 13 and 82, 1991.

Methodology: Data for 1960, 1970 and 1980 came from decennial censuses. The 1988 figures are based on population estimates produced by the U.S. Census Bureau.

Definitions: "Sex ratio" refers to the number of men per 100 women in a population.

Interpretation: Sex ratios be age have been relatively constant of the last 30 years up to age 60 to 64. Since 1960 the sex ratio at these ages has become smaller.

XII-9. METROPOLITAN AREAS
TEN LARGEST METROPOLITAN AREAS
1990

Metropolitan Area	Size
New York-Northern New Jersey-Long Island, NY-NJ-CT CMSA	18,087,251
Los Angles-Anaheim-Riverside, CA CMSA	14,531,529
Chicago-Gary-Lake County, IL-IN-WI CMSA	8,065,633
San Francisco-Oakland-San Jose, CA CMSA	6,253,311
Philadelphia-Wilmington-Trenton, PA-NJ-DE-MD CMSA	5,899,345
Detroit-Ann Arbor, MI CMSA	4,665,236
Boston-Lawrence-Salem, MA-NH CMSA	4,171,643
Washington, DC-MD-VA MSA	3,923,574
Dallas-Fort Worth, TX CMSA	3,885,415
Houston-Galveston-Brazoria, TX CMSA	3,711,043

Source: Based on data collected by the U.S. Bureau of the Census and published in **Census and You**, Vol. 26, No. 9 (September, 1991).

Methodology: Based on data collected by the Census Bureau through the 1990 census.

Definitions: "CMSA" is a Consolidated Metropolitan Statistical Area which refers to two or more contiguous MSAs grouped together because of their economic interdependence. "MSAs" are designated on the basis of size and economic interdependence. Counties or county equivalents are the "building blocks" of MSAs; that is, land area is added to MSA on a county-by-county basis. Data are for the resident population.

Qualifications: Data come from the 1990 census and are subject to some error. The overall undercount from the 1990 census is estimated to be less than two percent. However, for some MSAs, the undercount will be higher.

Interpretation: About 73 million people or 29% of the U.S. population, live in these 10 MSAs.

XII-10. CITY POPULATIONS
20 LARGEST U.S. CITIES
1990

City	Size
New York	7,322,564
Los Angeles	3,485,398
Chicago	2,783,726
Houston	1,630,553
Philadelphia	1,585,577
San Diego	1,110,549
Detroit	1,027,974
Dallas	1,006,877
Phoenix	983,403
San Antonio	935,933
San Jose	782,248
Baltimore	736,014
Indianapolis	731,327
San Francisco	723,959
Jacksonville	635,230
Columbus	632,910
Milwaukee	628,088
Memphis	610,337
Washington	606,900
Boston	574,283

Source: Based on data collected by the U.S. Bureau of the Census and published in **Census and You**, (July, 1991).

Methodology: Based on data collected by the Census Bureau through the 1990 census.

Definition: Data are for resident population. Resident population includes Armed Forces stationed in the state specified.

Qualifications: Decennial population censuses are carried out in the U.S. in years that end in zero. The 1990 census was the twenty-first taken. Recent censuses have inquired about a host of factors (e.g. income, commuting patterns and home ownership) beyond the simple counting of persons by age, race and sex required by the U.S. Constitution. Census population count data are subject to some error. The undercount for 1990 is likely to be less than two percent.

Interpretation: Eight U.S. cities had population of one million or more persons in 1990.

Demographics

XII-11. HOUSEHOLDS AND FAMILIES
SELECTED CHARACTERISTICS OF
HOUSEHOLDS AND FAMILIES
1960-1991

Household Type	Household Characteristics*			
	1960	1970	1980	1991
All Households	52,799	63,401	80,776	94,312
Average Size	3.33	3.14	2.76	2.63
Family Households	44,905	51,456	59,550	66,322
Percent Family Households	85.0%	81.1%	73.7%	70.3%
Average Size	3.67	3.58	3.29	3.18
Married Couples	39,329	44,755	49,112	52,147
Percent Married Couples	87.6%	87.0%	82.7%	78.6%

*Data are expressed in 1,000's except for percentages and averages.

Source: Based on data collected by the U.S. Bureau of the Census and published in **Statistical Abstract of the United States, 1991.**

Methodology: Data for 1960 through 1980 come from the decennial censuses. The 1991 data are from the Current Population Survey and subject to sampling error.

Definitions: A "household" consists of all persons occupying a housing unit. A "housing unit" is a house, apartment, group of rooms, or single room occupied as separate living quarters. Excluded are persons who live in group quarters (e.g. prisons, orphanages). A "family" is two or more persons related by birth, marriage, or adoption residing together in the same household. "Percent family households" refers to the percent of all households which are family households. "Percent of married couple households" is the proportion of all family households which are married couple households.

Qualifications: Include numbers of Armed Forces living off post or with their families on post.

Interpretation: Both average household size and family size have been declining over the last four decades. There has been a decline in the proportion of households that are families and married couple households.

XII-12. HOUSEHOLDS AND FAMILIES
AVERAGE SIZE OF HOUSEHOLDS AND FAMILIES
1940-1990

Year	Population Per Household		Population Per Family	
	All Ages	Under Age 18	All Ages	Under Age 18
1990	2.63	0.69	3.17	0.96
1985	2.69	0.72	3.23	0.98
1980	2.76	0.79	3.29	1.05
1975	2.94	0.93	3.42	1.18
1970	3.14	1.09	3.58	1.34
1965	3.29	1.21	3.70	1.44
1960	3.33	1.21	3.67	1.41
1955	3.33	1.14	3.59	1.30
1950	3.37	1.06	3.54	1.17
1940	3.67	1.14	3.76	1.24

Source: Based on data collected by the U.S. Bureau of the Census and published in "Household and Family Characteristics: March 1990 and 1989." **Current Population Reports**, Series P-20, No. 447, 1990.

Methodology: Data collected by means of the Decennial Census and the Current Population Survey, the U.S. Census Bureau's nationally representative sample survey conducted during intercensal time periods.

Definitions: A "household" consists of all persons occupying a housing unit. A housing unit is a house, apartment, group of rooms, or single room occupied as separate living quarters. Excluded are persons who live in group quarters (e.g. prisons, orphanages). A family is two or more persons related by birth, marriage, or adoption residing together in the same household.

Qualifications: Include numbers of Armed Forces living off post or with their families on post.

Interpretation: Households have lost more than one person on average since 1940. Over the same time interval, average family size has declined by more than one-half person.

XII-13. FAMILY SIZE
DISTRIBUTION FAMILIES BY TYPE AND SIZE
1991

Family Type Size	All Families*	Married Couple Families	Male Headed Families	Female Headed Families
Total	66,322	52,147	2,907	11,268
Two Persons	41.6%	39.5%	60.3%	46.9%
Three Persons	23.0	21.7	23.9	29.0
Four Persons	21.2	23.4	8.8	14.7
Five Persons	9.0	10.0	4.1	5.5
Six Persons	3.1	3.5	1.4	1.9
Seven or More Persons	1.9	1.9	1.5	2.0
Average per Family	3.18	3.24	2.78	3.00

*Numbers are expressed in 1,000s.

Source: Based on data collected by the U.S. Bureau of the Census and published in "Household and Family Characteristics: March 1990 and 1989." **Current Population Reports**, Series P-20, No. 458, 1992.

Methodology: Data collected by means of the Current Population Survey, the U.S. Census Bureau's nationally representative sample survey conducted during intercensal time periods.

Definitions: A "family" is two or more persons who reside together and are related by blood, marriage or adoption.

Qualifications: Include numbers of Armed Forces living off post or with their families on post.

Interpretation: Married couple families have the largest average size. There are over ten million female headed (husband not present) families.

XII-14. HOUSEHOLD INCOME
MEDIAN HOUSEHOLD INCOME
1970-1988

Year	Percent of Households With Incomes: Under $25,000	Over $50,000	Median
1988	45.9	20.8	$27,225
1987	46.0	20.3	27,139
1986	46.7	19.7	26,873
1985	48.4	18.2	25,967
1984	48.9	17.5	25,522
1983	50.5	16.2	24,964
1982	51.1	15.5	24,728
1981	51.0	15.1	24,823
1980	49.4	15.8	25,426
1975	48.5	15.2	25,947
1970	47.0	15.0	26,630

Source: Based on data collected by the U.S. Bureau of the Census and published in "Money Income and Poverty Status in the United States: 1988." **Current Population Reports**, Series P-60, No. 166, 1989.

Methodology: Data collected by means of the Current Population Survey, the U.S. Census Bureau's nationally representative sample survey conducted during intercensal time periods.

Definitions: Money income is the sum of the amounts received from wages and salaries, self-employment income (including losses), Social Security, Supplemental Security Income, public assistance, interest, dividends, royalties, estates or trusts, Veterans payments, unemployment and workers' compensation, private and government retirement and disability pensions, alimony, child support, and any other source of money income that was regularly received. A household is made up of all persons who occupy a housing unit. A housing unit is a house, apartment or other group of rooms, or a separate room intended for occupancy as separate living quarters.

Qualifications: These data are gathered through the Census Bureau's Current Population Survey and are subject to sampling and nonsampling error. The standard errors for the figures seen here range from $98 to $141. Underreporting of income is also a problem. In the early 1980s, independent estimates of total income derived by the Bureau of Economic Analysis were about 110 percent of the CPS figures. These figures are stated in 1988 dollars.

Interpretation: Median household income has increased by less than $1,000 in constant dollars since 1970. The percentage of households with incomes greater than $50,000 has risen by more than five percent.

XII-15. HOUSEHOLD INCOME
TOTAL INCOME BY HOUSEHOLD TYPE
1988

Household Type	Percent of Households With Incomes:		Median
	Under $25,000	Over $50,000	
All Households	45.9	20.8	$27,225
Family	36.8	26.0	32,491
Married Couple	29.9	30.4	36,436
Male Households (wife not present)	42.9	17.4	28,642
Female Households (husband not present)	68.4	7.3	16,051
Nonfamily Households	67.9	8.1	16,148

Source: Based on data collected by the U.S. Bureau of the Census and published in "Household and Family Characteristics: March 1990 and 1989." **Current Population Reports**, Series P-20, No. 447, 1990.

Methodology: Data collected by means of the Current Population Survey, the U.S. Census Bureau's nationally representative sample survey conducted during intercensal time periods.

Definitions: "Income" refers to money income and is the sum of the amounts received from wages and salaries, self-employment income (including losses), Social Security, Supplemental Security Income, public assistance, interest, dividends, royalties, estates or trusts, Veterans payments, unemployment and workers' compensation, private and government retirement and disability pensions, alimony, child support, and any other source of money income that was regularly received. A "household" is made up of all persons who occupy a housing unit. A housing unit is a house, apartment or other group of rooms, or a separate room intended for occupancy as separate living quarters. A "family" is two or more persons related by birth, marriage, or adoption living in the same housing unit.

Qualifications: These data are gathered through the Census Bureau's Current Population Survey and are subject to sampling and nonsampling error. The standard errors for the figures seen here range from $98 to $141. Underreporting of income is also a problem. In the early 1980s, independent estimates of total income derived by the Bureau of Economic Analysis were about 110 percent of the CPS figures.

Interpretation: Household income is considerably higher for family households than for nonfamily households. Within family households, husband-wife families have higher incomes than households with other structures.

XII-16. ASSET OWNERSHIP
HOUSEHOLD OWNING ASSETS BY TYPE OF ASSET AND AGE CATEGORY
1988

	Age Category				
	Less than 35 years	35 to 44 years	45 to 54 years	55 to 64 years	65 Years and over
Number of Households* (1,000s)	25,379	19,916	13,613	13,090	19,556
Percent Owning Interest earning assets at financial institutions	67.0%	72.5%	73.9%	75.0%	78.8%
Other interest earning assets	4.8	8.5	10.1	12.4	13.9
Regular checking accounts	45.0	50.6	56.4	49.8	43.6
Stocks & mutual fund shares	15.9	23.2	24.6	27.4	22.6
Own business or profession	9.9	16.3	18.2	16.0	5.6
Motor vehicles	87.8	90.2	90.7	89.6	75.0
Homes	39.6	66.6	74.0	78.5	74.7
Rental property	4.2	8.7	12.8	12.0	11.2
U.S. Savings Bonds	14.9	20.7	22.3	21.0	12.2
IRA or Keogh accounts	13.3	27.2	35.9	42.3	15.0

Source: Based on data collected by the U.S. Bureau of the Census and published in "Household Wealth and Asset Ownership: 1988." **Current Population Reports,** Series P-70, No. 22, 1990.

Methodology: Data collected by means of the Current Population Survey, the U.S. Census Bureau's nationally representative sample survey conducted during intercensal time periods.

Definitions: A "householder" is the first person in whose name the housing unit (e.g., home and apartment) is owned or rented as of the interview date. A "household" consists of all persons who occupy a housing unit. Survey respondents were asked if anyone in the household had the specific assets appearing in the table.

Qualifications: The data come from the Survey of Income and Program Participation (SIPP) and are subject to sampling and nonsampling error. The survey design calls for reinterviews of persons who were previously surveyed and the attrition from earlier ways has been about 18 percent. The standard errors for the data appearing in this table are 0.5% less. Data are restricted to the civilian, noninstitutionalized population and members of the Armed Forces living off post or with their families on post. Estimates exclude group quarters.

XII-17. POVERTY
TRENDS IN PERSONS BELOW POVERTY LEVEL
1960-1991

| | Persons in Families | | | | | |
| | All Persons | | All Families | | Female Headed Households | |
	Number*	Percent	Number*	Percent	Number*	Percent
1991	35,708	14.2%	27,143	12.8%	11,692	35.6%
1985	33,585	13.5	25,232	12.0	11,268	33.4
1980	29,272	13.0	22,601	11.5	10.120	36.7
1975	25,877	12.3	20,789	10.9	8,846	37.5
1970	25,420	12.6	20,405	10.8	7,503	38.1
1965	33,185	17.3	28,358	15.8	7,524	46.0
1960	39,851	22.2	34,925	20.7	7,247	48.9

*Numbers are expressed in 1,000's.

Source: Based on data collected by the U.S. Bureau of the Census and published in "Money Income and Poverty Status in the United States: 1988." **Current Population Reports**, Series P-60, No. 166, 1989 and "Poverty in the United States: 1991." **Current Population Reports**, Series P-60, No. 181, 1992.

Methodology: Data collected in the Current Population Survey, the U.S. Census Bureau's nationally representative sample survey conducted during intercensal time periods.

Definitions: "Poverty level" is determined by the calculation of an index which originated at the Social Security Administration in 1964 and was revised by Federal Interagency Committees in 1969 and 1980. It is based on money income and, therefore does not include the receipt of noncash benefits such as food stamps, Medicaid and public housing. Currently, there are 48 poverty thresholds in use based on different combinations of family size, number of children and other factors. The average poverty threshold for a family of four was $13,924 in 1991.

Interpretation: Since 1960 there has been a decline in the number of persons living at or below the poverty level. Female-headed families have more than three times the poverty rate reported for all families combined.

XII-18. IMMIGRATION
IMMIGRANTS BY CONTINENT OF BIRTH
1961-1990

	1961-1970	1971-1980	1981-1990
Europe	1,238,600*	801,300	761,550
Asia	445,300	1,633,800	2,738,157
North America	1,351,100	1,645,000	3,153,378
South America	228,300	284,400	461,847
Africa	39,300	91,500	176,893
Oceana	25,122	41,242	45,205
Other	29,900	23,000	
Total	3,321,700	4,493,300	7,338,062

*Data are rounded to nearest 100.

Sources: Based on data collected by the U.S. Immigration and Naturalization Service and published in 1991 **Statistical Yearbook of the Immigration and Naturalization Service.**

Methodology: These figures were compiled from the immigrant registry files of the Immigration and Naturalization Service.

Definitions: "Immigrants" are those foreign-born persons lawfully accorded the privilege of residing permanently in the United States. They may be issued immigrant visas by the Department of State overseas or adjusted to permanent resident status by the Immigration and Naturalization Service in the United States. The category "Europe" includes the former Soviet Union.

Qualifications: These data do not include persons who illegally reside in the United States.

Interpretation: The number of immigrants to the U.S. has increased over the last three decades. The number of immigrants from Asia has increased by a factor of four over the same time period, while the numbers from Europe, the historical source of U.S. immigrants, have declined substantially.

XII-19. IMMIGRATION
IMMIGRANTS BY AGE
1991

Age Category	Number	Percent
Under 5 years	36,669	2.0%
5-9 years	49,609	2.7
10-14 years	66,237	3.6
15-19 years	109,261	6.0
20-24 years	354,747	19.4
25-29 years	380,682	20.8
30-34 years	276,464	15.1
35-39 years	182,200	10.0
40-44 years	120,980	6.6
45-49 years	78,393	4.3
50-54 years	57,023	3.1
55-59 years	41,330	2.3
60-64 years	30,856	1.7
65-69 years	21,616	1.2
70-74 years	11,109	0.6
75-79 years	5,938	0.3
80 years and over	3,680	0.2
Not reported	373	–
Total	1,827,167	100.0
Median Age		28.8

Source: Based on data collected by the U.S. Immigration and Naturalization Service and published in 1991 **Statistical Yearbook of the Immigration and Naturalization Service.**

Methodology: These figures were compiled from the immigrant registry files of the Immigration and Naturalization Service.

Definitions: "Immigrants" are those foreign-born persons lawfully accorded the privilege of residing permanently in the United States. They may be issued immigrant visas by the Department of State overseas or adjusted to permanent resident status by the Immigration and Naturalization Service in the United States. A nonimmigrant is a person who seeks temporary entry to the United States for a specific purpose.

Qualifications: These data do not include persons who illegally reside in the United States. Percentages may not total to 100 due to rounding error.

Interpretation: The median age of immigrants is younger than that of the U.S. population as a whole. Immigrants are concentrated in the age cohorts 20 to 34.

XII-20. IMMIGRATION
IMMIGRANTS BY SELECTED STATES OF RESIDENCE
1991

State	Number	Percent
California	732,735	40.1%
Texas	212,600	11.6
New York	188,104	10.3
Florida	141,068	7.7
Illinois	73,388	4.0
New Jersey	56,164	3.0
Arizona	40,642	2.2
Washington	33,826	1.9
Massachusetts	27,020	1.5
Virginia	24,942	1.4

Source: Based on data collected by the U.S. Immigration and Naturalization Service and published in 1991 **Statistical Yearbook of the Immigration and Naturalization Service.**

Methodology: These figures were compiled from the immigrant registry files of the Immigration and Naturalization Service.

Definitions: "Immigrants" are those foreign-born persons lawfully accorded the privilege of residing permanently in the United States. They may be issued immigrant visas by the Department of State overseas or adjusted to permanent resident status by the Immigration and Naturalization Service in the United States. A nonimmigrant is a person who seeks temporary entry to the United States for a specific purpose.

Qualifications: These data do not include persons who illegally reside in the United States. Percentages do not total 100 because of omitted states.

Interpretation: Sixty-two percent of all immigrants intended to move to California, Texas, or New York in 1991.

XII-21. MOBILITY STATUS
MOBILITY STATUS AND TYPE OF MOVEMENT
1989-1990

Mobility Status	Percent
Nonmover	82.1%
Mover	17.9
Local Movement	10.6
Movement Between Counties	6.6
Within State	3.3
Between States	3.3
Movers from Abroad	0.6

Source: Based on data collected by the U.S. Bureau of the Census and published in "Geographical Mobility: March 1987 to March 1990." **Current Population Reports**, P-20, No. 456, 1991.

Methodology: Data collected in the Current Population Survey, the U.S. Census Bureau's nationally representative sample survey conducted during intercensal time periods. The CPS is an ongoing effort by the U.S. Bureau of the Census to gather social, economic, and demographic data during the intercensal time periods.

Definition: A "mover" is a person who in March 1989 lived in a different housing unit than they did in March 1990. "Local movement" is defined as a change of residence within the same county.

Qualification: Data come from the 1987 Current Population Survey (CPS) and are subject to sampling and nonsampling error.

Interpretation: Local movement (within counties) comprises about two-thirds of all geographic mobility. Only three percent of migration is from one state to another.

XII-22. GEOGRAPHIC MOBILITY
U.S. POPULATION MOVING ANNUALLY
1960-1990

Year	Percent
1989-90	17.9%
1984-85	19.4
1980-81	16.9
1970-71	18.5
1960-61	20.6

Source: Based on data collected by the U.S. Bureau of the Census and published in "Geographical Mobility: March 1987 to March 1990." **Current Population Reports**, P-20, No. 456, 1991.

Methodology: Data come from the Current Population Survey (CPS) and are subject to sampling and nonsampling error. The CPS is an ongoing effort by the U.S. Bureau of the Census to gather social, economic, and demographic data during the intercensal time periods.

Definitions: A "mover" is a person who currently lives in a different housing unit from that resided in at an earlier period of time (reference point). The reference point for these data is the earlier of the two years.

Interpretation: The level of geographic mobility has not varied significantly during the last 30 years.

XII-23. GEOGRAPHIC MOBILITY
MOBILITY STATUS OF PERSONS BY AGE
1989-1990

Age	Mobility Status		Mover from Abroad
	Nonmover	Mover	
1 to 4	76.2%	23.8%	0.5%
5 to 9	81.0	19.0	0.6
10 to 14	85.1	14.9	0.6
15 to 19	82.2	17.8	1.1
20 to 24	62.1	37.9	1.5
25 to 29	66.6	33.4	1.0
30 to 44	76.8	23.2	0.7
45 to 64	91.2	8.8	0.2
65 years and over	95.1	4.9	0.1
Total	82.1	17.9	0.6

Source: Based on data collected by the U.S. Bureau of the Census and published in "Geographical Mobility: March 1987 to March 1990." **Current Population Reports**, P-20, No. 456, 1991.

Methodology: Data come from the 1987 Current Population Survey (CPS) and are subject to sampling and nonsampling errors. The CPS is an ongoing effort by the U.S. Bureau of the Census to gather social, economic, and demographic data during the intercensal time periods.

Definition: A "mover" is a person who in March 1989 lived in a different housing unit than in March 1990.

Interpretation: About 18 percent of the U.S. population changed residences in a given year during the mid-1980s. The highest concentration of movement is among persons age 20 to 29 and 1 to 4.

Appendix

SOURCES FOR HEALTH DATA

INTRODUCTION

The primary purpose of this appendix is to provide an overview of the sources of data on health and health care of use to marketers, planners, administrators, and others interested in the field. Admittedly, an appendix such as this can become tedious reading when some of the data sets described seem to lack specific relevance to issues currently being confronted. The reader is, therefore, encouraged to focus first on the information sources that appear to be most relevant, and then to examine the others for ideas, insights, and information regarding trends that are perhaps indirectly related to the issues being addressed.

The sources of data discussed in this appendix are divided into four general categories: censuses, registration systems, surveys, and synthetically-produced data. Censuses, registries, and surveys are the more traditional sources of demographic data, although synthetically-produced statistics (including population estimates and projections) have become standard tools for most planning activities.

A number of the data sets described here are not what most users would label "health care data." However, health care data is an elusive label in that much of what affects the health care industry does not result directly from health-related events. Health care, in fact, developed a much greater sensitivity to the external environment during the 1980s. There has been an increase in a demand for data that in the past would not have been thought to be related to health care, including such topics as economics, urban development, and most importantly, demography. Therefore, this discussion has been expanded to include data sets that reflect the more general environment affecting health care-related activities.

GENERAL SOURCES

Although the sources provided in each section refer to the agencies and publications responsible for the specific data set being discussed, numerous compendia exist that users should find quite useful. The annual issues of **Health, United States,** published by the U.S. Department of Health and Human Services, present data on health status and determinants, the utilization of resources, health care resources, and health care expenditures. These data are mostly at the national level, although some state and regional data are available. The data are compiled from both governmental (e.g., National Center for Health Statistics) and private (e.g., American Medical Association) sources.

Other compendia include the **Statistical Abstract of the United States,** which is published every year by the Census Bureau. The **Abstract** contains detailed data for the nation as a whole for 31 different subject categories (e.g., vital statistics and health and nutrition), as well as some data for states and metropolitan areas. Most states publish a statistical abstract that provides similar data for that state and its counties and cities. The **County and City Data Book** is published by the Census Bureau every two years and includes 203 separate items for each county and 134 items for each city of 25,000 or more persons. Data of interest to health care analysts include population statistics, vital records, and hospital, physician, and nursing home statistics. This source also contains information on hospital insurance, supplementary medical insurance, and Social Security benefits. The **State and Metropolitan Area Data Book** is published by the Census Bureau every four years and includes 128 data items for each state, 298 variables for each Metropolitan Statistical Area (MSA), and 86 pieces of information for each MSA's central city. These compendia serve as general sources of information, and the references they cite provide direction to other data sets.

SPECIALIZED SOURCES

CENSUSES

A *census* of persons is technically a complete count of the population for a specific place at a specific time. The U.S. census of population is conducted every 10 years and the 1990 count was the twenty-first of the decennial censuses. Typical census items elicit data on the number of persons residing in each living unit (e.g., house, duplex, apartment, and dormitory) and the characteristics of those individuals. Other characteristics on which information is gathered include age, race, ethnicity, marital status, income, occupation, education, employment status, and industry of employment. There are also questions about the dwelling unit in which the respondent lives. Health-related items are noticeably absent from the Census. However, a new question in the 1990 census addressed functional disabilities and the ability to perform daily activities (e.g., dressing or bathing).

Census data are available for virtually every geographic unit, including states, counties, zip codes, metropolitan areas, cities, census tracts, block groups, block numbering areas, and blocks. Since 1970 most of these data have been available on computer tape and microfiche, though many users still rely on the large number of published reports. Census geography was dramatically improved for the 1990 census, and the new TIGER (Topologically Integrated Geographic Encoding and Referencing) system allows for the integration of geographic information and data collected as part of the 1990 census. The end result is the significantly enhanced ability to identify the demographic characteristics of a multitude of geographic units. In addition to the computer tape files available from the 1980 Census, 1990 data are available on CD-ROM and on floppy disk.

Economic censuses can be traced back to the early nineteenth century and are conducted every five years in years that end in 2 or 7. The types of businesses included are those engaged in retail trade, wholesale trade, service activities, mineral industries, transportation, construction, manufacturing, and agriculture, as well as governments. Aggregated information on businesses that engage in health-related activities is available from this source.

In general, the information collected from each establishment includes sales, employment, and payroll, though other, more specialized data are gathered. The data are available for a variety of geographic units, including states, metropolitan areas, counties, and incorporated places of 2,500 or more population. Formats include computer tape, microfiche, CD-ROM, and written reports. The tapes, microfiche, and reports may be obtained from the same sources and locations making available the population and housing data.

REGISTRATION SYSTEMS

A large amount of useful health-related data is collected through registration systems. A *registration system* involves the systematic registration, recording, and reporting of a broad range of events, institutions, and individuals. The implied characteristics of a registry include the regular and timely recording of the phenomenon in question. The best known registration activities in the United States are those related to *vital events*–births, deaths, marriages, divorces, and induced abortions. However, other registry data, such as those available from surveillance activities of the Centers for Disease Control and Prevention (CDCP), the Social Security Administration (SSA), and the Immigration and Naturalization Service (INS) can prove to be valuable, especially when examining changes in the level and distribution of the need for health care. In addition, lists maintained by professional associations such as the American Medical Association are placed in this category because such lists have many of the characteristics required of registries. The Medicare "registry" should also be mentioned since it is being utilized increasingly as a source of data on health care needs and utilization patterns.

VITAL STATISTICS

As noted above, *vital statistics* in the United States involves data collection for births, deaths, marriages, divorces, and induced abortions. Standard birth certificate information includes time and date of birth, place of occurrence and residence, birth weight, pregnancy complications, a pregnancy history for the mother, mother's and father's age and race (ethnicity in selected states), and mother's education and marital status. Data gathered on the standard death certificate include age, race (ethnicity in selected states), sex, home address, usual occupation, and industry of the decedent, along with the location where the death took place. In addition, information on disposition, immediate and secondary causes of death, and other significant conditions is collected. A separate certificate is used in the case of a fetal death.

Birth and death statistics are traditionally available in government publications, based on both place of occurrence of the event and place of residence of the effected individual. Considerable detail is provided for a wide range of geographies including states, MSAs, counties, and urban places. Data for different or smaller geographic areas may be available through state and local government agencies. Yearly summary reports are produced and published by the National Center for Health Statistics, though monthly summaries are also available through the monthly vital statistics reports. Micro data are available on computer tape, though not all data (a 50% sample of records is usual) and not all states and all variables are included. At the local level the county health department compiles both birth and death statistics and each state has an agency that compiles these data at the state level.

Reports of induced abortions are provided by the 13 states that make up the abortion registration area. The states that voluntarily participate in abortion data collection are Colorado, Indiana, Kansas, Missouri, Montana, New York, Oregon, Rhode Island, South Carolina, Tennessee, Utah, Vermont, and Virginia. The registration system works in the same way as those discussed above, with reports being submitted to state offices and records being forwarded to the National Center for Health Statistics. The information gathered includes a pregnancy history, type of procedure, and period of gestation, along with the woman's age, race, marital status, and education. Data for states are available in published format, and a microdata file for a sample of records is also available.

CDCP DISEASE SURVEILLANCE

The Centers for Disease Control and Prevention (CDCP) have been involved in disease-surveillance activities since the establishment of the Communicable Disease Center in 1946. Its initial agenda included the study of malaria, murine typhus, smallpox, and other diseases. Surveillance activities now include programs in human reproduction, environmental health, chronic disease, risk reduction, occupational safety and health, and infectious diseases. The purpose of the surveillance system is to provide weekly provisional information on the occurrence of diseases defined as "notifiable" by the Council of State and Territorial Epidemiologists (CSTE). Annual data are also available.

Notifiable disease reports are received by CDCP from 52 areas (Washington D.C. and New York City report separately) and five territories. A note of caution must be made regarding these data. As CDC discloses, diseases that cause severe clinical illness and are associated with serious consequences are probably reported quite accurately, while milder diseases are less likely to be reported. Data quality is significantly affected by the availability of diagnostic facilities and the priorities of officials who are responsible for reporting. As implied earlier, the number of diseases and conditions reported is quite large. Included for surveillance are anthrax, botulism, cholera, diphtheria, food-borne disease, leprosy, mumps, and toxic shock, among others.

These data are available weekly in **Morbidity and Mortality Weekly Report** (MMWR), a CDCP publication, as well as through an annual summary, **Summary of Notifiable Disease.**

IMMIGRATION DATA

Data regarding immigrants, legalization applications, refugees, asylum applicants, nonimmigrant entries, naturalizations, and enforcement are collected by the Immigration and Naturalization Service (INS) and made available by means of published reports and computer tape. These data are generated from immigrant visa information that, in theory, is available on everyone legally entering the United States. After a person is admitted to this country, visa and adjustment forms are forwarded to the INS data-capture facility for processing. Information collected includes port of admission, country of birth, last residence, nationality, age, sex, occupation, and the zip code of the immigrant's intended residence.

These data are made available through yearly statistical summaries, more frequent shorter reports, and computer tapes (which are available for 1972 through 1990). Each tape covers a three-year time period. While the published reports contain data for states and MSAs, tabulations by county and zip code are possible using the tapes.

HEALTH CARE MANPOWER

As discussed earlier, many health care manpower data sources fall into the category of registries. Manpower lists can be considered in this category since they are a mechanism for registering all persons who are practicing a given profession at a specific point in time. Like other registries, manpower registration involves the regular and timely recording of persons entering a given profession. Unlike some other registries, the maintenance of lists of persons who continue to practice is involved. Furthermore, these lists are made current by deleting such persons no longer practicing.

PHYSICIAN SUPPLY

During the 1980s, the demand for data on physicians grew tremendously. A master file of physicians has been maintained by the American Medical Association (AMA) since 1906. Currently, the file contains data on virtually every physician in the United States, regardless of AMA membership. The data are collected and updated on an ongoing basis, and the data base presently contains some 600,000 records. A file is initiated upon entry into medical school, and foreign medical graduates are added upon certification for residency training when they enter the country. A census of physicians is conducted every four years to update the files, though during the intercensal period changes are made via continuous checks of professional publications that note changes in physician activities.

A wide variety of information is gathered, including demographic (e.g., age, sex, and race) and specialty data. The master file is also used as a sampling frame for periodic surveys of physicians that collect detailed information on characteristics of physician practices, earnings, expenses, work patterns, and fees. Aggregated statistics from the master file are available for the entire nation, states, metropolitan areas, and counties in periodic publications such as the AMA's annual publication **Physician Characteristics and Distribution in the U.S.** and in secondary sources such as **Health, United States, Statistical Abstract of the U.S.,** and the **County and City Data Book.** Data from some secondary sources are available on computer tape. Portions of the master file can be purchased on tape, but only for selected purposes. The AMA also maintains a file on medical residents, but it is less accessible at present then the physician file.

Another major source of data on physicians is the MEDEC data base. This data base is maintained and updated annually by Medical Economics, Inc. The information included is based on data returned by physicians who receive Medical Economics' publication **Physician's Desk Reference.** The coverage of the MEDEC data base is not as extensive as that of the AMA master file, but some variables are included in the former that are not available in the AMA data base. The MEDEC data base is available for purchase and is also available through some desktop market analysis systems. In either case, the data should be used with caution, since problems in maintaining data bases of this type are significant.

State licensure agencies also maintain data bases on physicians registered in the particular state. While this information is often available to the public, mere registration in a jurisdiction does not necessarily indicate practice. Specialty boards and other organizations also maintain registries on their members or certification recipients. While this information is often available in printed directories, the availability of the actual data bases varies.

NURSE SUPPLY

Data on the number and characteristics of nurses are generated through the National Sample Survey of Registered Nurses conducted by the Bureau of Health Professions. Based on questionnaires sent to each licensed nurse in the United States, this serves as the only federal source of such data. Nurse supply estimates by states–including information on those who currently have licenses to practice, as well as those who are working part-time or full-time (and full-time equivalents)–are generated from a model that uses data from the National League for Nursing and the National Council of State Boards of Nursing. In addition, state licensure boards maintain data on active (and sometimes inactive) nurses within their jurisdictions. These data vary in accessibility, content, and format.

HEALTH CARE FACILITIES

The National Master Facility Inventory (NMFI) is a comprehensive file of inpatient facilities (including hospitals, nursing homes and related facilities, and other custodial or remedial care facilities) maintained by the National Center for Health Statistics. The NMFI is kept current by periodically adding the names and addresses of newly established facilities licensed by state boards and other agencies. Annual surveys are used to update information concerning existing facilities. Information available from this file includes size (number of beds), personnel, admissions, discharges, services offered, type of ownership, and type of certification. These data are available in various reports, although no systematic reporting mechanism exists. The secondary sources noted above also include these data. These data are also available on computer tape, although the last complete tape file is for 1976 and contains about 27,000 records.

Information is continuously gathered on hospitals by means of the annual hospital survey conducted by the American Hospital Association (AHA). Each year, a questionnaire is sent to the approximately 7,000 registered hospitals in the United States. The response rate is high–over 90%. Data are gathered on availability of services, utilization, financial information, hospital management, and personnel. These data are available for a variety of geographic units (including regions, divisions, states, counties and cities) through AHA published reports and computer diskettes and through secondary sources such as the **County and City Data Book**. The American Health Care Association maintains data on 10,000 nursing homes.

Since most health facilities are licensed by the state, information is usually available from the state agency charged with that responsibility. Increasingly, local organizations such as planning and regulatory agencies and business coalitions have begun to maintain facilities data bases. Some private data vendors have begun collecting and disseminating data on health care facilities. There are now vendors selling data on health maintenance organizations, minor emergency centers, free-standing surgery centers, and a variety of other types of facilities.

MENTAL HEALTH ORGANIZATIONS

An inventory of mental health organizations has been maintained historically by the National Institute of Mental Health (NIMH). Every two years, questionnaires have been sent to psychiatric hospitals, nonfederal general hospitals with psychiatric services, Veteran's Administration psychiatric services, residential treatment centers for emotionally disturbed children, freestanding outpatient psychiatric clinics, and other types of partial care organizations. These data are published every few years in **Mental Health, United States.** In 1993 NIMH was reorganized and at the time of the printing of this book, its new structure had not been finalized.

Since many mental health services are administered by state governments, the respective state agencies are a source of mental health statistics, although the data provided vary in terms of accessibility, content, and format. While rather detailed statistics have become available on ambulatory care services for physical illness, this is not the case for mental illness. The only significant sources of mental health outpatient statistics are the reports filed by comprehensive community mental health centers.

SURVEYS

Sample surveys are frequently used to supplement data from other sources. Information collected through sample surveys has several advantages over census and registry data. Two of the major advantages are more frequent data collection and more in-depth treatment of health-related issues. The relatively small sample sizes for such surveys have the additional advantages of quicker turnaround time and easier manipulation than large-scale operations such as the census. On the other hand, surveys have their disadvantages. Since they involve a sample, there is some slippage in accuracy relative to censuses. Perhaps the most serious shortcoming related to health care planning and marketing is the inability to compile adequate data for small geographic units due to small sample sizes. Also, special subject areas addressed by some surveys are not featured on a regular basis, so that the interval between surveys can become lengthy. Some of the more useful surveys are discussed below.

NATIONAL HEALTH INTERVIEW SURVEY (NATIONAL CENTER FOR HEALTH STATISTICS)

The National Health Interview Survey (NHIS) is an ongoing national survey of the U.S. noninstitutionalized civilian population. Each year, a multistage probability sample of between 36,000 and 46,000 households (92,000 to 135,000 persons) is generated for inclusion and interview. The data gathered are quite detailed and include demographic information on age, race, sex, marital status, occupation, and income. Health questions relate to physician visits, hospital stays, restricted-activity days, long-term activity limitation, and chronic conditions. Recently, questions regarding AIDS knowledge and attitudes have been added to the survey. Food nutrition knowledge, smoking and other tobacco use, cancer, and polio are also subjects sometimes addressed.

The data are available in published report form (**Current Estimates** reports, Series 10, and the **AdvanceData** series) and on computer tape. They have just recently been released on CD-ROM. The data tapes consist of five files, each related to a specific topic: health conditions, physician visits, hospital stays, household characteristics, and person characteristics. Geographic identification is limited to region and MSA if the person lived in one of the larger MSAs. The CD-ROM data are contained on a disk organized into nine files. The data are available for each year from 1969 through 1991.

NATIONAL HOSPITAL DISCHARGE SURVEY (NATIONAL CENTER FOR HEALTH STATISTICS)

The National Hospital Discharge Survey (NHDS) is a continuous nationwide survey of inpatient utilization of short stay hospitals. All hospitals with six or more beds reporting an average length of stay of less than 30 days are included in the sampling frame. A multistage probability sampling frame is used to select hospitals from the National Master Facility Inventory and discharge records from each of the hospitals. The resulting sample has ranged from 192,000 to 232,000 discharge records each year from 1970 to the present.

Information collected includes demographic, clinical, and financial characteristics of patients discharged from short-stay hospitals. The variables abstracted range from the age, race, sex, and marital status of the person discharged to source of payment, discharge status, diagnosis, and length of stay. Hospital information on bed size and type of ownership (voluntary nonprofit, government, and proprietary) are also gathered. Geographic specificity is limited to census division, region, and national summaries. These data are available on computer tape and through various reports produced by the National Center for Health Statistics (in Series 13 reports and in the **AdvanceData** series).

NATIONAL AMBULATORY MEDICAL CARE SURVEY (NATIONAL CENTER FOR HEALTH STATISTICS)

The National Ambulatory Medical Care Survey (NAMCS) is a nationwide survey designed to provide information about the provision and utilization of ambulatory health care services. The sampling frame is office visits made by ambulatory patients to physicians (other than those employed by the federal government) engaged in office practice. Telephone contacts and nonoffice visits are excluded. Three specialties (anesthesiology, pathology, and radiology) are excluded from the survey, since these practitioners generally do not provide direct patient care. A multistage probability sampling frame is used to select physicians from the master files maintained by the American Medical Association and the American Osteopathic Association. A sample of the records of these physicians for a randomly assigned one-week period are then examined. Recent samples contain about 70,000 records (earlier samples were smaller), and data are available for 1973, 1975 through 1981, and 1985 to the present.

Data regarding the age, race, ethnicity, and sex of the patient are gathered along with the reason for the visit, expected source(s) of payment, principal diagnosis, diagnostic services provided, and disposition of visit. Geographic identifiers include census region and whether or not the person was a resident of an MSA. Physician information collected includes specialty, type of practice, and type of doctor (M.D. or D.O.) The data can be found in **Vital and Health Statistics**, Series 13, **AdvanceData** reports, as well as on computer tape. The National Association of Health Data Organizations gathers data on actual and planned ambulatory care activities. Eighteen states routinely collect these data, which come primarily from hospital outpatient departments and ambulatory surgery facilities.

NATIONAL NURSING HOME SURVEY (NATIONAL CENTER FOR HEALTH STATISTICS)

The National Nursing Home Survey (NNHS) is a periodically-conducted national survey of nursing and related care homes, their residents, their discharges, and their staffs. Alaska and Hawaii are not included in the survey. The data are collected using a two-stage probability design. Once facilities are selected, residents and employees of each facility are sampled. Six separate questionnaires were used to gather data in the most recent survey. The first addresses characteristics of the facility and involves an interview with the administrator or a designee. The second focuses on cost data and is completed by the facility's accountant or bookkeeper and returned by mail. Information on the current and discharged residents is obtained by interviewing the staff person most familiar with the medical records of the residents. Additional resident data are gathered using telephone surveys of the residents' families. Full-time and part-time employees, including nurses, complete a nursing staff questionnaire.

This data set is quite large and for the 1985 survey included about 1,400 facilities, 5,100 discharges, 3,000 residents, and 14,000 staff records. Items included in the facility file range from number of beds and residents to admission policies and services provided. The discharge file contains information on the age, gender, and marital status of the person discharged, along with primary diagnosis at admission, total monthly charges for care, and the number of physician contacts. Resident files contain the same basic information along with data on quality of vision, frequency of visitors, and recreational activities. The staff file includes an occupational code and work experience along with general demographic characteristics.

The survey was conducted in 1973-74, 1977 and 1985. Data are available by region via the facility file and can be found in **AdvanceData** reports and **Vital and Health Statistics**, Series 12, 13, and 14, as well as on computer tape.

NATIONAL MEDICAL CARE UTILIZATION AND EXPENDITURE

SURVEY (NATIONAL CENTER FOR HEALTH STATISTICS)

The National Medical Care Utilization and Expenditure Survey (NMCUES) was first conducted in 1980 and 1981 with the purpose of gathering information on health status, access and use of medical services, associated charges, and sources of payment as well as insurance coverage. The survey contained three components: 6,000 households nationwide interviewed five times between 1980 and 1981; 4,000 state Medicaid households selected from Medicaid eligibility files in California, Michigan, New York, and Texas, again interviewed five times between 1980 and 1981; and an administrative-records sample of persons receiving Medicare and Medicaid payments.

The file for the nationwide household survey contains information on over 17,000 persons along with demographic information (e.g., age, race, sex, and education), medical visit and hospital stay data, and statistics regarding prescribed medicine, dental visits, and medical condition. The data are available on computer tape. In 1987, a separate expenditures survey, the National Medical Expenditure Survey, was conducted.

NATIONAL LONG-TERM CARE SURVEY (NATIONAL CENTER FOR HEALTH STATISTICS)

The National Long-Term Care Survey (NLTCS) is a joint effort on the part of Duke University and the Census Bureau to gather national-level data on long term care aspects of the older population. The major portion of the survey has focused on follow-up interviews with persons included in the first NLTCS survey in 1982. All of these persons were 65 years of age or older; the follow-ups were in 1984 and 1988. Attrition due to a variety of factors reduced the sample size from 31,934 in 1982 to 16,665 in 1988. A second, much smaller, component of the study involves a sample of persons aged 61 to 64 in 1982.

The survey has many components, focusing on issues ranging from household composition (if not living in an institutional setting) to the financial status of informal caregivers. Specific parts focus on activities of daily living, medical condition (e.g., diabetes), the need for special assistance, health insurance, health care costs, medical service providers, and institutionalized living.

CURRENT POPULATION SURVEY (U.S. BUREAU OF THE CENSUS)

The Current Population Survey (CPS) is the Census Bureau's device for gathering detailed demographic information between decennial censuses. The series generates topic-specific reports at regular intervals throughout the year. In addition, a microdata computer tape is available annually that contains information relevant to that specific year. The items collected include many of those gathered in the census of population and housing (e.g., age, race, and education). Of particular interest to the health care industry are the data on the extent and type of health insurance coverage for the total U.S. population. Cross-classifying responses to this inquiry with other social and economic variables can result in coverage information for a variety of subgroups. Health insurance is a relatively new inquiry and has been part of the CPS since 1980. This question was the basis for the recent estimate of 37 million persons who are lacking health insurance. Furthermore, during the third week of each September, a subsample of the larger CPS sample is queried regarding immigration.

These data are available through a variety of published reports as part of the Census Bureau's **Current Population Reports** series. The series generates topical reports at regular intervals throughout the year. In addition, a microdata computer tape and CD-ROM are available annually that contain information relevant to that specific year. Most published reports include geographic detail no lower than the regional level, due to the relatively small sample size. However, using the data set on computer tape the analyst can generate totals for smaller geographic units such as MSAs, although users are cautioned that smaller area estimates contain a great deal of variability.

CONSUMER EXPENDITURE SURVEY (U.S. DEPARTMENT OF LABOR)

The Bureau of Labor Statistics (BLS) has been collecting data on spending behavior and cost of living for nearly a century. Since 1980, the Consumer Expenditure Survey (CES) has gathered data on an ongoing basis; sample households are replaced by others as the cycle of data collection proceeds. Information gathered includes standard demographic factors (e.g., age, race, and education); income, including sources of income; and expenditures over a broad range of categories. Of particular interest to health care analysts are data regarding health care expenditures–money spent on health insurance, medical services, prescription drugs, and medical supplies.

The data are available in regularly published reports, and a microdata file may be purchased. Figures in the reports are presented by region and for the United States as a whole, though smaller geographic unit data may be produced from the data tapes. However, small sample size and the resulting instability of estimates must be considered. Some of these data are now being repackaged and sold in a more popular format.

NATIONAL SURVEY OF FAMILY GROWTH (NATIONAL CENTER FOR HEALTH STATISTICS)

The National Survey of Family Growth (NSFG) conducted by the National Center for Health Statistics is a periodic survey conducted to gather information on fertility, family planning, and aspects of maternal and child health that are closely related to childbearing. It is a multistage probability sample of civilian noninstitutionalized women aged 15 to 44. The survey has been conducted four times: June 1973 to February 1974 (Cycle I), January to September 1976 (Cycle II), August 1982 through February 1983 (Cycle III), and January to August 1988 (Cycle IV).

A wide range of information is collected through personal interviews including the age, race, marital status, education, income, and religion of each woman surveyed. Geographic specificity is limited to the census division lived in and metropolitan residence (yes or no). Family planning data collected range from age at first contraceptive visit and contractive use to sources of services and services used, including how such services were paid for. The data are available through **AdvanceData** and **Vital and Health Statistics** Series 23 reports as well as on computer tape.

SYNTHETIC DATA

Synthetic data are created by merging existing demographic data with assumptions about population change to produce estimates, projections, and forecasts. These data are particularly valuable given that census and survey activities are constricted because of budgeting and time considerations. The 1990 census is estimated to have cost $2.6 billion, a figure far too large to be incurred more often than once every 10 years.

POPULATION ESTIMATES AND PROJECTIONS

Population estimates for states, MSAs, and counties are prepared each year as a joint effort of the Census Bureau and the state agency designated by each state governor under the Federal-State Program for Local Population Estimates (FSCPE). The purpose of the program is to standardize data and procedures so that the best quality estimates can be derived. Some of the published estimates provide a population figure for the current year, one for the preceding year, and a change figure, while others also include components of change (births, deaths, and net migrants). For population projections, different information is available. One publication focuses totally on U.S. projections to the year 2080 by age, sex, and race, and provides data for three sets of fertility, mortality, and migration assumptions. Overall, the Census Bureau produces 30 different series of projections for each year.

Most states also generate population estimates and projections that are available through state agencies. However, these figures are often produced at irregular intervals and, thus, may be quite dated. The reader is also encouraged to evaluate the quality of these data to the best of his or her ability.

Population estimates and projections generated by government agencies have historically been the only ones available. Today, however, a number of data vendors also provide these figures. These vendor-generated data have the advantages of being available down to the census block group level (data for customized boundaries are also available) and are provided in greater detail (e.g., sex and age breakdowns) than government-produced figures. Virtually all vendors of demographic data offer estimates and projections.

OCCUPATIONAL PROJECTIONS

Occupational projections 10 to 15 years into the future for the United States are produced on a two-year cycle by the U.S. Bureau of Labor Statistics. Six models are created, each containing a host of variables reflecting different scenarios for growth in the total labor force, changes in the aggregate economy, industry demand, and industry employment, among other factors. Three sets of employment projections are created based upon differing sets of assumptions. Of interest here are the various categories of health-related occupations (which include dentists, physicians and surgeons, and therapists by specialty) and health care support occupations (which include dental and medical assistants, as well as nurse's aides).

These data are available through regularly published reports. The percentage distribution for the labor force (matrix coefficients) can also be obtained and these are sometimes used by other organizations to produce subnational projections.

Adapted from Louis G. Pol and Richard K. Thomas. 1992. *The Demography of Health and Health Care.* New York: Plenum Publishing Company.

NOTES

NOTES

NOTES

NOTES

NOTES

NOTES